What's the Matter?

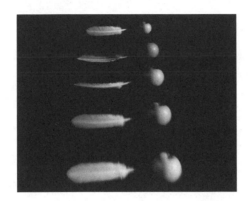

What's the Matter?

Readings in Physics

Foreword by Alan Lightman

Selected and Edited by

Donald H. Whitfield

with

James L. Hicks, *science consultant*

Published by the Great Books Foundation

with support from Harrison Middleton University

Published and distributed by

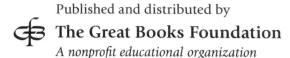 **The Great Books Foundation**

A nonprofit educational organization

35 East Wacker Drive, Suite 2300
Chicago, IL 60601-2205
www.greatbooks.org

First printing
9 8 7 6 5 4 3 2 1

Library of Congress Cataloging-in-Publication Data

What's the matter? readings in physics / foreword by Alan Lightman;
  selected and edited by Donald H. Whitfield, James L. Hicks
      p. cm.
  Includes bibliographical references.
   ISBN 1-880323-91-5 (alk. paper)
     1. Physics—history. 2. Physicists—History. 3. Physics—Study and teaching.
     4. Inquiry-based learning. I. Whitfield, Donald. II. Hicks, James L.

QC7.5.W53 2007
530.09—dc22   2005055073

Book cover and design: Think Design Group LLC

In memory of

Ewen M. Akin Jr., EdD

1930–2002

*Dr. Akin, an inspirational member of the board of directors
of the Great Books Foundation, was a committed educator in mind
and heart. An admired physics teacher and president of
Malcolm X College and Kennedy-King College, both in Chicago,
he was a man of exemplary character and a champion
of the mission of the Great Books Foundation.*

We physicists are always checking to see if there is something the matter with the theory. That's the game, because if there *is* something the matter, it's interesting!

—Richard Feynman, *QED: The Strange Theory of Light and Matter*

Alan Lightman is an adjunct professor of humanities at the Massachusetts Institute of Technology. He studied physics at Princeton University and the California Institute of Technology and has since combined the careers of scientist, educator, novelist, and essayist. Many of Dr. Lightman's writings, including the best-selling *Einstein's Dreams* (1993) and *The Discoveries: Great Breakthroughs in 20th-Century Science* (2005), emphasize the human side of scientific investigation.

Donald H. Whitfield is the director of higher education programs at the Great Books Foundation. He is a graduate of the great books program at St. John's College.

James L. Hicks has been an adjunct lecturer in education at Roosevelt University in Chicago. He taught physics for thirty-seven years at Barrington High School in Illinois; his innovative approach to science education was the subject of two documentaries. Among his numerous awards is the American Association of Physics Teachers (AAPT) Pre-College Award in 2004, the association's highest recognition for a high school teacher. He serves on AAPT's Committee on the History and Philosophy of Physics and on the editorial board of AAPT's journal, *The Physics Teacher.*

Harrison Middleton University is a great books, great ideas, great conversations, distance-learning university that offers undergraduate and graduate education in the humanities with concentrations in imaginative literature, natural sciences, philosophy and religion, social sciences, jurisprudence, and education. Harrison Middleton University promotes student-faculty scholarship through research, discussion, and the development of collaborative publications. For more information, go to www.chumsci.edu or call 1-877-248-6724.

Editorial Consultants: Mike Levine; Ashley Preston

About the
Great Books Foundation

What is the Great Books Foundation?

The Great Books Foundation is an independent, nonprofit educational organization whose mission is to help people learn how to think and share ideas. Toward this end, the Foundation offers workshops for leaders of and participants in Shared Inquiry discussion and publishes collections of classic and modern texts for both children and adults.

The Great Books Foundation was established in 1947 to promote liberal education for the general public. In 1962, the Foundation extended its mission to children with the introduction of Junior Great Books. Since its inception, the Foundation has helped thousands of people throughout the United States and in other countries begin their own discussion groups in schools, libraries, and community centers. Today, Foundation instructors conduct hundreds of workshops each year, in which educators and parents learn to lead Shared Inquiry discussion.

What resources are available to support my participation in Shared Inquiry?

The Great Books Foundation offers workshops in Shared Inquiry to help people get the most from discussion. Participants learn how to read actively, pose fruitful questions, and listen and respond to others effectively in discussion. All participants also practice leading a discussion and have an opportunity to reflect on the process with others. For more information about Great Books materials or workshops, call the Great Books Foundation at 1-800-222-5870 or visit our website at www.greatbooks.org.

Contents

Contents

Foreword

I vividly remember the occasion, years ago, when I took my two-year-old daughter to the ocean the first time. It was a mild, hazy day in June. We parked our car a half mile from the water and walked the rest of the way. A speckled pink crab shell lay on the sand and caught her attention. Then, a few hundred yards farther along, we heard the long roll of the waves. And I could tell that my daughter was curious about what made that sound she had never heard before. Holding her up with one arm, I pointed to the ocean. Her eyes followed along my arm, across the sand, and then out to the vast blue-green of the sea. For a moment she hesitated. I wasn't sure whether she would be puzzled or frightened by that first sight of infinity. Then she broke out into a radiant smile and giggled with pleasure.

In an article published in *Forum and Century* magazine in 1931, Albert Einstein wrote, "The most beautiful experience we can have is the mysterious. It is the fundamental emotion which stands at the cradle of true art and true science." On that day at the beach years ago, my daughter was experiencing the mysterious. What did Einstein mean by "the mysterious"? I don't think he meant that science is full of unpredictable or unknowable or supernatural forces. I believe that he meant a sense of awe, a sense that there are things larger than us, that we do not have all the answers at this moment. A sense that we can stand right at the edge between known and unknown and gaze into that cavern and be exhilarated rather than frightened.

An appreciation of the mysterious is part of the emotional force that propels scientists in their endeavors. Without that appreciation and the passion that comes with it, scientists would not work day and night on their research, often neglecting the rest of their lives. But, of course, such appreciation and passion also occur in other human activities, as Einstein suggests. In my opinion, what distinguishes science from other occupations are several features: the belief that the physical world is subject to cause-and-effect relationships, the belief that the physical world is governed by repeatable rules, and the adherence to concepts and theories that can be tested by experiment.

As far as the first feature, scientists would be permanently out of work if, for example, wheelbarrows could suddenly float for no reason at all. Scientists believe that every physical event has a physical cause, and that cause may be ultimately understood. Without cause-and-effect relationships, anything could happen at any moment. Likewise, anything could happen at any moment if the rules were constantly changing. If a 3-volt battery could barely power a flashlight on some days and yet run the floodlights in Yankee Stadium on other days, that behavior would represent a fatal problem for science. We don't know all the rules, and occasionally the rules must be modified, but science works on the assumption that the known rules of physics and chemistry and biology are reliable and repeatable.

Finally, an important defining aspect of science is its limitation to statements that can be tested. According to Karl Popper, who was an important early twentieth-century British philosopher of science, a *scientific* proposition is a statement that can be proven false. You can never prove a scientific concept or theory true, because you can never be sure that tomorrow you might not find a counterexample in nature. But you can certainly prove any scientific theory false. You can find a counterexample, an experiment that disagrees with the theory. And, according to Popper, unless you can at least imagine an experiment that might falsify the theory, that theory or statement is not scientific. It does not lie within the hallways of science.

Popper's restriction is tight, and it separates science from other areas of inquiry. There are many interesting questions that do not lie within the realm of science. For example: What is love? Or, would we be happier if we lived a thousand years? These questions are terribly interesting, but they lie outside the domain of science. One cannot prove wrong the statement that John is in love. Love is much too subjective and individual to be measured in such a way, even if we think we know John very well. (If we define love as the sudden increase in heartbeat above 120 beats per minute when John meets a certain person, then we could test whether John is in love. But such a definition would not satisfy most people.) Likewise, one cannot falsify the statement that we would be happier (or not happier) if we lived longer. Yet these are still fascinating questions, questions that provoke us and bring forth all kinds of creative thought and invention. Science is powerful, but it has limitations.

Even within the rather narrow territory of science, the manner of doing science has changed dramatically through the ages. The Greek scientist and philosopher Aristotle, one of the greatest early physicists, made a number of statements about the world that he never tested. For example, Aristotle gave several different proofs of why the earth is round. In the first proof, he argued that since the shadow of the earth during a lunar eclipse is always a curved segment of a circle, the earth must be round. That argument is certainly testable. In the second proof, he pointed out that stars rise and set sooner for people in the east than in the west. If the earth were flat from east to west, stars would rise as soon in the occident as in the orient. That argument is also testable. As his third proof, however, Aristotle proclaimed a philosophical argument: If the earth had been formed from smaller pieces sometime in the past, its pieces would fall toward a common center, thus making a sphere. Furthermore, according to Aristotle, a sphere is clearly the most perfect solid shape. Aristotle placed as much emphasis on this last, untestable proof as on the first two.

In the centuries following Aristotle, science was full of untested propositions. The situation began to change in the sixteenth century with the work of Francis Bacon and Galileo. These scientists established the idea that nature could be understood only by close observation. Rather than sit in your armchair and hold forth with sweeping principles, look in your microscope to see what is really there, look through your telescope, take out your ruler and clock and measure the trajectories of rolling balls. With these notions, science was placed on a firm empirical foundation.

Finally, in the twentieth century, Albert Einstein changed the mindset of science once again, at least in a manner that worked for him and a small number of theoretical scientists. Einstein studied nature not by close observation, as Bacon suggested, but by beginning with fundamental principles and postulates, creations from his own mind. Then he deduced the consequences of those principles, after which the consequences would be tested against experiment. Einstein's theory of special relativity, presented in 1905, was a prime example of his approach to science. Here, the great physicist began with the principle that all people and instruments in constant motion are equivalent to one another and measure the same laws of physics. From that foundational principle, Einstein deduced all the equations of special relativity, including the strange behavior of time. In the early 1930s, Einstein expressed his approach to science in this way: "We now know that science cannot grow out of empiricism alone, that in the constructions of science we need to use free invention which only *a posteriori* [later] can be confronted with experience." Einstein's method has been adopted by such leading twentieth-century physicists as Werner Heisenberg and Steven Weinberg. A major reason for this new approach— beginning with foundational principles rather than detailed observations of nature—is that modern science, and especially modern physics, has ventured into territories very far from our sensual experience with nature. The tiny world of the atom, where subatomic particles can be in two places at once, and the world of ultrahigh speed, where time stretches out, are far removed from our everyday experiences and sense perceptions.

Physics, the particular science represented in this book, has its own ways of thinking that distinguish it from other sciences. I was trained as a physicist, and I understand well how the physicist thinks about the world. The physicist is a reductionist. The physicist chisels away at a towering building until it is broken down into a heap of individual bricks and cement. What are the fundamental forces and particles of nature? asks the physicist. What are the eternal laws? Physicists make simplifications and idealizations and abstractions until the final problem is so simple that it can be solved by a mathematical law. For example, physicists reduce many phenomena to the model problem of a weight bobbing up and down on a spring, called the harmonic oscillator. The vibrations of atoms in molecules, the sloshing of water in a bowl, the quantum nature of empty space, can all be reduced to weights bobbing up and down on springs, which obey simple equations.

Biologists think differently. Because biology deals with living things, biologists hardly ever go below the level where life is relevant. (A notable exception is modern molecular biology, where physics, biology, and chemistry have merged.) And life requires the interaction between elements in a system. Thus, biology necessarily deals with *systems*. What is the system by which a living creature regulates and controls its internal processes? What is the system by which a living creature reproduces itself? What is the system by which a living creature gains and utilizes the energy required for life? Where physics might ponder the electrical force between two electrons, biology would be concerned with how the electrical charges on both sides of a cell membrane regulate the passage of substances across the membrane and thus connect the cell to the rest of the organism. Roughly speaking, physics has laws, while biology has concepts. Physicists seek simplicity, while biologists often seek complexity. Biology is more of an empirical science than physics because its concepts are close to the observed facts. There are many purely theoretical physicists but few purely theoretical biologists. Chemists lie somewhere in between, sometimes acting like biologists, sometimes like physicists.

A prime example of a law in physics is the conservation of energy. A moving hammer, a coiled spring, a weight suspended above the floor, boiling water, electricity flowing through a wire—all represent different forms of energy. A moving hammer can push a nail into a wall. A coiled spring can turn the hands of a clock. Boiling water can cook an egg. And so on. Energy is the ability to cause change, to push or pull, to do work. Despite the many forms that energy can take, scientists have found that the total energy of an isolated system never changes, with suitable quantitative definitions of each form of energy. That is the meaning of the word *conservation*. In an isolated region of space, cut off from its surroundings, various kinds of energy may change from one form to another, but the total amount of energy remains constant.

The conservation of energy is a strange and beautiful fact about nature. Physicists can use the law of the conservation of energy to make predictions about the world. For example, if I hold a paperweight of one kilogram at a height of one meter above the floor, that weight has a gravitational energy of about 9.8 joules. If I drop the weight, how fast will it be moving when it strikes the floor? When the weight strikes the floor, its energy will exist completely in the form of kinetic energy, or energy of motion. (Along the way to the floor, the weight has some gravitational energy and some kinetic energy.) The conservation of energy tells us that this kinetic energy at the floor must equal the initial gravitational energy, or 9.8 joules. For this amount of mass, that energy corresponds to a speed of about 14 meters per second. Even without dropping the weight, we can make this prediction. Such is the power of a conservation law in physics.

A surprisingly small number of questions have concerned physicists throughout the ages. What is the nature of matter and energy? What are the fundamental forces of nature? What are the fundamental particles, out of which all else can be built? What is the structure of the universe as a whole? How did the universe come into being? And, in the last hundred years, what kinds of symmetries does nature possess?

Of course, the stage on which these questions are pursued has both expanded and shrunk as new technologies have become available. The microscopes of the seventeenth century and the giant particle accelerators of the twentieth have allowed physicists to study smaller and smaller regions of space, just as the ever more capable telescopes on the ground and in space have allowed us to probe larger and larger regions of space.

By training and often by temperament, scientists are accustomed to concealing their excitement when publicly describing their work. But there are exceptions. Here are the written words of Galileo when he first discovered the four moons of Jupiter with his new telescope in the autumn of 1609: "But what greatly exceeds all admiration, and what especially impelled us to give notice to all astronomers and philosophers, is this, that we have discovered four wandering stars, known or observed by no one before us. These, like Venus and Mercury around the Sun, have their periods around a certain star [Jupiter]. . . . All these things were discovered and observed a few days ago by means of a glass contrived by me after I had been inspired by divine grace."

And here is Werner Heisenberg, one of the founders of quantum physics, describing in his memoir the transcendent moment in May 1925 when he realized what he had discovered: "It was almost three o'clock in the morning before the final result of my computations lay before me. . . . I had the feeling that, through the surface of atomic phenomena, I was looking at a strangely beautiful interior, and felt almost giddy at the thought that I now had to probe this wealth of mathematical structures nature had so generously spread out before me. I was far too excited to sleep."

Whether they vocalize it or not, all the great physicists in this book have most likely experienced the same exhilaration and mystery as a child on her first glimpse of the sea.

Alan Lightman

Introduction

All the ways of understanding the world that we call the sciences, whatever their subject matter, have made progress through an ongoing process of inquiry. The scientific knowledge that we encounter in books and the media is the result of scientists, over many centuries, asking questions about the natural world and proposing answers that in turn have suggested new questions for investigation. Some of this knowledge has proven so certain that it is stated in the form of principles and laws. Other knowledge is more provisional and is accompanied by speculative questions that point the way toward new lines of inquiry, defining the future directions of scientific research. Central to this progress is the lively and rigorous dialogue of scientists with both their contemporaries and their predecessors. Isaac Newton recognized this complex relationship when he said, "If I have seen further it is by standing upon the shoulders of Giants." *What's the Matter? Readings in Physics* has been designed to provide access to this continuing dialogue through the writings of many of the scientists who have seen unusually far and contributed to our knowledge of physical science. By seeing how scientists posed their questions and by following the reasoning that led to their answers, we can begin to understand how we have arrived at our current understanding of the physical world.

Physics is often called the most basic science because it seeks to know the underlying structure of the matter that makes up the universe as well as the fundamental rules by which the components of matter, whatever they may be, interact with one another. In addition, physics looks for a unified knowledge of the universe at all scales of space and time, from the subatomic level to the cosmic scale of galaxies, and from the beginning of the universe to its remote future. As Alan Lightman points out in the foreword to this book, physics strives to reduce our understanding of the countless phenomena of the world to the simplest possible principles, expressed in the clear and unambiguous language of mathematics. Since all the sciences deal with aspects of the material world, physics has a central place in all scientific explanations. This is reflected in the names of disciplines such as astrophysics, geophysics, and biophysics.

From a broader perspective, the theories and insights of physics, along with those of the other sciences, are among the most important human achievements, along with those of philosophy, theology, jurisprudence, art, and music. Scientific knowledge possesses value in its own right by satisfying our desire for greater understanding of the world, while also providing a model of how we can use reason to advance knowledge and to overcome ignorance and bias. At the same time, scientific knowledge carries immense responsibilities, not just for scientists but for everyone, making the need for scientific literacy more urgent than ever before. For citizens not to understand the knowledge that confers these responsibilities, as its results increasingly dominate our world, is as great a deficiency as not to be aware of the principles that have shaped our political institutions, and with consequences potentially just as dangerous. The selections "The Uncertainty of Science," by Richard Feynman, and "The Scientist's Responsibilities," by Albert Einstein, address these issues.

Because physics proposes answers to questions about the origin, development, and fate of the world, it frequently comes into conflict with other explanations of how the world came to be, whether based explicitly on religious doctrines or on teachings going by such names as creationism and intelligent design. One of the purposes of *What's the Matter?* is to provide a solid basis for understanding the kinds of explanations that physics gives and the way in which physics evaluates evidence for these explanations. A sound understanding of the characteristics and foundations of physics, including the nature of scientific reasoning and theories, will help the reader reflect thoughtfully on many of the ongoing controversies regarding the authority of science.

All the selections in *What's the Matter?* were written by scientists actively involved in inquiring about the physical world. Most of the selections are accounts of the author's own area of investigation, communicating the excitement of scientific research and discovery, and revealing much about the way scientists form their questions and pursue possible answers. The selections were chosen both because they are outstanding examples of scientific writing and because of their importance in the history of physics. In "The Science of Electromagnetism," James Clerk Maxwell says, "It is of great advantage to the student of any subject to read the original memoirs on that subject, for science is always most completely assimilated when it is in the nascent state." What Maxwell means is that we can best understand well-established scientific knowledge by reading and thinking about the original questions that scientists posed as they struggled to establish new concepts and principles. In doing so, even if the early ideas of scientists have been greatly revised or even discarded, we see that physics is as much a way of inquiring about the world as it is a body of accumulated knowledge.

The selections in *What's the Matter?* represent many different types of scientific writing. Some are essays about broad scientific topics, such as Alan Lightman's "Metaphor in Science." Others are detailed reports of experiments, such as Count Rumford's investigation of how friction generates heat, or Michael Faraday's research into how electrical currents are induced. Still others—such as Einstein's explanation of the theory of relativity, or Newton's discussion of the nature of time, space, and motion—trace the scientist's line of reasoning as he formulates fundamental physical principles. Many of the selections were chosen because they raise questions that apply generally to physics and science, even as they focus on an individual scientist's work on a specific problem. For example, Newton's formulation of the laws of motion may prompt us to ask what is meant by a law of physics and what evidence is necessary to give a statement the status of a physical law. The careful construction of experimental apparatus by Rumford, James Prescott Joule, and Faraday may lead us to investigate the criteria for a well-designed experiment. And Feynman's and Heisenberg's discussions of the uncertainty principle of quantum mechanics explicitly raise searching questions about how an observer's point of view influences the outcome and interpretation of an experiment, as well as the extent to which we can know the physical world.

The order of the selections in *What's the Matter?* emphasizes the continuity of the development of physics through the centuries, particularly the transition from classical Newtonian physics to the physics that developed from the theory of relativity and quantum theory in the first decades of the twentieth century. Since relativity and quantum theory dominate all branches of contemporary physics, more than a third of the selections focus on these topics. Many complex and rapidly evolving areas of current science—such as string theory, particle physics, dark matter, and gravitational waves—are only touched on in the selections. The editors of *What's the Matter?* have instead selected readings to lay a firm foundation in the basic concepts of physics necessary for an understanding of the topics on the frontiers of modern physics. Excellent books on these topics are listed after many of the selections. Although mathematics is of central importance to physics, and one of the goals of physics is to discover equations that express the most fundamental principles of the physical world, the selections in *What's the Matter?* contain very few mathematical expressions and require no more than an ability to do basic algebra. However, the relationship between mathematics and physics is of the greatest importance and is discussed in Steven Weinberg's "Beautiful Theories: Symmetry and Mathematics."

What's the Matter? is intended for both science students as well as general readers interested in exploring the ideas and development of physics. For students, this exploration may mean carefully thinking about the physical concepts that underlie the mathematical problem solving that often dominates physics courses. As part of a curriculum that recognizes the essential place of scientific knowledge among the other humanities, *What's the Matter?* opens up a larger inquiry into how the explanations of our world that science provides are distinct from those of, for example, literature, philosophy, or religion.

Using *What's the Matter?*

The core of *What's the Matter?* is the thirty-one original selections covering the entire span of physics, written by scientists ranging from Aristotle to Stephen Hawking, arranged in roughly chronological order. All the other features of the book are designed to help you read, think about, and discuss these selections.

Each selection is preceded by a brief quote about conducting scientific investigations of the physical world. These quotes are intended to raise general questions about the nature of physics and to stimulate thinking and discussion about the selection that follows.

Headnotes

A headnote precedes each selection. Because each scientist was immersed in the ideas and problems of his own time and place, it is helpful to know something about the scientific climate in which he worked. This may include assumptions about the physical world that were current at the time, the range of his own scientific work, and the kinds of scientific problems that he inherited from his predecessors and shared with his contemporaries. In addition, the selections sometimes include technical terminology or refer to unfamiliar ideas. The headnotes are intended to clarify some of these matters.

Content and Discussion Questions

Questions follow each selection; most selections have both content questions and discussion questions. These can be used as prompts while reading alone, as the basis of conversation in discussion groups, and as suggestions for classroom writing themes.

Content questions will help you to follow the line of scientific reasoning in each selection. These questions can be addressed by drawing on the ideas that the author has explicitly expressed; they do not require additional information, specialized knowledge, or complicated inferences. The purpose of these questions is to help clarify the details of the author's scientific argument—whether it consists of the description of a series of experiments, the explanation of a theory, or the terms of a speculative hypothesis—and to provide a solid basis for addressing the more challenging discussion questions.

While the content questions focus on what a writer says, the discussion questions explore what a writer means. Even though science writers generally intend to express their ideas clearly and without ambiguity, the complexity of these ideas will often suggest varying interpretations. In order to come to a deeper understanding of a reading, it is important to explore these interpretations and weigh them in light of evidence from the selection itself, in addition to examining the implications and consequences of what you think the writer is saying. Some of the discussion questions require going beyond the scientific details of the reading and can be addressed reasonably in many different ways. They ask you to evaluate your own convictions and opinions about broad issues concerning the nature of science in general and its relationship to other ways of understanding the world.

Suggestions for Further Reading

A brief list of books for further reading accompanies each selection. Generally, each list includes additional writings by the author of the selection, biographies of the author, and books about related topics. Some of these titles are classics that have stood the test of time; others are books about cutting-edge topics in scientific research that build on the ideas in the selection. At the end of *What's the Matter?* there is also a bibliography that includes several outstanding surveys of physics. Reading any of these surveys along with the selections in *What's the Matter?* will provide an excellent overview of the history and content of physics.

Notes on Key Terms and Concepts

Like the headnotes, this section is intended to clarify some of the terms and concepts used by the authors of the selections, in order to make their ideas more accessible. For this reason, the entries are referenced to one another and to the selections themselves, emphasizing that many concepts in physics are best understood in the context in which they have been developed and used.

Thematic Guide

Finally, the thematic guide offers suggestions for reading the selections topically and thematically. Although some readers may want to go through *What's the Matter?* from front to back, others will have different purposes and interests.

The first part of the thematic guide is aligned to the topics typically covered in physics courses and will be useful to teachers and students in finding readings to accompany various units in the curriculum, such as mechanics, electricity, or thermodynamics. Used in this way, along with a standard physics textbook, the readings in *What's the Matter?* can lead to a deeper understanding of scientific concepts.

The second part of the guide outlines five reading plans for exploring themes in the nature and development of physics through various sequences of selections. Reading and discussing the selections thematically can be a rewarding way to discover how science progresses through the interplay of ideas, and will suggest other ways of exploring the many interconnections among them.

About Shared
Inquiry Discussion

Shared Inquiry is the effort to achieve a more thorough understanding of a text by discussing questions, responses, and insights with others. For both the leader and the participants, careful listening is essential. The leader guides the discussion by asking questions about specific ideas and problems of meaning in the text, but does not seek to impose his or her own interpretation on the group.

During a Shared Inquiry discussion, group members consider a number of possible ideas and weigh the evidence for each. Ideas that are entertained and then refined or abandoned are not thought of as mistakes, but as valuable parts of the thinking process. Group members gain experience in communicating complex ideas and in supporting, testing, and expanding their thoughts. Everyone in the group contributes to the discussion, and while participants may disagree with one another, they treat one another's ideas respectfully.

Shared Inquiry discussion is a vital way to develop an understanding of the ideas in texts that have fundamentally shaped how people think about the world. By reading and thinking together about these important works, participants in Shared Inquiry discussion groups are joining a great conversation extending across the centuries.

What does Shared Inquiry contribute to the study of science?

Shared Inquiry focuses on the interpretation of texts, in the belief that many readers working together can achieve a more complete understanding than any one reader can alone. We hope that reading and discussing the selections in this anthology will not only increase your knowledge of physics, but also enhance your appreciation of the scientific process. By reading scientists' own explanations of their work, you can see the evolution of their ideas and the way in which they build on the work of colleagues both present and past. And because science advances by asking questions, posing hypotheses, and testing them, the parallels between the scientific method and Shared Inquiry discussion are strong.

Guidelines for leading and participating in discussion

Over the past fifty years, the Great Books Foundation has developed guidelines that distill the experience of many discussion groups, with participants of all ages. We have found that when groups adhere to the following procedures, discussions are most focused and fruitful:

1. **Read the selection before participating in the discussion.** This ensures that all participants are equally prepared to talk about the ideas in the work, and helps prevent talk that would distract the group from its purpose.
2. **Support your ideas with evidence from the text.** This keeps the discussion focused on understanding the selection and enables the group to weigh textual support for different answers and to choose intelligently among them.
3. **Discuss the ideas in the selection, and try to understand them fully before exploring issues that go beyond the selection.** Reflecting on a range of ideas and the evidence to support them makes the exploration of related issues more productive.
4. **Listen to others and respond to them directly.** Shared Inquiry is about the give-and-take of ideas, a willingness to listen to others and to talk with them respectfully. Directing your comments and questions to other group members, not always to the leader, will make the discussion livelier and more dynamic.

5. **Expect the leader to ask questions, rather than answer them.** The leader is a kind of chief learner, whose role is to keep discussion effective and interesting by listening and asking questions. The leader's goal is to help the participants develop their own ideas, with everyone (the leader included) gaining a new understanding in the process. When participants hang back and wait for the leader to suggest answers, discussion falters.

How to make discussions more effective

- **Ask questions when something is unclear.** Simply asking someone to explain what he or she means by a particular word, or to repeat a comment, can give everyone in the group time to think about the idea in depth.
- **Ask for evidence.** Asking "What in the text gave you that idea?" helps everyone better understand the reasoning behind an answer, and it allows the group to consider which ideas have the best support.
- **Ask for agreement and disagreement.** "Does your idea agree with hers, or is it different?" Questions of this kind help the group understand how ideas are related or distinct.
- **Reflect on discussion afterward.** Sharing comments about how the discussion went and ideas for improvement can make each discussion better than the last.

Room arrangement and group size

Ideally, everyone in a discussion should be able to see and hear everyone else. When it isn't possible to arrange the seating in a circle or horseshoe, encourage group members to look at the person talking, acknowledging one another and not just the leader.

In general, Shared Inquiry discussion is most effective in groups of ten to twenty participants. If a group is much bigger than twenty, it is important to ensure that everyone has a chance to speak. This can be accomplished by either dividing the group in half for discussion or by setting aside time at the end of discussion to go around the room and give each person a chance to make a brief final comment.

One of the ways of stopping science would be only to do experiments in the region where you know the law. But experimenters search most diligently, and with the greatest effort, in exactly those places where it seems most likely that we can prove our theories wrong. In other words, we are trying to prove ourselves wrong as quickly as possible, because only in that way can we find progress.

—Richard Feynman,
The Character of Physical Law

RICHARD FEYNMAN

The Uncertainty of Science

Along with many of the other scientists whose writings are included in *What's the Matter?* Richard Feynman (1918–1988) advanced our knowledge of the physical world by looking for solutions to problems formulated by his predecessors. At the same time, he opened entirely new lines of research that reflect the individuality of his approach to physics. Explaining what motivates scientists, he wrote, "With more knowledge comes a deeper, more wonderful mystery, luring one to penetrate deeper still. Never concerned that the answer may prove disappointing, with pleasure and confidence we turn over each new stone to find unimagined strangeness leading to more wonderful questions—certainly a grand adventure!"

When Feynman began his career in the 1930s at the Massachusetts Institute of Technology, the two revolutionary theories of twentieth-century physics, relativity and quantum mechanics, were already well advanced as a result of the work of such scientists as Albert Einstein, Max Planck, Niels Bohr, Werner Heisenberg, and Erwin Schrödinger. The theory of relativity was primarily concerned with the large-scale phenomena of cosmology as well as the redefinition of gravity in terms of the structure of space and time. Quantum mechanics, on the other hand, dealt with the subatomic world of elementary particles and the forces that determine their interactions. Both theories were already finding strong experimental confirmation and provided exciting new fields of research for young scientists such as Feynman. It was the array of interesting problems emerging from quantum mechanics, combined with the insights of relativity applied to phenomena at the subatomic level, that caught Feynman's attention and set him on the course of investigation that led to his major contributions in physics. While he was at MIT, Feynman developed his highly practical approach to physics research by making complex calculations of atomic properties using the theoretical equations of quantum theory, while giving little thought to the philosophical issues that this theory raised about the structure of the physical world.

Feynman was not only brilliant and original in his solutions to given scientific problems, but also highly creative in formulating new and interesting problems and research techniques as a result of these solutions. This was demonstrated while he was a graduate student at Princeton University working on a problem in electron theory. Although the solution of the central problem was not entirely successful, in pursuing it Feynman devised a valuable mathematical tool for summing up all the probable paths that an electron can take from one point to another in space and time.

In 1942, the United States initiated the Manhattan Project to develop atomic weapons, since many scientists—Einstein among them—had persuaded the government that Germany was involved in a similar effort. Feynman was persuaded to work at its main research center in New Mexico, where he was one of the youngest staff members. His outstanding performance attracted the attention of leading physicists, and he was persuaded after the war to continue his research, first at Cornell University and then at the California Institute of Technology.

Many of Feynman's important contributions to physics are in the field of quantum electrodynamics. Early quantum theory was deficient in explaining the interaction of subatomic particles, but quantum electrodynamics provides a way of understanding how electrons interact with other charged particles and with electromagnetic radiation. Experiments have proven quantum electrodynamics to be more accurate than any other physical theory, and it is one of the most important examples of how progress in physics comes about through successful theories that give unified explanations of a range of different phenomena—in this case, all those involving electricity and magnetism. Feynman shared the Nobel Prize in Physics in 1965 with Julian Schwinger and Tomonaga Shin'ichirō, both of whom had independently formulated quantum electrodynamics, though Feynman's version has found wide acceptance because of the practicality of its mathematical methods.

Although Feynman rarely became involved in public issues, one of his most prominent moments occurred when he demonstrated with devastating simplicity the technical reason for the 1986 explosion of the space shuttle *Challenger* while serving as a member of the investigating commission.

At Cal Tech, Feynman was considered an outstanding teacher, and his *Lectures on Physics* reflect his conviction that the essential way to pursue scientific knowledge is by continuously creating new problems to test. In the following essay, "The Uncertainty of Science," he asks us to consider the value of doubt and acknowledged ignorance as necessary conditions for progress in both science and other fields of human activity.

See also Feynman, pages 337–338.

The Uncertainty of Science

What is science? The word is usually used to mean one of three things, or a mixture of them. I do not think we need to be precise—it is not always a good idea to be too precise. Science means, sometimes, a special method of finding things out. Sometimes it means the body of knowledge arising from the things found out. It may also mean the new things you can do when you have found something out, or the actual doing of new things. This last field is usually called technology—but if you look at the science section in *Time* magazine you will find it covers about 50 percent of what new things are found out and about 50 percent what new things can be and are being done. And so the popular definition of science is partly technology, too.

I want to discuss these three aspects of science in reverse order. I will begin with the new things that you can do—that is, with technology. The most obvious characteristic of science is its application, the fact that as a consequence of science one has a power to do things. And the effect this power has had need hardly be mentioned. The whole industrial revolution would almost have been impossible without the development of science. The possibilities today of producing quantities of food adequate for such a large population, of controlling sickness—the very fact that there can

This selection is taken from part 1, "The Uncertainty of Science," of The Meaning of It All.

be free men without the necessity of slavery for full production—are very likely the result of the development of scientific means of production.

Now this power to do things carries with it no instructions on how to use it, whether to use it for good or for evil. The product of this power is either good or evil, depending on how it is used. We like improved production, but we have problems with automation. We are happy with the development of medicine, and then we worry about the number of births and the fact that no one dies from the diseases we have eliminated. Or else, with the same knowledge of bacteria, we have hidden laboratories in which men are working as hard as they can to develop bacteria for which no one else will be able to find a cure. We are happy with the development of air transportation and are impressed by the great airplanes, but we are aware also of the severe horrors of air war. We are pleased by the ability to communicate between nations, and then we worry about the fact that we can be snooped upon so easily. We are excited by the fact that space can now be entered; well, we will undoubtedly have a difficulty there, too. The most famous of all these imbalances is the development of nuclear energy and its obvious problems.

Is science of any value?

I think a power to do something is of value. Whether the result is a good thing or a bad thing depends on how it is used, but the power is a value . . . .

The next aspect of science is its contents, the things that have been found out. This is the yield. This is the gold. This is the excitement, the pay you get for all the disciplined thinking and hard work. The work is not done for the sake of an application. It is done for the excitement of what is found out. Perhaps most of you know this. But to those of you who do not know it, it is almost impossible for me to convey in a lecture this important aspect, this exciting part, the real reason for science. And without understanding this you miss the whole point. You cannot understand science and its relation to anything else unless you understand and appreciate the great adventure of our time. You do not live in your time unless you understand that this is a tremendous adventure and a wild and exciting thing.

Do you think it is dull? It isn't. Is it most difficult to convey, but perhaps I can give some idea of it. . . .

To give an example, I read Faraday's[1] *Chemical History of a Candle*, a set of six Christmas lectures for children. The point of Faraday's lectures was that no matter what you look at, if you look at it closely enough, you are involved in the entire universe. And so he got, by looking at every feature of the candle, into combustion, chemistry, etc. But the introduction of the book, in describing Faraday's life and some of his discoveries, explained that he had discovered that the amount of electricity necessary to perform electrolysis of chemical substances is proportional to the number of atoms which are separated, divided by the valence. It further explained that the principles he discovered are used today in chrome plating and the anodic coloring of aluminum, as well as in dozens of other industrial applications. I do not like that statement. Here is what Faraday said about his own discovery: "The atoms of matter are in some ways endowed or associated with electrical powers, to which they owe their most striking qualities, amongst them their mutual chemical affinity." He had discovered that the thing that determined how the atoms went together, the thing that determined the combinations of iron and oxygen which make iron oxide is that some of them are electrically plus and some of them are electrically minus, and they attract each other in definite proportions. He also discovered that electricity comes in units, in atoms. Both were important discoveries, but most exciting was that this was one of the most dramatic moments in the history of science, one of those rare moments when two great fields come together and are unified. He suddenly found that two apparently different things were different aspects of the same thing. Electricity was being studied, and chemistry was being studied. Suddenly they were two aspects of the same thing—chemical changes with the results of electrical forces. And they are still understood that way. So to say merely that the principles are used in chrome plating is inexcusable.

And the newspapers, as you know, have a standard line for every discovery made in physiology today: "The discoverer said that the discovery may have uses in the cure of cancer." But they cannot explain the value of the thing itself.

Trying to understand the way nature works involves a most terrible test of human reasoning ability. It involves subtle trickery, beautiful tightropes of logic on which one has to walk in order not to make a mistake in

1. [Michael Faraday (1791–1867), British scientist.]

predicting what will happen. The quantum mechanical and the relativity ideas are examples of this.

The third aspect of my subject is that of science as a method of finding things out. This method is based on the principle that observation is the judge of whether something is so or not. All other aspects and characteristics of science can be understood directly when we understand that observation is the ultimate and final judge of the truth of an idea. But "prove" used in this way really means "test," in the same way that a hundred-proof alcohol is a test of the alcohol, and for people today the idea really should be translated as, "The exception *tests* the rule." Or, put another way, "The exception proves that the rule is wrong." That is the principle of science. If there is an exception to any rule, and if it can be proved by observation, that rule is wrong.

The exceptions to any rule are most interesting in themselves, for they show us that the old rule is wrong. And it is most exciting, then, to find out what the right rule, if any, is. The exception is studied, along with other conditions that produce similar effects. The scientist tries to find more exceptions and to determine the characteristics of the exceptions, a process that is continually exciting as it develops. He does not try to avoid showing that the rules are wrong; there is progress and excitement in the exact opposite. He tries to prove himself wrong as quickly as possible.

The principle that observation is the judge imposes a severe limitation to the kind of questions that can be answered. They are limited to questions that you can put this way: "If I do this, what will happen?" There are ways to try it and see. Questions like "Should I do this?" and "What is the value of this?" are not of the same kind.

But if a thing is not scientific, if it cannot be subjected to the test of observation, this does not mean that it is dead, or wrong, or stupid. We are not trying to argue that science is somehow good and other things are somehow not good. Scientists take all those things that *can* be analyzed by observation, and thus the things called science are found out. But there are some things left out, for which the method does not work. This does not mean that those things are unimportant. They are, in fact, in many ways the most important. In any decision for action, when you have to make up your mind what to do, there is always a "should" involved, and this cannot be worked out from "If I do this, what will happen?" alone. You say, "Sure, you see what will happen, and then you decide whether you want it to happen or not." But that is the step the scientist cannot take. You can figure out what is going to happen, but then you have to decide whether you like it that way or not.

There are in science a number of technical consequences that follow from the principle of observation as judge. For example, the observation cannot be rough. You have to be very careful. There may have been a piece of dirt in the apparatus that made the color change; it was not what you thought. You have to check the observations very carefully, and then recheck them, to be sure that you understand what all the conditions are and that you did not misinterpret what you did. . . .

There are a number of special techniques associated with the game of making observations, and much of what is called the philosophy of science is concerned with a discussion of these techniques. The interpretation of a result is an example. To take a trivial instance, there is a famous joke about a man who complains to a friend of a mysterious phenomenon. The white horses on his farm eat more than the black horses. He worries about this and cannot understand it, until his friend suggests that maybe he has more white horses than black ones.

It sounds ridiculous, but think how many times similar mistakes are made in judgments of various kinds. You say, "My sister had a cold, and in two weeks . . . " It is one of those cases, if you think about it, in which there were more white horses. Scientific reasoning requires a certain discipline, and we should try to teach this discipline, because even on the lowest level such errors are unnecessary today.

Another important characteristic of science is its objectivity. It is necessary to look at the results of observation objectively, because you, the experimenter, might like one result better than another. You perform the experiment several times, and because of irregularities, like pieces of dirt falling in, the result varies from time to time. You do not have everything under control. You like the result to be a certain way, so the times it comes out that way, you say, "See, it comes out this particular way." The next time you do the experiment it comes out different. Maybe there was a piece of dirt in it the first time, but you ignore it.

These things seem obvious, but people do not pay enough attention to them in deciding scientific questions or questions on the periphery of science. There could be a certain amount of sense, for example, in the way you analyze the question of whether stocks went up or down because of what the President said or did not say.

Another very important technical point is that the more specific a rule is, the more interesting it is. The more definite the statement, the more interesting it is to test. If someone were to propose that the planets go around the sun because all planet matter has a kind of tendency for movement, a kind of motility, let us call it an "oomph," this theory could explain a number of other phenomena as well. So this is a good theory, is it not? No. It is nowhere near as good as a proposition that the planets move around the sun under the influence of a central force which varies exactly inversely as the square of the distance from the center. The second theory is better because it is so specific; it is so obviously unlikely to be the result of chance. It is so definite that the barest error in the movement can show that it is wrong; but the planets could wobble all over the place, and, according to the first theory, you could say, "Well, that is the funny behavior of the 'oomph.'"

So the more specific the rule, the more powerful it is, the more liable it is to exceptions, and the more interesting and valuable it is to check.

Words can be meaningless. If they are used in such a way that no sharp conclusions can be drawn, as in my example of "oomph," then the proposition they state is almost meaningless, because you can explain almost anything by the assertion that things have a tendency to motility. . . .

In all of this I have left out something very important. I said that observation is the judge of the truth of an idea. But where does the idea come from? The rapid progress and development of science requires that human beings invent something to test.

It was thought in the Middle Ages that people simply make many observations, and the observations themselves suggest the laws. But it does not work that way. It takes much more imagination than that. So the next thing we have to talk about is where the new ideas come from. Actually, it does not make any difference, as long as they come. We have a way of checking whether an idea is correct or not that has nothing to do with where it came from. We simply test it against observation. So in science we are not interested in where an idea comes from.

There is no authority who decides what is a good idea. We have lost the need to go to an authority to find out whether an idea is true or not. We can read an authority and let him suggest something; we can try it out and find out if it is true or not. If it is not true, so much the worse—so the "authorities" lose some of their "authority."

The relations among scientists were at first very argumentative, as they are among most people. This was true in the early days of physics, for example. But in physics today the relations are extremely good. A scientific argument is likely to involve a great deal of laughter and uncertainty on both sides, with both sides thinking up experiments and offering to bet on the outcome. In physics there are so many accumulated observations that it is almost impossible to think of a new idea which is different from all the ideas that have been thought of before and yet that agrees with all the observations that have already been made. And so if you get anything new from anyone, anywhere, you welcome it, and you do not argue about why the other person says it is so.

Many sciences have not developed this far, and the situation is the way it was in the early days of physics, when there was a lot of arguing because there were not so many observations. I bring this up because it is interesting that human relationships, if there is an independent way of judging truth, can become unargumentative.

Most people find it surprising that in science there is no interest in the background of the author of an idea or in his motive in expounding it. You listen, and if it sounds like a thing worth trying, a thing that could be tried, is different, and is not obviously contrary to something observed before, it gets exciting and worthwhile. You do not have to worry about how long he has studied or why he wants you to listen to him. In that sense it makes no difference where the ideas come from. Their real origin is unknown; we call it the imagination of the human brain, the creative imagination—it is known; it is just one of those "oomphs."

It is surprising that people do not believe that there is imagination in science. It is a very interesting kind of imagination, unlike that of the artist. The great difficulty is in trying to imagine something that you have never seen, that is consistent in every detail with what has already been seen, and that is different from what has been thought of; furthermore, it must be definite and not a vague proposition. That is indeed difficult.

Incidentally, the fact that there are rules at all to be checked is a kind of miracle; that it is possible to find a rule, like the inverse square law of gravitation, is some sort of miracle. It is not understood at all, but it leads to the possibility of prediction—that means it tells you what you would expect to happen in an experiment you have not yet done.

It is interesting, and absolutely essential, that the various rules of science be mutually consistent. Since the observations are all the same observations, one rule cannot give one prediction and another rule another prediction. Thus, science is not a specialist business; it is completely universal. . . .

The rules that describe nature seem to be mathematical. This is not a result of the fact that observation is the judge, and it is not a characteristic necessity of science that it be mathematical. It just turns out that you can state mathematical laws, in physics at least, which work to make powerful predictions. Why nature is mathematical is, again, a mystery.

I come now to an important point. The old laws may be wrong. How can an observation be incorrect? If it has been carefully checked, how can it be wrong? Why are physicists always having to change the laws? The answer is, first, that the laws are not the observations and, second, that experiments are always inaccurate. The laws are guessed laws, extrapolations, not something that the observations insist upon. They are just good guesses that have gone through the sieve so far. And it turns out later that the sieve now has smaller holes than the sieves that were used before, and this time the law is caught. So the laws are guessed; they are extrapolations into the unknown. You do not know what is going to happen, so you take a guess.

For example, it was believed—it was discovered—that motion does not affect the weight of a thing—that if you spin a top and weigh it, and then weigh it when it has stopped, it weighs the same. That is the result of an observation. But you cannot weigh something to the infinitesimal number of decimal places, parts in a billion. But we now understand that a spinning top weighs more than a top which is not spinning by a few parts in less than a billion. If the top spins fast enough so that the speed of the edges approaches 186,000 miles a second, the weight increase is appreciable—but not until then. The first experiments were performed with tops that spun at speeds much lower than 186,000 miles a second. It seemed then that the mass of the top spinning and not spinning was exactly the same, and someone made a guess that the mass never changes.

How foolish! What a fool! It is only a guessed law, an extrapolation. Why did he do something so unscientific? There was nothing unscientific about it; it was only uncertain. It would have been unscientific *not* to guess. It has to be done because the extrapolations are the only things that have any real value. It is only the principle of what you think will happen in a case you have not tried that is worth knowing about. Knowledge is of no real value if all you can tell me is what happened yesterday. It is necessary to tell what will happen tomorrow if you do something—not only necessary, but fun. Only you must be willing to stick your neck out.

Every scientific law, every scientific principle, every statement of the results of an observation is some kind of a summary that leaves out details, because nothing can be stated precisely. The man simply forgot—he should have stated the law "The mass doesn't change *much* when the speed isn't *too high.*" The game is to make a specific rule and then see if it will go through the sieve. So the specific guess was that the mass never changes at all. Exciting possibility! It does no harm that it turned out not to be the case. It was only uncertain, and there is no harm in being uncertain. It is better to say something and not be sure than not to say anything at all.

It is necessary and true that all of the things we say in science, all of the conclusions, are uncertain, because they are only conclusions. They are guesses as to what is going to happen, and you cannot know what will happen, because you have not made the most complete experiments.

It is curious that the effect on the mass of a spinning top is so small you may say, "Oh, it doesn't make any difference." But to get a law that is right, or at least one that keeps going through the successive sieves, that goes on for many more observations, requires a tremendous intelligence and imagination and a complete revamping of our philosophy, our understanding of space and time. I am referring to the relativity theory. It turns out that the tiny effects that turn up always require the most revolutionary modifications of ideas.

Scientists, therefore, are used to dealing with doubt and uncertainty. All scientific knowledge is uncertain. This experience with doubt and uncertainty is important. I believe that it is of very great value, and one that extends beyond the sciences. I believe that to solve any problem that has never been solved before, you have to leave the door to the unknown ajar. You have to permit the possibility that you do not have it exactly right. Otherwise, if you have made up your mind already, you might not solve it.

When the scientist tells you he does not know the answer, he is an ignorant man. When he tells you he has a hunch about how it is going to work, he is uncertain about it. When he is pretty sure of how it is going to work, and he tells you, "This is the way it's going to work, I'll bet," he still is in some doubt. And it is of paramount importance, in order to make progress, that we recognize this ignorance and this doubt. Because we have the doubt, we then propose looking in new directions for new ideas. The rate of the development of science is not the rate at which you make observations alone but, much more important, the rate at which you create new things to test.

If we were not able or did not desire to look in any new direction, if we did not have a doubt or recognize ignorance, we would not get any new ideas. There would be nothing worth checking, because we would know what is true. So what we call scientific knowledge today is a body of statements of varying degrees of certainty. Some of them are most unsure; some of them are nearly sure; but none is absolutely certain. Scientists are used to this. We know that it is consistent to be able to live and not know. Some people say, "How can you *live* without knowing?" I do not know what they mean. I always live without knowing. That is easy. How you get to know is what I want to know.

This freedom to doubt is an important matter in the sciences and, I believe, in other fields. It was born of a struggle. It was a struggle to be permitted to doubt, to be unsure. And I do not want us to forget the importance of the struggle and, by default, to let the thing fall away. I feel a responsibility as a scientist who knows the great value of a satisfactory philosophy of ignorance, and the progress made possible by such a philosophy—progress that is the fruit of freedom of thought. I feel a responsibility to proclaim the value of this freedom and to teach that doubt is not to be feared, but that it is to be welcomed as the possibility of a new potential for human beings. If you know that you are not sure, you have a chance to improve the situation. I want to demand this freedom for future generations.

Doubt is clearly a value in the sciences. Whether it is in other fields is an open question and an uncertain matter.

Discussion Questions

1. According to Feynman, how is the value of technology different from the value of the body of knowledge that results from the work of scientists such as Faraday? (16–17)

2. Is the "method of finding things out" that Feynman describes the only possible method of scientific investigation? (18)

3. Can the principle that observation is the judge of scientific truth establish new rules as well as it can test exceptions to existing rules? (18)

4. Is Feynman correct in thinking that the scientific method does not apply to answering questions of human choice and action? (18)

5. After conducting experiments and making observations, what special technique does a scientist use to form an interpretation of the results? (19)

6. In the examples given by Feynman, why is the inverse square law a more specific explanation for the movement of planets than the tendency called an "oomph"? (20)

7. Is it necessary for a physical law to be mathematical in order for it to be specific in Feynman's sense? (20)

8. What relation does Feynman think the scientist's creative imagination has to the accumulated observations that have been used to test previously existing ideas? (20–21)

9. What does Feynman mean when he says that the inverse square law of gravitation, which is successful in making predictions, "is not understood at all"? (21)

10. Is the universality of science that Feynman mentions a reflection of the nature of the physical world or does it result from the requirement that the rules of science should be mutually consistent? (22)

11. How does Feynman think a scientist extrapolates from observations in order to state a scientific law? (22–23)

12. Why does Feynman say that the extrapolations are "the only things that have any real value"? (22–23)

13. How can a scientist produce a law that will last through many successive observations? (23)

14. Is the uncertainty that Feynman says is so necessary for scientific progress compatible with the view that the goal of science is certainty? (23–24)

15. Do scientists have a particular responsibility to promote what Feynman calls their "satisfactory philosophy of ignorance" in fields outside science, such as religion and politics? (24)

Suggestions for Further Reading

By the author

Feynman, Richard P. *The Character of Physical Law*. New York: Modern Library, 1994. In these lectures, Feynman investigates how physicists formulate laws, focusing on the common features of these laws and how scientific progress is possible.

————. *The Meaning of It All: Thoughts of a Citizen Scientist*. Reading, MA: Perseus Books, 1998. This series of three lectures, from which the selection in *What's the Matter?* is taken, reflects Feynman's thoughts on the relationship between science, religion, and politics and expresses his conviction that the freedom to doubt is the basis of true progress in these areas of human concern.

————. *The Pleasure of Finding Things Out: The Best Short Works of Richard P. Feynman*. Edited by Jeffrey Robbins. Cambridge, MA: Perseus Books, 1999, 2000. This collection of essays and autobiographical reflections, conveyed with Feynman's characteristic blend of humor and seriousness, ranges from his early experiences working on the Manhattan Project to his report on the cause of the *Challenger* space shuttle explosion.

About the author

Gleick, James. Genius: *The Life and Science of Richard Feynman*. New York: Vintage, 1993. This biography captures both the scientific achievements and the personality of Feynman, in addition to providing a rich chronicle of his physicist colleagues and the era in which they worked.

About the topic

Derry, Gregory N. *What Science Is and How It Works.* Princeton, NJ: Princeton University Press, 1999, 2002. Starting with the conviction that science is based on the creative engagement of our minds with nature in order to understand our place in the world, the author shows readers what it means to think scientifically and how good science is conducted.

Lightman, Alan. *A Sense of the Mysterious: Science and the Human Spirit.* New York: Pantheon Books, 2005. Many of these essays, by an author who is both a physicist and a literary writer, offer insights into the ways that he and other scientists discover and investigate scientific problems.

Nature is the subject of our inquiry, and nature is a principle of change, so if we do not understand the process of change, we will not understand nature either.

—Aristotle, *Physics*

The Science of Nature

∽

Moving Things

The Western tradition of scientific investigation begins with Aristotle (384–322 BCE). For almost two thousand years, until the seventeenth century, his theories concerning the structure and meaning of the physical world dominated natural science. The longevity of Aristotle's ideas suggests that they are still worth considering. His book *Physics*, from which the following two selections are taken, presents a rigorously developed way of explaining the natural world and provides a contrasting perspective to the underlying assumptions of physics during the last three hundred and fifty years.

Aristotle was the son of the court physician to the king of Macedonia. Around 367 BCE, he was sent to study at Plato's Academy in Athens. At the Academy, Aristotle engaged in probing discussions of intellectual problems in political theory, ethics, literature, mathematics, and natural science. All these areas of thought were studied as branches of philosophy and were considered to be parts of an inquiry leading to a comprehensive knowledge of the world.

After Plato's death (347? BCE), Aristotle left Athens to travel and start academies in other parts of Greece. For three years he tutored the young Alexander the Great in Macedonia. When Aristotle returned to Athens in 335 BCE, he founded his own school, the Lyceum, based on his insights into how knowledge of all aspects of the world should be pursued. He emphasized formal logic, which he invented, as the basis for organizing this knowledge. During this period, Aristotle produced his major writings, including *Physics*, *Metaphysics*, *Ethics*, *Politics*, *Logic (Organon)*, and *Poetics*. Each of these books continues to have great influence in its own area of philosophical investigation. The works of Aristotle that have survived are thought to be detailed outlines of the lectures he delivered at the Lyceum. Almost a third of them are about natural science.

In Aristotle's time, there were many competing explanations of the physical world. He was the first to demonstrate how philosophers could build a theoretical framework for understanding all aspects of the physical world, based on just a few principles. Aristotle proposed that philosophers could accomplish this by combining careful observation of phenomena with the arguments of philosophy about how everything in the world must fit together to form an organic, logically consistent whole. For Aristotle, philosophy and natural science were closely related studies, and as late as the 1800s science was still referred to as natural philosophy. Philosophy provided the wider context for understanding explanations of the physical world. For example, Aristotle often made the argument that each thing in the world is directed by a purpose. This philosophical idea is one of the most important principles by which he forms his explanations of natural change and movement in the *Physics*. In addition, Aristotle was the first to clearly define the terms in which the physical world could be scientifically explained, emphasizing the central importance of such concepts as time, space, change, place, motion, cause, and nature.

Aristotle's *Physics* is both an introduction to his scientific method and an investigation of what causes physical things to change. Despite its title, the *Physics* does not resemble a modern physics textbook in content. In Greek, *physics* was an ordinary word referring in general to what we now call the natural world. Something immediately noticeable about the *Physics* is the absence of mathematics. Aristotle thought that to explain natural things, we must primarily consider all their qualities—their feel, their shape, their color, the appearance of their movement through space, and how they seem to change into one another. For him, applying mathematics to physical phenomena would reduce them to objects defined only by their spatial dimensions, their rate of movement, and their mechanical interactions. Mathematical physics based on careful quantitative measurement along with the techniques of algebra and calculus was not developed until the work of Galileo and Newton in the seventeenth century. The result was a shift to a new picture of the world based on methods and assumptions different from those of Aristotle, making possible scientific advancement of an entirely different kind than his approach could have accomplished.

The Science of Nature

In this selection, Aristotle suggests how we can inquire into the natural world in a scientific way. We all know the world in other ways, such as directly through our sense perceptions. We can also know something about the world through measuring it, assigning numbers to it, and using these numbers to describe the way things move and affect each other. But Aristotle is asking us to consider that scientific knowledge of the natural world comes through discovering the primary causes, or explanations, of things.

In any subject which has principles, causes, and elements, scientific knowledge and understanding stems from a grasp of these, for we think we know a thing only when we have grasped its first causes and principles and have traced it back to its elements. It obviously follows that if we are to gain scientific knowledge of nature as well, we should begin by trying to decide about its principles.

The natural way to go about this is to start with what is more intelligible and clear *to us* and move from there to what is clearer and more intelligible *in itself*. For the fact that something is intelligible to us does not mean that it is intelligible *tout court*.[1] So we have to proceed as I have said: we have to start with things which are less clear in themselves, but are clearer to us, and move from there to things which are clearer and more intelligible in themselves. The things which are immediately obvious and clear to us are usually mixed together; their elements and principles only become intelligible later, when one separates them. That is why we have to progress from the general to the particular; it is because it is whole entities

1. [Without qualification.]

This selection is taken from books 1 and 2 of the Physics.

that are more intelligible to the senses, and anything general is a kind of whole, in the sense that it includes a number of things which we could call its parts. In a way, the same relationship also obtains between names and definitions: a word means an undifferentiated whole (a circle, for instance), whereas the definition separates it into particulars. And little children initially call all men "father" and all women "mother," and only later distinguish who their fathers and mothers are.

~ ~ ~

Some things exist by nature, others are due to other causes. Natural objects include animals and their parts, plants, and simple bodies like earth, fire, air, and water; at any rate, we do say that these kinds of things exist naturally. The obvious difference between all these things and things which are not natural is that each of the natural ones contains within itself a source of change and of stability, in respect of either movement or increase and decrease or alteration. On the other hand, something like a bed or a cloak has no intrinsic impulse for change—at least, they do not under that particular description and to the extent that they are a result of human skill, but they do insofar as and to the extent that they are coincidentally made out of stone or earth or some combination of the two.

The nature of a thing, then, is a certain principle and cause of change and stability in the thing, and it is *directly* present in it—which is to say that it is present in its own right and not coincidentally. . . .

Nature, then, is as stated. The things which have a nature are those which have the kind of source I have been talking about. Each and every one of them is a substance, since substance is an underlying thing, and only underlying things can have a nature. They are all natural, and so is any property they have in their own right, such as the property fire has of moving upward. This property is not nature, and does not have a nature either, but it is due to nature and is natural.

Now, we have said what nature is and what "natural" and "due to nature" mean. It would be absurd, however, to try to *prove* that nature exists, since it is evident that there do exist many things of this sort. To rely on the non-obvious to establish the obvious is a sign of being incapable of distinguishing between what is and what is not intelligible in itself. This is a situation it is quite possible to be in: someone born blind, for instance, might reach conclusions about colors by a process of reasoning. Inevitably, then, people in this kind of situation argue only at the verbal level, but do not understand anything. . . .

↝ ↝ ↝

With these distinctions in place, we should look into the question of how many causes there are, and what they are like. For the point of our investigation is to acquire knowledge, and a prerequisite for knowing anything is understanding *why* it is as it is—in other words, grasping its primary cause. Obviously, then, this is what we have to do in the case of coming to be and ceasing to be, and natural change in general. Then, once we know the principles of these things, we can try to analyze anything we are looking into in terms of these principles.

One way in which the word *cause* is used is for that from which a thing is made and continues to be made—for example, the bronze of a statue, the silver of a bowl, and the genera of which bronze and silver are species.

A second way in which the word is used is for the form or pattern (i.e., the formula for what a thing is, both specifically and generically, and the terms which play a part in the formula). For example, the ratio 2:1, and number in general, cause the octave.

A third way in which the word is used is for the original source of change or rest. For example, a deviser of a plan is a cause, a father causes a child, and in general a producer causes a product and a changer causes a change.

A fourth way in which the word is used is for the end. This is what something is for, as health, for example, may be what walking is for. If asked, "Why is he walking?" we reply, "To get healthy," and in saying this we mean to explain the cause of his walking. And then there is everything which happens during the process of change (initiated by something else) that leads up to the end: for example, the end of health may involve slimming or purging or drugs or surgical implements; they are all for the same end, but they are different in that some are actions and some are implements.

These are more or less all the ways in which we use the word *cause*. The upshot is that there are a number of ways in which the word is used and also that a single thing has a number of causes, even without considering coincidence. For instance, both sculpturing and bronze are causally responsible for a statue, and are so for the statue in its own right, qua statue, although they are dissimilar *kinds* of causes, since one is a cause in the sense that matter is a cause, while the other is a cause in the sense that the source of change is a cause. . . .

~ ~ ~

It is clear, then, that there are causes and that there are as many of them as we have been saying, since there are just as many different kinds of question covered by the question "Why?" To ask "Why?" is ultimately equivalent *either* to asking "What is it?" (this is what the question comes to in the case of unchanging entities: in mathematics, for instance, it is ultimately equivalent to asking for a definition of *straight* or *commensurate* or whatever), *or* to asking "What initiated the change?" (as in "Why did they go to war?"—"Because they had been raided"), *or* to asking "What is the purpose?" (as in "To gain control"), *or* to asking, in the case of things that come to be, "What matter is involved?"

So it is clear that there are these causes and that there are this many of them. It is the job of the natural scientist, then, to understand all four of these causes; if he refers the question "Why?" to this set of four causes— matter, form, source of change, purpose—he will be explaining things in the way a natural scientist should.

In many cases, the last three of these causes come to the same thing. What a thing is and its purpose are the same, and the original source of change is, in terms of form, the same as these two: after all, it is a man who generates a man. This applies universally to everything which is changed itself when initiating change—and things which are *not* like this are not the province of natural science, because they do not initiate change by having change or a source of change within themselves, but do so without changing. . . .

In short, then, the question "Why?" is resolved by answering it in terms of a thing's matter, what it is, and its original source of change. This last is the normal practice of investigating the causes of events by asking, "What comes after what?"—that is, "What was it that first caused some effect, and what was it that was first affected?" and so on throughout a whole sequence. But there are two kinds of sources of natural change, and in one kind the source is not itself a natural object, in the sense that it does not contain its own source of change. In this latter category comes anything which causes change without itself changing (for example, that which is absolutely unchanging and is the primary entity in the whole universe) and what a thing is, or its form (since that is its end or purpose).

Since a thing's nature involves purpose, then, we also have to understand this cause. A complete elucidation of the question "Why?" involves explaining that from *this* there necessarily comes *that* (that that either comes from this in any case, or usually), and what must be present if the thing is to exist (analogous to the way the conclusion follows from the premises), and that this is what it is to be the thing, and that the thing is as it is because it is better that way—not better in any absolute sense, but better given what that particular thing actually is.

Content Questions

1. What does Aristotle think is necessary in order to have a scientific understanding of nature? (31)

2. According to Aristotle, how should we proceed in our search for the principles of nature? (31–32)

3. How are natural things different from things that are not natural? (32)

4. In what way does a bed or a cloak contain within itself a source of change? (32)

5. What does Aristotle mean by the difference between having a nature and "due to nature"? (32)

6. What are the four ways that Aristotle says the word *cause* is used? (33)

7. How can a single thing have a number of different causes? (33–34)

8. According to Aristotle, what questions should a natural scientist ask? (34)

9. Of the four causes, which one answers questions about a sequence of events? (34–35)

10. Which of the four causes explains why something is necessarily the way it is? (35)

Discussion Questions

1. Why does Aristotle say that, in investigating the natural world, we understand the principles of things only when we separate them from our initial sense perceptions? (31)

2. What is the difference between the internal "source of change and of stability" in something natural, and the workings of a machine? (32)

3. How are the changes in a natural object that come about through its internal source different from the changes that result from an external source? (32)

4. How could we discover whether something has natural properties, in the sense that Aristotle means? Could some observed properties help us decide whether or not something is natural? (32)

5. What is the relation of the four causes that Aristotle defines to the principles that he says a natural scientist should seek to discover? (33–34)

6. Are there some aspects of the natural world that might not be discovered through the four kinds of questions Aristotle sets out for the natural scientist to ask? (34)

7. Are the questions Aristotle suggests likely to lead to general physical laws, such as those for motion or heat? (34)

8. What does Aristotle mean when he says that a thing's nature involves purpose and that this cause must be present for a thing to exist? How is purpose a cause in explanations of the natural world? (34–35)

9. Why doesn't Aristotle recommend using quantitative measurements and mathematics to investigate the natural world? Is natural science possible without these tools?

10. Is there any difference between Aristotle's idea of what nature is and current scientific ideas of nature?

Moving Things

For Aristotle, many of the movements of natural objects can be explained by their inherent qualities. Natural objects are not simply bits of passive matter acted on by forces; instead, they act as they do because of what they are. Aristotle observes that objects with a predominantly fiery quality move upward; objects that are predominantly earthy move downward; and watery and airy objects are intermediate—consider condensation and evaporation. He calls these their natural movements. But Aristotle is also investigating the causes of movement when objects are pushed, pulled, or thrown contrary to their natural movements.

Everything that changes must be changed by something. For if the source of the change is not to be found within the changing object itself, it must obviously be changed by something other than itself, because the agent of change must under these circumstances be something different. . . .

❧ ❧ ❧

. . . Something which is potentially of a certain quality or quantity or in a certain place may by its nature be capable of being changed, when it has within itself, and not coincidentally, the source of the relevant kind of change. . . . Fire and earth are forcibly moved by something when they are moved unnaturally, but are moved naturally by something when the result is the actuality of what they already possessed in potential.

The difficulty in knowing what causes changes such as the upward movement of fire and the downward movement of earth is due to the

This selection is taken from books 7 and 8 of the Physics.

ambiguity of "potential." Someone who is learning something knows it potentially in a different sense from someone who already has that information but is not actually putting it to use. . . . Consider, for instance, someone who has passed from the state of potential he was in as a learner to a different potential state (the point being that someone who possesses knowledge but does not have it consciously in mind knows it potentially, but not in the same sense that he knew it potentially before he had learned it); when he is in this state, as long as nothing stops him, he will actualize his knowledge and have it consciously in mind, and if he does not he will prove to be in the contradictory state, that of ignorance. The same goes for natural objects as well: something cold is potentially hot, and then it changes and becomes fire and burns things, as long as nothing stops it and prevents it from doing so. The same goes for heavy and light as well: something becomes light instead of heavy—becomes air, say, instead of water (for water is the first thing to be potentially light)—and it is at once light. So it will immediately actualize its potential, unless something stops it from doing so. But the actuality of anything light is to be in a certain place—that is, high up—and it is being stopped if it is in the opposite place. . . .

But this is exactly what we are trying to discover—why light things and heavy things move to their own places. And the reason is that it is their nature to tend in certain directions, that this is what it is to be light and heavy; what it is to be light is defined by an upward tendency and what it is to be heavy is defined by a downward tendency. However, as I have already said, there are a number of different ways in which something may be potentially light and potentially heavy. When something is water, it is potentially light in one sense, and there is also a sense in which it is still potentially light when it is air, because it may be prevented from being high up. If whatever is preventing it from being high up is removed, however, it becomes actually light and continually rises higher and higher. . . .

Now, if someone moves the obstacle or hindrance, there is a sense in which he is causing the object to change and a sense in which he is not. For example, someone who pulls away a supporting pillar or who takes the stone out of a wineskin under water is only coincidentally causing the object to move; likewise, when a ball bounces off a wall, it is not the wall but the thrower of the ball who causes it to move. Although it is clear, then, that none of these things is a self-mover, each of them does contain with itself a source of movement; it is a source which enables them to be affected, however, rather than to cause movement or to act.

Everything that changes, then, does so either thanks to its own nature or because it is forced to do so, contrary to its nature; everything which is forced to change contrary to its nature is changed by something—that is, by something other than itself; and as for things which are changed naturally, those which are changed by themselves are changed by something and so are those (like light things and heavy things) which are not changed by themselves. For you could say that they were changed either by whatever it was that produced them and made them light or heavy, or by whatever it was that got rid of the obstacles and hindrances. It follows, then, that everything that changes is changed by something.

However, there are two ways in which this can happen. In the first case, the agent of change is not itself responsible for the change, but there is something else which causes the agent to change and so is responsible for the change. In the second case, the agent is itself responsible for the change, and there are again two ways in which this can happen: the agent is either immediately next to the final object or there are a number of intermediate agents in between. An example of the latter is when a stone is moved by a stick, which is moved by a hand, which is moved by a person, who no longer causes movement by being moved by something else.

We describe both the final and the first agents as agents of change, but a first agent of change is, properly speaking, more of an agent of change, because it is responsible for changing the final agent, and not vice versa, and because the first agent is needed for the final agent to be an agent of change, but the converse is not true. The stick, for example, will not cause movement unless the person causes it to move. Now, everything that changes has to be changed by something, and this something must either be changed by something else or not; if it is changed by something else, there must eventually be a first agent of change which is not changed by something else, whereas if the immediate agent of change is the first agent of change, there need not be any other agent. The point is that it is impossible for there to be an infinite series of agents of change which are themselves changed by something else, because an infinite series has no first term. Therefore, if everything that changes is changed by something, and if the first agent is changed, but not by something other than itself, it necessarily follows that it is changed by itself. . . .

. . . It would be a good idea to resolve a certain difficulty concerning movement. Given that, with the exception of self-movers, every moving object is moved by something, how is it that some things—things that are thrown, for instance—have continuity of movement when that which initiated the movement is no longer in contact with them? If the mover also causes something else to move—the air, for instance, which causes movement by being in motion itself—it remains equally impossible for the air to be in motion when the first cause of movement is no longer in contact with it or causing it to move. No, all the things that are moving must move at the same time as the first mover and must have stopped moving when the first mover stopped imparting motion, and this is so even if, like a lodestone, the first mover makes what it has moved capable of causing movement itself. So what we have to say is that although the first cause of movement imparts the ability to cause movement to the air or the water (or whatever else it may be that is, by its nature, capable of causing movement and of being moved), nevertheless the air or water or whatever does not stop causing movement and being moved at the same time as the first mover stops; it may stop being moved as soon as the cause of movement stops imparting movement, but it retains its ability to cause movement. That is why it imparts movement to something else which is consecutive to it, and the same goes for this in turn. The process of stopping begins when each consecutive member of the series has less power to cause movement, and the motion finally comes to an end when the previous member of the series no longer makes the next one a cause of movement, but only makes it move. The movement of these last two members of the series, the mover and the moved, necessarily ends simultaneously, and so the whole movement comes to an end.

So this kind of movement occurs in things which are capable of sometimes being in motion and sometimes being at rest. Despite appearances, it is not continuous motion; for the objects are either successive or in contact, since no single mover is involved, but a number of movers, one after another. . . . As things are, though, the appearance is of a single thing which is moving continuously.

Content Questions

1. According to Aristotle, what direction of movement would be unnatural for something fiery? What direction would be unnatural for something earthy? (38–39)

2. What are the different ways in which something can be potentially light or potentially heavy? (39–40)

3. How does Aristotle explain why heavy and light things move to their own places? (39)

4. In what way does removing an obstacle cause the movement of an object? (39)

5. What are the different ways in which everything that changes is changed by something? (38–40)

6. In a sequence of events involving movement, why is the first agent of change more of an agent of change than the last agent? (40)

7. What is Aristotle's question concerning things that appear to have continuity of movement? (41)

8. What does Aristotle say causes something that is thrown to continue its movement? (41)

9. If the first cause of movement stops moving, why do successive causes of movement, such as air or water, continue to have an effect? When do these effects stop? (41)

10. What reasons does Aristotle have for saying that continuous movement is only an appearance? (41)

Discussion Questions

1. What does Aristotle mean by the "source of the change"? (38)

2. When Aristotle speaks of fire and earth having natural movements, is he just describing the way they appear to move, or is he offering an explanation based on principles and causes? (38)

3. How would Aristotle say a natural scientist should determine whether something watery has the potential to change into something airy? (39)

4. What is the difference between saying that something moves downward because of its heaviness and saying that it falls because of the force of gravity? (39)

5. In Aristotle's example of a ball that bounces off a wall, why does he say that only the thrower of the ball causes the movement and not the wall? (39)

6. Since Aristotle does not introduce the idea of force acting on bodies, how would he explain what happens when a stick moves a stone? (40)

7. Why does Aristotle say that, in a chain of events, there must be a first agent of change? (40) Is this a consideration in current scientific explanations of the natural world?

8. Why does Aristotle think that the continuous movement of a projectile is impossible unless the projectile remains in contact with something that is also moving? (41)

9. How would Aristotle respond to the modern idea of inertia, in which objects in motion or at rest do not change their state unless acted on by a force?

10. Aristotle says that what appears to be the continuous movement of a projectile is actually discontinuous. (41) Does he seem to reach this conclusion through careful observation or through abstract reasoning? How do these two activities each contribute to any investigation of the natural world?

Suggestions for Further Reading

By the author

Aristotle. *Introduction to Aristotle.* Edited by Richard McKeon. Reprint. New York: Modern Library, 1992. McKeon, the editor and author of the excellent introductory essays in this anthology of Aristotle's major works, reminds us that "Aristotle is himself the best introduction to what Aristotle thought and meant."

————. *Physics.* Translated by Robin Waterfield. Oxford: Oxford University Press, 1996, 1999. This translation of the complete text of the *Physics,* from which the selections in *What's the Matter?* are taken, is in clear, modern English and fills some of the gaps in Aristotle's often abbreviated style of writing. An excellent introduction and notes clarify many of Aristotle's more difficult ideas.

Sachs, Joe. *Aristotle's Physics: A Guided Study*. New Brunswick, NJ: Rutgers University Press, 1995. This volume contains an innovative translation of the complete *Physics* along with running commentary designed to help readers follow the lines of Aristotle's reasoning. The introduction is particularly good for its discussion of nonmathematical physics in relation to twentieth-century science.

About the author

Ackrill, J. L. *Aristotle the Philosopher*. Oxford: Oxford University Press, 1981. The author, an outstanding translator and scholar of Aristotle's works, shows how Aristotle's ideas continue to stimulate exciting philosophical discussion and how we can argue with and learn from him.

Barnes, Jonathan. *Aristotle: A Very Short Introduction*. Oxford: Oxford University Press, 2000. This overview by a prominent professor of classical philosophy discusses the most important aspects of Aristotle's ideas with a strong emphasis on his theories of how knowledge of the world is acquired.

About the topic

Cohen, I. Bernard. *The Birth of a New Physics*. Rev. and updated. New York: W. W. Norton & Company, 1985. This history traces the development of modern physics from the revolutionary work of Galileo, Kepler, and Newton in reaction to the dominant ideas of Aristotle and his followers.

I seem to discern the firm belief that in philosophizing one must support oneself upon the opinion of some celebrated author, as if our minds ought to remain completely sterile and barren unless wedded to the reasoning of some other person. . . . That is not how matters stand. Philosophy is written in this grand book, the universe, which stands continually open to our gaze.

—Galileo, *The Assayer*

Falling Bodies and Projectiles

The work of Galileo Galilei (1564–1642) brought about fundamental changes both in how scientists investigate the physical world and in the ideas that nonscientists have about the nature of that world. Some of these changes were the result of his observations of celestial objects with the newly invented telescope. But the most far-reaching changes that Galileo initiated came from his emphasis on performing carefully contrived experiments in which quantities are measured and physical laws formulated in the language of mathematics. He defined the objects of investigation for physics as idealized events limited to the primary measurable aspects of things, such as their position, shape, volume, weight, and speed. Galileo introduced the approach to science in which an investigator constantly questions the meaning of observations, experimental results, and authoritative knowledge in order to find physical principles that will hold up to repeated scrutiny. Because the world into which Galileo was born in 1564 in Pisa, Italy, was dominated by dogmatic authority in science, supported by the powerful institutions of the church and the universities, his life became a struggle to establish new principles for unprejudiced scientific investigation.

When Galileo began his teaching career as a mathematician at the University of Pisa in 1589, physics was taught as a branch of philosophy, mainly derived from the work of Aristotle. Aristotelian physics was based on the principle that motion and change occur because objects have inherent qualities that make them behave in a purposeful way. For example, a heavy object falls toward the earth because its natural place is as close as possible to the center of all heavy things. This emphasis on physical explanations based on philosophical arguments concerning the qualities of things largely precluded explanations based on new experiments involving quantitative measurements and mathematics. In addition, Aristotelian physics placed the earth at the center of the world, with the moon, sun, planets, and stars moving in circular orbits around it and made of unchanging material different from that of the earth.

At Padua, where he remained until 1610, Galileo pursued two lines of scientific investigation that together led him to question prevailing scientific doctrines. One involved experiments with bodies falling freely and rolling down inclined planes. The results were his discovery that, contrary to Aristotelian physics, all heavy bodies fall at the same rate regardless of their material qualities, and his mathematical formulation of laws of motion relating uniform acceleration to time and distance. A version of these experiments is described in the following selection. The other method of scientific investigation was his use of the telescope for astronomical observations. He was the first person to do this and published his findings in *The Starry Messenger* in 1610. Among his discoveries were the uneven contours of the moon's surface, Jupiter's moons, and moving spots on the surface of the sun, all indications that these objects are made of the same changeable material as the earth. If this were the case, he reasoned, the results of his experiments with moving bodies on earth might also apply to celestial objects, suggesting that scientific laws are universal. Because of his discoveries, Galileo became a strong advocate for the controversial heliocentric world system proposed by Copernicus seventy years earlier.

After his appointment as mathematician and philosopher at the Medici court in Florence, Galileo visited Rome in 1613 to convince the church to officially recognize the Copernican system. The resulting complex chain of events over the following twenty years, involving not only church officials but also academic authorities, culminated in his trial and conviction in 1633 by the Inquisition for teaching unorthodox theories. Before his conviction, Galileo wrote the widely read *Dialogue Concerning the Two Chief World Systems* (1632). While under house arrest—which lasted until his death, in 1642—Galileo wrote *Dialogues Concerning Two New Sciences* (1638), in which he summed up his discoveries about the principles of motion and laid a foundation for the work of Isaac Newton.

Galileo wrote the *Dialogue Concerning the Two Chief World Systems*, from which the following selection is taken, as a discussion among three speakers— Salviati, Simplicio, and Sagredo—who argue for and against the widely accepted geocentric system and the new Copernican heliocentric system. In their discussion, they investigate questions about the motion of objects and point the way to the concept of inertia and the new sciences of kinematics and dynamics, which are fundamental to modern physics.

Falling Bodies and Projectiles

Sagredo: Simplicio, begin producing those difficulties that seem to you to contradict this new arrangement of the universe.

Simplicio: The arrangement is not new; rather, it is most ancient, as is shown by Aristotle refuting it, the following being his refutations:

". . . Whether the earth is moved either in itself, being placed in the center, or in a circle, being removed from the center, it must be moved with such motion by force, for this is not its natural motion. Because if it were, it would belong also to all its particles. But every one of them is moved along a straight line toward the center." . . .

. . . [Aristotle] strengthens this with [an] argument taken from experiments with heavy bodies which, falling from a height, go perpendicularly to the surface of the earth. Similarly, projectiles thrown vertically upward come down again perpendicularly by the same line, even though they have been thrown to immense height. These arguments are necessary proofs that their motion is toward the center of the earth, which, without moving in the least, awaits and receives them. . . .

Salviati: The arguments produced on this matter are of two kinds. Some pertain to terrestrial events without relation to the stars, and others

This selection is taken from part 2, "The Second Day," of Dialogue Concerning the Two Chief World Systems.

are drawn from the appearances and observations of celestial things. Aristotle's arguments are drawn mostly from the things around us, and he leaves the others to the astronomers. Hence it will be good, if it seems so to you, to examine those taken from earthly experiments. . . . Therefore, Simplicio, present them, if you will; or, if you want me to relieve you of that burden, I am at your service.

Simplicio: It will be better for you to bring them up, for having given them greater study you will have them readier at hand, and in great number, too.

Salviati: As the strongest reason of all is adduced that of heavy bodies, which, falling down from on high, go by a straight and vertical line to the surface of the earth. This is considered an irrefutable argument for the earth being motionless. For if it made the diurnal rotation, a tower from whose top a rock was let fall, being carried by the whirling of the earth, would travel many hundreds of yards to the east in the time the rock would consume in its fall, and the rock ought to strike the earth that distance away from the base of the tower. This effect they support with another experiment, which is to drop a lead ball from the top of the mast of a boat at rest, noting the place where it hits, which is close to the foot of the mast; but if the same ball is dropped from the same place when the boat is moving, it will strike at that distance from the foot of the mast which the boat will have run during the time of fall of the lead, and for no other reason than that the natural movement of the ball when set free is in a straight line toward the center of the earth. This argument is fortified with the experiment of a projectile sent a very great distance upward; this might be a ball shot from a cannon aimed perpendicular to the horizon. In its flight and return this consumes so much time that in our latitude the cannon and we would be carried together many miles eastward by the earth, so that the ball, falling, could never come back near the gun, but would fall as far to the west as the earth had run on ahead. . . .

Simplicio: Oh, these are excellent arguments, to which it will be impossible to find a valid answer. . . .

Salviati: There is a considerable difference between the matter of the ship and that of the earth under the assumption that the diurnal motion belongs to the terrestrial globe. For it is quite obvious that just as the motion of the ship is not its natural one, so the motion of all the things in it is accidental; hence it is no wonder that this stone which was held at the top of the mast falls down when it is set free, without any compulsion to follow the motion of the ship. But the diurnal rotation is being taken as the terrestrial globe's own and natural motion, and hence that of all its parts, as a thing indelibly impressed upon them by nature. Therefore the rock at the top of the tower has as its primary tendency a revolution about the center of the whole in twenty-four hours, and it eternally exercises this natural propensity no matter where it is placed. To be convinced of this, you have only to alter an outmoded impression made upon your mind, saying: "Having thought until now that it is a property of the earth's globe to remain motionless with respect to its center, I have never had any difficulty in or resistance to understanding that each of its particles also rests naturally in the same quiescence. Just so, it ought to be that if the natural tendency of the earth were to go around its center in twenty-four hours, each of its particles would also have an inherent and natural inclination not to stand still but to follow that same course."

And thus without encountering any obstacle you would be able to conclude that since the motion conferred by the force of the oars upon a boat, and through the boat upon all things contained in it, is not natural but foreign to them, then it might well be that this rock, once separated from the boat, is restored to its natural state and resumes its exercise of the simple tendency natural to it. . . .

Simplicio: It would be necessary to be able to make such an experiment and then to decide according to the result. Meanwhile, the result on shipboard confirms my opinion up to this point.

Salviati: You may well say "up to this point," since perhaps in a very short time it will look different. And to keep you no longer on tenterhooks, as the saying goes, tell me, Simplicio: do you feel convinced that the experiment on the ship squares so well with our purpose that one may reasonably believe that whatever is seen to occur there must also take place on the terrestrial globe?

Simplicio: So far, yes; and though you have brought up some trivial disparities, they do not seem to me of such moment as to suffice to shake my conviction.

Salviati: Rather, I hope that you will stick to it, and firmly insist that the result on the earth must correspond to that on the ship, so that when the latter is perceived to be prejudicial to your case you will not be tempted to change your mind.

You say, then, that since when the ship stands still the rock falls to the foot of the mast, and when the ship is in motion it falls apart from there, then conversely, from the falling of the rock at the foot it is inferred that the ship stands still, and from its falling away it may be deduced that the ship is moving. And since what happens on the ship must likewise happen on the land, from the falling of the rock at the foot of the tower one necessarily infers the immobility of the terrestrial globe. Is that your argument?

Simplicio: That is exactly it, briefly stated, which makes it easy to understand.

Salviati: Now tell me: if the stone dropped from the top of the mast when the ship was sailing rapidly fell in exactly the same place on the ship to which it fell when the ship was standing still, what use could you make of this falling with regard to determining whether the vessel stood still or moved?

Simplicio: Absolutely none, just as by the beating of the pulse, for instance, you cannot know whether a person is asleep or awake, since the pulse beats in the same manner in sleeping as in waking.

Salviati: Very good. Now, have you ever made this experiment of the ship?

Simplicio: I have never made it, but I certainly believe that the authorities who adduced it had carefully observed it. Besides, the cause of the difference is so exactly known that there is no room for doubt.

Salviati: You yourself are sufficient evidence that those authorities may have offered it without having performed it, for you take it as certain without having done it, and commit yourself to the good faith of their dictum. Similarly it not only may be, but must be that they did the same thing, too—I mean, put faith in their predecessors, right on back without ever arriving at anyone who had performed it. For anyone who does will find that the experiment shows exactly the opposite of what is written; that is, it will show that the stone always falls in the same place on the ship, whether the ship is standing still or moving with any speed you please. Therefore, the same cause holding good on the earth as on the ship, nothing can be inferred about the earth's motion or rest from the stone falling always perpendicularly to the foot of the tower.

Simplicio: If you had referred me to any other agency than experiment, I think that our dispute would not soon come to an end, for this appears to me to be a thing so remote from human reason that there is no place in it for credulity or probability.

Salviati: For me there is, just the same.

Simplicio: So you have not made a hundred tests, or even one? And yet you so freely declare it to be certain? I shall retain my incredulity, and my own confidence that the experiment has been made by the most important authors who make use of it, and that it shows what they say it does.

Salviati: Without experiment, I am sure that the effect will happen as I tell you, because it must happen that way; and I might add that you yourself also know that it cannot happen otherwise, no matter how you may pretend not to know it—or give that impression. But I am so handy at picking people's brains that I shall make you confess this in spite of yourself. . . .

Simplicio: I shall reply as best I can, certain that I shall be put to little trouble, for of the things I hold to be false, I believe I can know nothing, seeing that knowledge is of the true and not of the false.

Salviati: I do not want you to declare or reply anything that you do not know for certain. Now tell me: Suppose you have a plane surface as smooth as a mirror and made of some hard material like steel. This is not parallel to the horizon but somewhat inclined, and upon it you have placed a ball which is perfectly spherical and of some hard and heavy material like bronze. What do you believe this will do when released? Do you not think, as I do, that it will remain still?

Simplicio: If that surface is tilted?

Salviati: Yes, that is what was assumed.

Simplicio: I do not believe that it would stay still at all; rather, I am sure that it would spontaneously roll down.

Salviati: Pay careful attention to what you are saying, Simplicio, for I am certain that it would stay wherever you placed it.

Simplicio: Well, Salviati, so long as you make use of assumptions of this sort I shall cease to be surprised that you deduce such false conclusions.

Salviati: Then you are quite sure that it would spontaneously move downward?

Simplicio: What doubt is there about this?

Salviati: And you take this for granted not because I have taught it to you—indeed, I have tried to persuade you to the contrary—but all by yourself, by means of your own common sense.

Simplicio: Oh, now I see your trick; you spoke as you did in order to get me out on a limb, as the common people say, and not because you really believed what you said.

Salviati: That was it. Now how long would the ball continue to roll, and how fast? Remember that I said a perfectly round ball and a highly polished surface, in order to remove all external and accidental impediments. Similarly I want you to take away any impediment of the air caused by its resistance to separation, and all other accidental obstacles, if there are any.

Simplicio: I completely understood you, and to your question I reply that the ball would continue to move indefinitely, as far as the slope of the surface extended, and with a continually accelerated motion. For such is the nature of heavy bodies, which *vires acquirunt eundo,*[1] and the greater the slope, the greater would be the velocity.

Salviati: But if one wanted the ball to move upward on this same surface, do you think it would go?

Simplicio: Not spontaneously, no; but drawn or thrown forcibly, it would.

Salviati: And if it were thrust along with some impetus impressed forcibly upon it, what would its motion be, and how great?

Simplicio: The motion would constantly slow down and be retarded, being contrary to nature, and would be of longer or shorter duration according to the greater or lesser impulse and the lesser or greater slope upward.

Salviati: Very well; up to this point you have explained to me the events of motion upon two different planes. On the downward inclined plane, the heavy moving body spontaneously descends and continually accelerates, and to keep it at rest requires the use of force. On the upward slope, force is needed to thrust it along or even to hold it still, and motion which is impressed upon it continually diminishes until it is entirely annihilated. You say also that a difference in the two

1. [Gain strength as they go.—Trans.]

instances arises from the greater or lesser upward or downward slope of the plane, so that from a greater slope downward there follows a greater speed, while on the contrary upon the upward slope a given movable body thrown with a given force moves farther according as the slope is less.

Now tell me what would happen to the same movable body placed upon a surface with no slope upward or downward.

Simplicio: Here I must think a moment about my reply. There being no downward slope, there can be no natural tendency toward motion, and there being no upward slope, there can be no resistance to being moved, so there would be an indifference between the propensity and the resistance to motion. Therefore it seems to me that it ought naturally to remain stable. . . .

Salviati: I believe it would do so if one set the ball down firmly. But what would happen if it were given an impetus in any direction?

Simplicio: It must follow that it would move in that direction.

Salviati: But with what sort of movement? One continually accelerated, as on the downward plane, or increasingly retarded, as on the upward one?

Simplicio: I cannot see any cause for acceleration or deceleration, there being no slope upward or downward.

Salviati: Exactly so. But if there is no cause for the ball's retardation, there ought to be still less for its coming to rest, so how far would you have the ball continue to move?

Simplicio: As far as the extension of the surface continued without rising or falling.

Salviati: Then if such a space were unbounded, the motion on it would likewise be boundless? That is, perpetual?

Simplicio: It seems so to me, if the movable body were of durable material.

Salviati: That is of course assumed, since we said that all external and accidental impediments were to be removed, and any fragility on the part of the moving body would in this case be one of the accidental impediments.

Now tell me, what do you consider to be the cause of the ball moving spontaneously on the downward inclined plane, but only by force on the one tilted upward?

Simplicio: That the tendency of heavy bodies is to move toward the center of the earth, and to move upward from its circumference only with force; now the downward surface is that which gets closer to the center, while the upward one gets farther away.

Salviati: Then in order for a surface to be neither downward nor upward, all its parts must be equally distant from the center. Are there any such surfaces in the world?

Simplicio: Plenty of them; such would be the surface of our terrestrial globe if it were smooth, and not rough and mountainous as it is. But there is that of the water, when it is placid and tranquil.

Salviati: Then a ship, when it moves over a calm sea, is one of these movables which courses over a surface that is tilted neither up nor down, and if all external and accidental obstacles were removed, it would thus be disposed to move incessantly and uniformly from an impulse once received?

Simplicio: It seems that it ought to be.

Salviati: Now as to that stone which is on top of the mast: Does it not move, carried by the ship, both of them going along the circumference of a circle about its center? And consequently is there not in it an ineradicable motion, all external impediments being removed? And is not this motion as fast as that of the ship?

Simplicio: All this is true, but what next?

Salviati: Go on and draw the final consequence by yourself, if by yourself you have known all the premises.

Simplicio: By the final conclusion you mean that the stone, moving with an indelibly impressed motion, is not going to leave the ship but will follow it, and finally will fall at the same place where it fell when the ship remained motionless. And I, too, say that this would follow if there were no external impediments to disturb the motion of the stone after it was set free. But there are two such impediments: one is the inability of the movable body to split the air with its own impetus alone, once it has lost the force from oars which it shared as part of the ship while it was on the mast; the other is the new motion of falling downward, which must impede its other, forward, motion.

Salviati: As for the impediment of the air, I do not deny that to you, and if the falling body were of very light material, like a feather or a tuft of wool, the retardation would be quite considerable. But in a heavy stone it is insignificant, and if . . . the force of the wildest wind is not enough to move a large stone from its place, just imagine how much the quiet air could accomplish upon meeting a rock which moved no faster than the ship! All the same, as I said, I concede to you the small effect which may depend upon such an impediment, just as I know you will concede to me that if the air were moving at the same speed as the ship and the rock, this impediment would be absolutely nil.

As for the other, the supervening motion downward, in the first place it is obvious that these two motions (I mean the circular around the center and the straight motion toward the center) are not contraries, nor are they destructive of one another, nor incompatible. As to the moving body, it has no resistance whatever to such a motion, for you yourself have already granted the resistance to be against motion which increases the distance from the center, and the tendency to be toward motion which approaches the center. From this it follows necessarily that the moving body has neither a resistance nor a propensity to motion which does not approach toward or depart from the center, and in consequence no cause for diminution in the property impressed upon it. Hence the cause of motion is not a single one which must be weakened by the new action, but there exist two distinct causes. Of these, heaviness attends only to the drawing of the movable body toward the center, and impressed force only to its being led around the center, so no occasion remains for any impediment.

Simplicio: This argument is really very plausible in appearance, but actually it is offset by a difficulty which is hard to overcome. You have made an assumption throughout which will not lightly be granted by the Peripatetic school, being directly contrary to Aristotle. You take it as well known and evident that the projectile when separated from its origin retains the motion which was forcibly impressed upon it there. Now, this impressed force is as detestable to the Peripatetic philosophy as is any transfer of an accidental property from one subject to another. In their philosophy it is held, as I believe you know, that the projectile is carried by the medium, which in the present instance is the air. Therefore if that rock which was dropped from the top of the mast were to follow the motion of the ship, this effect would have to be attributed to the air, and not to the impressed force, but you assume that the air does not follow the motion of the ship, and is quiet.

Furthermore, the person letting the stone fall does not need to fling it or give it any impetus with his arm but has only to open his hand and let it go. So the rock cannot follow the motion of the boat either through any force impressed upon it by its thrower or by means of any assistance from the air, and therefore it will remain behind.

Salviati: It seems to me that what you are saying is that there is no way for the stone to be projected, not being thrown by anybody's arm.

Simplicio: This motion cannot properly be called one of projection.

Salviati: Then what Aristotle says about the motion of projectiles, the things moved by projection, and their movers is quite beside our purpose, and if it has nothing to do with us, why do you bring it up?

Simplicio: I adduce it for the sake of that impressed force which you introduced and gave a name to but which, since it does not exist in the world, cannot act at all, since *non entium nullae sunt operationes*.[2] Hence the cause of motion must be attributed to the medium, not only for projectiles, but for all other motions that are not natural ones. Due consideration has not been given to this, so what has been said up to this point remains ineffective.

Salviati: Patience; all in good time. Tell me: Seeing that your objection is based entirely upon the nonexistence of impressed force, then if I were to show you that the medium plays no part in the continuation of motion in projectiles after they are separated from their throwers, would you allow impressed force to exist? Or would you merely move on to some other attack directed toward its destruction?

Simplicio: If the action of the medium were removed, I do not see how recourse could be had to anything else than the property impressed by the motive force.

Salviati: It will be best, so as to get as far away as possible from any reason for arguing about it forever, to have you explain as clearly as you can just what the action of the medium is in maintaining the motion of the projectile.

Simplicio: Whoever throws the stone has it in his hand; he moves his arm with speed and force; by its motion not only the rock but the surrounding air is moved; the rock, upon being deserted by the hand, finds itself in air which is already moving with impetus, and by that

2. [The nonexistent performs no actions.—Trans.]

it is carried. For if the air did not act, the stone would fall from the thrower's hand to his feet.

Salviati: And you are so credulous as to let yourself be persuaded of this nonsense, when you have your own senses to refute it and to learn the truth? Look here: A big stone or a cannonball would remain motionless on a table in the strongest wind. . . . Now do you believe that if instead this had been a ball of cork or cotton, the wind would have moved it?

Simplicio: I am quite sure the wind would have carried it away, and would have done this the faster, the lighter the material was. For we see this in clouds being borne with a speed equal to that of the wind which drives them.

Salviati: And what sort of thing is the wind?

Simplicio: The wind is defined as merely air in motion.

Salviati: So then the air in motion carries light materials much faster and farther than it does heavy ones?

Simplicio: Certainly.

Salviati: But if with your arm you had to throw first a stone and then a wisp of cotton, which would move the faster and the farther?

Simplicio: The stone, by a good deal; the cotton would merely fall at my feet.

Salviati: Well, if that which moves the thrown thing after it leaves your hand is only the air moved by your arm, and if moving air pushes light material more easily than heavy, why doesn't the cotton projectile go farther and faster than the stone one? There must be something conserved in the stone, in addition to any motion of the air. Besides, if two strings of equal length were suspended from that rafter, with a lead ball attached to the end of one and a cotton ball to the other, and then if both were drawn an equal distance from the perpendicular and set free, there is no doubt that each would move toward the perpendicular and, propelled by its own impetus, would go beyond that by a certain interval and afterward return. Which of these pendulums, do you believe, would continue to move the longer before stopping vertically?

Simplicio: The lead ball would go back and forth a great many times; the cotton ball, two or three at most.

Salviati: So that whatever the cause of that impetus and mobility, it is conserved longer in the heavy material than in the light. Now I come to

59

the next point, and ask you why the air does not carry away the citron on that table right now.

Simplicio: Because the air itself is not moving.

Salviati: So the person who does the throwing must give the air that motion with which it subsequently moves the thing thrown. But since this force is incapable of being impressed (for you said that an accidental property cannot be made to pass from one subject to another), how can it go from the arm to the air? Or perhaps the arm and the air are not different subjects?

Simplicio: The answer is that the air, being neither heavy nor light in its own domain, is so disposed as to receive every impulse very readily, and to conserve it, too.

Salviati: Well, if the pendulums have just shown us that the less a moving body partakes of weight, the less apt it is to conserve motion, how can it be that the air, which has no weight at all in air, is the only thing that does conserve the motion acquired? I believe, and I know that you also believe at this moment, that no sooner does the arm stop than the air around it stops. Let us go into that room and agitate the air as much as possible with a towel; then, stopping the cloth, have a little candle flame brought immediately into the room, or set flying a bit of gold leaf in it, and you will see from the quiet wandering of either one that the air has been instantly restored to tranquillity. I could give you many experiments, but if one of these is not enough, the case is quite hopeless.

Sagredo: What an incredible stroke of luck it is that when an arrow is shot against the wind, the slender thread of air driven by the bowstring goes along with the arrow! But there is another point of Aristotle's which I should like to understand, and I beg Simplicio to oblige me with an answer.

If two arrows were shot with the same bow, one in the usual way and one sideways—that is, putting the arrow lengthwise along the cord and shooting it that way—I should like to know, which one would go the farther? Please reply, even though the question may seem to you more ridiculous than otherwise; forgive me for being, as you see, something of a blockhead, so that my speculations do not soar very high.

Simplicio: I have never seen an arrow shot sideways, but I think it would not go even one-twentieth the distance of one shot point-first.

Sagredo: Since that is just what I thought, it gives me occasion to raise a question between Aristotle's dictum and experience. For as to experience, if I were to place two arrows upon that table when a strong wind was blowing, one in the direction of the wind and the other across it, the wind would quickly carry away the latter and leave the former. Now apparently the same ought to happen with two shots from a bow, if Aristotle's doctrine were true, because the one going sideways would be spurred on by a great quantity of air moved by the bowstring—as much as the whole length of the arrow—whereas the other arrow would receive the impulse from only as much air as there is in the tiny circle of its thickness. I cannot imagine the cause of such a disparity, and should like very much to know it.

Simplicio: The cause is obvious to me; it is because the arrow shot point foremost has to penetrate only a small quantity of air, and the other has to cleave as much as its whole length.

Sagredo: Oh, so when arrows are shot they have to penetrate the air? If the air goes with them, or rather if it is the very thing which conducts them, what penetration can there be? Do you not see that in such a manner the arrow would be moving faster than the air? Now what conferred this greater velocity upon the arrow? Do you mean to say that the air gives it a greater speed than its own?

You know perfectly well, Simplicio, that this whole thing takes place just exactly opposite to what Aristotle says, and that it is as false that the medium confers motion upon the projectile as it is true that it is this alone which impedes it. Once you understand this, you will recognize without any difficulty that when the air really does move, it carries the arrow along with it much better sideways than point-first, because there is lots of air driving it in the former case and little in the latter. But when shot from the bow, since the air stands still, the sidewise arrow strikes against much air and is much impeded, while the other easily overcomes the obstacles of the tiny amount of air that opposes it.

Salviati: How many propositions I have noted in Aristotle (meaning always in his science) that are not only wrong, but wrong in such a way that their diametrical opposites are true, as happens in this instance! But keeping to our purpose, I believe that Simplicio is convinced that from seeing the rock always fall in the same place, nothing can be guessed about the motion or stability of the ship. If what had been said previously was not enough, this experience concerning the medium can make the whole thing certain. From this experience it may be seen that, at most, the falling body might drop behind if it were made of light material and the air did not follow the ship's motion, but if the air were moving with equal speed, no imaginable difference could be found in this or in any other experiment you please, as I shall soon explain to you. Now, if in this example no difference whatever appears, what is it that you claim to see in the stone falling from the top of the tower, where the rotational movement is not adventitious and accidental to the stone but natural and eternal, and where the air as punctiliously follows the motion of the earth as the tower does that of the terrestrial globe? Do you have anything else to say, Simplicio, on this particular?

Simplicio: No more, except that so far I do not see the mobility of the earth to be proved.

Salviati: I have not claimed to prove it yet, but only to show that nothing can be deduced from the experiments offered by its adversaries as one argument for its motionlessness.

Content Questions

1. How does the observation that falling bodies and projectiles seem to follow straight lines toward the center of the earth support Aristotle's refutation of the theory that the earth is in motion? (49–50)

2. What reason is there to think that the lead ball dropped from the top of the mast of the moving ship would strike at a distance from the foot of the mast? (50)

3. According to Salviati, what is the "considerable difference" between the example of dropping a lead ball from the mast of a moving ship and that of dropping it from the top of a tower? (50)

4. How does Simplicio infer from the example of the moving ship that the "terrestrial globe" is not moving? (51–52)

5. What reasons does Salviati offer to Simplicio to convince him that his faith in the opinions of his predecessors is unfounded? (52–53)

6. What assumptions about the behavior of heavy bodies are behind Simplicio's explanation to Salviati of "the events of motion upon two different planes"? (54)

7. In Salviati's thought experiments about rolling balls, as well as plane and spherical surfaces, what are the "external and accidental impediments" that have been removed? (54)

8. What argument does Salviati offer in response to Simplicio's objection that the falling motion of the stone from the mast "must impede its other, forward, motion"? (56)

9. How does Simplicio's explanation of movement of the medium of air work as an alternative to Salviati's idea of an impressed force? (57–58)

10. Why does Salviati suggest that "there must be something conserved in the stone" in offering his explanation for the movement of projectiles? (59)

11. What is the question that Sagredo says he is raising "between Aristotle's dictum and experience"? (61)

12. By the end of the discussion, what does Salviati claim to have shown about the arguments for the motionlessness of the earth? (61–62)

Discussion Questions

1. At the beginning of the dialogue, what justification do Simplicio and Salviati have for basing their arguments on the assumption that objects have natural motions? (50–51)

2. Why does Galileo have Simplicio say he is convinced of the outcome of the ship experiment without having performed it because "the cause of the difference is so exactly known"? (52)

3. According to Salviati, how should a scientist decide when to retest received knowledge by experiment and when to accept it as indisputably established? (52–53)

4. After having Salviati suggest that a physical experiment be performed, why does Galileo have Salviati say to Simplicio that he is certain of the result "without experiment" and that Simplicio knows "it cannot happen otherwise"? (53)

5. Why does Galileo have Salviati begin his questioning of Simplicio by tricking him into admitting that assumptions contrary to common sense are misleading? (53–54)

6. How can an ideal thought experiment such as Salviati's establish anything about the physical world if "all external and accidental impediments" are imagined as having been removed? (54) What advantages for explaining the physical world would there be in not taking into consideration these impediments?

7. What are some of the aspects of a physical event that a scientist might consider in trying to form an explanation of what happens? How should a scientist decide which aspects to focus on and which to disregard? (54)

8. What is the source of the knowledge of causes that Salviati and Simplicio use to predict what will happen to the ball on the plane in the thought experiment? (54–56)

9. If Salviati and Simplicio need a cause to explain why the ball moves upward or downward on the inclined plane, why don't they seem to need a cause for the ball's "boundless" motion on a level plane? (55)

10. How is the incessant and uniform motion of the ship on a spherical surface the same or different from the concept of inertia? (56)

11. What evidence does Salviati have that the motion of the body falling from the mast of the ship has "two distinct causes"? (57)

12. What do Salviati and Simplicio mean by an "impressed force"? (57–58)

13. Is there any advantage to explaining the motion of a projectile by means of a medium that sustains the motion, as Simplicio claims? (58)

14. Is Sagredo correct in saying, "You know perfectly well, Simplicio, that this whole thing takes place just exactly opposite to what Aristotle says"? (61)

15. Does the inconclusiveness of this dialogue demonstrate the strength or the weakness of the characters' scientific investigation? (62)

Suggestions for Further Reading

By the author

Galileo. *Dialogue Concerning the Two Chief World Systems—Ptolemaic and Copernican.* Translated by Stillman Drake. New York: Modern Library, 2001. This book, from which the selection in *What's the Matter?* is taken, provoked Galileo's trial by the Inquisition for promoting Copernicus's heliocentric system. This edition includes an insightful foreword by Einstein.

———. *Discoveries and Opinions of Galileo.* Translated by Stillman Drake. New York: Anchor Books, 1957, 1990. This collection contains four of Galileo's most important shorter writings, including *The Starry Messenger,* in which he reports the first observations with a telescope of the moon, planets, and stars.

———. *Two New Sciences: Including Centers of Gravity and Force of Percussion.* Translated by Stillman Drake. 2nd ed. Toronto: Wall & Thompson, 1989. In this pathbreaking work written toward the end of his life, Galileo combines lively dialogues and mathematical proofs to formulate for the first time the laws of motion relating time, distance, and acceleration. Much of modern physics begins here.

About the author

Drake, Stillman. *Galileo: A Very Short Introduction.* Oxford: Oxford University Press, 2001. The foremost contemporary scholar and translator of Galileo's work provides in this brief book an overview of Galileo's life and scientific accomplishments.

Sobel, Dava. *Galileo's Daughter: A Historical Memoir of Science, Faith, and Love.* New York: Walker & Company, 1999; New York: Penguin Books, 2000. This is a biography of Galileo himself as much as of his daughter, whose letters to her father serve as a focus for portraying the social, intellectual, and spiritual forces that influenced his trial by the Inquisition.

About the topic

Cohen, I. Bernard. *The Birth of a New Physics.* Rev. and updated. New York: W. W. Norton & Company, 1985. This lively history of the beginnings of modern science focuses on the revolutionary work of Galileo, Kepler, and Newton. Through close attention to the details of their scientific investigations, the author challenges us to think about how they created the worldview that we now take for granted.

The whole difficulty of philosophy appears
to turn upon this: that from the phenomena
of motion we may investigate the forces of
nature, and then from these forces we may
demonstrate the rest of the phenomena.

—Isaac Newton, *Principia*

Forces

↬

Laws of Motion

↬

Time, Space, and Motion

↬

Rules of Doing Philosophy

The great changes in natural science in the seventeenth century are often described as the scientific revolution. Outmoded ways of explaining the physical world gave way to a new approach emphasizing the methods of modern science, including observation, experimentation, quantitative measurement, and the mathematical formulation of natural laws. The theoretical and experimental discoveries of Isaac Newton (1642–1727) were central to this revolution, as he synthesized and perfected the work of the innovative scientists who preceded him. Acknowledging his debt to them, Newton wrote, "If I have seen further, it is by standing upon the shoulders of Giants." However, many of Newton's achievements, including his laws of motion, theories of gravity and optics, and invention of calculus, are his own creations and opened up new ways of understanding the physical world.

Newton was raised on a farm in England but his mechanical ingenuity and scholarly interests were recognized, and a relative made it possible for him to study at the University of Cambridge, beginning in 1661. At that time, universities did not offer science courses, and the study of the natural world was considered a branch of philosophy. The doctrines of Aristotle and his followers dominated natural phi-losophy, maintaining that the earth is at the center of the universe, that the natural principles governing the earth and the heavens are fundamentally different, and that objects continue moving only if a cause sustains their motion. Newton's studies in natural philosophy covered none of the topics now basic to physics—concepts such as mass, force, gravity, inertia, and the idea that the movements of objects can be measured and predicted in terms of their mass and the forces impressed on them.

However, during the one hundred years preceding Newton, independent-minded scientists including Nicolaus Copernicus, Rene Descartes, Galileo, and Johannes Kepler had taken new directions in investigating the physical world and had begun to challenge Aristotelian doctrines. Newton immersed himself in these scientists' writings and embarked on a rigorous course of self-study, mastering their ideas and making them the basis of his own investigations. Each of these scientists had made discoveries that Newton perceived could be part of a comprehensive theory of the physical world, but which had not been brought together under one unifying set of principles. Kepler, following Copernicus's idea of a heliocentric world, had derived from astronomical data three laws that accurately described the elliptical orbits of the planets. Descartes had proposed that all motions in the physical world could be understood in terms of the mechanical interactions of objects that can be measured and quantified. Galileo, using the newly invented telescope, had observed that the moon and the planets appear to be made of the same materials as the earth. In addition, Galileo developed a new science of mechanics based on experimentation, formulated mathematical laws that describe accelerated motion, and suggested a principle of inertia according to which objects, once set in motion, keep moving with no need to find a cause to explain their continuing movement. All these scientists shared Newton's belief in the importance of careful observation and experimentation and regarded mathematics as the language of science.

As an undergraduate and later as a Cambridge professor, Newton conducted his scientific research in solitude, carefully guarding his discoveries. After his invention of the reflecting telescope—the result of his extensive investigations in optics—Newton was elected in 1671 as a member of the Royal Society, an association of prominent scientists who met to exchange ideas about new scientific developments. In order to answer his colleagues' questions about planetary motion, Newton proceeded to systematically bring together his discoveries concerning astronomy and the science of motion and forces in one book, *Philosophiae Naturalis Principia Mathematica (Mathematical Principles of Natural Philosophy)*, published in 1687. Starting with quantitative definitions of mass and forces, and stating three laws governing the motion of all objects, Newton built a complex structure of mathematical proofs culminating in his demonstration that gravity, the force of attraction between all bodies with mass, operates everywhere in the universe according to a simple inverse square law. He also laid the foundation of the modern science of mechanics and explained the movements of planets, moons, comets, and tides, providing a sound theoretical basis for Kepler's laws. Most important, in the *Principia* Newton demonstrated for the first time that the same natural laws apply to phenomena universally, from an apple's fall to the ground to the moon's orbiting of the earth. Even after Newton's ideas were challenged by the theory of relativity and quantum theory in the twentieth century, scientists have relied on his insight that well-established physical laws apply in all times and places, allowing scientists to extend their investigations to the entire universe.

The publication of the *Principia* brought wide fame to Newton, who left the academic world of Cambridge and moved to London, where he served as master of the Royal Mint and president of the Royal Society, and was knighted. Over the next two centuries, the mechanistic explanations of Newtonian physics came to embody a broad worldview. Its influence extended far beyond the realm of physical science, even being used as a model in attempts to make sense of human activities, including political, historical, and economic movements.

See also Newton / Young, pages 99–100.

Forces

In the following definitions and commentaries from the beginning of the Principia, *Newton specifies what he means by matter, motion, and force and suggests some of the implications for investigating the physical world. At the same time, Newton asserts that he is "considering these forces, not physically, but only mathematically." This selection raises many issues, from the nature of a definition itself to the differences and similarities in our understanding of these terms today.*

Definition 1

*The **quantity of matter** is the measure of the same arising from its density and magnitude conjointly.*

Air of double density, in a space that is also doubled, is quadrupled; in a tripled [space],[1] sextupled. The same is to be understood of snow and powdered substances condensed by compression or liquefaction. And the same account is given of all bodies which are condensed in various ways through various causes. In this I do not take account of the medium (if any) freely pervading the interstices of the parts. Further, in what follows, by the names *body* or *mass* I everywhere mean this quantity. It is apprehended through an individual body's weight. For it is found by experiments with pendulums carried out with the greatest accuracy to be proportional to weight.

1. [Bracketed material in this selection is from the translator.]

This selection is taken from "Definitions," of the Principia.

Definition 2

*The **quantity of motion** is the measure of the same arising from the velocity and the quantity of matter conjointly.*

The motion of the whole is the sum of the motions in the individual parts, and therefore in a body twice as big, with an equal velocity, it is doubled, and with a doubled velocity it is quadrupled.

Definition 3

*The **inherent force** of matter is the power of resisting, by which each and every body, to the extent that it can, perseveres in its state either of resting or of moving uniformly in a straight line.*

This is always proportional to its body, and does not differ in any way from the inertia of mass, except in the mode of conception. Through the inertia of matter it comes to be that every body is with difficulty disturbed from its state either of resting or of moving. Whence the inherent force can also be called by the extremely significant name *force of inertia*. A body exercises this force only in the alteration of its status by another force being impressed upon it, and this exercise falls under the diverse considerations of resistance and impetus: resistance, to the extent that a body resists an impressed force in order to preserve its state, and impetus, to the extent that the same body, in giving way with difficulty to the force of a resisting obstacle, endeavors to change the state of that obstacle. Common opinion attributes resistance to things at rest and impetus to things in motion, but motion and rest, as they are commonly conceived, are distinguished from each other only with respect [to each other], nor are those things really at rest which are commonly seen as if at rest.

Definition 4

Impressed force is an action exerted upon a body for changing its state either of resting or of moving uniformly in a straight line.

This force consists in the action alone, and does not remain in the body after the action. For the body continues in each new state through the force of inertia alone. Moreover, impressed force has various origins, such as from impact, from pressure, from centripetal force.

Definition 5

Centripetal force is that by which bodies are pulled, pushed, or in any way tend toward some point from all sides, as to a center.

Of this kind is gravity, by which bodies tend to the center of the earth; magnetic force, by which iron seeks a magnet; and that force, whatever it might be, by which the planets are perpetually drawn back from rectilinear motions and are driven to revolve in curved lines. A stone, whirled around in a sling, attempts to depart from the hand that drives it around, and by its attempt stretches out the sling, doing so more strongly as it revolves more swiftly, and as soon as it is released, it flies away. The force contrary to that attempt, by which the sling perpetually draws the stone back to the hand and retains it in its orbit, I call *centripetal*, because it is directed toward the hand as to the center of the orbit. And the account of all bodies that are driven in a gyre is the same. They all attempt to recede from the centers of the orbits, and in the absence of some force contrary to that attempt, by which they are pulled together and kept in their orbits, and which I therefore call centripetal, they will go off in straight lines with uniform motion.

If a projectile were deprived of the force of gravity, it would not be deflected toward the earth, but would go off in a straight line toward the heavens, doing so with a uniform motion, provided that the resistance of the air be removed. It is drawn back by its gravity from the rectilinear path and is perpetually bent toward the earth, more or less according to its gravity and the velocity of motion. Where its gravity is less in proportion to the quantity of matter, or where the velocity with which it is propelled greater, it will deviate correspondingly less from the rectilinear path, and will travel farther.

If a lead ball, propelled by gunpowder from the summit of some mountain in a horizontal line with a given velocity, were to travel in a curved line for the distance of two miles before it fell to earth, it would travel about twice as far with double the velocity, and about ten times as far with ten times the velocity, provided that the resistance of the air be removed. And by increasing the velocity, the distance to which it is propelled may be increased at will, and the curvature of the line which it describes may be diminished, so that it would finally fall at a distance of ten or thirty or ninety degrees, or it might even go around the whole earth, or, at last, go off toward the heavens, continuing on *in infinitum* with the motion with which it departed. And by the same account, by which a projectile may be deflected into an orbit by the force of gravity and may go around the whole earth, the moon too, whether by the force of gravity (provided it be heavy) or by another force of whatever kind, by which it is urged toward the earth, can be always pulled back toward the earth from its rectilinear path, and deflected into its orbit; and without such a force the moon cannot be held back in its orbit.

This force, if it were less than required, would not sufficiently deflect the moon from the rectilinear path; and if greater than required, would deflect it more than sufficiently and would lead it down from its orbit toward the earth. It is indeed requisite that it be of exactly the right magnitude, and it is for the mathematicians to find the force by which a body can be accurately kept back in any given orbit you please with a given velocity, and in turn to find the curvilinear line into which a body departing from any given place you please with a given velocity would be deflected by a given force.

᠕   ᠕   ᠕

. . . I am considering these forces, not physically, but only mathematically. Therefore, the reader should beware of thinking that by words of this kind I am anywhere defining a species or manner of action, or a cause or physical account, or that I am truly and physically attributing forces to centers (which are mathematical points) if I should happen to say either that centers attract, or that forces belong to centers.

Content Questions

1. In his definition of quantity of matter, what does Newton mean by "density" and "magnitude"? What does it mean for the measure of the quantity of matter to arise "conjointly" from density and magnitude? (73)

2. According to Newton's first definition, how can two quantities of matter be compared? How many times greater would air of double density be in a space that is quadrupled? (73)

3. According to the first definition, are a body's mass and weight the same thing? (73)

4. According to Newton's second definition, what is the relation of a body's quantity of motion to its density and magnitude? (74)

5. How is it possible for the quantities of motion of two different bodies to be the same if their velocities and quantities of matter are different? (74)

6. According to Newton's third definition, how is a body's inherent force related to its density and magnitude? (74)

7. When does a body at rest or moving uniformly in a straight line exercise its "force of inertia"? (74)

8. How can a body's exercise of inherent force be considered as both resistance and impetus? Why does Newton think that considering inherent force in both these ways is contrary to "common opinion"? (74)

9. Why does Newton say, "Nor are those things really at rest which are commonly seen as if at rest"? (74)

10. How does impressed force relate to inherent force? (74)

11. After it has completed its action, what effect does impressed force have on a body's new state? (74)

12. Under what conditions might the action of an impressed force not result in motion? (74)

13. According to Newton's definitions, why would a stone whirled in a sling, a projectile, or the moon "go off in straight lines with uniform motion" if they were to be deprived of centripetal force? (75)

14. In what way does a body's quantity of motion affect how it responds to a centripetal force? (74–75)

15. How does Newton's description of a falling projectile help explain why the moon maintains its orbit around the earth? (75–76)

Discussion Questions

1. Why does Newton begin the *Principia* with definitions? Do the definitions establish that the things defined actually exist?

2. Why does Newton define quantity of matter and quantity of motion, but not matter and motion themselves? Are Newton's first and second definitions different from or similar to current definitions of mass and momentum? (73–74)

3. What do the concepts of inherent force and impressed force have in common that makes Newton define both of them as forces? (74)

4. In his definition of impressed force, what does Newton mean by an action? Why does he say that the force "does not remain in the body after the action"? (74)

5. Why doesn't Newton attribute the centripetal force affecting the moon and the planets in their orbits to gravity? (75–76)

6. What would mathematicians have to demonstrate in order to establish that the centripetal force deflecting the moon from a rectilinear path is the same as the force of gravity affecting a projectile on earth? (75–76)

7. What does Newton mean when he says, "I am considering these forces, not physically, but only mathematically"? (76) How can discovering the mathematical principles of forces help scientists form a more complete picture of the physical world?

Laws of Motion

In stating the three laws of motion, Newton uses the definitions in the preceding selection to specify fundamental relationships between motions and forces. He asserts that the relationships expressed by the laws actually exist and can be clearly understood from our experience of the physical world. In Corollary 1, which follows the laws and depends on them for its proof, Newton demonstrates how he uses geometrical propositions to establish complex relationships among forces. His use of definitions, scientific laws, and mathematical proofs raises questions about how they are related to one another and to the world that physics seeks to explain.

Law 1

Every body continues in its state of resting or of moving uniformly in a straight line, except insofar as it is driven by impressed forces to alter its state.

Projectiles continue in their motions except insofar as they are slowed by the resistance of the air and insofar as they are driven downward by the force of gravity. A top, whose parts, by cohering, perpetually draw themselves back from rectilinear motions, does not stop rotating, except insofar as it is slowed by the air. And the greater bodies of the planets and comets preserve their motions, both progressive and circular, carried out in spaces of less resistance, for a longer time.

This selection is taken from "Axioms, or Laws of Motion," of the Principia.

Law 2

The change of motion is proportional to the motive force impressed, and takes place following the straight line in which that force is impressed.

If some force should generate any motion you please, a double [force][1] will generate a double [motion], and a triple [force] a triple [motion], whether it has been impressed all at once, or gradually and successively. And because this motion is always directed in the same way as the generating force, if the body was previously in motion, then this [impressed] motion is either added to its motion (if they have the same sense) or subtracted (if contrary), or joined on obliquely (if oblique) and compounded with it according to the determination of the two.

Law 3

To an action there is always a contrary and equal reaction; or, the mutual actions of two bodies upon each other are always equal and directed to contrary parts.

Whatever pushes or pulls something else is pushed or pulled by it to the same degree. If one pushes a stone with a finger, his finger is also pushed by the stone. If a horse pulls a stone tied to a rope, the horse will also be equally pulled (so to speak) to the stone; for the rope, being stretched in both directions, will by the same attempt to slacken itself urge the horse toward the stone, and the stone toward the horse, and will impede the progress of the one to the same degree that it promotes the progress of the other. If some body, striking upon another body, should change the latter's motion in any way by its own force, the same body (because of the equality of the mutual pushing) will also in turn undergo the same change in its own motion, in the contrary direction, by the force of the other. These actions produce equal changes, not of velocities, but of motions—that is, in bodies that are unhindered in any other way. For changes in velocities made thus in opposite directions are inversely proportional to the bodies, because the motions are equally changed. This law applies to attractions as well.

1. [Bracketed material in this selection is from the translator.]

Corollary 1

A body [urged] by forces joined together describes the diagonal of a parallelogram in the same time in which it describes the sides separately.

Suppose that, in a given time, by the force *M* alone, impressed at place *A*, a body would be carried with uniform motion from *A* to *B*, and by the force *N* alone, impressed at the same place, it would be carried from *A* to *C*. Let the parallelogram *ABCD* be completed, and that body will be carried by both forces in the same time on the diagonal from *A* to *D*.

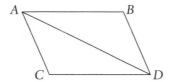

For because the force *N* acts along the line *AC* parallel to *BD*, this force, by law 2, will not at all change the velocity of approach to that line *BD* generated by the other force. Therefore, the body will arrive at the line *BD* in the same time whether force *N* be impressed or not; and therefore, at the end of that time, it will be found somewhere on that line *BD*. By the same argument, at the end of the same time, it will be found somewhere on the line *CD*, and for that reason it must necessarily be found at the intersection of the two lines *D*. But, by law 1, it will proceed with a rectilinear motion from *A* to *D*.

Content Questions

1. What is common to the velocity of a body in "its state of resting or of moving uniformly in a straight line"? (79)

2. According to Law 1, how is a body's state altered when it is "driven by impressed forces"? Why is Law 1 sometimes called the law of inertia? (79)

3. According to Newton's commentary on Law 1, how do air resistance and gravity each alter the state of a projectile? What is the net effect of these two forces on the projectile? (79)

4. In Definition 2 of "Forces," Newton defines quantity of motion as compounded of velocity and mass. How does this definition explain what he means in Law 2 by "change of motion," assuming that the mass of a body in motion remains constant? (80)

5. Why is the familiar equation $F = ma$ (force = mass × acceleration) an expression of Law 2? What relation does the equation show between a body's change of motion and its mass, and between its change of motion and the impressed force? (80)

6. In his commentary to Law 2, what does Newton mean when he states, "This motion is always directed in the same way as the generating force"? Under what condition will the motion generated by an impressed motive force be subtracted from the motion of a moving body? (80)

7. In Law 2, what does Newton mean when he states that the motion generated by an impressed force is compounded with the motion of a body? In what ways does the compounding of motions affect a body's velocity? (80)

8. According to Law 3, what is the difference between an action and a reaction? What does Newton mean when he says that the mutual actions of two bodies are "directed to contrary parts"? (80)

9. How does Newton's example of the horse, the stone, and the rope illustrate that forces always occur in pairs? (80)

10. What does Newton mean when he states in his commentary to Law 3 that mutual actions produce equal changes, "not of velocities, but of motions"? (80)

11. If "motions are equally changed" when bodies interact, why will a person hit by a moving car generally suffer more damage than the car? (80)

12. What are the two parts of the proposition that Newton proves in Corollary 1? In the statement of the proposition, what does Newton mean by "forces joined together"? (81)

13. Why does Newton first prove that the force *N* acting along the line *AC* will not change the body's velocity of approach to the line *BD* generated by force *M*? How does he use Law 2 to prove this? (81)

14. What is the argument proving that the body must be found "somewhere on the line *CD*"? How does Newton reach the conclusion that the body must be found at *D*? (81)

15. How does Newton use Law 1 to prove that in moving from *A* to *D*, the body describes the diagonal of the parallelogram *ABCD*? (81)

Discussion Questions

1. In physics, how is a law different from a definition?

2. What does Newton mean by motion? How is motion different from simply the movement of objects in space?

3. Why doesn't Newton offer proofs of the assertions he makes in his laws of motion, as he does for the proposition about joined forces in Corollary 1?

4. How do scientists establish that a statement about how the physical world operates is a law of nature? Under what circumstances can a law of nature be discarded after scientists have accepted it as valid?

5. How are laws of nature different from other kinds of laws, such as those made by legislatures to govern society?

Time, Space, and Motion

Physics is concerned with explaining relationships among objects in motion and at rest. In the following selection, Newton first carefully defines the basic terms—time, space, place, and motion—used to describe these relationships. He also focuses on the distinction between the absolute and the relative, raising questions about why he thinks this distinction is important in physics and how scientific observations and experiments can differentiate between the two. At the beginning of the twentieth century, Einstein reanalyzed the concepts of space, time, and motion in developing his theory of relativity.

Time, space, place, and motion are very familiar to everyone. It should nevertheless be noted that these are not commonly conceived of otherwise than from their relation to sensible objects. And from this there arise certain prejudices, for the removal of which it is useful for these same [terms][1] to be distinguished into absolute and relative, true and apparent, mathematical and common.

I. Absolute, true, and mathematical time, in itself and by its nature without relation to anything external, flows uniformly, and by another name is called *duration*. Relative, apparent, and common [time] is the perceptible and external measure (whether accurate or varying in rate) of any duration you please by means of motion, which is commonly used in place of true time, such as an hour, a day, a month, a year.

1. [Bracketed material in this selection is from the translator.]

This selection is taken from "Definitions," of the Principia.

II. Absolute space, by its nature, without relation to anything external, always remains similar and motionless. Relative [space] is any movable measure or dimension you please of this space, which [measure] is defined by our senses through its position with respect to bodies, and is commonly taken in place of motionless space, such as the dimension of subterranean, aerial, or celestial space defined through its position with respect to the earth. Absolute and relative space are the same in form and size, but do not always remain the same in number. For if the earth, for example, were to move, the space of our air, which relatively and with respect to our earth always stays the same, will be now one part of absolute space in which the air moves across, now another part of it, and thus, absolutely, it will perpetually change.

III. Place is the part of space which a body occupies, and is absolute or relative according to the space. It is a part, I say, of space, not the location of a body, or the enclosing surface. For the places of equal solids are always equal; the surfaces, however, are nearly always unequal because of the dissimilarity of figures. Locations, on the other hand, do not, properly speaking, have quantity, nor are they so much places as properties of places. The motion of the whole is the same as the sum of the motions of the parts: that is, the translation of the whole from its place is the same as the sum of the translations of the parts from their places. Consequently, the place of the whole is the same as the sum of the places of the parts, and for that reason it is internal and in the whole body.

IV. Absolute motion is the translation of a body from absolute place to absolute place; relative [motion is the translation of a body] from relative [place] to relative [place]. Thus in a boat which is carried with sails set, the relative place of a body is that region of the boat in which the body is, or that part of the whole concavity which the body fills, and which to that extent moves along with the boat; and relative rest is the body's continuing to remain in the same region of the boat or part of the concavity. But true rest is the body's continuing to remain in the same motionless part of that space in which the boat itself along with its concavity and all its contents moves. Whence if the earth is really at rest, a body which is relatively at rest in the boat will move truly and absolutely with that velocity with which the boat moves upon the earth. If on the contrary the earth also moves, the true and absolute motion of the body arises partly from the true motion of the earth in motionless space, partly from the relative motion of the boat upon the earth; and if the body also moves relatively in the boat, its true motion arises partly from the true motion of the earth in motionless space, partly from the relative motions of the boat upon the earth and of the body in the boat; and from these relative motions there arises the body's relative motion upon the earth. . . .

. . . All motions can be accelerated and retarded, but the flow of absolute time cannot be changed. The duration or perseverance of the existence of things is the same whether the motions are fast or slow or none. . . .

As the order of the parts of time is unchangeable, so also is the order of the parts of space. If these move from their places, they will also (so to speak) move from themselves. For times and spaces are in a way the places of themselves and of all things. Everything without exception is located in time according to order of succession, in space according to order of place. It is of their essence that they be places, and it is absurd for primary places to move. These are therefore absolute places, and translations from these places are alone absolute motions.

However, because these parts of space cannot be seen and cannot be distinguished from each other by our senses, we introduce perceptible measures in their stead. For from the positions and distances of things from some body, which we see as motionless, we define all places universally, and thereafter we also estimate all motions as well with respect to the places mentioned previously, insofar as we conceive the bodies to be carried away from them. We thus use relative places and motions in place of absolute ones, and this is not an inconvenience in human affairs. In philosophical matters, however, an abstraction from the senses must be made. For it can happen that there is no body really at rest, to which places and motions may be referred.

Further, absolute and relative motions are distinguished from each other through their properties and causes and effects. It is a property of rest that bodies really at rest are at rest among themselves. Therefore, since it is possible that some body in the regions of the fixed stars, or far beyond, be absolutely at rest, while it cannot be known from the position of bodies with respect to each other in our regions whether one of them may preserve its given position with respect to that distant [body], true rest cannot be defined from the position of the latter [bodies] among themselves. . . .

The causes by which true and relative motions are distinguished from each other are the forces impressed upon bodies for generating motions. True motion is neither generated nor changed except by forces impressed upon the moved body itself. But relative motion can be generated and changed without forces being impressed upon this body. For it suffices that they be impressed only upon other bodies to which it is related, so that, when they give way, that relation, of which the relative rest or motion of this [body] consists, is changed. Again, true motion is always changed by forces impressed upon the moved body, but relative motion is not necessarily changed by these forces. For if the same forces were impressed upon other bodies as well, to which there is a relation, in such a way that the relative position be preserved, the relation in which the relative motion consists will be preserved. Therefore, every relative motion can be changed while the true motion is preserved, and can be preserved while the true motion is changed, and for that reason true motion consists not at all in relations of this sort.

The effects by which absolute and relative motions are distinguished from each other are the forces of receding from the axis of circular motion. For in purely relative circular motion, these forces are none, but in true and absolute [circular motion] they are greater or less according to the quantity of motion.

Suppose that a pail should hang from a very long cord, and be driven continually in a circular path until the cord becomes somewhat stiff from twisting, and [the pail] next be filled with water, and be at rest along with the water, and then be driven by some sudden force in a circular path with a contrary motion, persevering in that motion for a long time as the cord untwists. At the beginning, the surface of the water will be flat, as it was before the motion of the vessel, but after the vessel, by a force gradually impressed upon the water, makes it too begin to rotate perceptibly, it will itself gradually withdraw from the middle and will climb up to the sides of the vessel, adopting a concave form (as I have myself experienced); and, with an ever increasing motion, will climb more and more, until it makes its revolutions in an equal time with the vessel, and comes to rest relative to it. This climbing is an indicator of a striving to withdraw from the axis of motion, and through such a striving the true and absolute circular motion of the water, here completely contrary to relative motion, comes to be known and is measured. At first, where the relative motion of the water in the vessel was greatest, that motion did not arouse any striving to withdraw from the axis: the water was not seeking the circumference by climbing up the sides of the vessel, but stayed flat, and for that reason its true circular motion had not yet begun. Later, however, where the relative motion of the water decreased, its ascent up the sides of the vessel was an indicator of the striving to withdraw from the axis, and this striving showed its true circular motion, which was ever increasing, and was finally made greatest where the water came to rest relatively in the vessel. Therefore, this striving will not depend upon the translational motion of the water with respect to the surrounding bodies, and consequently, true circular motion cannot be defined by such translations.

The true circular motion of any revolving [body] is unique, corresponding to a unique striving which is its own, as it were, and is commensurate with the effect. Relative motions, however, are countless, in accord with the various relations with external [bodies], and, like relations, they are entirely bereft of true effects, except insofar as they participate in that true and unique motion. Hence also, in the system of those people who would have our heavens rotate in an orb beneath the heavens of the fixed stars, and bear the planets along with them, the individual parts of the heavens, and the planets which are indeed relatively at rest in the heavens nearest them, in truth move. For they change their positions with respect to each other (unlike what happens in those truly at rest), and, being carried along with the heavens, they participate in their motion, and, like the parts of all revolving things, strive to recede from their axes.

Relative quantities are therefore not those quantities themselves whose names they display, but are those perceptible measures of them (whether true or erroneous) which are commonly used in place of the measured quantities. And if the meanings of words should be defined from usage, then by those names *time*, *space*, *place*, and *motion*, these perceptible measures should properly be understood, and the discussion will be out of the ordinary and purely mathematical if the quantities measured be understood here.

Content Questions

1. What does Newton mean when he says that time, space, place, and motion "are not commonly conceived of otherwise than from their relation to sensible objects"? (84)

2. Why do seconds, centuries, and millennia refer to relative rather than absolute times? (84)

3. What does Newton mean when he says that absolute and relative space "are the same in form and size, but do not always remain the same in number"? (85)

4. Why does Newton say that "equal solids are always equal," even though their surfaces may be unequal? (85)

5. In Newton's example of the moving boat, what is the relation of a body truly at rest to the boat as it sails onward? (85)

6. Why does the true motion of an object moving relatively in the boat arise partly from the earth's true motion and partly from the relative motions of both the boat and the body? (86)

7. Why does Newton reject the possibility that true rest can be defined from the relative positions of bodies among themselves? (86)

8. How can the relative motion of a body be changed without forces being impressed on the body itself? How can its relative motion remain the same if forces are impressed on it? (87)

9. According to Newton, why is true motion only generated or changed by forces impressed on the moved body itself? (87)

10. In Newton's experiment of the spinning bucket, what is the effect on the water when the relative motion is greatest? (87)

11. Why does the water "begin to rotate perceptibly" and climb the walls of the bucket? If the bucket suddenly disappeared, what would be the direction of motion of each part of the water? (87)

12. What does the concave shape of the water suggest about the water's acceleration as it recedes from the axis of circular motion? (87)

13. According to Newton, when is it possible in the experiment to measure the absolute circular motion of the water? (87–88)

14. Why does Newton conclude that the water's ascent up the sides of the bucket "showed its true circular motion"? (88)

15. What does Newton mean by the "perceptible measures" of time, space, place, and motion? (88)

Discussion Questions

1. Why does Newton differentiate between absolute and relative time, space, place, and motion? What "prejudices" does he think will be removed by making these distinctions? (84)

2. Even though Newton defines absolute and relative time, space, place, and motion, why doesn't he define time, space, and motion themselves? (84–85) Should all concepts in physics be defined, or can some concepts remain undefined?

3. Why does Newton think that absolute and relative motions can be distinguished from each other by "the forces of receding from the axis of circular motion"? (87) What does Newton mean when he says that "the true circular motion of any revolving [body] is unique"? (88)

4. Is Newton justified in concluding that the ascent of water up the sides of the bucket demonstrates the water's absolute circular motion? (87–88)

5. In forming scientific explanations of the physical world, should physicists be concerned with absolute quantities in addition to relative quantities and the "perceptible measures of them"? (88) How could the distinctions between absolute and relative quantities be useful to them?

Rules of Doing Philosophy

In Newton's time, the physical sciences were called natural philosophy. In the following selection, Newton presents a set of philosophical guidelines and principles that can be applied to the scientific investigation of the natural world. His rules raise fundamental questions about how scientists should assign causes to natural phenomena and which qualities of physical bodies are essential in explaining the world. In addition, these rules open up more general questions about the nature of scientific reasoning and methods.

Rule 1

That there ought not to be admitted any more causes of natural things than those which are both true and sufficient to explain their phenomena.

Philosophers state categorically: Nature does nothing in vain, and vain is that which is accomplished with more that can be done with less. For Nature is simple, and does not indulge herself in superfluous causes.

Rule 2

Accordingly, to natural effects of the same kind the same causes should be assigned, as far as possible.

As, for example, respiration in humans and in animals, the descent of stones in Europe and in America, light in a cooking fire and in the sun, the reflection of light on earth and in the planets.

This selection is taken from "Rules of Philosophizing," of the Principia.

Rule 3

The qualities of bodies that do not suffer intensification and remission, and that pertain to all bodies upon which experiments can be carried out, are to be taken as qualities of bodies universally.

For the qualities of bodies are apprehended only through experience, and are accordingly to be declared general whenever they generally square with experiments; and those which cannot be diminished cannot be removed. It is certain that against the tenor of experiments, dreams are not to be rashly contrived, nor is a retreat to be made from the analogy of Nature, since she is wont to be simple and ever consonant with herself. The extension of bodies is apprehended only through the senses, nor is it perceived in all things. But because it belongs to all perceptible bodies, it is affirmed to be universal. We experience many bodies to be hard. Hardness of the whole, moreover, arises from hardness of the parts, and thence we rightly conclude that the undivided particles, not only of these bodies which are perceived, but also of all others, are hard. We conclude that all bodies are impenetrable, not by reason, but by perception. Those that we handle are found to be impenetrable, and thence we conclude that impenetrability is a property of bodies universally. That all bodies are movable, and that by certain forces (which we call the forces of inertia) they persevere in motion or rest, we gather from these very properties in bodies that we see. Extension, hardness, impenetrability, movability, and the force of inertia of the whole arise from the extension, hardness, impenetrability, movability, and forces of inertia of the parts, and thence we conclude that all the least parts of all bodies are extended and hard and impenetrable and movable and endowed with forces of inertia. And this is the foundation of all of philosophy. Moreover, that parts of bodies that are divided and mutually contiguous can be separated from each other we come to know from the phenomena, and that undivided parts can by reason be divided up into smaller parts is certain from mathematics. But whether those distinct and hitherto undivided parts can be divided by the forces of nature and separated from each other is uncertain. And if it were to be established by but a single experiment that by breaking a hard, solid body some undivided particle were to suffer division, we would conclude, by the force of this rule, not only that the divided parts are separable, but also that the undivided ones can be divided *in infinitum*.

Finally, if it be established universally by experiments and astronomical observations that all bodies on the surface of the earth are heavy toward the earth, and this according to the quantity of matter in each, and that the moon is heavy toward the earth according to the quantity of its matter, and that our sea in turn is heavy toward the moon, and that all the planets are heavy toward each other, and that the gravity of comets toward the sun is similar, it will have to be said, by this rule, that all bodies gravitate toward each other. For the argument from phenomena for universal gravitation will be even stronger than that for the impenetrability of bodies, concerning which we have absolutely no experiment in the heavenly bodies; nay, not even an observation. Nevertheless, I do not at all assert that gravity is essential to bodies. By "inherent force" [*vis insita*][1] I understand only the force of inertia. This is inalterable. Gravity is diminished in receding from earth.

Rule 4

In experimental philosophy, propositions gathered from the phenomena by induction are to be taken as true, whether exactly or approximately, contrary hypotheses notwithstanding, until other phenomena appear through which they are either rendered more accurate or liable to exceptions.

This must be done lest an argument from induction be nullified by hypotheses.

---

1. [Bracketed material in this selection is from the translator.]

Content Questions

1. According to Rule 1, how does nature's simplicity determine which causes scientists should admit into their explanations of natural things? (91)

2. How are the examples given in Rule 2 "natural effects of the same kind"? (91)

3. In Rule 3, what does Newton mean by "qualities of bodies"? (92)

4. In order to be declared general, how must the qualities of bodies "generally square with experiments"? (92)

5. According to Newton, why are extension, hardness, impenetrability, movability, and the force of inertia "qualities of bodies universally"? What are some qualities of bodies that Newton would not consider universal? (92)

6. Why doesn't Newton consider gravity a universal quality of bodies? (93)

7. In Rule 4, what does Newton mean by "propositions gathered from the phenomena by induction"? (93)

8. What is Newton warning against when he says that Rule 4 must be followed "lest an argument from induction be nullified by hypotheses"? (93)

Discussion Questions

1. According to Rule 1, how can a scientist decide which causes of natural things are "both true and sufficient to explain their phenomena"? (91)

2. Can the philosophical principle that "Nature does nothing in vain" be verified scientifically? (91) Why would this principle be useful to scientists in their investigations of the physical world?

3. Why does Newton qualify the application of Rule 2 by adding "as far as possible"? (91)

4. Would the science of physics be possible if the examples Newton gives in Rule 2 were not natural effects of the same kind? (91)

5. In experimental physics, why is it important to determine which qualities pertain to bodies "universally"? (92)

6. Since experiments examine only a finite number of phenomena, how can scientists determine the universal qualities of bodies? (92)

7. Why does Newton say that it is "the foundation of all of philosophy" to conclude that the "least parts of all bodies" have the same qualities as the wholes of which they are part? (92)

8. According to Newton, why does Rule 3 allow us to conclude from "but a single experiment" that the undivided parts of bodies "can be divided *in infinitum*"? (92)

9. Why does Newton say that it might be possible to make an "argument from phenomena" for universal gravitation, even though gravity itself is not a universal quality of bodies? How does Newton think that the application of Rule 3 could establish universal gravitation? (93)

10. Why does Newton consider the impenetrability of bodies a universal quality, even though "we have absolutely no experiment in the heavenly bodies; nay, not even an observation" to establish it? (93)

11. What does Newton mean when he says, in Rule 4, that scientists should take inductive propositions as true, even though it is understood that other phenomena may appear that make the propositions "liable to exceptions"? (93)

12. Why does Newton call his four statements "rules"? Why doesn't he call them rules of doing *natural* philosophy, since they seem to be guidelines for scientific investigations?

Suggestions for Further Reading

By the author

Cohen, I. Bernard, and Richard S. Westfall, eds. *Newton: Texts, Backgrounds, Commentaries.* New York: W. W. Norton & Company, 1995. In this anthology, two of the most eminent Newton scholars have assembled selections from the full range of Newton's writings, framed by outstanding introductory essays and notes.

Densmore, Dana. *Newton's "Principia": The Central Argument.* 3rd ed. Translated by William H. Donahue. Santa Fe, NM: Green Lion Press, 2003. This volume, from which the selections in *What's the Matter?* are taken, combines Donahue's excellent translation of the *Principia* with extensive commentary and notes by Densmore. In a spirit of inquiry, it provides the best way to approach Newton's lengthy and challenging book and helps readers appreciate Newton's achievement in establishing universal gravitation.

————. *Selections from Newton's "Principia"*. Translated by William H. Donahue. Santa Fe, NM: Green Lion Press, 2004. Containing essential excerpts from Newton's *Principia*—including the selections in *What's the Matter?*—this book is drawn from Densmore's longer work (cited above) and serves well as an introduction to Newton's ideas.

About the author

Gleick, James. *Isaac Newton.* New York: Pantheon Books, 2003. This well-researched biography by a noted science writer shows the genesis of Newton's mature ideas and places his accomplishments in their historical scientific context.

Westfall, Richard S. *The Life of Isaac Newton.* Cambridge: Cambridge University Press, 1994. This condensed version of Westfall's definitive biography of Newton, *Never at Rest* (1980), explores all aspects of Newton's scientific work and gives a good sense of the character of the man himself.

About the topic

Fritzsch, Harald. *An Equation That Changed the World: Newton, Einstein, and the Theory of Relativity.* Translated by Karin Heusch. Chicago: University of Chicago Press, 1994, 1997. In this series of lively fictitious dialogues, Newton and Einstein discuss how Newton's ideas of the universe have been modified and extended by modern physics.

The best and safest method of philosophizing seems to be, first, to inquire diligently into the properties of things and to establish those properties by experiments, and to proceed later to hypotheses for the explanation of things themselves. For hypotheses ought to be applied only in the explanation of the properties of things, and not made use of in determining them; except insofar as they may furnish experiments.

—Isaac Newton in a letter to Henry Oldenburg, June 10, 1672

ISAAC NEWTON ⌒ THOMAS YOUNG

On Light

Light seems to have always held a deep fascination for humans. Both insubstantial and pervasive, it hovers between the world of solid, material objects and some ethereal realm where matter dissolves into pure luminescence. It conveys information about the world to us though our most valued sense organs, and its dramatic daily recurrence at sunrise dispels the unseen dangers that lurk in the dark of night. It is metaphorically embedded in everyday language in such words as *illuminating* and *enlightening* and stands for understanding and clarity of thought. Light figures prominently in the myths and stories that humans have told through the centuries, representing what is good and beneficial in contrast to the powers of darkness. At the beginning of the Book of Genesis, God's first commandment when he begins to create the world is "Let there be light!" recognizing that light is somehow primary and essential to the structure of the physical world. From ancient through modern times, scientists have continually proposed and debated theories of light, leading in the twentieth century to fundamental insights concerning the nature of the physical world.

The following selection consists of two excerpts, one from the *Opticks* (1704) of Isaac Newton (1642–1727), the other from "On the Nature of Light and Colors," a lecture by Thomas Young (1773–1829). Each scientist makes his case for a different explanation of light, building his arguments on rich analogies from common experience and on an appeal to crucial experiments to determine the truth of his claims. Although Young lived many years after Newton, his scientific training was dominated by the principles of classical Newtonian physics. The two excerpts can be read as a kind of dialogue between Newton and Young, showing the arguments and evidence scientists use to evaluate opposing theories, and raising questions about the purpose of scientific investigations of the natural world.

One important reason for Newton's stature in the development of modern science was his great ability as both an experimental and a theoretical scientist. Many of his most important early experiments were in optics. When Newton began his scientific career in the mid-1600s, leading scientists of the time had advanced theories about the nature of light and color. Their interest in light was not simply an isolated concern, but part of an attempt to discern the underlying structure of the physical world as a whole, as well as to formulate mathematical laws of optics that would be helpful in constructing instruments for scientific investigations.

The focus of Newton's experiments was the investigation of the nature of color. Some scientists held that sunlight is essentially homogeneous and that colors are produced by modifications to its rays. Newton conducted a series of experiments with prisms demonstrating that sunlight is composed of distinct components, each of which is a separate color. Because each component of sunlight seems to possess fixed qualities that determine its color, Newton was led to think of light as consisting of streams of separate particles, or *corpuscles*, governed by the laws of motion that apply to all physical objects. This theory of the nature of light was in contrast to that of scientists who thought that light consists of waves propagated in a subtle, pervasive medium. One result of Newton's optical experiments was his invention of the reflecting telescope, designed to eliminate the chromatic aberration produced by lenses. It was this invention, built by himself in his workshop, that first brought Newton to the attention of the prominent scientists of the Royal Society. Newton published the results of his early experiments in his book the *Opticks*. Its sound mathematical principles of optics, combined with the authority conferred by Newton's fame, gave weight to its more speculative theories of the nature of light.

Young was highly accomplished in many fields of learning, including medicine, linguistics, and most areas of scientific investigation. His independence of mind led him to question Newton's particle theory of light and to conduct a series of experiments that provided strong evidence that light is propagated as waves. Young noticed that beams of light passing through two closely spaced slits produce light and dark bands on a screen. Making an analogy to the way that waves of water reinforce and cancel out one another, he interpreted the bands as overlapping waves of light. Other scientists confirmed Young's wave theory, which became the dominant explanation of light in the nineteenth century and the basis for James Clerk Maxwell's model of electromagnetic waves.

In the twentieth century, the debate about the nature of light was reopened with Einstein's theory that under some circumstances, light behaves like particles. The wave-particle duality of light became a critical concept in the development of quantum theory and led to an important reinterpretation of Young's double-slit experiment. (See Feynman, "Quantum Behavior," pages 337–338.)

See also Newton, pages 69–71.

The Particle Theory of Light

Isaac Newton

Query 28. Are not all hypotheses erroneous, in which light is supposed to consist in pression[1] or motion, propagated through a fluid medium? For in all these hypotheses the phenomena of light have been hitherto explained by supposing that they arise from new modifications of the rays, which is an erroneous supposition.

   If light consisted only in pression propagated without actual motion, it would not be able to agitate and heat the bodies which refract and reflect it. If it consisted in motion propagated to all distances in an instant, it would require an infinite force every moment, in every shining particle, to generate that motion. And if it consisted in pression or motion, propagated either in an instant or in time, it would bend into the shadow. For pression or motion cannot be propagated in a fluid in right lines, beyond an obstacle which stops part of the motion, but will bend and spread every way into the quiescent medium which lies beyond the obstacle. Gravity tends downward, but the pressure of water arising from gravity tends every way with equal force, and is propagated as readily, and with as much force sideways as downward, and through crooked passages as through straight ones. The waves on the surface of stagnating water, passing by the sides of a broad obstacle which stops part of them, bend afterward and dilate themselves gradually into the quiet water behind the obstacle. The waves, pulses, or vibrations of the air, wherein sounds consist, bend manifestly,

1. [*pression:* pressure.]

This selection is taken from book 3 of the Opticks.

though not so much as the waves of water. For a bell or a cannon may be heard beyond a hill which intercepts the sight of the sounding body, and sounds are propagated as readily through crooked pipes as through straight ones. But light is never known to follow crooked passages nor to bend into the shadow. For the fixed stars by the interposition of any of the planets cease to be seen. And so do the parts of the sun by the interposition of the Moon, Mercury, or Venus. The rays which pass very near to the edges of any body are bent a little by the action of the body, . . . but this bending is not toward but from the shadow, and is performed only in the passage of the ray by the body, and at a very small distance from it. So soon as the ray is past the body, it goes right on. . . .

. . . And against filling the heavens with fluid mediums, unless they be exceedingly rare, a great objection arises from the regular and very lasting motions of the planets and comets in all manner of courses through the heavens. For thence it is manifest, that the heavens are void of all sensible resistance, and by consequence of all sensible matter. . . .

. . . A dense fluid can be of no use for explaining the phenomena of nature, the motions of the planets and comets being better explained without it. It serves only to disturb and retard the motions of those great bodies, and make the frame of nature languish. And in the pores of bodies, it serves only to stop the vibrating motions of their parts, wherein their heat and activity consists. And as it is of no use, and hinders the operations of nature, and makes her languish, so there is no evidence for its existence, and therefore it ought to be rejected. And if it be rejected, the hypotheses that light consists in pression or motion, propagated through such a medium, are rejected with it.

And for rejecting such a medium, we have the authority of those the oldest and most celebrated philosophers of Greece and Phoenicia, who made a vacuum, and atoms, and the gravity of atoms, the first principles of their philosophy; tacitly attributing gravity to some other cause than dense matter. Later philosophers banish the consideration of such a cause out of natural philosophy, feigning hypotheses for explaining all things mechanically, and referring other causes to metaphysics. Whereas the main business of natural philosophy is to argue from phenomena without feigning hypotheses, and to deduce causes from effects, till we come to the very first cause, which certainly is not mechanical; and not only to unfold the mechanism of the world, but chiefly to resolve these and such like questions. What is there in places almost empty of matter, and whence is it that the Sun and planets gravitate toward one another, without dense matter between them? Whence is it that nature doth nothing in vain, and whence arises all that order and beauty which we see in the world? To what end are comets, and whence is it that planets move all one and the same way in orbs concentric, which comets move all manner of ways in orbs very eccentric; and what hinders the fixed stars from falling upon one another? How came the bodies of animals to be contrived with so much art, and for what ends were their several parts? Was the eye contrived without skill in optics, and the ear without knowledge of sounds? How do the motions of the body follow from the will, and whence is the instinct in animals? Is not the sensory of animals that place to which the sensitive substance is present, and into which the sensible species of things are carried through the nerves and brain, that there they may be perceived by their immediate presence to that substance? And these things being rightly dispatched, does it not appear from phenomena that there is a Being incorporeal, living, intelligent, omnipresent, who in infinite space, as it were in his sensory, sees the things themselves intimately, and thoroughly perceives them, and comprehends them wholly by their immediate presence to himself: of which things the images only carried through the organs of sense into our little sensoriums, are there seen and beheld by that which in us perceives and thinks. And though every true step made in this philosophy brings us not immediately to the knowledge of the first cause, yet it brings us nearer to it, and on that account is to be highly valued.

Query 29. Are not the rays of light very small bodies emitted from shining substances? For such bodies will pass through uniform mediums in right lines without bending into the shadow, which is the nature of the rays of light. They will also be capable of several properties, and be able to conserve their properties unchanged in passing through several mediums, which is another condition of the rays of light. Pellucid substances act upon the rays of light at a distance in refracting, reflecting, and inflecting them, and the rays mutually agitate the parts of those substances at a distance for heating them; and this action and reaction at a distance very much resembles an attractive force between bodies. If refraction be performed by attraction of the rays, the sines of incidence must be to the sines of refraction in a given proportion, . . . and this rule is true by experience. The rays of light in going out of glass into a vacuum are bent toward the glass; and if they fall too obliquely on the vacuum, they are bent backward into the glass, and totally reflected; and this reflection cannot be ascribed to the resistance of an absolute vacuum, but must be caused by the power of the glass attracting the rays at their going out of it into the vacuum, and bringing them back. For if the farther surface of the glass be moistened with water or clear oil, or liquid and clear honey, the rays which would otherwise be reflected will go into the water, oil, or honey; and therefore are not reflected before they arrive at the farther surface of the glass, and begin to go out of it. If they go out of it into the water, oil, or honey, they go on, because the attraction of the glass is almost balanced and rendered ineffectual by the contrary attraction of the liquid. But if they go out of it into a vacuum which has no attraction to balance that of the glass, the attraction of the glass either bends and refracts them, or brings them back and reflects them. . . . Nothing more is requisite for producing all the variety of colors, and degrees of refrangibility, than that the rays of light be bodies of different sizes, the least of which may take violet the weakest and darkest of the colors, and be more easily diverted by refracting surfaces from the right course; and the rest as they are bigger and bigger, may make the stronger and more lucid colors, blue, green, yellow, and red, and be more and more difficultly diverted.

The Wave Theory of Light

Thomas Young

The nature of light is a subject of no material importance to the concerns of life or to the practice of the arts, but it is in many other respects extremely interesting, especially as it tends to assist our views both of the nature of our sensations and of the constitution of the universe at large. The examination of the production of colors, in a variety of circumstances, is intimately connected with the theory of their essential properties and their causes; and we shall find that many of these phenomena will afford us considerable assistance in forming our opinion respecting the nature and origin of light in general.

It is allowed, on all sides, that light either consists in the emission of very minute particles from luminous substances, which are actually projected, and continue to move, with the velocity commonly attributed to light, or [it consists] in the excitation of an undulatory motion, analogous to that which constitutes sound, in a highly light and elastic medium pervading the universe; but the judgments of philosophers of all ages have been much divided with respect to the preference of one or the other of these opinions. . . .

We shall proceed to examine in detail the manner in which the two principal hypotheses respecting light may be applied to its various properties and affections; and in the first place to the simple propagation of light in right lines through a vacuum, or a very rare homogeneous medium. In this circumstance there is nothing inconsistent with either hypothesis;

This selection is take from lecture 39 of A Course of Lectures on Natural Philosophy and the Mechanical Arts.

but it undergoes some modifications, which require to be noticed, when a portion of light is admitted through an aperture and spreads itself in a slight degree in every direction. In this case it is maintained by Newton that the margin of the aperture possesses an attractive force, which is capable of inflecting the rays. But there is some improbability in supposing that bodies of different forms and of various refractive powers should possess an equal force of inflection, as they appear to do in the production of these effects; and there is reason to conclude from experiments that such a force, if it existed, must extend to a very considerable distance from the surfaces concerned, at least a quarter of an inch, and perhaps much more, which is a condition not easily reconciled with other phenomena. In the Huygenian system of undulation,[1] this divergence or diffraction is illustrated by a comparison with the motions of waves of water and of sound, both of which diverge when they are admitted into a wide space through an aperture, so much indeed that it has usually been considered as an objection to this opinion, that the rays of light do not diverge in the degree that would be expected if they were analogous to the waves of water. But as it has been remarked by Newton that the pulses of sound diverge less than the waves of water, so it may fairly be inferred that in a still more highly elastic medium, the undulations, constituting light, must diverge much less considerably than either.

With respect, however, to the transmission of light through perfectly transparent mediums of considerable density, the system of emanation labors under some difficulties. It is not to be supposed that the particles of light can perforate with freedom the ultimate atoms of matter, which compose a substance of any kind; they must, therefore, be admitted in all directions through the pores or interstices of those atoms. . . . It is certain that some substances retain all their properties when they are reduced to the thickness of the ten millionth of an inch at most, and we cannot therefore suppose the distances of the atoms of matter in general to be so great as the hundred millionth of an inch. Now if ten feet of the most transparent water transmits, without interruption, one half of the light that enters it, each section or stratum of the thickness of one of these pores of matter must intercept only about one twenty thousand millionth, and so much

---

1. [*Huygenian system of undulation*: a wave theory of light proposed by the Dutch scientist Christiaan Huygens (1629–1695).]

must the space or area occupied by the particles be smaller than the interstices between them, and the diameter of each atom must be less than the hundred and forty thousandth part of its distance from the neighboring particles: so that the whole space occupied by the substance must be as little filled as the whole of England would be filled by a hundred men, placed at the distance of about thirty miles from each other. This astonishing degree of porosity is not indeed absolutely inadmissible, and there are many reasons for believing the statement to agree in some measure with the actual constitution of material substances; but the Huygenian hypothesis does not require the disproportion to be by any means so great, since the general direction and even the intensity of an undulation would be very little affected by the interposition of the atoms of matter, while these atoms may at the same time be supposed to assist in the transmission of the impulse, by propagating it through their own substance. . . .

A very striking circumstance, respecting the propagation of light, is the uniformity of its velocity in the same medium. According to the projectile hypothesis, the force employed in the free emission of light must be about a million million times as great as the force of gravity at the earth's surface; and it must either act with equal intensity on all the particles of light, or must impel some of them through a greater space than others if its action be less powerful, since the velocity is the same in all cases. For example, if the projectile force is weaker with respect to red light than with respect to violet light, it must continue its action on the red rays to a greater distance than on the violet rays. There is no instance in nature besides of a simple projectile moving with a velocity uniform in all cases, whatever may be its cause, and it is extremely difficult to imagine that so immense a force of repulsion can reside in all substances capable of becoming luminous, so that the light of decaying wood, or of two pebbles rubbed together, may be projected precisely with the same velocity as the light emitted by iron burning in oxygen gas, or by the reservoir of liquid fire on the surface of the sun. Another cause would also naturally interfere with the uniformity of the velocity of light, if it consisted merely in the motion of projected corpuscles of matter; . . . if any of the stars were 250 times as great in diameter as the sun, its attraction would be so strong as to destroy the whole momentum of the corpuscles of light proceeding from it and to render the star invisible at a great distance; and although there is no reason to imagine that any of the stars are actually of this magnitude, yet some of them are probably many times greater than our sun, and therefore large enough to produce such a retardation in the motion of their light as would materially alter its effects. It is almost unnecessary to observe that the uniformity of the velocity of light, in those spaces which are free from all material substances, is a necessary consequence of the Huygenian hypothesis, since the undulations of every homogeneous elastic medium are always propagated, like those of sound, with the same velocity, as long as the medium remains unaltered.

On either supposition, there is no difficulty in explaining the equality of the angles of incidence and reflection; for these angles are equal as well in the collision of common elastic bodies with others incomparably larger, as in the reflections of the waves of water and of the undulations of sound. And it is equally easy to demonstrate that the sines of the angles of incidence and refraction must be always in the same proportion at the same surface, whether it be supposed to possess an attractive force, capable of acting on the particles of light, or to be the limit of a medium through which the undulations are propagated with a diminished velocity. . . .

The partial reflection from all refracting surfaces is supposed by Newton to arise from certain periodical retardations of the particles of light, caused by undulations, propagated in all cases through an ethereal medium. The mechanism of these supposed undulations is so complicated, and attended by so many difficulties, that the few who have examined them have been in general entirely dissatisfied with them. . . . . It may, therefore, safely be asserted that in the projectile hypothesis this separation of the rays of light of the same kind by a partial reflection at every refracting surface remains wholly unexplained. In the undulatory system, on the contrary, this separation follows as a necessary consequence. It is simplest to consider the ethereal medium which pervades any transparent substance, together with the material atoms of the substance, as constituting together a compound medium denser than the pure ether, but not more elastic; and by comparing the contiguous particles of the rarer and the denser medium with common elastic bodies of different dimensions, we may easily determine not only in what manner, but almost in what degree, this reflection must take place in different circumstances. Thus, if one of two equal bodies strikes the other, it communicates to it its whole motion without any reflection. But a smaller body striking a larger one is reflected, with the more force as the difference of their magnitude is greater; and a larger body, striking a smaller one, still proceeds with a diminished velocity, the remaining motion constituting, in the case of an undulation falling on a rarer medium, a part of a new series of motions which necessarily returns backward with the appropriate velocity. We may observe a circumstance nearly similar to this last in a portion of mercury spread out on a horizontal table; if a wave be excited at any part, it will be reflected from the termination of the mercury almost in the same manner as from a solid obstacle. . . .

In order to explain, in the system of emanation, the dispersion of the rays of different colors by means of refraction, it is necessary to suppose that all refractive mediums have an elective attraction, acting more powerfully on the violet rays, in proportion to their mass, than on the red. But an elective attraction of this kind is a property foreign to mechanical philosophy, and when we use the term in chemistry, we only confess our incapacity to assign a mechanical cause for the effect, and refer to an analogy with other facts, of which the intimate nature is perfectly unknown to us. It is not indeed very easy to give a demonstrative theory of the dispersion of colored light upon the supposition of undulatory motion, but we may derive a very satisfactory illustration from the well-known effects of waves of different breadths. The simple calculation of the velocity of waves, propagated in a liquid perfectly elastic, or incompressible, and free from friction, assigns to them all precisely the same velocity, whatever their breadth may be: the compressibility of the fluids actually existing introduces, however, a necessity for a correction according to the breadth of the wave, and it is very easy to observe, in a river or a pond of considerable depth, that the wider waves proceed much more rapidly than the narrower. We may, therefore, consider the pure ethereal medium as analogous to an infinitely elastic fluid, in which undulations of all kinds move with equal velocity, and material transparent substances, on the contrary, as resembling those fluids, in which we see the large waves advance beyond the smaller; and by supposing the red light to consist of larger or wider undulations and the violet of smaller, we may sufficiently elucidate the greater refrangibility of the red than of the violet light.

It is not, however, merely on the ground of this analogy that we may be induced to suppose the undulations constituting red light to be larger than those violet light. A very extensive class of phenomena leads us still more directly to the same conclusion: they consist chiefly of the production of colors . . . by diffraction or inflection, [neither] of which have been explained, upon the supposition of emanation, in a manner sufficiently minute or comprehensive to satisfy the most candid even of the advocates for the projectile system; while on the other hand [both] of them may be at once understood, from the effect of the interference of double lights, in a manner nearly similar to that which constitutes in sound the sensation of a beat, when two strings, forming an imperfect unison, are heard to vibrate together.

Supposing the light of any given color to consist of undulations of a given breadth or of a given frequency, it follows that these undulations must be liable to those effects which we have already examined in the case of the waves of water and the pulses of sound. It has been shown that two equal series of waves, proceeding from centers near each other, may be seen to destroy each other's effects at certain points, and at other points to redouble them; and the beating of two sounds has been explained from a similar interference. We are now to apply the same principles to the alternate union and extinction of colors.

In order that the effects of two portions of light may be thus combined, it is necessary that they be derived from the same origin and that they arrive at the same point by different paths, in directions not much deviating from each other. This deviation may be produced in one or both of the portions by diffraction, by reflection, by refraction, or by any of these effects combined; but the simplest case appears to be when a beam of homogeneous light falls on a screen in which there are two very small holes or slits, which may be considered as centers of divergence, from whence the light is diffracted in every direction. In this case, when the two newly formed beams are received on a surface placed so as to intercept them, their light is divided by dark stripes into portions nearly equal, but becoming wider as the surface is more remote from the apertures, so as to subtend very nearly equal angles from the apertures at all distances, and wider also in the same proportion as the apertures are closer to each other. The middle of the two portions is always light, and the bright stripes on each side are at such distances that the light, coming to them from one of the apertures, must have passed through a longer space than that which comes from the other, by an interval which is equal to the breadth of one, two, three, or more of the supposed undulations, while the intervening dark spaces correspond to a difference of half a supposed undulation, of one and a half, of two and a half, or more. . . .

The comparison of the results of this theory with experiments fully establishes their general coincidence. . . .

   . . . The full confirmation or decided rejection of the theory . . . can be expected from time and experience alone. If it be confuted, our prospects will again be confined within their ancient limits, but if it be fully established, we may expect an ample extension of our views of the operations of nature, by means of our acquaintance with a medium so powerful and so universal as that to which the propagation of light must be attributed.

Content Questions

1. Why does Newton reject the hypothesis that light consists of waves propagated through a fluid medium? What exception does he admit to his claim that light rays do not bend? (101–102)

2. How do the motions of planets and comets provide a reason for Newton to deny that light is motion through a fluid medium? (102)

3. What does Newton think is "the main business of natural philosophy"? Why does he think that "feigning hypotheses" is contrary to the business of natural philosophy? (102)

4. How are the questions about the world that Newton poses different from those that only "unfold the mechanism of the world"? Where does Newton think his questions should lead natural philosophy? (102–103)

5. How do the perceptions of Newton's "Being incorporeal" differ from the perceptions of humans? (103)

6. How does Newton explain the passage of light through transparent substances? (103–104)

7. What property of bodies is important to Newton's theory of refraction? In the experiment Newton describes, why does he moisten the surface of the glass with various substances such as water, oil, and honey? (103–104)

8. How does Newton account for some colors being "stronger and more lucid" than others? (104)

9. Why does Young question Newton's explanation of what happens when light "spreads itself" as it passes through an aperture? (106)

10. How does Young use Newton's own comparison of the difference between the divergence of sound waves and water waves to support the wave theory of light? (106)

11. Why does Young favor the wave hypotheses, even though he is able to make an argument supporting the particle theory of light in terms of the porosity of matter? (106–107)

12. Why does Young think that the uniformity of light's velocity in the same medium supports the wave theory of light? (107)

13. According to Young, how does partial reflection from a refracting surface occur? (108)

14. Why does Young think that it is difficult to demonstrate the "dispersion of colored light upon the supposition of undulatory motion"? (109)

15. How does Young think that the pattern of light and dark stripes he observed in his experiment establishes the wave theory of light? (110)

Discussion Questions

1. What are the differences between Newton's and Young's reasons for investigating the nature of light? Would Young say that "feigning hypotheses" is not the business of natural philosophy? (102, 105)

2. Why does Young reject Newton's complicated mechanism for explaining reflection from refracting surfaces? (108) If different theories account equally well for the same phenomenon, how should scientists decide which one to adopt?

3. Why do both Newton and Young assume that if light is like a wave, it must be propagated in a physical medium? (101, 108)

4. In speculating on Newton's explanation of the dispersion of light rays of different colors, what does Young mean when he says, "An elective attraction of this kind is a property foreign to mechanical philosophy"? (109)

5. How do Newton's and Young's explanations of the nature and behavior of light depend on analogies with more familiar physical phenomena? How can analogies of this sort both assist and mislead scientists in their investigations?

Suggestions for Further Reading

By the author

Cohen, I. Bernard, and Richard S. Westfall, eds. *Newton: Texts, Backgrounds, Commentaries.* New York: W. W. Norton & Company, 1995. The writings in this anthology, which are accompanied by outstanding introductory essays and notes, include the essential passages from Newton's work in optics.

Newton, Isaac. *Opticks*. New York: Dover Publications, 1952. In this book, from
which the selection in *What's the Matter?* is taken, Newton describes his own
groundbreaking experiments with light, lenses, and colors, while at the same
time providing a survey of the arguments for and against the wave and particle
theories of light.

Sepper, Dennis L. *Newton's Optical Writings: A Guided Study.* New Brunswick, NJ:
Rutgers University Press, 1994. Focusing on excerpts from Newton's writings on
optics and the properties of light, this guided study clarifies difficult passages and
explains Newton's work in the scientific context of his times.

About the topic

Baierlein, Ralph. *Newton to Einstein: The Trail of Light.* Cambridge: Cambridge
University Press, 1992, 2001. Starting with Newton's work in optics, this
outstanding textbook leads readers from the development of the wave theory of
light and its relation to electromagnetism to Einstein's theory of special relativity.
Included are biographical profiles, detailed descriptions of key experiments, and
challenging questions for further investigation.

Feynman, Richard P. *QED: The Strange Theory of Light and Matter.* Princeton, NJ:
Princeton University Press, 1985, 1988. In this collection of lectures on quantum
electrodynamics (QED), the field that he helped to establish, Feynman shows how
quantum theory forms the basis for an explanation of the behavior of light and its
interaction with electrons.

Park, David. *The Fire Within the Eye: A Historical Essay on the Nature and Meaning
of Light.* Princeton, NJ: Princeton University Press, 1997, 1999. This highly readable
history of ideas about the nature of light and vision provides a thorough account
of philosophical, theological, and scientific theories from ancient Greece until
modern times.

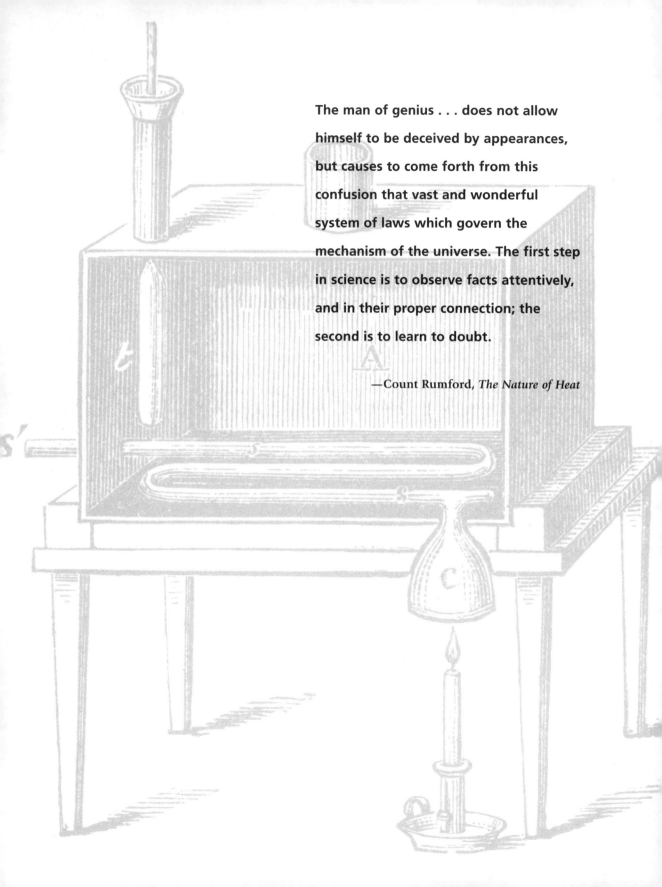

The man of genius . . . does not allow himself to be deceived by appearances, but causes to come forth from this confusion that vast and wonderful system of laws which govern the mechanism of the universe. The first step in science is to observe facts attentively, and in their proper connection; the second is to learn to doubt.

—Count Rumford, *The Nature of Heat*

COUNT RUMFORD (BENJAMIN THOMPSON)

Heat and Friction

One of the central concerns of physics is to find explanations for the ordinary phenomena that we observe. What qualifies as an adequate explanation has changed numerous times through the centuries as theoretical ideas about the structure of the world have altered. These changes have occurred mainly because of innovative reasoning combined with new observations based on carefully contrived experiments. The scientific work of Count Rumford (Benjamin Thompson, 1753–1814) offers outstanding examples of how scientific experiments can best be conducted as well as fundamental insights about the nature of heat that later scientists found invaluable for their own research. Rumford's explanations of heat were part of a movement in physics away from attributing material substance to physical phenomena—a movement also advanced by Thomas Young, Antoine Laurent Lavoisier, Michael Faraday, and James Clerk Maxwell with respect to light, fire, magnetism, and electricity. Rumford provided the foundation for the development of clear definitions of the concepts of energy and work by Robert Mayer, James Prescott Joule, and others that led to the exact formulation of the mechanical equivalent of heat and the law of energy conservation.

Although Rumford is remembered today mainly for his scientific work, his extremely varied career as statesman, military officer, inventor, and administrator provides a framework for understanding his highly practical and detailed methods of conducting scientific research. Born Benjamin Thompson in New England, Rumford sided with the British during the American Revolution and, as a result, spent most of his life as an exile in Europe. He rose to positions of significant influence in the governments of England and Bavaria, receiving the honorary title of Count Rumford in Bavaria. He devised numerous plans for social improvement, many based on technological innovations such as better designs for the fireplace, the chimney, and the coffeepot.

In England, Rumford was elected as a fellow of the prestigious Royal Society, an organization that provided a gathering place for scientists to exchange ideas and evaluate the work of their colleagues. Rumford's fellowship gave him the opportunity to associate with major British scientists and also a forum in which to present many reports of his experimental work. In 1799, Rumford led the establishment of the Royal Institution, which continues today to provide the Royal Society with an extensive laboratory for original research, as well as programs for public education in science.

Rumford was avidly curious about the workings of nature and early in life acquired an interest in the phenomena associated with heat. Although there is nothing more common to us than the sensations of hot and cold, it is difficult to give a clear scientific answer to the question "What is heat?" Two explanations of heat were current in eighteenth-century physics. According to one, heat is the result of the motion of an object's particles—the greater the frictional motion, the greater the heat. The other explanation conceives of heat as a material substance, called *caloric*, a fluid that flows into and out of objects. As caloric flows in, the heat of an object increases and it expands; as it flows out, the object becomes cooler and contracts. Both explanations rely on underlying mechanisms to account for heat. In the following excerpt, from Rumford's 1798 paper "An Experimental Enquiry Concerning the Source of the Heat Which Is Excited by Friction," he reports how he tested the validity of the caloric explanation of heat.

In this paper, Rumford asks us to consider the importance of experiments carefully designed to produce exact measurements of the heat generated by the relative motion of metal surfaces in contact with each other. Observing that there appears to be a connection between the heat produced and the mechanical work that produces it, he attempts to derive a quantitative value for their equivalence. In addition, Rumford presents a model of the interplay of experimental observation, the detailed organization of quantitative data, and well-reasoned interpretation. He also emphasizes that the goal of scientific experimentation is to formulate general laws of how natural phenomena behave.

Heat and Friction

It frequently happens that in the ordinary affairs and occupations of life, opportunities present themselves of contemplating some of the most curious operations of nature, and very interesting philosophical experiments might often be made, almost without trouble or expense, by means of machinery contrived for the mere mechanical purposes of the arts and manufactures.

I have frequently had occasion to make this observation, and am persuaded that a habit of keeping the eyes open to everything that is going on in the ordinary course of the business of life has oftener led, as it were by accident, or in the playful excursions of the imagination, put into action by contemplating the most common appearances, to useful doubts and sensible schemes for investigation and improvement than all the more intense meditations of philosophers in the hours expressly set apart for study. . . .

Being engaged lately in superintending the boring of cannon in the workshops of the military arsenal at Munich, I was struck with the very considerable degree of Heat which a brass gun acquires in a short time in being bored, and with the still more intense Heat (much greater than that of boiling water, as I found by experiment) of the metallic chips separated from it by the borer.

The more I meditated on these phenomena, the more they appeared to me to be curious and interesting. A thorough investigation of them seemed even to bid fair to give a further insight into the hidden nature of Heat, and to enable us to form some reasonable conjectures respecting the existence, or nonexistence, of an *igneous fluid*—a subject on which the opinions of philosophers have in all ages been much divided. . . .

From *whence comes* the Heat actually produced in the mechanical operation above mentioned?

Is it furnished by the metallic chips which are separated by the borer from the solid mass of metal?

If this were the case, then, according to the modern doctrines of latent Heat, and of caloric, the *capacity for Heat* of the parts of the metal, so reduced to chips, ought not only to be changed, but the change undergone by them should be sufficiently great to account for *all* the Heat produced.

But no such change had taken place; for I found, upon taking equal quantities, by weight, of these chips, and of thin slips of the same block of metal separated by means of a fine saw, and putting them at the same temperature (that of boiling water) into equal quantities of cold water (that is to say, at the temperature of 59.5°F), [that] the portion of water into which the chips were put was not, to all appearance, heated either less or more than the other portion, in which the slips of metal were put.

This experiment being repeated several times, the results were always so nearly the same that I could not determine whether any or what change had been produced in the metal, *in regard to its capacity for Heat*, by being reduced to chips by the borer.

Hence it is evident that the Heat produced could not possibly have been furnished at the expense of the latent Heat of the metallic chips. But, not being willing to rest satisfied with these trials, however conclusive they appeared to me to be, I had recourse to the following still more decisive experiment.

Taking a cannon (a brass six-pounder), cast solid, and rough as it came from the foundry (see fig.1),[1] and fixing it (horizontally) in the machine used for boring, and at the same time finishing the outside of the cannon by turning (see fig. 2), I caused its extremity to be cut off, and, by turning down the metal in that part, a solid cylinder was formed, 7.75 inches

1. [All figures referred to in this selection appear on pages 130–131.]

in diameter and 9.8 inches long, which, when finished, remained joined to the rest of the metal (that which, properly speaking, constituted the cannon) by a small cylindrical neck only 2.2 inches in diameter and 3.8 inches long.

This short cylinder, which was supported in its horizontal position and turned round its axis by means of the neck by which it remained united to the cannon, was now bored with the horizontal borer used in boring cannon; but its bore, which was 3.7 inches in diameter, instead of being continued through its whole length (9.8 inches) was only 7.2 inches in length, so that a solid bottom was left to this hollow cylinder, which bottom was 2.6 inches in thickness.

This cavity is represented by dotted lines in figure 2, as also in figure 3, where the cylinder is represented on an enlarged scale.

This cylinder being designed for the express purpose of generating Heat *by friction*, by having a blunt borer forced against its solid bottom at the same time that it should be turned round its axis by the force of horses, in order that the Heat accumulated in the cylinder might from time to time be measured, a small round hole (see *d, e,* fig. 3), 0.37 of an inch only in diameter and 4.2 inches in depth, for the purpose of introducing a small cylindrical mercurial thermometer, was made in it, on one side, in a direction perpendicular to the axis of the cylinder and ending in the middle of the solid part of the metal which formed the bottom of its bore.

The solid contents of this hollow cylinder, exclusive of the cylindrical neck by which it remained united to the cannon, were 385.75 cubic inches, English measure, and it weighed 113.13 lb., avoirdupois, as I found on weighing it at the end of the course of experiments made with it, and after it had been separated from the cannon with which, during the experiments, it remained connected.

Experiment No. 1

This experiment was made in order to ascertain how much Heat was actually generated by friction, when a blunt steel borer being so forcibly shoved (by means of a strong screw) against the bottom of the bore of the cylinder that the pressure against it was equal to the weight of about 10,000 lb., avoirdupois, the cylinder was turned round on its axis (by the force of horses) at the rate of about thirty-two times in a minute.

This machinery, as it was put together for the experiment, is represented by figure 2; *w* is a strong horizontal iron bar, connected with proper machinery carried round by horses, by means of which the cannon was made to turn round its axis.

To prevent, as far as possible, the loss of any part of the Heat that was generated in the experiment, the cylinder was well covered up with a fit coating of thick and warm flannel, which was carefully wrapped round it and defended it on every side from the cold air of the atmosphere. This covering is not represented in the drawing of the apparatus, figure 2.

I ought to mention that the borer was a flat piece of hardened steel, 0.63 of an inch thick, 4 inches long, and nearly as wide as the cavity of the bore of the cylinder, namely, 3.5 inches. Its corners were rounded off at its end so as to make it fit the hollow bottom of the bore, and it was firmly fastened to the iron bar (*m*) which kept it in its place. The area of the surface by which its end was in contact with the bottom of the bore of the cylinder was nearly 2.33 inches. This borer, which is distinguished by the letter *n*, is represented in most of the figures.

At the beginning of the experiment, the temperature of the air in the shade, as also that of the cylinder, was just 60°F.

At the end of thirty minutes, when the cylinder had made 960 revolutions about its axis, the horses being stopped, a cylindrical mercurial thermometer, whose bulb was 0.32 of an inch in diameter and 3.25 inches in length, was introduced into the hole made to receive it, in the side of the cylinder, when the mercury rose almost instantly to 130°.

Though the Heat could not be supposed to be quite equally distributed in every part of the cylinder, yet, as the length of the bulb of the thermometer was such that it extended from the axis of the cylinder to near its surface, the Heat indicated by it could not be very different from that of the *mean temperature* of the cylinder, and it was on this account that a thermometer of that particular form was chosen for this experiment. . . .

Having taken away the borer, I now removed the metallic dust, or, rather, scaly matter, which had been detached from the bottom of the cylinder by the blunt steel borer in this experiment; and, having carefully weighed it, I found its weight to be 837 grains, troy.

Is it possible that the very considerable quantity of Heat that was produced in this experiment (a quantity which actually raised the temperature of above 113 lb. of gunmetal at least 70 degrees of Fahrenheit's thermometer and which, of course, would have been capable of melting 6.5 lb. of ice, or of causing near 5 lb. of ice-cold water to boil) could have been furnished by so inconsiderable a quantity of metallic dust? And this merely in consequence of *a change* of its capacity for Heat?

As the weight of this dust (837 grains, troy) amounted to no more that 1/948th part of that of the cylinder, it must have lost no less than 948 degrees of Heat to have been able to have raised the temperature of the cylinder one degree; and consequently it must have given off 66,360 degrees of Heat to have produced the effects which were actually found to have been produced in the experiment!

But without insisting on the improbability of this supposition, we have only to recollect that from the results of actual and decisive experiments, made for the express purpose of ascertaining that fact, the capacity for Heat of the metal of which great guns are cast *is not sensibly changed* by being reduced to the form of metallic chips in the operation of boring cannon; and there does not seem to be any reason to think that it can be much changed, if it be changed at all, in being reduced to much smaller pieces by means of a borer that is less sharp.

If the Heat, or any considerable part of it, were produced in consequence of a change in the capacity for Heat of a part of the metal of the cylinder, as such change could only be *superficial*, the cylinder would by degrees by *exhausted*, or the quantities of Heat produced in any given short space of time would be found to diminish gradually in successive experiments. To find out if this really happened or not, I repeated the last-mentioned experiment several times with the utmost care, but I did not discover the smallest sign of exhaustion in the metal, notwithstanding the large quantities of Heat actually given off.

Finding so much reason to conclude that the Heat generated in these experiments, or *excited*, as I would rather choose to express it, was not furnished *at the expense of the latent Heat* or *combined caloric* of the metal, I pushed my inquiries a step further, and endeavored to find out whether the air did, or did not, contribute anything in the generation of it.

Experiment No. 2

As the bore of the cylinder was cylindrical, and as the iron bar (*m*), to the end of which the blunt steel borer was fixed, was square, the air had free access to the inside of the bore, and even to the bottom of it, where the friction took place by which the Heat was excited.

As neither the metallic chips produced in the ordinary course of the operation of boring brass cannon, not the finer scaly particles produced in the last-mentioned experiments by the friction of the blunt borer, showed any signs of calcination, I did not see how the air could possibly have been the cause of the Heat that was produced; but in an investigation of this kind, I thought that no pain should be spared to clear away the rubbish and leave the subject as naked and open to inspection as possible.

In order, by one decisive experiment, to determine whether the air of atmosphere had any part or not in the generation of the Heat, I contrived to repeat the experiment under circumstances in which *it was evidently impossible for it to produce any effect whatever.* By means of a piston exactly fitted to the mouth of the bore of the cylinder, through the middle of which piston the square iron bar, to the end of which the blunt steel borer was fixed, passed in a square hole made perfectly airtight, the access of the external air to the inside of the bore of the cylinder was effectually prevented. (In figure 3, this piston (*p*) is seen in its place; it is likewise shown in figures 7 and 8.)

I did not find, however, by this experiment, that the exclusion of the air diminished, in the smallest degree, the quantity of Heat excited by the friction.

There still remained one doubt, which, though it appeared to me to be so slight as hardly to deserve any attention, I was however desirous to remove. The piston which closed the mouth of the bore of the cylinder, in order that it might be airtight, was fitted into it with so much nicety, by means of its collars of leather, and pressed against it with so much force that, notwithstanding its being oiled, it occasioned a considerable degree of friction when the hollow cylinder was turned round its axis. Was not the Heat produced, or at least some part of it, occasioned by this friction of the piston? And as the external air had free access to the extremity of the bore, where it came in contact with the piston, is it not possible that this air may have had some share in the generation of the Heat produced?

Experiment No. 3

A quadrangular oblong deal box (see fig. 4), watertight, 11.5 English inches long, 9.4 inches wide, and 9.6 inches deep (measured in the clear), [was] provided with holes or slits in the middle of each of its ends just large enough to receive the one, the square iron rod to the end of which the blunt steel borer was fastened, [and] the other, the small cylindrical neck which joined the hollow cylinder to the cannon. When this box (which was occasionally closed above by a wooden cover or lid moving on hinges) was put into its place—that is to say, when, by means of the two vertical openings or slits in its two ends (the upper parts of which openings were occasionally closed by means of narrow pieces of wood sliding in vertical grooves), the box (g, h, i, k, fig. 3) was fixed to the machinery in such a manner that its bottom (i, k) [was] in the plane of the horizon—its axis coincided with the axis of the hollow metallic cylinder. It is evident, from the description, that the hollow metallic cylinder would occupy the middle of the box without touching it on either side (as it is represented in figure 3), and that on pouring water into the box and filling it to the brim, the cylinder would be completely covered and surrounded on every side by that fluid. And further, as the box was held fast by the strong square iron rod (m) which passed in a *square hole* in the center of one of its ends (fig. 4), while the round or cylindrical neck, which joined the hollow cylinder to the end of the cannon, could turn round freely on its axis in the *round hole* in the center of the other end of it, it is evident that the machinery could be put in motion without the least danger of forcing the box out of its place, throwing the water out of it, or deranging any part of the apparatus.

Everything being ready, I proceeded to make the experiment I had projected in the following manner.

The hollow cylinder having been previously cleaned out, and the inside of its bore wiped with a clean towel till it was quite dry, the square iron bar, with the blunt steel borer fixed to the end of it, was put into its place, the mouth of the bore of the cylinder being closed at the same time by means of the circular piston, through the center of which the iron bar passed.

This being done, the box was put in its place, and, the joinings of the iron rod and of the neck of the cylinder with the two ends of the box having been made watertight by means of collars of oiled leather, the box was filled with cold water (viz., at the temperature of 60°), and the machine was put in motion.

The result of this beautiful experiment was very striking, and the pleasure it afforded me amply repaid me for all the trouble I had had in contriving and arranging the complicated machinery used in making it.

The cylinder, revolving at the rate of about thirty-two times in a minute, had been in motion but a short time, when I perceived, by putting my hand into the water and touching the outside of the cylinder, that Heat was generated, and it was not long before the water which surrounded the cylinder began to be sensibly warm.

At the end of one hour I found, by plunging a thermometer into the water in the box (the quantity of which fluid amounted to 18.77 lb., avoirdupois) that its temperature had been raised no less than 47 degrees, being now 107° of Fahrenheit's scale. . . .

At the end of two hours, reckoning from the beginning of the experiment, the temperature of the water was found to be raised to 178°.

At 2 hours 20 minutes it was at 200°, and at 2 hours 30 minutes it ACTUALLY BOILED!

It would be difficult to describe the surprise and astonishment expressed in the countenances of the bystanders on seeing so large a quantity of cold water heated, and actually made to boil, without any fire.

Though there was, in fact, nothing that could justly be considered as surprising in this event, yet I acknowledge fairly that it afforded me a degree of childish pleasure, which, were I ambitious of the reputation of a *grave philosopher*, I ought most certainly rather to hide than to discover.

The quantity of Heat excited and accumulated in this experiment was very considerable, for not only the water in the box, but also the box itself (which weighed 15.25 lb.), and the hollow metallic cylinder, and that part of the iron bar which, being situated within the cavity of the box, was immersed in the water, were heated 150 degrees of Fahrenheit's scale, viz., from 60° (which was the temperature of the water and of the machinery at the beginning of the experiment) to 210°, the Heat of boiling water at Munich. . . .

As the machinery used in this experiment could easily be carried round by the force of one horse (though, to render the work lighter, two horses were actually employed in doing it), these computations show further how large a quantity of Heat might be produced, by proper mechanical contrivance, merely by the strength of a horse, without fire, light, combustion, or chemical decomposition; and, in a case of necessity, the Heat thus produced might be used in cooking victuals.

But no circumstances can be imagined in which this method of procuring Heat would not be disadvantageous, for more Heat might be obtained by using the fodder necessary for the support of a horse as fuel. . . .

In the experiment no. 1, the quantity of Heat generated in *half an hour* was found to be equal to that which would be required to heat 5 lb., avoirdupois, of ice-cold water 180 degrees, or cause it to boil.

According to the result of the experiment no. 3, the Heat generated in *half an hour* would have caused 5.31 lb. of ice-cold water to boil. But in this last-mentioned experiment, the Heat generated being more effectually confined, less of it was lost, which accounts for the difference of the results of the two experiments. . . .

～　～　～

By meditating on the results of all these experiments, we are naturally brought to that great question which has so often been the subject of speculation among philosophers; namely—

What is Heat? Is there any such thing as an *igneous fluid*? Is there anything that can with propriety be called *caloric*?

We have seen that a very considerable quantity of Heat may be excited in the friction of two metallic surfaces, and given off in a constant stream or flux *in all directions* without interruption or intermission, and without any signs of diminution or exhaustion.

From whence came the Heat which was continually given off in this manner in the foregoing experiments? Was it furnished by the small particles of metal, detached from the larger solid masses, on their being rubbed together? This, as we have already seen, could not possibly have been the case.

Was it furnished by the air? This could not have been the case, for in [one] of the experiments, the machinery being kept immersed in water, the access of the air of the atmosphere was completely prevented.

Was it furnished by the water which surrounded the machinery? That this could not have been the case is evident: *first*, because this water was continually *receiving Heat* from the machinery, and could not at the same time be *giving to* and *receiving Heat from* the same body; and *second*, because there was no chemical decomposition of any part of this water. Had any such decomposition taken place (which, indeed, could not reasonably have been expected), one of its component elastic fluids (most probably inflammable air) must at the same time have been set at liberty and, in making its escape into the atmosphere, would have been detected; but though I frequently examined the water to see if any air bubbles rose up through it, and had even made preparations for catching them, in order to examine them, if any should appear, I could perceive none, nor was there any sign of decomposition of any kind whatever, or other chemical process, going on in the water.

Is it possible that the Heat could have been supplied by means of the iron bar to the end of which the blunt steel borer was fixed? Or by the small neck of gunmetal by which the hollow cylinder was united to the cannon? These suppositions appear more improbable even than any of those before mentioned, for Heat was continually going off, or *out of the machinery*, by both these passages, during the whole time the experiment lasted.

And, in reasoning on this subject, we must not forget to consider that most remarkable circumstance, that the source of the Heat generated by friction, in these experiments, appeared evidently to be *inexhaustible*.

It is hardly necessary to add that anything which any *insulated* body, or system of bodies, can continue to furnish *without limitation* cannot possibly be *a material substance*, and it appears to me to be extremely difficult, if not quite impossible, to form any distinct idea of anything capable of being excited and communicated in the manner the Heat was excited and communicated in these experiments, except it be MOTION.

I am very far from pretending to know how, or by what means or mechanical contrivance, that particular kind of motion in bodies which has been supposed to constitute Heat is excited, continued, and propagated. . . .

But although the mechanism of Heat should, in fact, be one of those mysteries of nature which are beyond the reach of human intelligence, this ought by no means to discourage us or even lessen our ardor in our attempts to investigate the laws of its operations. How far can we advance in any of the paths which science has opened to us before we find ourselves enveloped in those thick mists which on every side bound the horizon of the human intellect? But how ample and how interesting is the field that is given us to explore!

Nobody, surely, in his sober senses, has ever pretended to understand the mechanism of gravitation, and yet what sublime discoveries was our immortal Newton enabled to make merely by the investigation of the laws of its action!

The effects produced in the world by the agency of Heat are probably *just as extensive*, and quite as important, as those which are owing to the tendency of the particles of matter toward each other, and there is no doubt but its operations are, in all cases, determined by laws equally immutable.

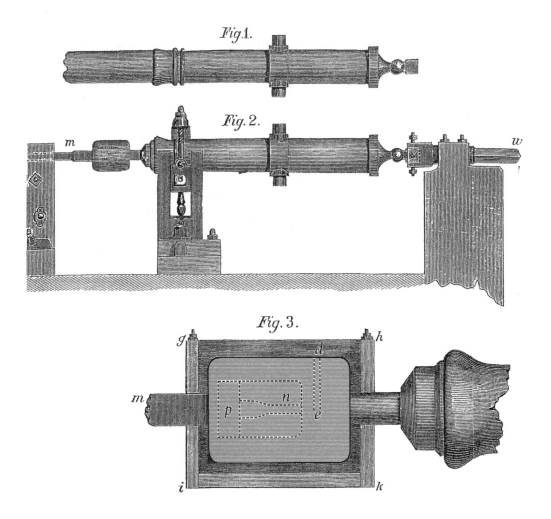

Fig.1.

Fig.2.

Fig.3.

Description of the Figures

Figure 1 shows the cannon used in the foregoing experiments in the state it was in when it came from the foundry.

Figure 2 shows the machinery used in experiments No. 1 and No. 2. The cannon is seen fixed in the machine used for boring cannon.

w is a strong iron bar (which, to save room in the drawing, is represented as broken off), which bar, being united with machinery (not expressed in the figure) that is carried round by horses, causes the cannon to turn round its axis.

m is a strong iron bar, to the end of which the blunt borer is fixed; which, by being forced against the bottom of the bore of the short hollow cylinder that remains connected by a small cylindrical neck to the end of the cannon, is used in generating Heat by friction.

Figure 3 shows, on an enlarged scale, the same hollow cylinder that is represented on a smaller scale in the foregoing figure. It is here seen connected with the wooden box (*g, h, i, k*) used in experiments No. 3 and No. 4, when this hollow cylinder was immersed in water.

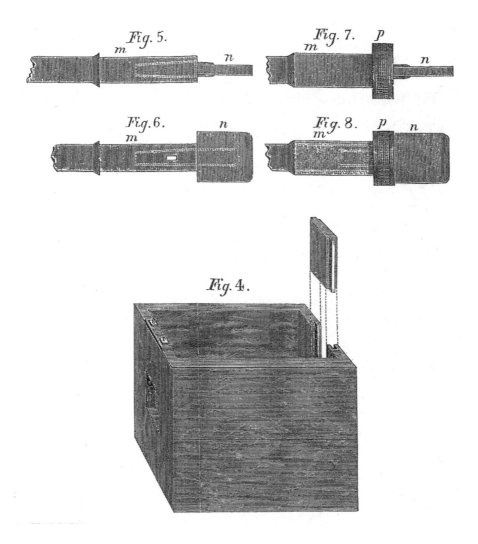

Fig. 5.

Fig. 7.

Fig. 6.

Fig. 8.

Fig. 4.

p, which is marked by dotted lines, is the piston which closed the end of the bore of the cylinder.

n is the blunt borer seen sidewise.

d, e, is the small hole by which the thermometer was introduced that was used for ascertaining the Heat of the cylinder. To save room in the drawing, the cannon is represented broken off near its muzzle, and the iron bar to which the blunt borer is fixed is represented broken off at *m*.

Figure 4 is a perspective view of the wooden box, a section of which is seen in the foregoing figure. (See *g, h, i, k,* fig. 3.)

Figures 5 and 6 represent the blunt borer *n*, joined to the iron bar *m*, to which it was fastened.

Figures 7 and 8 represent the same borer, with its iron bar, together with the piston which, in experiments No. 2 and No. 3, was used to close the mouth of the hollow cylinder.

Content Questions

1. What questions about heat does Rumford want to investigate based on what he observed when brass cannons were being bored? (120)

2. According to the "modern doctrines of latent Heat" that Rumford mentions, what is the source of heat produced in the mechanical operation of boring cannons? (120)

3. How does comparing the effect of the heated metal chips and that of metal slips on cold water lead Rumford to suspect there is a problem with the caloric theory of heat? (120)

4. What is the purpose of Rumford's experimental apparatus involving metal cylinders and a rotating blunt borer in contact with metal surfaces? (120–121)

5. In experiment no. 1, which features of the procedure help answer Rumford's question about how much heat was generated by friction? (121–123)

6. Which results of experiment no. 1 lead Rumford to conclude that the heat produced "was not furnished *at the expense of the latent Heat* or *combined caloric* of the metal"? (123)

7. Why does Rumford think it necessary to carry out experiment no. 2, and what does he conclude from its results? (123–124)

8. In experiment no. 3, what is the purpose of the water-filled box, and how does it provide a way of investigating the quantity of heat produced? (125–126)

9. What is the difference between the two arguments Rumford makes for why the water in his experiment could not be the source of the heat that is produced? (127–128)

10. How does the apparent inexhaustibility of the heat produced in Rumford's experiments lead him to reason that heat is not a material substance but must be excited by motion? (128)

Discussion Questions

1. What are the "playful excursions of the imagination, put into action by contemplating the most common appearances," that Rumford says will lead a scientist to worthwhile investigations of nature? (119)

2. Does Rumford begin his investigations into the "hidden nature of Heat" with any theory of his own in mind, or is he only trying to test the existing theory that heat is an *"igneous fluid"*? (120)

3. Why is Rumford not "willing to rest satisfied" with his initial trial concerning the heat capacity of the metal chips, even though the experiment was repeated several times and seemed to yield conclusive results? (120)

4. In reporting his findings, why does Rumford give the exact dimensions and weight of his experimental apparatus? (120–121)

5. If Rumford is testing the theory that heat is a material substance given up and absorbed by objects, why does he perform experiments that produce heat only by means of friction? (121)

6. Why does Rumford prefer to say that the heat produced is *"excited"* rather than "generated"? (123)

7. What does it mean for a scientist to say, as Rumford does about experiment no. 2, that he is conducting a "decisive experiment"? (124) In contrast, what does Rumford mean in calling experiment no. 3 "beautiful"? (126)

8. In experiments no. 1 and no. 3, why does Rumford carefully measure and report the change of temperature of the metal and water over time? What relation does he assume between temperature and amount of heat produced? (126–127)

9. What do the results of experiment no. 3 imply about the relationship between mechanical work performed and quantity of heat produced? (126–127)

10. What relationship do the results of Rumford's experiments imply among the various ways that heat can be produced: by means of mechanical motion, fire, light, combustion, and chemical decomposition? (126–127)

11. Is Rumford justified in coming to the conclusion that because the source of heat appears to be inexhaustible, it must be motion and not a material substance? (128)

12. Do Rumford's conclusions prove that the caloric theory is false? Do they prove that the alternative theory of heat as motion is true? (128)

13. What does Rumford mean by the "mechanism of Heat"? (128)

14. Is it possible for science to investigate the laws of the physical world without understanding the underlying mechanisms of the phenomena being investigated? (128–129)

15. Should a scientist set limits, as Rumford does, on the reach of human intelligence in investigating and understanding the physical world? (128–129)

Suggestions for Further Reading

About the author

Brown, G. I. *Scientist, Soldier, Statesman, Spy: Count Rumford.* Thrupp, UK: Sutton Publishing Limited, 2001. As the title suggests, Count Rumford (Benjamin Thompson) had an unusually varied career. This brief biography captures his many-sided inventiveness and contains a good discussion of theories of heat at the time Rumford conducted his experiments.

About the topic

Chang, Hasok. *Inventing Temperature: Measurement and Scientific Progress.* Oxford: Oxford University Press, 2004. Before heat could be studied scientifically, scientists such as Rumford needed a way to accurately measure temperature. This history traces the practical and conceptual problems that had to be solved before temperature scales and instruments could be constructed.

Crease, Robert P. *The Prism and the Pendulum: The Ten Most Beautiful Experiments in Science.* New York: Random House, 2003, 2004. In calling one of his experiments beautiful, Rumford was emphasizing the aesthetic appeal of science, which is often overlooked. This book provides detailed narratives of experiments that not only established important scientific principles but also were elegantly designed.

Harré, Rom. *Great Scientific Experiments: Twenty Experiments That Changed Our View of the World.* Mineola, NY: Dover Publications, 2002. Like Rumford's inquiries about heat, the experiments covered in this book are models of how scientific investigation should be conducted. Each chapter focuses on the work of an individual scientist and discusses the subsequent influence of his landmark experiment.

Segrè, Gino. *A Matter of Degrees: What Temperature Reveals About the Past and Future of Our Species, Planet, and Universe.* New York: Viking, 2002; New York: Penguin Books, 2003. From the formation of the universe through the development of life on earth, this book looks at the many ways in which temperature provides a fundamental measurement for understanding the world.

Von Baeyer, Hans Christian. *Warmth Disperses and Time Passes: The History of Heat.* New York: Modern Library, 1999. This readable and entertaining history begins with the work of Rumford and focuses on the scientists who developed thermodynamics.

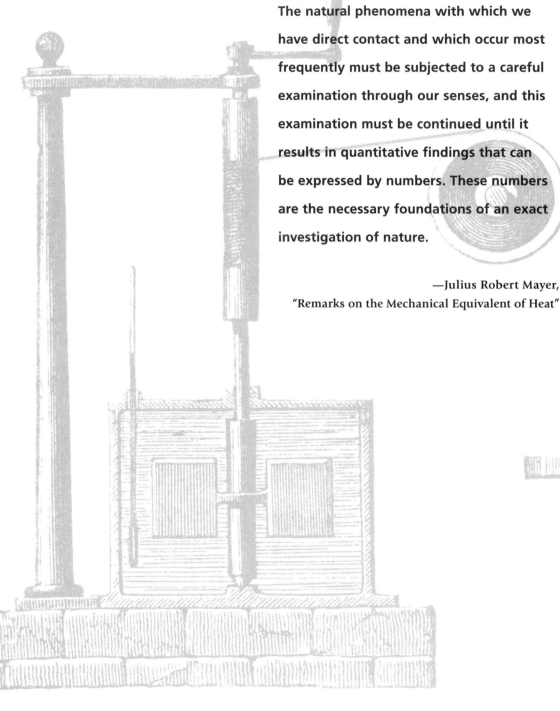

The natural phenomena with which we have direct contact and which occur most frequently must be subjected to a careful examination through our senses, and this examination must be continued until it results in quantitative findings that can be expressed by numbers. These numbers are the necessary foundations of an exact investigation of nature.

—Julius Robert Mayer,
"Remarks on the Mechanical Equivalent of Heat"

JAMES PRESCOTT JOULE

The Mechanical Equivalent of Heat

The word *energy* is so commonly used that we rarely think about its abstract scientific meaning. Although it is not hard to point to sources of energy, such as oil, electricity, the sun, and the food we eat, defining energy itself is difficult. This is because we primarily observe and measure energy through its effects; additionally, it is capable of assuming many different forms, as when a dam's turbine and generator convert the kinetic energy of water to electricity. Today, energy is usually defined indirectly as the capacity of an object with mass for doing work. But scientific insight was necessary to first conceive of the idea of energy as essential to understanding the physical world.

In the early nineteenth century, new technologies prompted scientific interest in conversion processes. Scientists observed that phenomena involving chemicals, heat, electricity, magnetism, and motion could be converted into each other. Some processes were being applied to the solution of practical problems, such as the steam engine's production of motion from heat, and the generation of electrical currents from chemical reactions in batteries. However, until the concept of energy was developed, scientists had no way to explain what was common to all these conversion processes; they needed a combination of sound theoretical ideas and precise quantitative experimental data.

Two discoveries by Count Rumford—that heat is not a substance and that a measurable amount of heat is produced from a measurable quantity of motion— contributed an important insight. These discoveries implied not only that there was something converted from one form to another in this process, but also that something was conserved. What exactly was converted and conserved was the concern of the theoretical scientist Robert Julius Mayer. In 1842, Mayer asserted that all forms of what he called *living force*, and which we now call energy, can be converted into each other, and that heat is a form of energy. Furthermore, he claimed that in conversion processes, the total amount of energy remains unchanged. Mayer was one of the first scientists to propose the principle of the conservation of energy, but his work was based on logical speculation rather than experiment. It was the work of James Prescott Joule (1818–1889) that provided the quantitative data necessary to confirm Mayer's theories.

Although Joule had little formal education in science, his work in his family's brewery contributed to his skill in making exact measurements with extremely precise thermometers. In his early experiments, Joule used an arrangement of falling weights to rotate a wire coil in a strong magnetic field, generating an electrical current. He then measured the amount of heat produced by the current that corresponded to the mechanical motion of the weights, precisely determining something that Mayer had theoretically proposed—the mechanical equivalent of heat. Joule later conducted hundreds of experiments with various conversion processes, the most famous of which involved the direct heating of water by the motion of immersed paddle wheels. He expressed his consistent quantitative results for the mechanical equivalent of heat in terms of work units (foot-pounds) per British thermal unit (the amount of heat required to raise one pound of water 1° Fahrenheit). The average value that he found was very close to the one now accepted (778 foot-pounds per BTU) and attests to Joule's extraordinary ability as an experimental scientist. In his honor, the standard unit of energy in physics is named the *joule*.

Joule's work demonstrated that in conversion processes, nature, like a good bookkeeper, accounts for all energy, which is neither created nor destroyed. Although he did not arrive at a fully developed concept of energy, his discoveries led directly to the formulation of the law of energy conservation, now known as the first law of thermodynamics. As with all great advances in physics, this law provided a principle that unified aspects of the physical world previously regarded as only loosely related, and gave central importance to the concept of energy.

In the following selection, Joule's description of the reasoning behind his discovery of the mechanical equivalent of heat emphasizes how a scientist's investigations are often guided by a profound confidence in the orderliness of the universe.

The Mechanical Equivalent of Heat

In our notion of matter, two ideas are generally included, namely those of *impenetrability* and *extension*. By the extension of matter we mean the space which it occupies; by its impenetrability we mean that two bodies cannot exist at the same time in the same place. Impenetrability and extension cannot with much propriety be reckoned among the *properties* of matter, but deserve rather to be called its *definitions*, because nothing that does not possess the two qualities bears the name of matter. If we conceive of impenetrability and extension we have the idea of matter, and of matter only.

Matter is endowed with an exceedingly great variety of wonderful properties, some of which are common to all matter, while others are present variously, so as to constitute a difference between one body and another. Of the first of these classes, the attraction of gravitation is one of the most important. We observe its presence readily in the solid bodies, the component parts of which are . . . held together by this force. If we break the body in pieces, and remove the separate pieces to a distance from each other, they will still be found to attract each other, though in

This section is taken from "On Matter, Living Force, and Heat" and "On the Mechanical Equivalent of Heat."

139

a very slight degree, owing to the force being one which diminishes very rapidly as the bodies are removed further from one another. The larger the bodies are, the more powerful is the force of attraction subsisting between them. Hence, although the force of attraction between small bodies can only be appreciated by the most delicate apparatus except in the case of contact, that which is occasioned by a body of immense magnitude, such as the earth, becomes very considerable. This attraction of bodies toward the earth constitutes what is called their *weight* or *gravity*, and is always exactly proportional to the quantity of matter. Hence, if any body be found to weigh 2 lb., while another weighs only 1 lb., the former will contain exactly twice as much matter as the latter; and this is the case, whatever the bulk of bodies may be: 2 lb. of air contains exactly twice the quantity of matter that 1 lb. of lead does.

Matter is something endowed with other kinds of attraction besides the attraction of gravitation; sometimes it also possesses the faculty of *repulsion*, by which force the particles tend to separate farther from each other. Wherever these forces exist, they do not supersede the attraction of gravitation. Thus the weight of a piece of iron or steel is in no way affected by imparting to it the magnetic virtue.

Besides the force of gravitation, there is another very remarkable property displayed in an equal degree be every kind of matter—its perseverance in any condition, whether of rest or motion, in which it may have been placed. This faculty has received the name of *inertia*, signifying passiveness, or the inability of any thing to change its own state. It is in consequence of this property that a body at rest cannot be set in motion without the application of a certain amount of force to it, and also that when the body has been set in motion it will never stop of itself, but continue to move straight forward with a uniform velocity until acted upon by another force, which, if applied contrary to the direction of motion, will retard it, if in the same direction will accelerate it, and if sideways will cause it to move in a curved direction. In the case in which the force is applied contrary in direction, but equal in degree to that which set the body first in motion, it will be entirely deprived of motion, whatever time may have elapsed since the first impulse, and to whatever distance the body may have traveled.

From these facts it is obvious that the force expended in setting a body in motion is carried by the body itself, and exists with it and in it, throughout the whole course of its motion. This force possessed by moving bodies is termed by mechanical philosophers *vis vira*, or "living force." The term may be deemed by some inappropriate, inasmuch as there is no life, properly speaking, in question; but it is *useful*, in order to distinguish the moving force from that which is stationary in its character, as the force of gravity. When, therefore, . . . I employ the term *living force*, you will understand that I simply mean the force of bodies in motion. The living force of bodies is regulated by their weight and by the velocity of their motion. You will readily understand that if a body of a certain weight possesses a certain quantity of living force, twice as much living force will be possessed by a body of twice the weight, provided both bodies move with equal velocity. But the law by which the *velocity* of a body regulates its living force is not so obvious. At first sight, one would imagine that the living force would be simply proportional to the velocity, so that if a body moved twice as fast as another, it would have twice the impetus, or living force. Such, however, is not the case; for if three bodies of equal weight move with the respective velocities of 1, 2, and 3 miles per hour, their living forces will be found to be proportional to those numbers multiplied by themselves, viz., to 1×1, 2×2, and 3×3, or 1, 4, and 9, the squares of 1, 2, and 3. This remarkable law may be proved in several ways. A bullet fired from a gun at certain velocity will pierce a block of wood to only one-quarter of the depth it would if propelled at twice the velocity. Again, if a cannonball were found to fly at a certain velocity when propelled by a given charge of gunpowder, and if it were required to load the cannon so as to propel the ball with twice that velocity, it would be found necessary to employ four times the weight of power previously used. Thus, also, it will be found that a railway train going at 70 miles per hour possesses 100 times the impetus, or living force, that it does when traveling at 7 miles per hour.

A body may be endowed with living force in several ways. It may receive it by the impact of another body. Thus, if a perfectly elastic ball be made to strike another similar ball of equal weight at rest, the striking ball will communicate the whole of its living force to the ball struck, and, remaining at rest itself, will cause the other ball to move in the same direction and with the same velocity that it did itself before the collision. Here we see an instance of the facility with which living force may be transferred from one body to another. A body may also be endowed with living force by means of the action of gravitation upon it through a certain distance. If I hold a ball at a certain height and drop it, it will have acquired, when it arrives at the ground, a degree of living force proportional to its weight and the height from which it has fallen. We see, then, that living force may be produced by the action of gravity through a given distance or space. We may therefore say that the former is of equal value, or *equivalent*, to the latter. Hence, if I raise a weight of 1 lb. to the height of one foot, so that gravity may act on it through that distance, I shall communicate to it that which is of equal value or equivalent to a certain amount of living force; if I raise the weight to twice the height, I shall communicate to it the equivalent of twice the quantity of living force. Hence, also, when we compress a spring, we communicate to it the equivalent of a certain amount of living force; for in that case we produce molecular attraction between the particles of the spring through the distance they are forced asunder, which is strictly analogous to the production of the attraction of gravitation through a certain distance.

You will at once perceive that the living force of which we have been speaking is one of the most important qualities with which matter can be endowed, and, as such, that it would be absurd to suppose that it can be destroyed, or even lessened, without producing the equivalent of attraction through a given distance of which we have been speaking. You will therefore be surprised to hear that until very recently the universal opinion has been that living force could be absolutely and irrevocably destroyed at anyone's option. Thus, when a weight falls to the ground, it has been generally supposed that its living force is absolutely annihilated, and that the labor which may have been expended in raising it to the elevation from which it fell has been entirely thrown away and wasted, without the production of any permanent effect whatever. We might reason, a priori, that such absolute destruction of living force cannot possibly take place, because it is manifestly absurd to suppose that the powers with which God has endowed matter can be destroyed any more than that they can be created by man's agency; but we are not left with this argument alone, decisive as it must be to every unprejudiced mind. The common experience of everyone teaches that living force is not *destroyed* by the friction or collision of bodies. We have reason to believe that the manifestations of living force on our globe are, at the present time, as extensive as those which have existed at any time since its creation, or, at any rate, since the deluge—that the winds blow as strongly, and the torrents flow with equal impetuosity, now as at the remote period of 4,000 or even 6,000 years ago; and yet we are certain that, through that vast interval of time, the motions of the air and of the water have been incessantly obstructed and hindered by friction. We may conclude, then, with certainty, that these motions of air and water, constituting living force, are not *annihilated* by friction. We lose sight of them, indeed, for a time, but we find them again reproduced. Were it not so, it is perfectly obvious that long ere this, all nature would have come to a dead standstill. What, then, may we inquire, is the cause of this apparent anomaly? How comes it to pass that, though in almost all natural phenomena we witness the arrest of motion and the apparent destruction of living force, we find that no waste or loss of living force has actually occurred? Experiment has enabled us to answer these questions in a satisfactory manner; for it has shown that, wherever living force is *apparently* destroyed, an equivalent is produced which in process of time may be reconverted into living force. This equivalent is *heat*. Experiment has shown that wherever living force is apparently destroyed or absorbed, heat is produced. The most frequent way in which living force is thus converted into heat is by means of friction. Wood rubbed against wood or against any hard body, metal rubbed against metal or against any other body—in short, all bodies, solid or even liquid, rubbed against each other—are invariably heated, sometimes even so far as to become red-hot. In all these instances the quantity of heat produced is invariably in proportion to the exertion employed in rubbing the bodies together—that is, the living force absorbed. By fifteen or twenty smart and quick strokes of hammer on the end of an iron rod of about a quarter of an inch in diameter placed upon an anvil, an expert blacksmith will render that end of the iron visibly red-hot. Here heat is produced by the absorption of the living force of the descending hammer in the soft iron; which is proved to be the case from the fact that the iron cannot be heated if it be rendered hard and elastic, so as to transfer living force of the hammer to the anvil.

The general rule, then, is that wherever living force is *apparently* destroyed, whether by percussion, friction, or any similar means, an extract equivalent of heat is restored. The converse of this proposition is also true, namely, that heat cannot be lessened or absorbed without the production of living force, or its equivalent attraction through space. Thus, for instance, in the steam engine it will be found that the power gained is at the expense of the heat of the fire—that is, that the heat occasioned by the combustion of the coal would have been greater had a part of it not been absorbed in producing and maintaining the living force of the machinery. It is right, however, to observe that this has not as yet been demonstrated by experiment. But there is no room to doubt that experiment would prove the correctness of what I have said, for I have myself proved that a conversion of heat into living force takes place in the expansion of air, which is analogous to the expansion of steam in the cylinder of the steam engine. But the most convincing proof of the conversion of heat into living force has been derived from my experiments with the electromagnetic engine, a machine composed of magnets and bars of iron set in motion by an electrical battery. I have proved by actual experiment that, in exact proportion to the force with which this machine works, heat is abstracted from the electrical battery. You see, therefore, that living force may be converted into heat, and that heat may be converted into living force, or its equivalent attraction through space. All three, therefore—namely, heat, living force, and attraction through space (to which I might also add light) . . . —are mutually convertible into one another. In these conversions nothing is ever lost. The same quantity of heat will always be converted into the same quantity of living force. We can therefore express the equivalency in definite language applicable at all times and under all circumstances. Thus the attraction of 817 lb. through the space of one foot is equivalent to, and convertible into, the living force possessed by a body of the same weight of 817 lb. when moving with the velocity of eight feet per second, and this living force is again convertible into the quantity of heat which can increase the temperature of one pound of water by one degree Fahrenheit. The knowledge of the equivalency of heat to mechanical power is of great value in solving a great number of interesting and important questions. In the case of steam engine, by ascertaining the quantity of heat produced by the combustion of coal, we can find out how much of it is converted into mechanical power, and thus come to a conclusion [about] how far the steam engine is susceptible of further improvements. Calculations made upon this principle have shown that at least ten times as much power might be produced as is now obtained by the combustion of coal. Another interesting conclusion is that the animal frame, though destined to fulfill so many other ends, is as a machine more perfect than the best-contrived steam engine—that is, is capable of more work with the same expenditure of fuel. . . .

. . . We find a vast variety of phenomena connected with the conversion of living force and heat into one another which speak in language, which cannot be misunderstood, of the wisdom and beneficence of the Great Architect of nature. The motion of air which we call *wind* arises chiefly from the intense heat of the torrid zone compared with the temperature of the temperate and frigid zones. Here we have an instance of heat being converted into the living force of currents of air. These currents of air, in their progress across the sea, lift up its waves and propel the ships, while in passing across the land they shake the trees and disturb every blade of grass. The waves by their violent motion, the ships by their passage through a resisting medium, and the trees by rubbing of their branches together and the friction of their leaves against themselves and the air, each and all of them generate heat equivalent to the diminution of the living force of the air which they occasion. The heat thus restored may again contribute to raise fresh currents of air; and thus the phenomena may be repeated in endless succession and variety.

When we consider our own animal frames, "fearfully and wonderfully made," we observe in the motion of our limbs a continual conversion of heat into living force, which may be either converted back again into heat or employed in producing an attraction through space, as when a man ascends a mountain. Indeed the phenomena of nature, whether mechanical, chemical, or vital, consist almost entirely in a continual conversion of attraction through space, living force, and heat into one another. Thus it is that order is maintained in the universe—nothing is deranged, nothing ever lost, but the entire machinery, complicated as it is, works smoothly and harmoniously. And though, as in the awful vision of Ezekiel, "wheel may be in the middle of wheel," and everything may appear complicated and involved in the apparent confusion and intricacy of an almost endless variety of causes, effects, conversions, and arrangements, yet is the most perfect regularity preserved—the whole being governed by the sovereign will of God.

A few words may be said, in conclusion, with respect to the real nature of heat. The most prevalent opinion, until of late, has been that it is a *substance* possessing, like all other matter, impenetrability and extension. We have, however, shown that heat can be converted into living force and into attraction through space. It is perfectly clear, therefore, that unless matter can be converted into attraction through space, which is too absurd an idea to be entertained for a moment, the hypothesis of heat being a substance must fall to the ground. Heat must therefore consist of either living force or of attraction through space. In the former case we can conceive the constituent particles of heated bodies to be, either in whole or in part, in a state of motion. In the latter we may suppose the particles to be removed by the process of heating, so as to exert attraction through greater space. I am inclined to believe that both of these hypotheses will be found to hold good—that in some instances, particularly in the case of *sensible* heat, or such as is indicated by the thermometer, heat will be found to consist in the living force of the particles of the bodies in which it is induced; while in others, particularly in the case of *latent* heat, the phenomena are produced by the separation of particle from particle, so as to cause them to attract one another through a greater space. We may conceive, then, that the communication of heat to body consists, in fact, in the communication of impetus, or living force, to its particles. . . .

~ ~ ~

For a long time it had been a favorite hypothesis that heat consists of a force of power belonging to bodies, but it was reserved for Count Rumford to make the first experiments decidedly in favor of that view. That justly celebrated natural philosopher demonstrated by his ingenious experiments that the very great quantity of heat excited by the boring of cannon could not be ascribed to a change taking place in the calorific capacity of the metal, and he therefore concluded that the motion of the borer was communicated to the particles of metal, thus producing the phenomena of heat. . . .

One of the most important parts of Count Rumford's paper, though one to which little attention has hitherto been paid, is that in which he makes an estimate of the quantity of mechanical force required to produce a certain amount of heat. Referring to his third experiment, he remarks that the "total quantity of ice-cold water which, with the heat actually generated by friction, and accumulated in 2 hours and 30 minutes, might have been heated 180°F, or made to boil, equals 26.58 lb." On the next page he states that "the machinery used in the experiment could easily be carried round by the force of one horse (though, to render the work lighter, two horses were actually employed in doing it)." Now, the power of a horse is estimated by Watt at 33,000 foot-pounds per minute, and therefore if continued for two hours and a half will amount to 4,950,000 foot-pounds, which, according to Count Rumford's experiment, will be equivalent to 26.58 lb. of water raised 180°F. Hence the heat required to raise a pound of water 1°F will be equivalent to the force represented by 1,034 foot-pounds. This result is not very widely different from that which I have deduced from my own experiments . . . , viz., 772 foot-pounds; and it must be observed that the excess of Count Rumford's equivalent is just such as might have been anticipated from the circumstance, which he himself mentions, that "no estimate was made of the heat accumulated in the wooden box, nor of that dispersed during the experiment." . . .

In 1834 Dr. Faraday demonstrated the "Identity of the Chemical and Electrical Forces." This law, along with others subsequently discovered by that great man, showing the relations which subsist between magnetism, electricity, and light, have enabled him to advance this idea that the so-called imponderable bodies are merely the exponents of different forms of force. . . .

My own experiments in reference to the subject were commenced in 1840, in which year I communicated to the Royal Society my discovery of the law of the heat evolved by voltaic electricity, a law from which the immediate deductions were drawn—first, that the heat evolved by any voltaic pair is proportional . . . to its intensity or electromotive force; and second, that the heat evolved by the combustion of a body is proportional to the intensity of its affinity for oxygen. I thus succeeded in establishing relations between heat and chemical affinity. In 1843 I showed that the heat evolved by magnetoelectricity is proportional to the force absorbed, and that the force of the electromagnetic engine is derived from the force of chemical affinity in the battery, a force which otherwise would be evolved in the form of heat. From these facts I considered myself justified in announcing "that the quantity of heat capable of increasing the temperature of a pound of water by one degree of Fahrenheit's scale is equal to, and may be converted into, a mechanical force capable of raising 838 lb. to the perpendicular height of one foot."

In a subsequent paper, read before the Royal Society in 1844, I endeavored to show that the heat absorbed and evolved by the rarefaction and condensation of air is proportional to the force evolved and absorbed in those operations. The quantitative relation between force and heat deduced from these experiments is almost identical with that derived from the electromagnetic experiments just referred to. . . .

From the explanation given by Count Rumford of the heat arising from the friction of solids, one might have anticipated, as a matter of course, that the evolution of heat would also be detected in the friction of liquid and gaseous bodies. . . . Nevertheless, the scientific world, pre-occupied with the hypothesis that heat is a substance, . . . has almost unanimously denied the possibility of generating heat in that way. . . . In 1843 I announced the fact that "heat is evolved by the passage of water through narrow tubes," and that each degree of heat per pound of water required for its evolution in this way a mechanical force represented by 770 foot-pounds. Subsequently, in 1845 and 1847, I employed a paddle wheel to produce the fluid friction, and obtained the equivalents 781.5, 782.1, and 787.6 respectively from the agitation of water, sperm oil, and mercury. Results so closely coinciding with one another, and with those previously derived from experiments with elastic fluids and the electro-magnetic machine, left no doubt in my mind as to the existence of an equivalent relation between force and heat: but still it appeared of the highest importance to obtain that relation with still greater accuracy. This I have attempted in the present paper.

Content Questions

1. Why does Joule think that impenetrability and extension must be considered definitions, rather than properties, of matter? (139)

2. Among the "exceedingly great variety of wonderful properties" that matter may have, why does Joule emphasize the force of gravity and inertia? (139–140)

3. What does Joule think happens to the force that is applied to a body, setting it in motion? (140)

4. What does Joule mean by the term *vis viva* (living force)? Why does he think this term is useful? (141) What term is now used in place of *living force*?

5. How does Joule arrive at the law by which the velocity of a body regulates its living force? (141)

6. What are the ways that a body can be "endowed with living force," with respect to its motion and to its position? (141–142)

7. According to Joule, how can living force be equivalent to "the action of gravity through a given distance or space"? (142)

8. What reason does Joule think common opinion had for holding that living force can be "absolutely and irrevocably destroyed at anyone's option"? According to Joule, why can't living force be destroyed? (142–143)

9. What reasons does Joule give for claiming that, when living force is apparently destroyed, an equivalent is produced in the form of heat? (143)

10. In the mutual convertibility of living force, heat, and attraction through space into each other, what does Joule mean when he says that "nothing is ever lost"? (144)

11. Why does Joule claim that "the animal frame . . . is as a machine more perfect than the best-contrived steam engine"? (144)

12. Based on his observation of natural phenomena, what does Joule think is the result of the "continual conversion of attraction through space, living force, and heat into one another"? (145)

13. Why does Joule conclude that heat is not a substance? (145–146)

14. Why does Joule think that one of the most important parts of Count Rumford's paper is his calculation of the horsepower used in his experiment? (146)

15. How do the results of Joule's experiment using a paddle wheel to produce friction lead him to conclude that there is "an equivalent relation between force and heat?" (148)

Discussion Questions

1. In the term *living force,* does Joule intend us to understand "force" in the same way as when he speaks of the force of gravity or a force expended in setting a body in motion? (141) In science, should a term be used that is in some way inappropriate, even though it is also useful?

2. What does Joule mean by the "quantity" of living force? How does he think that the living force of bodies is regulated by their weight? Should he make a distinction between weight and mass? (141)

3. When Joule says that living force and the action of gravity through a given distance are equivalent, is he saying that they are the same? (142) In science, can things be equivalent, though not identical?

4. Why does Joule argue that it is evident to everyone from common experience that "living force is not *destroyed* by the friction or collision of bodies"? (142) Is it in fact evident?

5. Why does Joule think that nature has not come to a "dead standstill"? How does he think that scientific experiment can reveal "the cause of this apparent anomaly"? (143)

6. How does understanding the operation of machinery such as steam engines help Joule to think about the conversion of living force into various forms? Why is heat so important to him in trying to explain these conversions? (143–144)

7. What does Joule mean by the term *conversion* when he speaks of heat, living force, and attraction through space as being "mutually convertible"? (144)

8. Is it scientifically valid for Joule to conclude that "a continual conversion of attraction through space, living force, and heat into one another" explains the maintenance of order in the universe? (145)

9. When Joule says that the universe is "governed by the sovereign will of God," is he offering this as a conclusion confirmed by what he has discovered about nature as a scientist? (145) Should scientists introduce religious principles into their scientific arguments?

10. How does Joule's theory that bodies consist of particles support his hypothesis that heat can be either living force or attraction through space? (145–146)

11. What does Joule mean by the mechanical equivalent of heat? (147–148)

12. Why doesn't Joule state his conclusion about the "equivalent relation between force and heat" as a conservation law? Is he lacking some concept, terminology, or data that would allow him to formulate his ideas in a form that we would now call the first law of thermodynamics? (148)

Suggestions for Further Reading

About the topic

Carnot, Sadi. *Reflections on the Motive Power of Fire: And Other Papers on the Second Law of Thermodynamics.* Mineola, NY: Dover Publications, 2005. Carnot's experiments preceded those of Joule, and his papers examine the relation between heat and work in mechanical engines. Carnot's discoveries helped to formulate the law of energy conservation and pointed the way to the second law of thermodynamics.

Goldstein, Martin, and Inge F. Goldstein. *The Refrigerator and the Universe: Understanding the Laws of Energy.* Cambridge, MA: Harvard University Press, 1993, 1995. Along with its excellent presentation of the three laws of thermodynamics, this book shows the extent to which thermodynamics can be used to gain understanding of a wide range of phenomena in physics, chemistry, biology, geology, and cosmology.

Lightman, Alan. *Great Ideas in Physics: The Conservation of Energy, the Second Law of Thermodynamics, the Theory of Relativity, and Quantum Mechanics.* 3rd ed. New York: McGraw-Hill, 2000. The chapter on the conservation of energy is highly recommended for its discussion of essential concepts such as the definition of energy, the role of mathematics in formulating physical laws, and the philosophical implications of conservation laws.

Lindley, David. *Degrees Kelvin: A Tale of Genius, Invention, and Tragedy.* Washington, D.C.: Joseph Henry Press, 2004, 2005. This biography of Kelvin, a contemporary of Joule who played a central role in the creation of the fields of thermodynamics and electromagnetism, traces the story of his life during the time when physics was becoming a specialized discipline.

Planck, Max. *Treatise on Thermodynamics.* Reprint. Mineola, NY: Dover Publications, 1990. Although Planck's work in thermodynamics led to the revolutionary discovery of quantum physics and its reliance on statistical methods to explain microscopic phenomena, in this elegant explanation of the principles of heat Planck takes a classical, macroscopic approach without appealing to interpretations based on molecular motion.

Von Baeyer, Hans Christian. *Warmth Disperses and Time Passes: The History of Heat.* New York: Modern Library, 1999. Besides providing a detailed description of Joule's experiments, this lively history discusses the important discoveries in thermodynamics of James Clerk Maxwell and his famous thought experiment, called "Maxwell's demon."

Entropy is an appreciation of arrangement and organization; it is subjective in the same sense that the constellation Orion is subjective. That which is arranged is objective, so too are the stars composing the constellation; but the association is the contribution of the mind which surveys.

—Arthur Eddington,
The Nature of the Physical World

ARTHUR EDDINGTON

Entropy: The Running-Down of the Universe

The second law of thermodynamics and the concept of entropy provide scientific explanations of familiar physical events: heated ice melts, smoke disperses, broken dishes do not repair themselves, scattered billiard balls do not spontaneously return to their original positions. If we observed these events going in reverse, as if time ran backward, we would think that some principle of how the world operates had changed. In each case, things go from a more orderly state to one less orderly; we know that to restore order, it is necessary to expend energy and perform work. In the nineteenth century, scientists investigating what happens when heat energy is transformed into work developed explanations of these events and established the branch of physics called thermodynamics. Their discoveries led to several equivalent statements of the second law of thermodynamics and closely paralleled the discovery of the principle of energy conservation, the first law of thermodynamics.

In analyzing the efficiency of the steam engine in the early 1800s, the French engineer Sadi Carnot discovered there are natural limits to the quantity of work that can be derived from an engine's energy source, regardless of design improvements to the engine. The British scientist Lord Kelvin (William Thomson) recognized that there is also a qualitative difference between the energy an engine uses to operate and the unusable energy it dissipates as heat. He concluded that the reason one must refuel an engine is that it cannot continue to operate without an external source of high-quality, concentrated energy. Building on these insights, the German physicist Rudolf Clausius proposed that some energy used in physical processes degrades irretrievably to a form no longer useful for producing work, even though the total quantity of energy is conserved. To account for processes that spontaneously go in one direction but are never observed in reverse, such as a spoon becoming hot in a cup of tea, in 1865 Clausius introduced a new concept to physics, which he called *entropy*. Entropy is a measure of the extent to which any physical process is reversible or irreversible. In the examples mentioned above, entropy has increased. The result of Clausius's discoveries was one statement of the second law of thermodynamics: in closed systems without external sources of usable energy, entropy always increases. Clausius concluded that although the total amount of energy in the universe is constant, the amount of usable energy decreases over time and the entropy of the universe as a whole tends toward a maximum value.

The work of Kelvin and Clausius represented great advances in understanding how physical events unfold through energy transformations. However, in the late nineteenth century the Austrian physicist Ludwig Boltzmann explained the physical mechanism for the tendency of energy to dissipate and of entropy to increase. Boltzmann believed in the atomic theory of matter and its conception of energy as molecular motion. He interpreted the second law of thermodynamics and entropy in terms of the statistical probability that there are vastly more ways for random molecular motion to be disordered than ordered. The second law became a statement of the immense odds against order naturally emerging from disorder, with entropy being a measure of the probable disorder in physical events. These two principles are central to all fields of science. They account for the changes and evolution of the world, from subatomic particles to galaxies, including the work of life forms maintaining themselves through processes that counteract entropy.

Arthur Eddington (1882–1944) was a British astronomer, physicist, and mathematician whose work helped bring about fundamental changes in how scientists viewed the universe during the period when the theory of relativity and quantum theory were first developed. Eddington contributed to the understanding of the structure and subatomic energy sources of stars, and Albert Einstein considered him the foremost interpreter of his theory of relativity. In 1919, Eddington conducted experiments confirming predictions of the general theory of relativity about the bending of light paths in gravitational fields, leading to the theory's wider acceptance. He also wrote a series of popular science books for general readers explaining the new ideas of astronomy, cosmology, and physics, including entropy and the second law of thermodynamics.

In the following selection, taken from *The Nature of the Physical World* (1928), Eddington considers why the second law of thermodynamics holds "the supreme position among the laws of nature," and why "the chain of deductions from this simple law have been almost illimitable." Because the second law and entropy are deeply connected with the direction in time of physical events, he raises searching questions about the beginning, the evolution, and the final state of the universe.

Entropy: The Running-Down of the Universe

Shuffling

If you take a pack of cards as it comes from the maker and shuffle it for a few minutes, all trace of the original systematic order disappears. The order will never come back however long you shuffle. Something has been done which cannot be undone, namely, the introduction of a random element in place of arrangement.

Illustrations may be useful even when imperfect, and therefore I have slurred over two points, which affect the illustration rather than the application which we are about to make. It was scarcely true to say that the shuffling cannot be undone. *You* can sort out the cards into their original order if you like. But in considering the shuffling which occurs in the physical world we are not troubled by a deus ex machina like you. I am not prepared to say how far the human mind is bound by the conclusions we shall reach. So I exclude you—at least I exclude that activity of your mind which you employ in sorting the cards. I allow you to shuffle them because you can do that *absent-mindedly*.

Secondly, it is not quite true that the original order never comes back. There is a ghost of a chance that someday a thoroughly shuffled pack will

This selection is taken from chapter 4, "The Running-Down of the Universe," of The Nature of the Physical World.

be found to have come back to the original order. That is because of the comparatively small number of cards in the pack. In our applications the units are so numerous that this kind of contingency can be disregarded.

We shall put forward the contention that

> whenever anything happens which cannot be undone, it is always reducible to the introduction of a random element analogous to that introduced by shuffling.

Shuffling is the only thing which nature cannot undo.

When Humpty Dumpty had a great fall—

> All the king's horses and all the king's men
> Cannot put Humpty Dumpty together again.

Something had happened which could not be undone. The fall could have been undone. It is not necessary to invoke the king's horses and the king's men; if there had been a perfectly elastic mat underneath, that would have sufficed. At the end of his fall Humpty Dumpty had kinetic energy which, properly directed, was just sufficient to bounce him back onto the wall again. But the elastic mat being absent, an irrevocable event happened at the end of the fall—namely, the introduction of a *random element* into Humpty Dumpty.

But why should we suppose that shuffling is the *only* process that cannot be undone?

> The Moving Finger writes; and, having writ,
> Moves on: nor all thy Piety and Wit
> Can lure it back to cancel half a Line.

When there is no shuffling, is the Moving Finger stayed? The answer of physics is unhesitatingly yes. To judge of this we must examine those operations of nature in which no increase of the random element can possibly occur. These fall into two groups. Firstly, we can study those laws of nature which control the behavior of a single unit. Clearly no shuffling can occur in these problems; you cannot take the king of spades away from the pack and shuffle him. Secondly, we can study the processes of nature in a crowd which is already so completely shuffled that there is no room for any further increase of the random element. If our contention is right, everything that occurs in these conditions is capable of being undone. We shall consider the first condition immediately; the second must be deferred until page [167].

Any change occurring to a body which can be treated as a single unit can be undone. The laws of nature admit of the undoing as easily as of the doing. The earth describing its orbit is controlled by laws of motion and of gravitation; these admit of the earth's actual motion, but they also admit of the precisely opposite motion. In the same field of force the earth could retrace its steps; it merely depends on how it was started off. It may be objected that we have no right to dismiss the starting off as an inessential part of the problem; it may be as much a part of the coherent scheme of nature as the laws controlling the subsequent motion. Indeed, astronomers have theories explaining why the eight planets all started to move the same way round the sun. But that is a problem of eight planets, not of a single individual—a problem of the pack, not of the isolated card. So long as the earth's motion is treated as an isolated problem, no one would dream of putting into the laws of nature a clause requiring that it must go *this* way round and not the opposite.

There is similar reversibility of motion in fields of electric and magnetic force. Another illustration can be given from atomic physics. The quantum laws admit of the emission of certain kinds and quantities of light from an atom; these laws also admit of absorption of the same kinds and quantities, i.e., the undoing of the emission. I apologize for an apparent poverty of illustration; it must be remembered that many properties of a body, e.g., temperature, refer to its constitution as a large number of separate atoms, and therefore the laws controlling temperature cannot be regarded as controlling the behavior of a single individual.

The common property possessed by laws governing the individual can be stated more clearly by a reference to time. A certain sequence of states running from past to future is the *doing* of an event; the same sequence running from future to past is the *undoing* of it—because in the latter case we turn round the sequence so as to view it in the accustomed manner, from past to future. So if the laws of nature are indifferent as to the doing and undoing of an event, they must be indifferent as to a direction of time from past to future. That is their common feature, and it is seen at once when (as usual) the laws are formulated mathematically. There is no more distinction between past and future than between right and left. In algebraic symbolism, left is $-x$, right is $+x$; past is $-t$, future is $+t$. This holds for all laws of nature governing the behavior of noncomposite individuals—the "primary laws," as we shall call them. There is only one law of nature—the second law of thermodynamics—which recognizes a distinction between past and future more profound than the difference of plus and minus. It stands aloof from all the rest. But this law has no application to the behavior of a single individual, and, as we shall see later, its subject matter is the random element in a crowd.

Whatever the primary laws of physics may say, it is obvious to ordinary experience that there is a distinction between past and future of a different kind from the distinction of left and right. . . .

Now the primary laws of physics taken one by one all declare that they are entirely indifferent as to which way you consider time to be progressing, just as they are indifferent as to whether you view the world from the right or the left. This is true of the classical laws, the relativity laws, and even the quantum laws. It is not an accidental property; the reversibility is inherent in the whole conceptual scheme in which these laws find a place. Thus the question whether the world does or does not "make sense" is outside the range of these laws. We have to appeal to the one outstanding law—the second law of thermodynamics—to put some sense into the world. It opens up a new province of knowledge, namely, the study of organization, and it is in connection with organization that a direction of time flow and a distinction between doing and undoing appears for the first time.

Time's Arrow

. . . Let us draw an arrow arbitrarily. If as we follow the arrow we find more and more of the random element in the state of the world, then the arrow is pointing toward the future; if the random element decreases, the arrow points toward the past. That is the only distinction known to physics. This follows at once if our fundamental contention is admitted that the introduction of randomness is the only thing which cannot be undone.

I shall use the phrase *time's arrow* to express this one-way property of time which has no analogue in space. It is a singularly interesting property from a philosophical standpoint. We must note that

1. It is vividly recognized by consciousness.

2. It is equally insisted on by our reasoning faculty, which tells us that a reversal of the arrow would render the external world nonsensical.

3. It makes no appearance in physical science except in the study of organization of a number of individuals. Here the arrow indicates the direction of progressive increase of the random element.

Let us now consider in detail how a random element brings the irrevocable into the world. When a stone falls, it acquires kinetic energy, and the amount of the energy is just that which would be required to lift the stone back to its original height. By suitable arrangements the kinetic energy can be made to perform this task; for example, if the stone is tied to a string, it can alternately fall and reascend like a pendulum. But if the stone hits an obstacle, its kinetic energy is converted into heat energy. There is still the same quantity of energy, but even if we could scrape it together and put it through an engine, we could not lift the stone back with it. What has happened to make the energy no longer serviceable?

Looking microscopically at the falling stone, we see an enormous multitude of molecules moving downward with equal and parallel velocities—an organized motion like the march of a regiment. We have to notice two things, the *energy* and the *organization of the energy*. To return to its original height the stone must preserve both of them.

When the stone falls on a sufficiently elastic surface, the motion may be reversed without destroying the organization. Each molecule is turned backward and the whole array retires in good order to the starting point—

> The famous Duke of York
>> With twenty thousand men,
> He marched them up to the top of the hill
>> And marched them down again.

History is not made that way. But what usually happens at the impact is that the molecules suffer more or less random collisions and rebound in all directions. They no longer conspire to make progress in any one direction; they have lost their organization. Afterward they continue to collide with one another and keep changing their directions of motion, but they never again find a common purpose. Organization cannot be brought about by continued shuffling. And so, although the energy remains quantitatively sufficient (apart from unavoidable leakage which we suppose made good), it cannot lift the stone back. To restore the stone we must supply extraneous energy which has the required amount of organization.

Here a point arises which unfortunately has no analogy in the shuffling of a pack of cards. No one (except a conjurer) can throw two half-shuffled packs into a hat and draw out one pack in its original order and one pack fully shuffled. But we can and do put partly disorganized energy into a steam engine and draw it out again partly as fully organized energy of motion of massive bodies and partly as heat energy in a state of still worse disorganization. Organization of energy is negotiable, and so is the disorganization or random element; disorganization does not forever remain attached to the particular store of energy which first suffered it but may be passed on elsewhere. We cannot here enter into the question why there should be a difference between the shuffling of energy and the shuffling of material objects, but it is necessary to use some caution in applying the analogy on account of this difference. As regards heat energy, the temperature is the measure of its degree of organization; the lower the temperature, the greater the disorganization.

Coincidences

There are such things as chance coincidences; that is to say, chance can deceive us by bringing about conditions which look very unlike chance. In particular, chance might imitate organization, whereas we have taken organization to be the antithesis of chance or, as we have called it, the "random element." This threat to our conclusions is, however, not very serious. *There is safety in numbers.*

Suppose that you have a vessel divided by a partition into two halves, one compartment containing air and the other empty. You withdraw the partition. For the moment all the molecules of air are in one half of the vessel; a fraction of a second later they are spread over the whole vessel and remain so ever afterward. The molecules will not return to one half of the vessel; the spreading cannot be undone—unless other material is introduced into the problem to serve as a scapegoat for the disorganization and carry off the random element elsewhere. This occurrence can serve as a criterion to distinguish past and future time. If you observe first the molecules spread through the vessel and (as it seems to you) an instant later the molecules all in one half of it—then your consciousness is going backward, and you had better consult a doctor.

Now, each molecule is wandering round the vessel with no preference for one part rather than the other. On the average it spends half its time in one compartment and half in the other. There is a faint possibility that at one moment all the molecules might in this way happen to be visiting the one half of the vessel. You will easily calculate that if n is the number of molecules (roughly a quadrillion), the chance of this happening is $(1/2)^n$. The reason why we ignore this chance may be seen by a rather classical illustration. If I let my fingers wander idly over the keys of a typewriter it *might* happen that my screed made an intelligible sentence. If an army of monkeys were strumming on typewriters they *might* write all the books in the British Museum. The chance of their doing so is decidedly more favorable than the chance of the molecules returning to one half of the vessel.

When numbers are large, chance is the best warrant for certainty. Happily, in the study of molecules and energy and radiation in bulk, we have to deal with a vast population, and we reach a certainty which does not always reward the expectations of those who court the fickle goddess.

In one sense the chance of the molecules returning to one half of the vessel is too absurdly small to think about. Yet in science we think about it a great deal, because it gives a measure of the irrevocable mischief we did when we casually removed the partition. Even if we had good reasons for wanting the gas to fill the vessel, there was no need to waste the organization; as we have mentioned, it is negotiable and might have been passed on somewhere where it was useful.[1] When the gas was released and began to spread across the vessel, say from left to right, there was no immediate increase of the random element. In order to spread from left to right, left-to-right velocities of the molecules must have preponderated, that is to say, the motion was partly organized. Organization of position was replaced by organization of motion. A moment later the molecules struck the farther wall of the vessel, and the random element began to increase.

---

1. If the gas in expanding had been made to move a piston, the organization would have passed into the motion of the piston.

But before it was destroyed, the left-to-right organization of molecular velocities was the exact numerical equivalent of the lost organization in space. By that we mean that the chance against the left-to-right preponderance of velocity occurring by accident is the same as the chance against segregation in one half of the vessel occurring by accident.

The adverse chance here mentioned is a preposterous number which (written in the usual decimal notation) would fill all the books in the world many times over. We are not interested in it as a practical contingency, but we are interested in the fact that it is definite. It raises "organization" from a vague descriptive epithet to one of the measurable quantities of exact science. We are confronted with many kinds of organization. The uniform march of a regiment is not the only form of organized motion; the organized evolutions of a stage chorus have their natural analogue in sound waves. A common measure can now be applied to all forms of organization. Any loss of organization is equitably measured by the chance against its recovery by an accidental coincidence. The chance is absurd regarded as a contingency, but it is precise as a measure.

The practical measure of the random element which can increase in the universe but can never decrease is called *entropy*. Measuring by entropy is the same as measuring by the chance explained in the last paragraph, only the unmanageably large numbers are transformed (by a simple formula) into a more convenient scale of reckoning. Entropy continually increases. We can, by isolating parts of the world and postulating rather idealized conditions in our problems, arrest the increase, but we cannot turn it into a decrease. That would involve something much worse than a violation of an ordinary law of nature, namely, an improbable coincidence. The law that entropy always increases—the second law of thermodynamics— holds, I think, the supreme position among the laws of nature. If someone points out to you that your pet theory of the universe is in disagreement with Maxwell's equations—then so much the worse for Maxwell's equations. If it is found to be contradicted by observation—well, these experimentalists do bungle things sometimes. But if your theory is found to be against the second law of thermodynamics I can give you no hope; there is nothing for it but to collapse in deepest humiliation. This exaltation of the second law is not unreasonable. There are other laws which we have strong reason to believe in, and we feel that a hypothesis which violates them is highly improbable, but the improbability is vague and does not confront us as a paralyzing array of figures, whereas the chance against a breach of the second law (i.e., against a decrease of the random element) can be stated in figures which are overwhelming.

I wish I could convey to you the amazing power of this conception of entropy in scientific research. From the property that entropy must always increase, practical methods of measuring it have been found. The chain of deductions from this simple law have been almost illimitable, and it has been equally successful in connection with the most recondite problems of theoretical physics and the practical tasks of the engineer. Its special feature is that the conclusions are independent of the nature of the microscopic processes that are going on. It is not concerned with the nature of the individual; it is interested in him only as a component of a crowd. Therefore the method is applicable in fields of research where our ignorance has scarcely begun to lift, and we have no hesitation in applying it to problems of the quantum theory, although the mechanism of the individual quantum process in unknown and at present unimaginable.

Primary and Secondary Law

I have called the laws controlling the behavior of single individuals "primary laws," implying that the second law of thermodynamics, although a recognized law of nature, is in some sense a secondary law. This distinction can now be placed on a regular footing. Some things never happen in the physical world because they are *impossible*; others because they are *too improbable*. The laws which forbid the first are the primary laws; the laws which forbid the second are the secondary laws. It has been the conviction of nearly all physicists[2] that at the root of everything there is a complete scheme of primary law governing the career of every particle or constituent of the world with an iron determinism. This primary scheme is all-sufficing, for since it fixes the history of every constituent of the world, it fixes the whole world history.

But for all completeness primary law does not answer every question about nature which we might reasonably wish to put. Can a universe evolve backward, i.e., develop in the opposite way to our own system?

---

2. There are, however, others besides myself who have recently begun to question it.

Primary law, being indifferent to a time direction, replies, "Yes, it is not impossible." Secondary law replies, "No, it is too improbable." The answers are not really in conflict; but the first, though true, rather misses the point. This is typical of some much more commonplace queries. If I put *this* saucepan of water on *this* fire, will the water boil? Primary law can answer definitely if it is given the chance, but it must be understood that "this" translated into mathematics means a specification of the positions, motions, etc., of some quadrillions of particles and elements of energy. So in practice the question answered is not quite the one that is asked: if I put *a* saucepan resembling this one in a few major respects on *a* fire, will the water boil? Primary law replies, "It may boil; it may freeze; it may do pretty well anything. The details given are insufficient to exclude any result as impossible." Secondary law replies plainly, "It will boil because it is too improbable that is should do anything else." Secondary law is not in conflict with primary law, nor can we regard it as essential to complete a scheme of law already complete in itself. It results from a different (and rather more practical) conception of the aim of our traffic with secrets of nature.

The question whether the second law of thermodynamics and other statistical laws are mathematical deductions from the primary laws, presenting their results in a conveniently usable form, is difficult to answer, but I think it is generally considered that there is an unbridgeable hiatus. At the bottom of all the questions settled by secondary law there is an elusive conception of "a priori probability of states of the world" which involves an essentially different attitude to knowledge from that presupposed in the construction of the scheme of primary law.

Thermodynamic Equilibrium

Progress of time introduces more and more of the random element into the constitution of the world. There is less of chance about the physical universe today than there will be tomorrow. It is curious that in this very matter-of-fact branch of physics, developed primarily because of its importance for engineers, we can scarcely avoid expressing ourselves in teleological language. We admit that the world contains both chance and design, or, at any rate, chance and the antithesis of chance. This antithesis is emphasized by our method of measurement of entropy; we assign to the organization or nonchance element a measure which is, so to speak, proportional to the strength of our disbelief in a chance origin for it. "A fortuitous concourse of atoms"—that bugbear of the theologian—has a very harmless place in orthodox physics. The physicist is acquainted with it *as a much-prized rarity*. Its properties are very distinctive, and unlike those of the physical world in general. The scientific name for a fortuitous concourse of atoms is *thermodynamic equilibrium*.

Thermodynamic equilibrium is the other case which we promised to consider in which no increase in the random element can occur, namely, that in which the shuffling is already as thorough as possible. We must isolate a region of the universe, arranging that no energy can enter or leave it, or at least that any boundary effects are precisely compensated. The conditions are ideal, but they can be reproduced with sufficient approximation to make the ideal problem relevant to practical experiment. A region in the deep interior of a star is an almost perfect example of thermodynamic equilibrium. Under these isolated conditions the energy will be shuffled as it is bandied from matter to ether and back again, and very soon the shuffling will be complete.

The possibility of the shuffling becoming complete is significant. If after shuffling the pack you tear each card in two, a further shuffling of the half cards becomes possible. Tear the cards again and again; each time there is further scope for the random element to increase. With infinite divisibility there can be no end to the shuffling. The experimental fact that a definite state of equilibrium is rapidly reached indicates that energy is not infinitely divisible, or at least that it is not infinitely divided in the natural processes of shuffling. Historically this is the result from which the quantum theory first arose. . . .

In such a region we lose time's arrow. You remember that the arrow points in the direction of increase of the random element. When the random element has reached its limit and become steady the arrow does not know which way to point. It would not be true to say that such a region is timeless; the atoms vibrate as usual like little clocks; by them we can measure speeds and durations. Time is still there and retains its ordinary properties, but it has lost its arrow; like space it extends, but it does not "go on." . . .

~ ~ ~

I am not sure that I am logical but I cannot feel the difficulty of an infinite future time very seriously. The difficulty about A.D. ∞ will not happen until we reach A.D. ∞, and presumably in order to reach A.D. ∞ the difficulty must first have been surmounted. It should also be noted that according to the second law of thermodynamics the whole universe will reach thermodynamic equilibrium at a not infinitely remote date in the future. Time's arrow will then be lost altogether, and the whole conception of progress toward a future fades away.

But the difficulty of an infinite past is appalling. It is inconceivable that we are the heirs of an infinite time of preparation; it is not less inconceivable that there was once a moment with no moment preceding it.

This dilemma of the beginning of time would worry us more were it not shut out by another overwhelming difficulty lying between us and the infinite past. We have been studying the running-down of the universe; if our views are right, somewhere between the beginning of time and the present day we must place the winding up of the universe.

Traveling backward into the past we find a world with more and more organization. If there is no barrier to stop us earlier, we must reach a moment when the energy of the world was wholly organized with none of the random element in it. It is impossible to go back any further under the present system of natural law. I do not think the phrase "wholly organized" begs the question. The organization we are concerned with is exactly definable, and there is a limit at which it becomes perfect. There is not an infinite series of states of higher and still higher organization; nor, I think, is the limit one which is ultimately approached more and more slowly. Complete organization does not tend to be more immune from loss than incomplete organization.

There is no doubt that the scheme of physics as it has stood for the last three-quarters of a century postulates a date at which either the entities of the universe were created in a state of high organization, or preexisting entities were endowed with that organization which they have been squandering ever since. Moreover, this organization is admittedly the antithesis of chance. It is something which could not occur fortuitously. . . .

Turning again to the other end of time, there is one school of thought which finds very repugnant the idea of a wearing out of the world. This school is attracted by various theories of rejuvenescence. Its mascot is the phoenix. Stars grow cold and die out. May not two dead stars collide, and be turned by the energy of the shock into fiery vapor from which a new sun—with planets and with life—is born? This theory, very prevalent in the last century, is no longer contemplated seriously by astronomers. There is evidence that the present stars at any rate are products of one evolutionary process which swept across primordial matter and caused it to aggregate; they were not formed individually by haphazard collisions having no particular time connection with one another. But the phoenix complex is still active. Matter, we believe, is gradually destroyed and its energy set free in radiation. Is there no counterprocess by which radiation collects in space, evolves into electrons and protons, and begins star building all over again? This is pure speculation, and there is not much to be said on one side or the other as to its truth. But I would mildly criticize the mental outlook which *wishes* it to be true. However much we eliminate the minor extravagances of nature, we do not by these theories stop the inexorable running-down of the world by loss of organization and increase of the random element. Whoever wishes for a universe which can continue indefinitely in activity must lead a crusade against the second law of thermodynamics; the possibility of re-formation of matter from radiation is not crucial, and we can await conclusions with some indifference.

At present we can see no way in which an attack on the second law of thermodynamics could possibly succeed, and I confess that personally I have no great desire that it should succeed in averting the final running-down of the universe. I am no phoenix worshipper. This is a topic on which science is silent, and all that one can say is prejudice. But since prejudice in favor of a never-ending cycle of rebirth of matter and worlds is often vocal, I may perhaps give voice to the opposite prejudice. I would feel more content that the universe should accomplish some great scheme of evolution and, having achieved whatever may be achieved, lapse back into chaotic changelessness, than that its purpose should be banalized by continual repetition. I am an Evolutionist, not a Multiplicationist. It seems rather stupid to keep doing the same thing over and over again.

Content Questions

1. What does it mean to say that shuffling something, such as a pack of cards, introduces a "random element"? According to Eddington, what determines whether something that has been shuffled has more or less chance of coming back to its original order? (157–158)

2. Why does Eddington examine natural operations in which the random element cannot increase? (158–159)

3. What is the "common property possessed by laws governing the individual"? What aspect of ordinary experience is unrecognized by these laws? (159)

4. What does the second law of thermodynamics introduce into physics, in order to address the question of whether the world makes sense? (160)

5. How does time's arrow indicate whether we are looking to the future or to the past? (160–161)

6. In Eddington's example of the falling stone, why does some of the energy become "no longer serviceable," even though the total quantity of energy remains the same? Why is extraneous energy necessary to restore the stone to its original position? (161)

7. According to Eddington, how does the operation of the steam engine demonstrate that "organization of energy is negotiable"? (162)

8. In explaining why the random element is not a serious threat to certainty in the study of molecules, energy, and radiation, why does Eddington say, "*There is safety in numbers*"? In Eddington's example of the divided vessel, what is it that reduces the chance that all the air molecules will ever again be in one compartment after the partition is removed? (162–163)

9. How does Eddington define entropy? What is the relation of entropy to the second law of thermodynamics? (164)

10. How do primary and secondary laws differ in their answers to questions about how the physical world operates? (165–166)

11. When Eddington asks whether a saucepan of water will boil, why does primary law answer that "the details given are insufficient to exclude any result as impossible"? What enables secondary law to give a more definite answer? (166)

12. What is thermodynamic equilibrium? What happens to the random element when thermodynamic equilibrium is reached? (166–167)

13. Why is time's arrow lost in a region of thermodynamic equilibrium? (167)

14. What does Eddington mean by "the running-down of the universe"? (168)

15. Why does Eddington think it is unlikely that matter is re-formed from radiation, even without scientific evidence to support or deny it? (168–169)

Discussion Questions

1. What does Eddington mean when he says that he has slurred over two points concerning shuffling "which affect the illustration rather than the application"? In science, how can an analogy to something familiar, such as shuffling, "be useful even when imperfect"? (157)

2. If the primary laws of physics do not recognize the obvious distinction between past and future, how can they be useful in helping us to understand the world? What does Eddington mean when he says, "The question whether the world does or does not 'make sense' is outside the range of these laws"? (160)

3. Why does Eddington say that the increase or decrease of the random element indicated by time's arrow is "the only distinction known to physics"? (160)

4. In Eddington's example of the falling stone, why is it important to notice that kinetic energy is converted into heat energy? Why can't continued shuffling restore the organization of the stone's energy? (161–162)

5. How is it possible for chance to bring about "conditions which look very unlike chance"? (162)

6. Why does Eddington say that we are not interested in adverse chance as a "preposterous number . . . but we are interested in the fact that it is definite"? (164)

7. How is entropy a "common measure" that can be applied to "all forms of organization"? (164)

8. How is the increase of entropy related to the number of random events in a physical system? What reasoning would lead to the principle that in the universe entropy continually increases, but never decreases? (164)

9. What does Eddington mean when he says that an improbable coincidence is "much worse than a violation of an ordinary law of nature"? (164)

10. What leads Eddington to assert that the second law of thermodynamics holds "the supreme position among the laws of nature"? (164)

11. What does Eddington mean when he says that primary law is complete and "all-sufficing"? If this is the case, why can't primary law "answer every question about nature which we might reasonably wish to put"? (165–166)

12. How can physics include both primary and secondary law if Eddington is correct in saying that each reflects a different conception of our aims in investigating nature? (166)

13. How are the properties of thermodynamic equilibrium "unlike those of the physical world in general"? Why would scientists value thermodynamic equilibrium as a *"much-prized rarity"* in their experimental investigations? (167)

14. Why is Eddington so confident that an attack on the second law of thermodynamics could not succeed? (169) When should scientists accept a principle as so well established that it is futile to question it further?

15. When Eddington says that he would prefer the universe to evolve and "lapse back into chaotic changelessness" rather than repeat itself, why does he call his statement a prejudice about "a topic on which science is silent"? (169) Are the prejudices that scientists hold about the nature and purpose of the physical world impediments to scientific progress?

Suggestions for Further Reading

By the author

Eddington, Arthur S. *The Nature of the Physical World.* Ann Arbor: University of Michigan Press, 1958. In this series of lectures, from which the selection in *What's the Matter?* is taken, Eddington, one of the leading scientists of the early twentieth century, discusses how relativity, quantum theory, and statistical mechanics have forced us to reexamine the philosophical assumptions of classical physics and our place in the universe.

About the topic

Atkins, P. W. *The 2nd Law: Energy, Chaos, and Form.* New York: W. H. Freeman and Company, 1994. The subject of this richly illustrated and beautifully written book is the universality of the second law of thermodynamics and how it provides the principle by which we understand all processes of physical change in the world.

Coveney, Peter, and Roger Highfield. *The Arrow of Time.* London: W. H. Allen, 1990; New York: Fawcett Columbine, 1991. This wide-ranging book focuses on the second law of thermodynamics and explores the mysterious contradiction between the apparent irreversibility of time and the fact that the fundamental laws of science do not distinguish between past and future.

Lightman, Alan. *Great Ideas in Physics: The Conservation of Energy, the Second Law of Thermodynamics, the Theory of Relativity, and Quantum Mechanics.* 3rd ed. New York: McGraw-Hill, 2000. The chapter on the second law of thermodynamics includes an interesting discussion of how scientists at first resisted its implications and how thinkers in the humanities have tried to come to terms with it.

Prigogine, Ilya, and Isabelle Stengers. *Order Out of Chaos: Man's New Dialogue with Nature.* New York: Bantam Books, 1984. Written by Nobel laureate Prigogine, who was central to the development of chaos theory, this book is both a discussion of how order can arise in a world subject to entropy as well as a history of what the author calls "the precarious cultural position of science."

Von Baeyer, Hans Christian. *Warmth Disperses and Time Passes: The History of Heat.* New York: Modern Library, 1999. This lively history of the science of thermodynamics includes the story of Maxwell's attempt to expose flaws in the second law of thermodynamics through his thought experiment known as "Maxwell's demon."

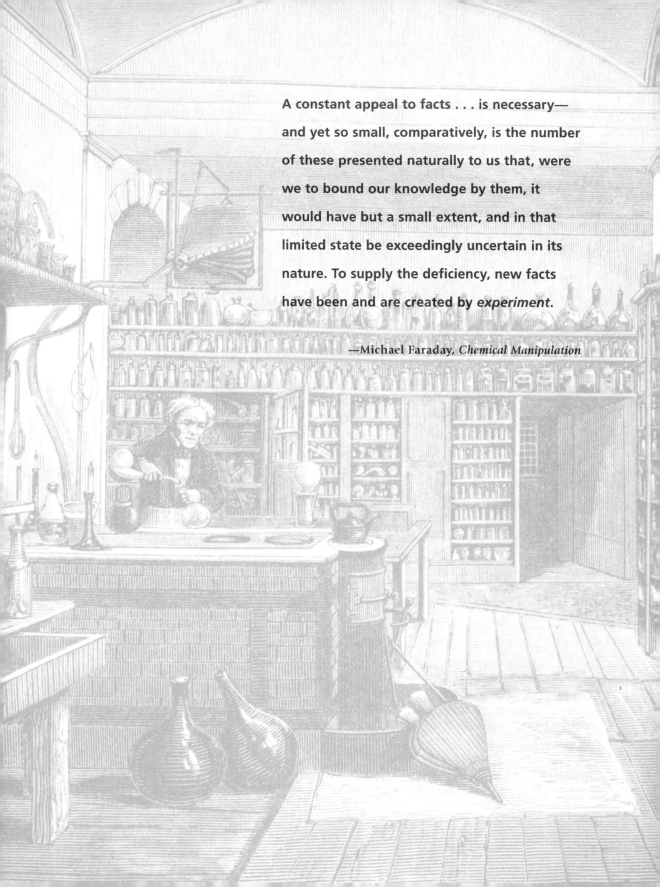

A constant appeal to facts . . . is necessary—
and yet so small, comparatively, is the number
of these presented naturally to us that, were
we to bound our knowledge by them, it
would have but a small extent, and in that
limited state be exceedingly uncertain in its
nature. To supply the deficiency, new facts
have been and are created by *experiment*.

—Michael Faraday, *Chemical Manipulation*

MICHAEL FARADAY

Induction of Electric Currents

⌣

On the Physical Lines of Magnetic Force

In the mid-nineteenth century, scientists' investigations of electrical, magnetic, and optical phenomena were brought together in the electromagnetic field theory. This theory, one of science's most important explanations of the natural world's underlying unity, is the prototype for the field theories of twentieth-century physics, including relativity, quantum mechanics, and the Standard Model of particle physics. The theory's basic concepts—fields and lines of force—were developed by Michael Faraday (1791–1867) and later extended and put into mathematical form by James Clerk Maxwell.

Faraday was born into a poor family in London and apprenticed to a bookbinder at the age of fourteen. He had little formal education, acquiring much of his knowledge, particularly of science, by reading books brought into the shop. One remarkable lack in Faraday's learning, considering his scientific accomplishments, was mathematics, of which he understood only the most basic principles. Faraday attended public lectures by the famous scientist Sir Humphrey Davy, taking meticulous notes that he later showed to Davy. As a result, Davy hired him as a laboratory assistant at the Royal Institution, where Faraday remained for his entire career as a researcher and lecturer, as well as superintendent of the laboratory.

When Faraday began his investigations of electricity and magnetism, scientists understood how such phenomena behave, but were uncertain about their nature and the connections between them. It was well known that magnets attract and repel through space. Knowledge of electrical phenomena was largely confined to bodies charged with static electricity, their ability to attract and repel suggesting a relationship between electricity and magnetism. Scientists speculated that electricity and magnetism were fluid substances that infiltrated a body, giving it positive and negative charges and polarities. Current electricity, available today through electrical devices, was almost unknown outside the scientific laboratory. Only after Alessandro Volta invented the electrical battery, in 1800, was a source of sustainable electric current available, making possible many of Faraday's experiments.

Before Faraday, the scientists who had been most successful in explaining electricity and magnetism, such as Charles Augustin de Coulomb and André Marie Ampère, used analytical mathematics to formulate laws of electrical and magnetic force, based on the Newtonian idea that forces act at a distance along straight lines. Their approach to physics emphasized finding mathematical rules for how phenomena behave, rather than observing the nature of physical reality that the mathematical rules represent. In 1820, Hans Christian Oersted discovered that a magnetic compass needle is deflected by a force that acts circularly around a wire carrying an electric current, a phenomenon that was difficult for scientists to explain in Newtonian terms. Many scientists, including Faraday, were stimulated by Oersted's discovery to further investigate the relation of electricity to magnetism.

Following his early research in chemistry—to which he made important contributions—Faraday turned his attention to electricity, building on Oersted's experiments. He demonstrated that the magnetic field around a wire carrying a current causes rotational motion in a magnet, suggesting a connection between magnetic, electrical, and mechanical force. In 1831, Faraday demonstrated the symmetrical effect: the induction of an electric current in a coil of wire by a magnet moving through, but not touching, the coil. Because the current was induced when the magnet moved, Faraday reasoned that it resulted from changes in the region surrounding the coil and magnet. He hypothesized that what was changing in this region, or *field*, was the flux through the coil of lines of influence created by the magnet. Faraday's concept of fields introduced new ways of understanding electricity and magnetism, and his emphasis on the action of forces in the field, often along curved lines, differed profoundly from scientists who followed the approach of Newtonian physics. These scientists considered the electrical and magnetic bodies as the sole centers of forces that in some unknown way act instantaneously across the empty spaces between them, while Faraday proposed that the forces reside in the field and are transmitted by it in finite, measurable time intervals. Furthermore, Faraday held that electricity and magnetism were not fluid substances, but manifestations of changing conditions in the field.

Faraday's outstanding experimental and theoretical work was motivated by his conviction that there is a discoverable unity underlying all natural forces; he found credible evidence that current electricity, static electricity, and magnetism are manifestations of a single force, electromagnetism. One of his most significant experiments demonstrated that magnetism rotates light, suggesting a further unity of electromagnetic and optical phenomena, an idea fully developed by Maxwell in the concept of electromagnetic waves.

Faraday was deeply religious and belonged to a Christian sect that advocated a very simple way of life. He declined to benefit financially from the practical applications of his many discoveries, which included the principles of the electric motor and the electric generator. Throughout his career, Faraday delivered renowned public lectures at the Royal Institution, most notably the series published as *A Course of Six Lectures on the Chemical History of a Candle* (1861). Rather than write a single summary of his scientific discoveries in electricity and magnetism, he collected and arranged the reports of his investigations into *Experimental Researches in Electricity* (1839–1855), from which the following selections are taken.

Induction of Electric Currents

The following selection is the beginning of Faraday's Experimental Researches in Electricity. *Faraday starts with a series of experiments wherein he investigates the conditions under which an electric current in a conductor induces a current in another conductor without touching it. By describing the successive ways he arranges and modifies his laboratory equipment in response to his interpretation of the results, Faraday demonstrates how a scientist puts questions to nature and builds on nature's replies, forming further questions for experimental investigation. Faraday's discoveries concerning induction were the first step leading to his hypothesis of electrical and magnetic fields.*

(The system of numbered paragraphs in this selection is Faraday's own and extends throughout his entire book, tying together the reports of his research over a period of twenty years into a carefully cross-referenced and continuous whole.)

1. The power which electricity of tension[1] possesses of causing an opposite electrical state in its vicinity has been expressed by the general term *induction*, which, as it has been received into scientific language, may also, with propriety, be used in the same general sense to express the power which electrical currents may possess of inducing any particular state upon matter in their immediate neighborhood, otherwise indifferent. It is with this meaning that I purpose using it in the present paper.

2. Certain effects of the induction of electrical currents have already been recognized and described: as those of magnetization; Ampère's experiments of bringing a copper disc near to a flat spiral; his repetition with electromagnets of Arago's extraordinary experiments; and perhaps a few

---

1. [*electricity of tension:* static electricity.]

This selection is taken from series 1 of Experimental Researches in Electricity.

others.[2] Still it appeared unlikely that these could be all the effects which induction by currents could produce, especially as, upon dispensing with iron, almost the whole of them disappear, while yet an infinity of bodies, exhibiting definite phenomena of induction with electricity of tension, still remain to be acted upon by the induction of electricity in motion.

3. Further: Whether Ampère's beautiful theory[3] were adopted, or any other, or whatever reservation were mentally made, still it appeared very extraordinary, that as every electric current was accompanied by a corresponding intensity of magnetic action at right angles to the current, good conductors of electricity, when placed within the sphere of this action, should not have any current induced through them, or some sensible effect produced equivalent in force to such a current.

4. These considerations, with their consequence, the hope of obtaining electricity from ordinary magnetism, have stimulated me at various times to investigate experimentally the inductive effect of electric currents. I lately arrived at positive results; and not only had my hopes fulfilled, but obtained a key which appeared to me to open out a full explanation of Arago's magnetic phenomena, and also to discover a new state, which may probably have great influence in some of the most important effects of electric currents.

5. These results I purpose describing, not as they were obtained, but in such a manner as to give the most concise view of the whole.

↬   ↬   ↬

6. About 26 feet of copper wire one-twentieth of an inch in diameter were wound round a cylinder of wood as a helix, the different spires of which were prevented from touching by a thin interposed twine. This helix was covered with calico and then a second wire applied in the same manner. In this way twelve helixes were superposed, each containing an average length of wire of 27 feet, and all in the same direction. The first, third,

2. [*Ampère's and Arago's experiments:* demonstrations by the French physicists André Marie Ampère (1775–1836) and François Jean Arago (1786–1853) showing that when a suspended magnet and a metal disc are placed close together but not touching, and one is moved relative to the other, the stationary one also moves.]
3. [*Ampère's beautiful theory:* the hypothesis that the particles of matter making up a magnet contain microscopic electric currents.]

fifth, seventh, ninth, and eleventh of these helixes were connected at their extremities end to end so as to form one helix; the others were connected in a similar manner, and thus two principal helixes were produced, closely interposed, having the same direction, not touching anywhere, and each containing 155 feet in length of wire.

7. One of these helixes was connected with a galvanometer[4], the other with a voltaic battery[5] of ten pairs of plates four inches square, with double coppers and well charged, yet not the slightest sensible deflection of the galvanometer needle could be observed.

8. A similar compound helix, consisting of six lengths of copper and six of soft iron wire, was constructed. The resulting iron helix contained 214 feet of wire, the resulting copper helix 208 feet, but whether the current from the trough was passed through the copper or the iron helix, no effect upon the other could be perceived at the galvanometer.

9. In these and many similar experiments no difference in action of any kind appeared between iron and other metals.

10. Two hundred and three feet of copper wire in one length were coiled round a large block of wood; another 203 feet of similar wire were interposed as a spiral between the turns of the first coil, and metallic contact everywhere prevented by twine. One of these helixes was connected with a galvanometer, and the other with a battery of 100 pairs of plates four inches square, with double coppers and well charged. When the contact was made, there was a sudden and very slight effect at the galvanometer, and there was also a similar slight effect when the contact with the battery was broken. But while the voltaic current was continuing to pass through the one helix, no galvanometrical appearances or any effect like induction upon the other helix could be perceived, although the active power of the battery was proved to be great, by its heating the whole of its own helix, and by the brilliancy of the discharge when made through charcoal.

---

4. [*galvanometer:* an instrument for measuring an electric current by means of the influence of the magnetism produced by a current on a sensitive magnetic indicator needle; similar to a modern ammeter.]

5. [*voltaic battery:* an apparatus capable of producing a continuous electric current, consisting of a series of parallel pairs of metal plates—usually one plate of copper and one of zinc—in a trough filled with a weak acid solution.]

11. Repetition of the experiments with a battery of 120 pairs of plates produced no other effects, but it was ascertained, both at this and the former time, that the slight deflection of the needle occurring at the moment of completing the connection was always in one direction, and that the equally slight deflection produced when the contact was broken was in the other direction, and also that these effects occurred when the first helixes were used. (6, 8)

12. The results which I had by this time obtained with magnets led me to believe that the battery current through one wire did, in reality, induce a similar current through the other wire, but that it continued for an instant only, and partook more of the nature of the electrical wave passed through from the shock of a common Leyden jar[6] than the current from a voltaic battery, and therefore might magnetize a steel needle, although it scarcely affected the galvanometer.

13. This expectation was confirmed: for on substituting a small hollow helix, formed round a glass tube, for the galvanometer; introducing a steel needle; making contact as before between the battery and the inducing wire (7, 10); and then removing the needle before the battery contact was broken, it was found magnetized.

14. When the battery contact was first made, then an unmagnetized needle introduced into the small indicating helix (13), and lastly the battery contact broken, the needle was found magnetized to an equal degree apparently as before, but the poles were of the contrary kind.

15. The same effects took place on using the large compound helixes first described. (6, 8)

16. When the unmagnetized needle was put into the indicating helix, before contact of the inducing wire with the battery, and remained there until the contact was broken, it exhibited little or no magnetism, the first effect having been nearly neutralized by the second (13, 14). The force of the induced current upon making contact was found always to exceed that of the induced current at breaking of contact, and if therefore the contact was made and broken many times in succession, while the needle remained in the indicating helix, it at last came out not unmagnetized, but a needle magnetized as if the induced current upon making contact had

6. [*Leyden jar:* a device for collecting, storing, and discharging static electric charge; similar to a modern capacitor.]

acted alone on it. This effect may be due to the accumulation (as it is called) at the poles of the unconnected pile, rendering the current upon first making contact more powerful than what it is afterward, at the moment of breaking contact.

17. If the circuit between the helix or wire under induction and the galvanometer or indicating spiral was not rendered complete *before* the connection between the battery and the inducing wire was completed or broken, then no effects were perceived at the galvanometer. Thus, if the battery communications were first made, and then the wire under induction connected with the indicating helix, no magnetizing power was there exhibited. But still retaining the latter communications, when those with the battery were broken, a magnet was formed in the helix, but of the second kind (14), i.e., with poles indicating a current in the same direction to that belonging to the battery current, or to that always induced by that current at its cessation.

18. In the preceding experiments the wires were placed near to each other, and the contact of the inducing one with the battery made when the inductive effect was required, but as the particular action might be supposed to be exerted only at the moments of making and breaking contact, the induction was produced in another way. Several feet of copper wire were stretched in wide zigzag forms, representing the letter *W*, on one surface of a broad board; a second wire was stretched in precisely similar forms on a second board, so that when brought near the first, the wires should everywhere touch, except that a sheet of thick paper was interposed. One of these wires was connected with the galvanometer, and the other with a voltaic battery. The first wire was then moved toward the second, and as it approached, the needle was deflected. Being then removed, the needle was deflected in the opposite direction. By first making the wires approach and then recede, simultaneously with the vibrations of the needle, the latter soon became very extensive, but when the wires ceased to move from or toward each other, the galvanometer needle soon came to its usual position.

19. As the wires approximated, the induced current was in the *contrary* direction to the inducing current. As the wires receded, the induced current was in the *same* direction as the inducing current. When the wires remained stationary, there was no induced current.

20. When a small voltaic arrangement was introduced into the circuit between the galvanometer (10) and its helix or wire, so as to cause a permanent deflection of 30° or 40°, and then the battery of 100 pairs of plates connected with the inducing wire, there was an instantaneous action, as before (11), but the galvanometer needle immediately resumed and retained its place unaltered, notwithstanding the continued contact of the inducing wire with the trough: such was the case in whichever way the contacts were made.

21. Hence it would appear that collateral currents, either in the same or in opposite directions, exert no permanent inducing power on each other, affecting their quantity or tension.

22. I could obtain no evidence by the tongue, by spark, or by heating fine wire or charcoal of the electricity passing through the wire under induction; neither could I obtain any chemical effects, though the contacts with metallic and other solutions were made and broken alternately with those of the battery so that the second effect of induction should not oppose or neutralize the first (13, 16).

23. This deficiency of effect is not because the induced current of electricity cannot pass fluids, but probably because of its brief duration and feeble intensity, for on introducing two large copper plates into the circuit on the induced side (20), the plates being immersed in brine but prevented from touching each other by an interposed cloth, the effect at the indicating galvanometer or helix occurred as before. The induced electricity could also pass through a voltaic trough (20). When, however, the quantity of interposed fluid was reduced to a drop, the galvanometer gave no indication.

24. Attempts to obtain similar effects by the use of wires conveying ordinary electricity[7] were doubtful in the results. A compound helix similar to that already described, containing eight elementary helixes (6), was used. Four of the helixes had their similar ends bound together by wire, and the two general terminations thus produced connected with the small magnetizing helix containing an unmagnetized needle (13). The other four helixes were similarly arranged, but their ends connected with a Leyden jar. On passing the discharge, the needle was found to be a magnet, but it appeared probable that a part of the electricity of the jar

7. [*ordinary electricity:* static electricity.]

had passed off to the small helix, and so magnetized the needle. There was indeed no reason to expect that the electricity of a jar possessing as it does great tension would not diffuse itself through all the metallic matter interposed between the coatings.

25. Still it does not follow that the discharge of ordinary electricity through a wire does not produce analogous phenomena to those arising from voltaic electricity, but as it appears impossible to separate the effects produced at the moment when the discharge begins to pass, from the equal and contrary effects produced when it ceases to pass (16), inasmuch as with ordinary electricity these periods are simultaneous, so there can be scarcely any hope that in this form of the experiment they can be perceived.

26. Hence it is evident that currents of voltaic electricity present phenomena of induction somewhat analogous to those produced by electricity of tension, although, as will be seen hereafter, many differences exist between them. The result is the production of other currents (but which are only momentary), parallel, or tending to parallelism, with the inducing current. By reference to the poles of the needle formed in the indicating helix (13, 14) and to the deflections of the galvanometer needle (11), it was found in all cases that the induced current, produced by the first action of the inducing current, was in the contrary direction to the latter, but that the current produced by the cessation of the inducing current was in the same direction (19). For the purpose of avoiding periphrasis, I propose to call this action of the current from the voltaic battery *volta-electric induction.* The properties of the second wire, after induction has developed the first current, and while the electricity from the battery continues to flow through its inducing neighbor (10, 18), constitute a peculiar electric condition, the consideration of which will be resumed hereafter. All these results have been obtained with a voltaic apparatus consisting of a single pair of plates.

Content Questions

1. Why does Faraday use the general term *induction* for both the power of electricity of tension (static electricity) and the power of electrical currents? (179–180)

2. What are the "considerations" that led Faraday to investigate the inductive effect of electrical currents? (180)

3. In his experiments with helixes, why does Faraday make sure that the wires are prevented from touching each other by using twine and calico cloth to separate them? (180–181)

4. Why does Faraday interpret the deflection of the galvanometer needle as an indication that electrical induction is occurring? (181)

5. In the course of carrying out his experiments, what reason does Faraday discover for whether the galvanometer needle is deflected? (182)

6. What is Faraday's reasoning in substituting the "small hollow helix" and the steel needle for the galvanometer as a way of detecting electrical induction? (182)

7. How is the magnetization of the needle related to the sequence in which Faraday makes and breaks the connection of the helix to the battery? (182)

8. Why does Faraday conduct the experiment in which a wire carrying a current is moved back and forth in relation to another wire connected to a galvanometer? (183)

9. How does the experiment with moving wires give stronger evidence than Faraday's earlier experiments with helixes that an electrical current is being induced? (183)

10. What evidence does Faraday have that the "brief duration and feeble intensity" of the induced electricity makes it impossible for him to detect its chemical effects? (184)

11. After his inconclusive attempt to demonstrate that "ordinary electricity" (static electricity) can produce effects analogous to those "arising from voltaic electricity," why does Faraday say that there is "scarcely any hope" that such effects can be perceived in the experiment he conducted? (184–185)

12. What relation does Faraday imply between the effect on the wire under induction by the "first action of the inducing current," and the effect produced by the approach of a wire with constant current as described in paragraph 19? (185)

Discussion Questions

1. What does Faraday mean when he says that induction occurs in the "immediate neighborhood" of the inducing electrical currents? (179) What problems might arise for a scientist trying to explain how electricity is transmitted by induction, rather than by conduction?

2. Why does Faraday think that it would be "very extraordinary" if a current were not induced in an electric conductor placed within a magnet's sphere of action? (180) Why would a scientist hold the conviction that the physical world can be explained in terms of symmetrical relationships?

3. Why does Faraday describe the results of his experiments "not as they were obtained, but in such a manner as to give the most concise view of the whole"? (180) Why does Faraday provide a narrative of all his results, rather than just stating the positive ones?

4. Why does Faraday conduct variations of his experiment using different kinds and lengths of wire, different batteries, and different connections of the wires to the batteries and galvanometer? (180–181)

5. In his experiments, why is Faraday interested in the direction of the effects, whether it is the deflection of the galvanometer needle, the poles of the magnetized steel needle, or the electrical current in the moving wires? What does Faraday mean when he says that electrical currents are in the same or in a contrary direction to each other? (183)

6. When Faraday finds a reliable way to produce a persistent induced current by moving the wires in relation to each other, why doesn't he speculate on the underlying cause of what occurs? (183) In conducting experimental research, at what stage should a scientist move beyond descriptions and begin to form explanatory theories?

7. Why is Faraday interested in finding out whether there are analogies between the induction phenomena of current (voltaic) electricity and of static (ordinary) electricity? (184–185)

On the Physical Lines
of Magnetic Force

Faraday wrote this selection twenty years after the preceding one, near the end of his career as an experimental and theoretical scientist. Using his knowledge of how one can map the magnetic lines of force in the space surrounding a magnet, Faraday speculates whether these lines have a physical character like other natural objects, raising the question of what scientists mean when they say that something has a physical nature. Faraday's analogies between the way static electricity, electrical currents, and magnetism "act manifestly at a distance" show him pursuing a primary goal of science, which is to discover unity underlying different natural phenomena.

I have recently been engaged in describing and defining the lines of magnetic force, i.e., those lines which are indicated in a general manner by the disposition of iron filings or small magnetic needles, around or between magnets; and I have shown, I hope satisfactorily, how these lines may be taken as exact representations of the magnetic power, both as to disposition and amount; also how they may be recognized by a moving wire[1] in a manner altogether different in principle from the indications given by a magnetic needle, and in numer-

---

1. [*moving wire*: an instrument for detecting magnetic field lines, consisting of a loop of conducting wire attached to a galvanometer. When the loop is moved back and forth along a magnet, crossing the field lines, an electric current is induced in the wire and detected by the galvanometer.]

This selection is take from Experimental Researches in Electricity.

ous cases with great and peculiar advantages. The definition then given had no reference to the physical nature of the force at the place of action, and will apply with equal accuracy whatever that may be, and this being very thoroughly understood, I am now about to leave the strict line of reasoning for a time, and enter upon a few speculations respecting the physical character of the lines of force, and the manner in which they may be supposed to be continued through space. We are obliged to enter into such speculations with regard to numerous natural powers, and, indeed, that of gravity is the only instance where they are apparently shut out.

It is not to be supposed for a moment that speculations of this kind are useless, or necessarily hurtful, in natural philosophy. They should ever be held as doubtful, and liable to error and to change, but they are wonderful aids in the hands of the experimentalist and mathematician. For not only are they useful in rendering the vague idea more clear for the time, giving it something like a definite shape, that it may be submitted to experiment and calculation, but they lead on, by deduction and correction, to the discovery of new phenomena, and so cause an increase and advance of real physical truth, which, unlike the hypothesis that led to it, becomes fundamental knowledge not subject to change. Who is not aware of the remarkable progress in the development of the nature of light and radiation in modern times, and the extent to which that progress has been aided by the hypotheses both of emission and undulation? Such considerations form my excuse for entering now and then upon speculations, but though I value them highly when cautiously advanced, I consider it as an essential character of a sound mind to hold them in doubt, scarcely giving them the character of opinions, but esteeming them merely as probabilities and possibilities, and making a very broad distinction between them and the facts and laws of nature. . . .

~ ~ ~

Many powers act manifestly at a distance. Their physical nature is incomprehensible to us; still we may learn much that is real and positive about them, and among other things something of the condition of the space between the body acting and that acted upon, or between the two mutually acting bodies. Such powers are presented to us by the phenomena of gravity, light, electricity, magnetism, etc. These when examined will be found to present remarkable differences in relation to their respective lines of forces and, at the same time that they establish the existence of real physical lines in some cases, will facilitate the consideration of the question as applied especially to magnetism.

When two bodies, *a, b,* gravitate toward each other, the line in which they act is a straight line, for such is the line which either would follow if free to move. The attractive force is not altered, either in *direction* or *amount,* if a third body is made to act by gravitation or otherwise upon either or both of the two first. A balanced cylinder of brass gravitates to the earth with a weight exactly the same whether it is left like a pendulum freely to hang toward it or whether it is drawn aside by other attraction or by tension, whatever the amount of the latter may be. A new gravitating force may be exerted upon *a,* but that does not in the least affect the amount of power which it exerts toward *b.* We have no evidence that *time* enters in any way into the exercise of this power, whatever the distance between the acting bodies, as that from the sun to the earth or from star to star. We can hardly conceive of this force in one particle by itself; it is when two or more are present that we comprehend it, yet in gaining this idea we perceive no difference in the character of the power in the different particles; all of the same kind are *equal, mutual,* and *alike.* In the case of gravitation, no effect which sustains the idea of an independent or physical line of force is presented to us, and as far as we at present know, the line of gravitation is merely an ideal line representing the direction in which the power is exerted.

Take the sun in relation to another force which it exerts upon the earth, namely, its illuminating or warming power. In this case, rays (which are lines of force) pass across the intermediate space, but then we may affect these lines by different media applied to them in their course. We may alter their direction either by reflection or refraction; we may make them pursue curved or angular courses. We may cut them off at their origin and then search for and find them before they have attained their object. They have a relation to *time,* and occupy eight minutes in coming from the sun to the earth, so that they may exist independently either of their source or their final home and have in fact a clear, distinct physical existence. They are in extreme contrast with the lines of gravitating power in this respect, as they are also in respect of their condition at their terminations. The two bodies terminating a line of gravitating force are alike in their actions in every respect, and so the line joining them has like relations in both directions. The two bodies at the terminals of a ray are utterly unlike in action; one is a source, the other a destroyer of the line, and the line itself has the relation of a stream flowing in one direction. In these two cases of gravity and radiation, the difference between an abstract and a physical line of force is immediately manifest.

Turning to the case of static electricity we find here attractions (and other actions) at a distance as in the former cases, but when we come to compare the attraction with that of gravity, very striking distinctions are presented which immediately affect the question of a physical line of force. In the first place, when we examine the bodies bounding or terminating the lines of attraction, we find them as before, mutually and equally concerned in the action, but they are not alike: on the contrary, though each is endued with a force which speaking generally is of the like nature, still they are in such contrast that their actions on a third body in a state like either of them are precisely the reverse of each other—what the one attracts the other repels, and the force makes itself evident as one of those manifestations of power endued with a dual and antithetical condition. Now, with all such dual powers, attraction cannot occur unless the two conditions of force are present and in face of each other through the lines of force. Another essential limitation is that these two conditions must be exactly equal in amount, not merely to produce the effects of attraction, but in every other case; for it is impossible to arrange things so that there shall be present or be evolved more electric power of the one kind than of the other. Another limitation is that they must be in physical relation to each other, and that when a positive and a negative electrified surface are thus associated, we cannot cut off this relation except by transferring the forces of these surfaces to equal amounts of the contrary forces provided elsewhere. Another limitation is that the power is definite in amount. If a ball *a* be charged with 10 of positive electricity, it may be made to act with that amount of power on another ball *b* charged with 10 of negative electricity, but if 5 of its power be taken up by a third ball *c* charged with negative electricity, then it can only act with 5 of power on ball *a*, and that ball must find or evolve 5 of positive power elsewhere: this is quite unlike what occurs with gravity, a power that presents us with nothing dual in its character. Finally, the electric force acts in curved lines. If a ball be electrified positively and insulated in the air, and a round metallic plate be placed about twelve or fifteen inches off, facing it and uninsulated, the latter will be found, by the necessity mentioned above, in a negative condition, but it is not negative only on the side facing the ball, but on the other or outer face also, as may be shown by a carrier applied there, or by a strip of gold or silver leaf hung against that outer face. Now, the power affecting this face does not pass through the uninsulated plate, for the thinnest gold leaf is able to stop the inductive action, but round the edges of the face, and therefore acts in curved lines. All these points indicate the existence of physical lines of electric force—the absolutely essential relation of positive and negative surfaces to each other, and their dependence on each other contrasted with the known mobility of the forces, admit of no other conclusion. The action also in curved lines must depend upon a physical line of force. And there is a third important character of the force leading to the same result, namely, its affection by media having different specific inductive capacities.

When we pass to dynamic electricity the evidence of physical lines of force is far more patent. A voltaic battery having its extremities connected by a conducting medium has what has been expressively called a current of force running round the circuit, but this current is an axis of power having equal and contrary forces in opposite directions. It consists of lines of force which are compressed or expanded according to the transverse action of the conductor, which change in direction with the form of the conductor, which are found in every part of the conductor, and [which] can be taken out from any place by channels properly appointed for the purpose; and nobody doubts that they are physical lines of force.

Finally as regards a magnet, which is the object of the present discourse. A magnet presents a system of forces perfect in itself and able, therefore, to exist by its own mutual relations. It has the dual and antithetical character belonging to both static and dynamic electricity, and this is made manifest by what are called its polarities, i.e., by the opposite powers of like kind found at and toward its extremities. These powers are found to be absolutely equal to each other; one cannot be changed in any degree as to amount without an equal change to the other, and this is true when the opposite polarities of a magnet are not related to each other, but to the polarities of other magnets. The polarities, or the *northness* and *southness*, of a magnet are not only related to each other, through or within the magnet itself, but are also related externally to opposite polarities (in the manner of static electric induction), or they cannot exist, and this external relation involves and necessitates an exactly equal amount of the new opposite polarities to which those of the magnet are related. So that if the force of magnet a is related to that of another magnet b, it cannot act on a third magnet c without being taken off from b, to an amount proportional to its action on c. The lines of magnetic force are shown by the moving wire to exist both within and outside of the magnet; also they are shown to be closed curves passing in one part of their course through the magnet, and the amount of those within the magnet at its equator is exactly equal in force to the amount in any section including the whole of those on the outside. The lines of force outside a magnet can be affected in their direction by the use of various media placed in their course. A magnet can in no way be procured having only one magnetism, or even the smallest excess of northness or southness one over the other. When the polarities of a magnet are not related externally to the force of other magnets, then they are related to each other: i.e., the northness and southness of an isolated magnet are exterally dependent on and sustained by each other.

Now all these facts, and many more, point to the existence of physical lines of force external to the magnets as well as within. They exist in curved as well as in straight lines, for if we conceive of an isolated straight bar magnet, or more especially of a round disk of steel magnetized regularly so that its magnetic axis shall be in one diameter, it is evident that the polarities must be related to each other externally by curved lines of force, for no straight line can at the same time touch two points having northness and southness. Curved lines of force can, as I think, only consist with physical lines of force.

The phenomena exhibited by the moving wire confirm the same conclusion. As the wire moves across the lines of force, a current of electricity passes or tends to pass through it, there being no such current before the wire is moved. The wire when quiescent has no such current, and when it moves it need not pass into places where the magnetic force is greater or less. It may travel in such a course that if a magnetic needle were carried through the same course it would be entirely unaffected magnetically, i.e., it would be a matter of absolute indifference to the needle whether it were moving or still. Matters may be so arranged that the wire when still shall have the same diamagnetic force as the medium surrounding the magnet, and so in no way cause disturbance of the lines of force passing through both; and yet when the wire moves, a current of electricity shall be generated in it. The mere fact of motion cannot have produced this current: there must have been a state or condition around the magnet and sustained by it, within the range of which the wire was placed, and this state shows the physical constitution of the lines of magnetic force.

What this state is, or upon what it depends, cannot as yet be declared. It may depend upon the ether, as a ray of light does, and an association has already been shown between light and magnetism. It may depend upon a state of tension, or a state of vibration, or perhaps some other state analogous to the electric current, to which the magnetic forces are so intimately related. Whether it of necessity requires matter for its sustentation will depend upon what is understood by the term *matter*. If that is to be confined to ponderable or gravitating substances, then matter is not essential to the physical lines of magnetic force any more than to a ray of light or heat, but if in the assumption of an ether we admit it to be a species of matter, then the lines of force may depend upon some function of it. Experimentally mere space is magnetic, but then the idea of such mere space must include that of the ether, when one is talking on that belief, or if hereafter any other conception of the state or condition of space rise up, it must be admitted into the view of that, which just now in relation to experiment is called mere space. On the other hand it is, I think, an ascertained fact that ponderable matter is not essential to the existence of physical lines of magnetic force.

Content Questions

1. What is Faraday able to discover about lines of magnetic force through his "strict line of reasoning"? What does he propose that his "speculations" might add to this knowledge? (188–189)

2. How does Faraday think that speculations about "natural powers" are "wonderful aids in the hands of the experimentalist and mathematician"? (189)

3. What does Faraday mean when he says that natural powers such as gravity, light, electricity, and magnetism "act manifestly at a distance?" (189)

4. Why does Faraday conclude that "in the case of gravitation, no effect which sustains the idea of an independent or physical line of force is presented to us"? (190)

5. What evidence does Faraday give for his statement: "In these two cases of gravity and radiation, the difference between an abstract and a physical line of force is immediately manifest"? (191)

6. In the case of static electricity, how do the "dual powers" that Faraday describes affect the interactions of the bodies at the terminations of the lines of force? (191)

7. How do the effects induced by static electricity provide Faraday with evidence that its force acts in curved lines? (191–192)

8. How does the relation of an electrical current to its conductor support Faraday's assertion that the lines of force of dynamic electricity are physical? (192)

9. According to Faraday, how is the magnetic system of forces similar to and different from static electricity? (192)

10. What is Faraday's argument for why a magnet's external lines of force must be curved? How do "the phenomena exhibited by the moving wire confirm the same conclusion"? (193–194)

11. What does Faraday think is necessary to produce an electric current, other than the motion of a wire in the vicinity of a magnet? Why does he think this additional factor provides strong evidence that the lines of magnetic force are physical? (193–194)

12. What is Faraday trying to account for in speculating about the nature of "the ether" and of "mere space"? (194)

Discussion Questions

1. What does Faraday mean by the "physical character" of lines of magnetic force? How would physical lines of magnetic force differ from Faraday's earlier definition of magnetic lines of force as "exact representations of the magnetic power, both as to disposition and amount"? (188–189)

2. Why does Faraday say that we are obliged to enter into speculations about natural powers? (189)

3. Why aren't the results of experimentation and what Faraday calls a "strict line of reasoning" adequate for understanding how the physical world operates? (189)

4. How can contradictory models of the physical world, such as the ones that Faraday mentions for the nature of light, lead to progress in scientific knowledge and to "an increase and advance of real physical truth?" (189)

5. How does Faraday think that a scientific understanding of natural powers is possible if "their physical nature is incomprehensible to us"? (189)

6. When Faraday contrasts radiation's lines of force with gravity's lines of force, why does he emphasize that radiation requires time for its effects to occur? (190)

7. Why does Faraday emphasize that the power of static electric attraction is "definite in amount" in attempting to establish that its lines of force are physical? (191)

8. When Faraday asserts, "A magnet presents a system of forces perfect in itself and able, therefore, to exist by its own mutual relations," how do these characteristics strengthen the argument that magnetic lines of force are physical? (192)

9. In speaking of the apparent curvature of magnetic lines of force, why does Faraday say that curved lines of force can be consistent only with physical lines of force? (193)

10. How do Faraday's speculations on what occurs when a wire moves across lines of magnetic force help explain the results of his experiments on the induction of electrical currents? (193–194)

11. Is Faraday saying that the "state or condition around the magnet and sustained by it" is identical to or distinct from the physical lines of magnetic force? What reason might he have for assuming that the state must depend on anything at all, such as the ether, "a state of tension," or some form of matter that is not ponderable? (194)

12. Does Faraday mean for us to think of physical lines of force as natural objects, just like the bodies with which the lines of force are associated? (194)

Suggestions for Further Reading

By the author

Faraday, Michael. *The Chemical History of a Candle.* Mineola, NY: Dover Publications, 2002. In this series of popular lectures, Faraday demonstrates that during the time a candle burns, "there is not a law under which any part of this universe is governed that does not come into play and is not touched upon."

————. *The Forces of Matter.* Buffalo, NY: Prometheus Books, 1993. This series of lectures for the general public, complete with descriptions of Faraday's demonstrations, presents a unified picture of the physical forces—including gravity, chemical affinity, heat, magnetism, and electricity—that become apparent when matter interacts with matter.

Fisher, Howard J. *Faraday's Experimental Researches in Electricity: Guide to a First Reading.* Santa Fe, NM: Green Lion Press, 2001. This volume, from which the selections in *What's the Matter?* are taken, provides the best way to approach Faraday's major work. Substantial portions of Faraday's text are accompanied by introductions and notes designed to help readers understand the technical details of his experiments and also appreciate his method of conducting research, as relayed in his own words.

Fisher, Howard J. *Faraday's Experimental Researches in Electricity: The First Series.* Santa Fe, NM: Green Lion Press, 2004. This study module, drawn from the longer volume cited above, contains the selection on electrical induction included in *What's the Matter?* Fisher's introductory essay, "Thinking About Electricity," is a model of how to approach the ideas and procedures of scientists who worked in earlier times.

About the author

Cantor, Geoffrey, David Gooding, and Frank A. J. L. James. *Michael Faraday.* Amherst, NY: Humanity Books, 1996. This brief biography of Faraday not only covers the events of his life but also gives a detailed picture of the relation of his experimental work and popular lecturing to the scientific community of his time.

Thomas, John Meurig. *Michael Faraday and the Royal Institution: The Genius of Man and Place.* London: Taylor & Francis, 1991. This history explores the close relationship Faraday had with the Royal Institution, where he was an experimental scientist, administrator, and lecturer for more than forty years.

If the skill of the mathematician has enabled the experimentalist to see that the quantities which he has measured are connected by necessary relations, the discoveries of physics have revealed to the mathematician new forms of quantities which he could never have imagined for himself.

—James Clerk Maxwell,
"Address to the Mathematical and Physical
Sections of the British Association"

JAMES CLERK MAXWELL

The Science of Electromagnetism

*

Electricity and Electromotive Force

*

A Dynamical Theory of the Electromagnetic Field

Until the second half of the nineteenth century, scientists' investigations of distinct physical phenomena such as heat, magnetism, electricity, optics, and gases were generally known as natural philosophy and not identified as branches of a single science. However, discoveries of fundamental connections among different phenomena led to the development of the discipline we now call physics and to the founding of research laboratories where scientists work on problems involving all areas of physics. The accomplishments of James Clerk Maxwell (1831–1879) as an experimental and theoretical scientist were important to the emergence of physics as a well-defined science, and his discoveries provided new ways of conceiving the physical world, pointing toward the paths physics followed in the twentieth century.

Maxwell was born in Scotland and his early interest in physical science was strongly encouraged by his father. When Maxwell entered the University of Cambridge in 1850, the Royal Society, Great Britain's leading scientific organization, already had published two of his scientific papers. At Cambridge, Maxwell excelled in mathematics, which he focused on because the university considered training in theoretical reasoning, rather than laboratory work, to be the foundation of an education in natural philosophy. After receiving his degree, Maxwell became a professor of natural philosophy, and in 1871 he accepted the newly created position of professor of physics at Cambridge. He assumed the responsibility for designing and staffing the new Cavendish Laboratory, which became one of the world's great centers of physics research. In his inaugural lecture, Maxwell emphasized that physicists must help their students "bring the theoretical part of [their] training into contact with the practical." He stressed that physics students need to overcome the difficulty of recognizing abstract relations learned from books in the concrete objects before them, "wrenching the mind away from the symbols to the objects, and from the objects back to the symbols." Maxwell himself combined deep physical intuition with a powerful grasp of mathematical methods, allowing him to gain insights that blended the concrete and the abstract.

In Maxwell's time, scientists had successfully explained the properties of gases by assuming that a gas is composed of huge numbers of rapidly moving particles. To simplify descriptions of the particles' movements, scientists assumed they all have the same velocity. This made no physical sense to Maxwell, who reasoned that the particles must move at many different velocities because of their repeated collisions. By applying the mathematical tools of statistical analysis, Maxwell generated a bell-shaped frequency curve representing the range of velocities. He thus arrived at results that agreed with the laws of gas behavior, suggesting that his abstract mathematical model was analogous to a mechanical model of the actual behavior of gases. Maxwell's application of statistical methods in physics, further developed by Ludwig Boltzmann in Germany, became known as statistical mechanics, leading to advances in thermodynamics and offering evidence that matter is composed of molecules and atoms. The development of statistical mechanics was an important extension of Newtonian laws of motion to physical systems composed of elements too numerous to consider individually. In the twentieth century, as physicists investigated the realm of subatomic particles where classical mechanics does not apply, the statistical methods initiated by Maxwell became fundamental to atomic science, quantum theory, and most other areas of research.

Although Maxwell made contributions to many areas of physics, his discoveries in electromagnetism are his greatest achievement. Maxwell's investigations built on the work of Michael Faraday, who had established that magnetism and electricity are not distinct phenomena, but are fundamentally connected, since magnetic effects accompany electric currents and moving magnets induce electric currents in conductors. Because many of these effects seem to take place across empty space, Faraday had proposed that they are propagated through lines of force that form fields in the vicinity of magnetic and electrified objects. He thought of these lines of force as physically real and saw them as mechanical systems, subject to the classical laws of motion that govern all physical bodies. This idea was contrary to the thinking of many scientists, who assumed that electric and magnetic effects occur instantaneously as action at a distance, without any physical means of transmission. Maxwell, following Faraday's lead and using the mathematical tools that Faraday lacked, successfully showed how the concept of fields could provide a model for electromagnetic phenomena. Using this model, Maxwell derived a set of general field equations that describes all known electromagnetic interactions—one of the greatest achievements in physics. Furthermore, Maxwell demonstrated theoretically that electromagnetic radiation is propagated as waves traveling at a constant velocity exactly the same as that of light, showing that light is an electromagnetic wave and unifying the study of optics and electromagnetism. Heinrich Hertz later conducted experiments that demonstrated the existence of a wide spectrum of electromagnetic waves, including radio waves, leading to immense technological advances.

Maxwell's electromagnetic field theory marks a fundamental shift in how physics represents the physical world. Classical physics emphasized separate objects and their motions, and held that forces that come into play when objects interact are centered in the objects themselves. Field theory introduced a picture of the world emphasizing the continuous range of physical quantities, including forces, in the spaces surrounding objects. In the twentieth century, field theory became central to all branches of physics, including general relativity and quantum theory, leading scientists to search for a unified field theory bringing together all the forces of nature.

The Science of Electromagnetism

In the following selection, Maxwell describes how he will develop a mathematical theory of electromagnetism, based on Faraday's hypothesis that there are fields consisting of physical lines of force in the space surrounding electrical and magnetic objects. He contrasts his own theory with those of scientists who assume that forces act on bodies across distances with no intervening medium to transmit the forces. In doing so, Maxwell asks us to consider the nature of the assumptions scientists make concerning "what actually takes place" in the physical world as they formulate the laws and theories of physics.

The fact that certain bodies, after being rubbed, appear to attract other bodies, was known to the ancients. In modern times, a great variety of other phenomena have been observed, and have been found to be related to these phenomena of attraction. They have been classed under the name of *electric* phenomena, amber, ἤλεκτρσν, having been the substance in which they were first described.

Other bodies, particularly the lodestone, and pieces of iron and steel which have been subjected to certain processes, have also been long known to exhibit phenomena of action at a distance. These phenomena, with others related to them, were found to differ from the electric phenomena, and have been classed under the name of *magnetic* phenomena, the lodestone, μάγνης, being found in the Thessalian Magnesia.

This selection is taken from part 1, chapter 1, and part 4, chapter 6, of A Treatise on Electricity and Magnetism *(3rd ed.).*

These two classes of phenomena have since been found to be related to each other, and the relations between the various phenomena of both classes, so far as they are known, constitute the science of electromagnetism.

In the following treatise I propose to describe the most important of these phenomena, to show how they may be subjected to measurement, and to trace the mathematical connections of the quantities measured. Having thus obtained the data for a mathematical theory of electromagnetism, and having shown how this theory may be applied to the calculation of phenomena, I shall endeavor to place in as clear a light as I can the relations between the mathematical form of this theory and that of the fundamental science of dynamics, in order that we may be in some degree prepared to determine the kind of dynamical phenomena among which we are to look for illustrations or explanations of the electromagnetic phenomena. . . .

The most important aspect of any phenomenon from a mathematical point of view is that of a measurable quantity. I shall therefore consider electrical phenomena chiefly with a view to their measurement, describing the methods of measurement, and defining the standards on which they depend.

In the application of mathematics to the calculation of electrical quantities, I shall endeavor in the first place to deduce the most general conclusions from the data at our disposal, and in the next place to apply the results to the simplest cases that can be chosen. I shall avoid, as much as I can, those questions which, though they have elicited the skill of mathematicians, have not enlarged our knowledge of science.

The internal relations of the different branches of the science which we have to study are more numerous and complex than those of any other science hitherto developed. Its external relations, on the one hand to dynamics, and on the other to heat, light, chemical action, and the constitution of bodies, seem to indicate the special importance of electrical science as an aid to the interpretation of nature.

It appears to me, therefore, that the study of electromagnetism in all its extent has now become of the first importance as a means of promoting the progress of science.

The mathematical laws of the different classes of phenomena have been to a great extent satisfactorily made out.

The connections between the different classes of phenomena have also been investigated, and the probability of the rigorous exactness of the experimental laws have been greatly strengthened by a more extended knowledge of their relations to each other.

Finally, some progress has been made in the reduction of electromagnetism to a dynamical science, by showing that no electromagnetic phenomenon is contradictory to the supposition that it depends on purely dynamical action.

What has been hitherto done, however, has by no means exhausted the field of electrical research. It has rather opened up that field, by pointing out subjects of inquiry, and furnishing us with means of investigation. . . .

I have therefore thought that a treatise would be useful which should have for its principal object to take up the whole subject in a methodical manner, and which should also indicate how each part of the subject is brought within the reach of methods of verification by actual measurement.

The general complexion of the treatise differs considerably from that of several excellent electrical works, published, most of them, in Germany, and it may appear that scant justice is done to the speculations of several eminent electricians and mathematicians. One reason of this is that before I began the study of electricity I resolved to read no mathematics on the subject till I had first read through Faraday's *Experimental Researches in Electricity*. I was aware that there was supposed to be a difference between Faraday's way of conceiving phenomena and that of the mathematicians, so that neither he nor they were satisfied with each other's language. I had also the conviction that this discrepancy did not arise from either party being wrong. . . .

As I proceeded with the study of Faraday, I perceived that his method of conceiving the phenomena was also a mathematical one, though not exhibited in the conventional form of mathematical symbols. I also found that these methods were capable of being expressed in the ordinary mathematical forms, and thus compared with those of the professed mathematicians.

For instance, Faraday, in his mind's eye, saw lines of force traversing all space where the mathematicians saw centers of force attracting at a distance: Faraday saw a medium where they saw nothing but distance: Faraday sought the seat of the phenomena in real actions going on in the medium, they were satisfied that they had found it in a power of action at a distance impressed on the electric fluids.

When I had translated what I considered to be Faraday's ideas into a mathematical form, I found that in general the results of the two methods coincided, so that the same phenomena were accounted for, and the same laws of action deduced by both methods, but that Faraday's methods resembled those in which we begin with the whole and arrive at the parts by analysis, while the ordinary mathematical methods were founded on the principle of beginning with the parts and building up the whole by synthesis.

I also found that several of the most fertile methods of research discovered by the mathematicians could be expressed much better in terms of ideas derived from Faraday than in their original form. . . .

Great progress has been made in electrical science, chiefly in Germany, by cultivators of the theory of action at a distance, . . . depending either directly on the relative velocity of the particles, or on the gradual propagation of something, whether potential or force, from the one particle to the other. The great success which these eminent men have attained in the application of mathematics to electrical phenomena, gives, as is natural, additional weight to their theoretical speculations, so that those who, as students of electricity, turn to them as the greatest authorities in mathematical electricity, would probably imbibe, along with their mathematical methods, their physical hypotheses.

These physical hypotheses, however, are entirely alien from the way of looking at things which I adopt, and one object which I have in view is that some of those who wish to study electricity may, by reading this treatise, come to see that there is another way of treating the subject, which is no less fitted to explain the phenomena, and which, though in some parts it may appear less definite, corresponds, as I think, more faithfully with our actual knowledge, both in what it affirms and in what it leaves undecided.

In a philosophical point of view, moreover, it is exceedingly important that two methods should be compared, both of which have succeeded in explaining the principal electromagnetic phenomena, and both of which have attempted to explain the propagation of light as an electromagnetic phenomenon and have actually calculated its velocity, while at the same time the fundamental conceptions of what actually takes place, as well as most of the secondary conceptions of the quantities concerned, are radically different.

I have therefore taken the part of an advocate rather than that of a judge, and have rather exemplified one method than attempted to give an impartial description of both. . . .

I have confined myself almost entirely to the mathematical treatment of the subject, but I would recommended the student, after he has learned, experimentally if possible, what are the phenomena to be observed, to read carefully Faraday's *Experimental Researches in Electricity*. He will there find a strictly contemporary historical account of some of the greatest electrical discoveries and investigations, carried on in an order and succession which could hardly have been improved if the results had been known from the first, and expressed in the language of a man who devoted much of his attention to the methods of accurately describing scientific operations and their results.

It is of great advantage to the student of any subject to read the original memoirs on that subject, for science is always most completely assimilated when it is in the nascent state, and in the case of Faraday's *Researches* this is comparatively easy, as they are published in a separate form, and may be read consecutively. If by anything I have here written I may assist any student in understanding Faraday's modes of thought and expression, I shall regard it as the accomplishment of one of my principal aims—to communicate to others the same delight which I have found myself in reading Faraday's *Researches*. . . .

The discovery by Oersted[1] of the magnetic action of an electric current led by a direct process of reasoning to that of magnetization by electric currents, and of the mechanical action between electric currents. It was not, however, till 1831 that Faraday, who had been for some time endeavoring to produce electric currents by magnetic or electric action, discovered the conditions of magnetoelectric induction. The method which Faraday employed in his researches consisted in a constant appeal to experiment as a means of testing the truth of his ideas, and a constant cultivation of ideas under the direct influence of experiment. . . .

1. [Hans Christian Oersted (1777–1851), Danish scientist.]

The experimental investigation by which Ampère[2] established the laws of the mechanical action between electric currents is one of the most brilliant achievements in science.

The whole, theory and experiment, seems as if it had leaped, full grown and full armed, from the brain of the "Newton of electricity." It is perfect in form, and unassailable in accuracy, and it is summed up in a formula from which all the phenomena may be deduced, and which must always remain the cardinal formula of electrodynamics.

The method of Ampère, however, though cast into an inductive form, does not allow us to trace the formation of the ideas which guided it. We can scarcely believe that Ampère really discovered the law of action by means of the experiments which he describes. We are led to suspect what, indeed, he tells us himself, that he discovered the law by some process which he has not shown us, and that when he had afterward built up a perfect demonstration he removed all traces of the scaffolding by which he had raised it.

Faraday, on the other hand, shows us his unsuccessful as well as his successful experiments, and his crude ideas as well as his developed ones, and the reader, however inferior to him in inductive power, feels sympathy even more than admiration, and is tempted to believe that, if he had the opportunity, he too would be a discoverer. Every student should therefore read Ampère's research as a splendid example of scientific style in the statement of a discovery, but he should also study Faraday for the cultivation of a scientific spirit, by means of the action and reaction which will take place between the newly discovered facts as introduced to him by Faraday and the nascent ideas in his own mind.

It was perhaps for the advantage of science that Faraday, though thoroughly conscious of the fundamental forms of space, time, and force, was not a professed mathematician. He was not tempted to enter into the many interesting researches in pure mathematics which his discoveries would have suggested if they had been exhibited in a mathematical form, and he did not feel called upon either to force his results into a shape acceptable to the mathematical taste of the time, or to express them in a form which mathematicians might attack. He was thus left at leisure to do his proper work, to coordinate his ideas with his facts, and to express them in natural, untechnical language.

2. [André Marie Ampère (1775–1836), French scientist.]

It is mainly with the hope of making these ideas the basis of a mathematical method that I have undertaken this treatise.

We are accustomed to consider the universe as made up of parts, and mathematicians usually begin by considering a single particle, and then conceiving its relation to another particle, and so on. This has generally been supposed the most natural method. To conceive of a particle, however, requires a process of abstraction, since all our perceptions are related to extended bodies, so that the idea of the *all* that is in our consciousness at a given instant is perhaps as primitive an idea as that of any individual thing. Hence there may be a mathematical method in which we proceed from the whole to the parts instead of from the parts to the whole. For example, Euclid, in his first book, conceives a line as traced out by a point, a surface as swept out by a line, and a solid as generated by a surface. But he also defines a surface as the boundary of a solid, a line as the edge of a surface, and a point as the extremity of a line. . . .

In electrical investigations we may use formulas in which the quantities involved are the distances of certain bodies, and the electrifications or currents in these bodies, or we may use formulas which involve other quantities, each of which is continuous through all space.

The mathematical process employed in the first method is integration along lines, over surfaces, and throughout finite spaces; those employed in the second method are partial differential equations and integrations throughout all space.

The method of Faraday seems to be intimately related to the second of these modes of treatment. He never considers bodies as existing with nothing between them but their distance, and acting on one another according to some function of that distance. He conceives all space as a field of force, the lines of force being in general curved, and those due to any body extending from it on all sides, their directions being modified by the presence of other bodies. He even speaks of the lines of force belonging to a body as in some sense part of itself, so that in its action on distant bodies it cannot be said to act where it is not. This, however, is not a dominant idea with Faraday. I think he would rather have said that the field of space is full of lines of force, whose arrangement depends on that of the bodies in the field, and that the mathematical and electrical action on each body is determined by the lines which abut on it.

Content Questions

1. According to Maxwell, how has the science of electromagnetism helped to unify our understanding of the physical world? (205–206)

2. What are the steps that Maxwell proposes to follow in his *Treatise* in order to show the relation of his theory to the "fundamental science of dynamics"? What does he hope to accomplish by showing this relation? (205–206)

3. What differences does Maxwell find between the way that Faraday imagines the action of electromagnetic forces and the way that the mathematicians imagine them? (207–208)

4. How did Maxwell show that the results of Faraday and the mathematicians coincide, even though they each use different methods? (207–208)

5. What does Maxwell think his own method of conceiving electromagnetic phenomena will add to the method of Faraday and the method of the mathematicians? (208)

6. According to Maxwell, how do Ampère's reports of his experiments and discoveries differ from Faraday's reports? What benefit does Maxwell see for science students in reading Faraday's *Researches* that they might not find in reading Ampère? (210)

7. Why does Maxwell think that it was a great advantage to science that Faraday was not "a professed mathematician"? (210)

8. In considering how mathematics can be used to explain the physical world, why does Maxwell think that "there may be a mathematical method in which we proceed from the whole to the parts instead of from the parts to the whole"? (211)

9. What is the difference between the two kinds of formulas used in electrical investigations described by Maxwell? How do these methods reflect different ways of imagining what takes place when electromagnetic forces act? (211)

10. According to Maxwell, how is Faraday's method of conceiving electromagnetic phenomena consistent with the mathematical method that uses quantities "continuous through all space"? (211)

Discussion Questions

1. Why does Maxwell emphasize the measurement of quantities in developing his theory of electromagnetism? (206) Is it possible to have a scientific explanation of how the physical world operates without making quantitative measurements?

2. What does Maxwell mean by "a mathematical point of view" in investigating natural phenomena? (206) How does mathematics help physicists gain greater understanding of the physical world?

3. According to Maxwell, what is the relationship between measuring and calculating physical quantities? (206) In testing a scientific theory, why is it important to be able to calculate physical quantities?

4. Why does Maxwell think that it is important to reduce electromagnetism to a "dynamical science"? (206–207)

5. Why does Maxwell consider Faraday's method of conceiving electromagnetic phenomena mathematical, even though it is "not exhibited in the conventional form of mathematical symbols"? (207)

6. Why is Maxwell concerned that students who turn to scientists they regard as "the greatest authorities in mathematical electricity" might "imbibe, along with their mathematical methods, their physical hypotheses"? (208)

7. Even though some scientists had great success explaining electromagnetic phenomena based on the theory of action at a distance, why does Maxwell want to offer another explanation? How should scientists decide among hypotheses that are based on radically different "fundamental conceptions of what actually takes place," yet are equally successful in accounting for phenomena? (208)

8. Why does Maxwell say, "It is of great advantage to the student of any subject to read the original memoirs on that subject, for science is always most completely assimilated when it is in the nascent state"? (209) Would it be better for students to first read scientific books that reflect fully developed and well-established knowledge?

9. Why does Maxwell think that Faraday's scientific method benefited from not being "exhibited in a mathematical form"? (210–211) How can the formal mathematics of scientific theories lead scientists to discover successful new methods of experimental investigation?

10. According to Maxwell, what advantage does Faraday's explanation of the electrical action of bodies in terms of fields of force have over explanations based on the idea of action at a distance? (211) What difficulties would theories based on action at a distance raise for scientific explanations of the physical world?

Electricity and Electromotive Force

In this selection, Maxwell begins his inquiry into the nature of electricity with well-established experimental observations of bodies exhibiting electrical behavior. Without coming to final conclusions, he shows us the kinds of questions that must be asked to determine whether electricity belongs in any of the known categories of measurable physical quantities, such an energy, mass, or force. Because Maxwell knows that electric currents can perform mechanical work and that work involves energy, he asks whether the operation of an electromotive force can be understood, like ordinary mechanical force, in terms of the principles of dynamics.

Before we proceed to the investigation of the law of electrical force, let us enumerate the facts we have already established.

By placing any electrified system inside an insulated hollow conducting vessel, and examining the resultant effect on the outside of the vessel, we ascertain the character of the total electrification of the system placed inside, without any communication of electricity between the different bodies of the system.

The electrification of the outside of the vessel may be tested with great delicacy by putting it in communication with an electroscope.

We may suppose the electroscope to consist of a strip of gold leaf hanging between two bodies charged, one positively, and the other negatively. If the gold leaf becomes electrified it will incline toward the body

This selection is taken from part 1, chapter 1, and part 4, chapter 6, of A Treatise on Electricity and Magnetism *(3rd ed.).*

whose electrification is opposite to its own. By increasing the electrification of the two bodies and the delicacy of the suspension, an exceedingly small electrification of the gold leaf may be detected. . . .

This method was used by Faraday in his very admirable demonstration of the laws of electrical phenomena.

The total electrification of a body, or system of bodies, remains always the same, except insofar as it receives electrification from or gives electrification to other bodies.

In all electrical experiments the electrification of bodies is found to change, but it is always found that this change is due to want of perfect insulation, and that as the means of insulation are improved, the loss of electrification becomes less. We may therefore assert that the electrification of a body placed in a perfectly insulating medium would remain perfectly constant.

When one body electrifies another by conduction, the total electrification of the two bodies remains the same, that is, the one loses as much positive or gains as much negative electrification as the other gains of positive or loses of negative electrification.

For if the two bodies are enclosed in the hollow vessel, no change of the total electrification is observed.

When electrification is produced by friction, or by any other known method, equal quantities of positive and negative electrification are produced.

For the electrification of the whole system may be tested in the hollow vessel, or the process of electrification may be carried on within the vessel itself, and however intense the electrification of the parts of the system may be, the electrification of the whole, as indicated by the gold leaf electroscope, is invariably zero.

The electrification of a body is therefore a physical quantity capable of measurement, and two or more electrifications can be combined experimentally with a result of the same kind as when two quantities are added algebraically. We therefore are entitled to use language fitted to deal with electrification as a quantity as well as a quality, and to speak of any electrified body as "charged with a certain quantity of positive or negative electricity."

While admitting electricity, as we have now done, to the rank of a physical quantity, we must not too hastily assume that it is, or is not, a substance, or that it is, or is not, a form of energy, or that it belongs to any known category of physical quantities. All that we have hitherto proved is that it cannot be created or annihilated, so that if the total quantity of electricity within a closed surface is increased or diminished, the increase or diminution must have passed in or out through the closed surface.

This is true of matter. . . .

It is not true of heat, for heat may be increased or diminished within a closed surface, without passing in or out through the surface, by the transformation of some other form of energy into heat, or of heat into some other form of energy.

It is not true even of energy in general if we admit the immediate action of bodies at a distance. For a body outside the closed surface may make an exchange of energy with a body within the surface. But if all apparent action at a distance is the result of the action between the parts of an intervening medium, it is conceivable that in all cases of the increase or diminution of the energy within a closed surface we may be able, when the nature of this action of the parts of the medium is clearly understood, to trace the passage of the energy in or out through that surface.

There is, however, another reason which warrants us in asserting that electricity, as a physical quantity, synonymous with the total electrification of a body, is not, like heat, a form of energy. An electrified system has a certain amount of energy, and this energy can be calculated by multiplying the quantity of electricity in each of its parts by another physical quantity, called the *potential*[1] of that part, and taking half the sum of the products. The quantities *electricity* and *potential*, when multiplied together, produce the quantity *energy*. It is impossible, therefore, that electricity and energy should be quantities of the same category, for electricity is only one of the factors of energy, the other factor being *potential*.

Energy, which is the product of these factors, may also be considered as the product of several other pairs of factors, such as:

---

1. [A number representing the measure of the potential for a charged body to acquire the potential energy stored in the region around another charged body, not to be confused with potential energy itself.]

A force	× a distance through which the force is to act.
A mass	× gravitation acting through a certain height.
A mass	× half the square of its velocity.
A pressure	× a volume of fluid introduced into a vessel at that pressure.
A chemical affinity	× a chemical change, measured by the number of electrochemical equivalents which enter into combination.

If we ever should obtain distinct mechanical ideas of the nature of electric potential, we may combine these with the idea of energy to determine the physical category in which electricity is to be placed.

↬ ↬ ↬

. . . When an electric current exists in a conducting circuit, it has a capacity for doing a certain amount of mechanical work, and this independently of any external electromotive force maintaining the current. Now, capacity for performing work is nothing else than energy, in whatever way it arises, and all energy is the same in kind, however it may differ in form. The energy of an electric current is either of that form which consists in the actual motion of matter, or of that which consists in the capacity for being set in motion, arising from forces acting between bodies placed in certain positions relative to each other.

The first kind of energy, that of motion, is called *kinetic energy*, and when once understood it appears so fundamental a fact of nature that we can hardly conceive the possibility of resolving it into anything else. The second kind of energy, that depending on position, is called *potential energy*, and is due to the action of what we call forces, that is to say, tendencies toward change of relative position. With respect to these forces, though we may accept their existence as a demonstrated fact, yet we always feel that every explanation of the mechanism by which bodies are set in motion forms a real addition to our knowledge.

The electric current cannot be conceived except as a kinetic phenomenon. Even Faraday, who constantly endeavored to emancipate his mind from the influence of those suggestions which the words *electric current* and *electric fluid* are too apt to carry with them, speaks of the electric current as "something progressive, and not a mere arrangement."

The effects of the current, such as electrolysis, and the transfer of electrification from one body to another, are all progressive actions which require time for their accomplishment, and are therefore of the nature of motions.

As to the velocity of the current, we have shown that we know nothing about it; it may be the tenth of an inch in an hour, or a hundred thousand miles in a second. So far are we from knowing its absolute value in any case, that we do not even know whether what we call the positive direction is the actual direction of the motion or the reverse.

But all that we assume here is that the electric current involves motion of some kind. That which is the cause of electric currents has been called *electromotive force.* This name has long been used with great advantage, and has never led to any inconsistency in the language of science. Electromotive force is always to be understood to act on electricity only, not on the bodies in which the electricity resides. It is never to be confounded with ordinary mechanical force, which acts on bodies only, not on the electricity in them. If we ever come to know the formal relation between electricity and ordinary matter, we shall probably also know the relation between electromotive force and ordinary force.

When ordinary force acts on a body, and when the body yields to the force, the work done by the force is measured by the product of the force into the amount by which the body yields. Thus, in the case of water forced through a pipe, the work done at any section is measured by the fluid pressure at the section multiplied into the quantity of water which crosses the section.

In the same way the work done by an electromotive force is measured by the product of the electromotive force into the quantity of electricity which crosses a section of the conductor under the action of the electromotive force.

The work done by an electromotive force is of exactly the same kind as the work done by an ordinary force, and both are measured by the same standards or units.

Part of the work done by an electromotive force acting on a conducting circuit is spent in overcoming the resistance of the circuit, and this part of the work is thereby converted into heat. Another part of the work is spent in producing the electromagnetic phenomena observed by Ampère, in which conductors are made to move by electromagnetic forces. The rest of the work is spent in increasing the kinetic energy of the current, and the effects of this part of the action are shown in the phenomena of the induction of currents observed by Faraday.

We therefore know enough about electric currents to recognize, in a system of material conductors carrying currents, a dynamical system which is the seat of energy, part of which may be kinetic and part potential.

The nature of the connections of the parts of this system is unknown to us, but as we have dynamical methods of investigation which do not require a knowledge of the mechanism of the system, we shall apply them to this case.

Content Questions

1. In Maxwell's description of the experimental apparatus for examining electrified systems, why does he specify that the hollow vessel into which the electrified system is placed is insulated? (215)

2. Why is the electroscope used to test the electrification of the outside of the insulated vessel containing the electrified system? (215–216)

3. According to Maxwell, what are the conditions under which the electrification of a body or system of bodies changes? (216)

4. What experimental indications suggest to Maxwell that electrification is a conserved quantity? (216)

5. What differences between heat and electricity make Maxwell reluctant to claim whether electricity "is, or is not, a form of energy"? (217)

6. Why does Maxwell point to the way in which the energy of an electrified system is calculated as evidence that electricity is not a form of energy? What does Maxwell think we would have to know about the factors in the calculation to determine "the physical category in which electricity is to be placed"? (217–218)

7. According to Maxwell and Faraday, what form does an electric current's energy take? What does Faraday mean when he says that an electric current is "something progressive, and not a mere arrangement"? (218–219)

8. What assumptions about electric currents does Maxwell think are contained in the term *electromotive force*? Why can't electromotive force be considered an ordinary mechanical force? (219)

9. Why does Maxwell say that "the work done by an electromotive force is of exactly the same kind as the work done by an ordinary force"? (219)

10. What knowledge of electric currents does Maxwell have that enables him "to recognize, in a system of material conductors carrying currents, a dynamical system"? (220)

Discussion Questions

1. Why does Maxwell assert that we are "entitled to use language fitted to deal with electrification as a quantity as well as a quality"? (216) How does a scientist determine whether a natural phenomenon should be admitted "to the rank of a physical quantity"? (217)

2. What does Maxwell mean when he speaks of categories of physical quantities? (217) How does a scientist determine which category a physical quantity such as electricity, energy, potential, force, mass, or pressure belongs in?

3. Why does Maxwell say that every explanation "of the mechanism by which bodies are set in motion" is a "real addition to our knowledge"? (218) Why wouldn't a thorough description of the forces that cause motion be adequate for an understanding of the dynamics of the physical world?

4. Why would Faraday have "constantly endeavored to emancipate his mind from the influence of those suggestions which the words *electric current* and *electric fluid* are too apt to carry with them"? (218–219) What should a physicist consider when choosing words to describe natural phenomena?

5. Why does Maxwell think that "if we ever come to know the formal relation between electricity and ordinary matter" we will then probably understand the relationship between electromotive force and ordinary force? (219)

6. Why does Maxwell mention that the "same standards or units" are used to measure the work done by both electromotive and ordinary force? How would defining and measuring the work of the two forces in the same way help Maxwell build a dynamic theory of his new science of electromagnetism? (219)

A Dynamical Theory of the Electromagnetic Field

This selection is from the paper in which Maxwell first presents a detailed explanation of his field theory, drawing on evidence from the operation of electromotive force and analogies to the science of optics. He proposes the existence of a pervasive "ethereal medium" that is set in motion by electricity and magnetism and is capable of containing and transmitting electromagnetic energy. At the same time, Maxwell says that he has expressed his theory in the general equations of the electromagnetic field, asking us to consider how mechanical models and abstract mathematics are related to each other in scientific theories.

The most obvious mechanical phenomenon in electrical and magnetical experiments is the mutual action by which bodies in certain states set each other in motion while still at a sensible distance from each other. The first step, therefore, in reducing these phenomena into scientific form, is to ascertain the magnitude and direction of the force acting between the bodies, and when it is found that this force depends in a certain way upon the relative position of the bodies and on their electric or magnetic condition, it seems at first sight natural to explain the facts by assuming the existence of something either at rest or in motion in each body, constituting its electric or magnetic state, and capable of acting at a distance according to mathematical laws.

In this way mathematical theories of statical electricity, of magnetism, of the mechanical action between conductors carrying currents, and of the induction of currents have been formed. In these theories the force acting between the two bodies is treated with reference only to the condition of the bodies and their relative position, and without any express consideration of the surrounding medium.

These theories assume, more or less explicitly, the existence of substances the particles of which have the property of acting on one another at a distance by attraction or repulsion. The most complete development of a theory of this kind is that of M. W. Weber[1], who has made the same theory include electrostatic and electromagnetic phenomena.

In doing so, however, he has found it necessary to assume that the force between two electric particles depends on their relative velocity, as well as on their distance.

This theory, as developed by M. W. Weber and C. Neumann, is exceedingly ingenious, and wonderfully comprehensive in its application to the phenomena of statical electricity, electromagnetic attractions, induction of currents, and diamagnetic phenomena; and it comes to us with the more authority, as it has served to guide the speculations of one who has made so great an advance in the practical part of electric science, both by introducing a consistent system of units in electrical measurement and by actually determining electrical quantities with an accuracy hitherto unknown.

The mechanical difficulties, however, which are involved in the assumption of particles acting at a distance with forces which depend on their velocities are such as to prevent me from considering this theory as an ultimate one, though it may have been, and may yet be useful in leading to the coordination of phenomena.

I have therefore preferred to seek an explanation of the fact in another direction, by supposing them to be produced by actions which go on in the surrounding medium as well as in the excited bodies, and endeavoring to explain the action between distant bodies without assuming the existence of forces capable of acting directly at sensible distances.

The theory I propose may therefore be called a theory of the *electromagnetic field*, because it has to do with the space in the neighborhood of the electric or magnetic bodies, and it may be called a *dynamical theory*, because it assumes that in that space there is matter in motion, by which the observed electromagnetic phenomena are produced.

1. [Wilhelm Weber (1804–1891), German experimental and theoretical physicist.]

The electromagnetic field is that part of space which contains and surrounds bodies in electric or magnetic conditions.

It may be filled with any kind of matter, or we may endeavor to render it empty of all gross matter. . . .

There is always, however, enough matter left to receive and transmit the undulations of light and heat, and it is because the transmission of these radiations is not greatly altered when transparent bodies of measurable density are substituted for the so-called vacuum, that we are obliged to admit that the undulations are those of an ethereal substance, and not of the gross matter, the presence of which merely modifies in some way the motion of the ether.

We have therefore some reason to believe, from the phenomena of light and heat, that there is an ethereal medium filling space and permeating bodies, capable of being set in motion and of transmitting that motion from one part to another, and of communicating that motion to gross matter so as to heat it and affect it in various ways.

Now, the energy communicated to the body in heating it must have formerly existed in the moving medium, for the undulations had left the source of heat some time before they reached the body, and during that time the energy must have been half in the form of motion of the medium and half in the form of elastic resilience. . . .

We may therefore receive, as a datum derived from a branch of science independent of that with which we have to deal, the existence of a pervading medium, of small but real density, capable of being set in motion, and of transmitting motion from one part to another with great, but not infinite, velocity.

Hence the parts of this medium must be so connected that the motion of one part depends in some way on the motion of the rest; and at the same time these connections must be capable of a certain kind of elastic yielding, since the communication of motion is not instantaneous, but occupies time.

The medium is therefore capable of receiving and storing up two kinds of energy, namely, the *actual* energy depending on the motions of its parts, and *potential* energy, consisting of the work which the medium will do in recovering from displacement in virtue of its elasticity.

The propagation of undulations consists in the continual transformation of one of these forms of energy into the other alternately, and at any instant the amount of energy in the whole medium is equally divided, so that half is energy of motion, and half is elastic resilience.

A medium having such a constitution may be capable of other kinds of motion and displacement than those which produce the phenomena of light and heat, and some of these may be of such a kind that they may be evidenced to our senses by the phenomena they produce.

Now we know that the luminiferous medium is in certain cases acted on by magnetism; for Faraday discovered that when a plane polarized ray traverses a transparent diamagnetic medium[2] in the direction of the lines of magnetic force produced by magnets or currents in the neighborhood, the plane of polarization is caused to rotate.

This rotation is always in the direction in which positive electricity must be carried round the diamagnetic body in order to produce the actual magnetization of the field. . . .

. . . We have therefore warrantable grounds for inquiring whether there may not be a motion of the ethereal medium going on wherever magnetic effects are observed, and we have some reason to suppose that this motion is one of rotation, having the direction of the magnetic force as its axis.

We may now consider another phenomenon observed in the electro-magnetic field. When a body is moved across the lines of magnetic force it experiences what is called an *electromotive force*; the two extremities of the body tend to become oppositely electrified, and an electric current tends to flow through the body. When the electromotive force is sufficiently powerful, and is made to act on certain compound bodies, it decomposes them, and causes one of their components to pass toward one extremity of the body, and the other in the opposite direction.

Here we have evidence of a force causing an electric current in spite of resistance; electrifying the extremities of a body in opposite ways, a condition which is sustained only by the action of the electromotive force, and which, as soon as that force is removed, tends, with an equal and opposite force, to produce a countercurrent through the body and to restore the original electrical state of the body; and finally, if strong enough, tearing to pieces chemical compounds and carrying their components in opposite

2. [In this case, the glass through which the polarized light passes, and that has become temporarily and slightly magnetized under the influence of a strong magnetic field.]

directions, while their natural tendency is to combine, and to combine with a force which can generate an electromotive force in the reverse direction.

This, then, is a force acting on a body caused by its motion through the electromagnetic field, or by changes occurring in that field itself; and the effect of the force is either to produce a current and heat the body, or to decompose the body, or, when it can do neither, to put the body in a state of electric polarization—a state of constraint in which opposite extremities are oppositely electrified, and from which the body tends to relieve itself as soon as the disturbing force is removed.

According to the theory which I propose to explain, this electromotive force is the force called into play during the communication of motion from one part of the medium to another, and it is by means of this force that the motion of one part causes motion in another part. When electromotive force acts on a conducting circuit, it produces a current, which, as it meets with resistance, occasions a continual transformation of electrical energy into heat, which is incapable of being restored again to the form of electrical energy by any reversal of the process.

But when electromotive force acts on a dielectric[3] it produces a state of polarization of its parts similar in distribution to the polarity of the parts of a mass of iron under the influence of a magnet, and like the magnetic polarization, capable of being described as a state in which every particle has its opposite poles in opposite conditions.

In a dielectric under the action of electromotive force, we may conceive that the electricity in each molecule is so displaced that one side is rendered positively and the other negatively electrical, but that the electricity remains entirely connected with the molecule, and does not pass from one molecule to another. The effect of this action on the whole dielectric mass is to produce a general displacement of electricity in a certain direction. . . .

Here, then, we perceive another effect of electromotive force, namely, electric displacement, which according to our theory is a kind of elastic yielding to the action of the force, similar to that which takes place in structures and machines owing to the want of perfect rigidity of the connections. . . .

3. [*dielectric:* a substance that does not conduct electric current; an insulator.]

It appears therefore that certain phenomena in electricity and magnetism lead to the same conclusion as those of optics, namely, that there is an ethereal medium pervading all bodies, and modified only in degree by their presence; that the parts of this medium are capable of being set in motion by electric currents and magnets; that this motion is communicated from one part of the medium to another by forces arising from the connections of those parts; that under the action of these forces there is a certain yielding depending on the elasticity of these connections; and that therefore energy in two different forms may exist in the medium, the one form being the actual energy of motion of its parts, and the other being the potential energy stored up in the connections, in virtue of their elasticity.

Thus, then, we are led to the conception of a complicated mechanism capable of a vast variety of motion, but at the same time so connected that the motion of one part depends, according to definite relations, on the motion of other parts, these motions being communicated by forces arising from the relative displacement of the connected parts, in virtue of their elasticity. Such a mechanism must be subject to the general laws of dynamics, and we ought to be able to work out all the consequences of its motion, provided we know the form of the relation between the motions of the parts.

We know that when an electric current is established in a conducting circuit, the neighboring part of the field is characterized by certain magnetic properties, and that if two circuits are in the field, the magnetic properties of the field due to the two currents are combined. Thus each part of the field is in connection with both currents, and the two currents are put in connection with each other in virtue of their connection with the magnetization of the field. The first result of this connection that I propose to examine is the induction of one current by another, and by the motion of conductors in the field.

The second result, which is deduced from this, is the mechanical action between conductors carrying currents. . . .

I then apply the phenomena of induction and attraction of currents to the exploration of the electromagnetic field, and the laying down systems of lines of magnetic force which indicate its magnetic properties. By exploring the same field with a magnet, I show the distribution of its equipotential magnetic surfaces, cutting the lines of force at right angles.

In order to bring these results within the power of symbolical calculation, I then express them in the form of the general equations of the electromagnetic field. . . .

There are twenty of these equations in all, involving twenty variable quantities.

I then express in terms of these quantities the intrinsic energy of the electromagnetic field as depending partly on its magnetic and partly on its electric polarization at every point.

From this I determine the mechanical force acting, first, on a movable conductor carrying an electric current; secondly, on a magnetic pole; thirdly, on an electrified body.

The last result, namely, the mechanical force acting on an electrified body, gives rise to an independent method of electrical measurement founded on its electrostatic effects. . . .

The general equations are next applied to the case of a magnetic disturbance propagated through a nonconducting field, and it is shown that the only disturbances which can be so propagated are those which are transverse to the direction of propagation, and that the velocity of propagation is the velocity v, found from experiments such as those of Weber, which expresses the number of electrostatic units of electricity which are contained in one electromagnetic unit.

This velocity is so nearly that of light, that it seems we have strong reason to conclude that light itself (including radiant heat, and other radiations if any) is an electromagnetic disturbance in the form of waves propagated through the electromagnetic field according to electromagnetic laws. If so, the agreement between the elasticity of the medium as calculated from the rapid alternations of luminous vibrations, and as found by the slow processes of electrical experiments, shows how perfect and regular the elastic properties of the medium must be when not encumbered with any matter denser than air. . . .

~ ~ ~

I have on a former occasion attempted to describe a particular kind of motion and a particular kind of strain, so arranged as to account for the phenomena. In the present paper I avoid any hypothesis of this kind; and in using such words as *electric momentum* and *electric elasticity* in reference to the known phenomena of the induction of currents and the polarization of dielectrics, I wish merely to direct the mind of the reader to mechanical phenomena which will assist him in understanding the electrical ones. All such phrases in the present paper are to be considered as illustrative, not as explanatory.

In speaking of the energy of the field, however, I wish to be understood literally. All energy is the same as mechanical energy, whether it exists in the form of motion or in that of elasticity, or in any other form. The energy in electromagnetic phenomena is mechanical energy. The only question is, where does it reside? On the old theories it resides in the electrified bodies, conducting circuits, and magnets, in the form of an unknown quality called potential energy, or the power of producing certain effects at a distance. On our theory it resides in the electromagnetic field, in the space surrounding the electrified and magnetic bodies, as well as in those bodies themselves, and is in two different forms, which may be described without hypothesis as magnetic polarization and electric polarization, or, according to a very probable hypothesis, as the motion and the strain of one and the same medium.

The conclusions arrived at in the present paper are independent of this hypothesis, being deduced from experimental facts of three kinds:

1. The induction of the electric currents by the increase or diminution of neighboring currents according to the changes in the lines of force passing through the circuit.
2. The distribution of magnetic intensity according to the variations of a magnetic potential.
3. The induction (or influence) of statical electricity through dielectrics.

We may now proceed to demonstrate from these principles the existence and laws of the mechanical forces which act upon electric currents, magnets, and electrified bodies placed in the electromagnetic field.

Content Questions

1. According to Maxwell, why might it seem "natural" to explain the forces acting between bodies in electrical and magnetic experiments "with reference only to the condition of the bodies and their relative position"? Why did the mathematical theories that were formed to explain these phenomena assume the existence of "substances the particles of which have the property of acting on one another at a distance"? (223–224)

2. What prevents Maxwell from considering Weber's theory of electromagnetic phenomena to be the ultimate theory, even though Maxwell admits that it is "exceedingly ingenious, and wonderfully comprehensive"? (224)

3. When Maxwell designates his theory as dynamical, what new assumptions does he introduce about "the space in the neighborhood of the electric or magnetic bodies"? (224)

4. Why does the way heat and light are transmitted convince Maxwell that they are propagated in "a pervading medium, of small but real density, capable of being set in motion"? What does he mean when he calls it an "ethereal medium"? (225)

5. Why is the ability of the ethereal medium to receive and store energy essential to Maxwell's dynamical theory? (225)

6. Why does the result of Faraday's experiment with polarized light suggest to Maxwell that the ethereal medium "may be capable of other kinds of motion and displacement than those which produce the phenomena of light and heat"? (226)

7. According to Maxwell, what must occur for a body in the electromagnetic field to experience an electromotive force? What occurs when the initial electromotive force is removed? (226–227)

8. How does the electromotive force help Maxwell explain what happens when electrified or magnetic bodies appear to act on each other at a distance? (227)

9. Why does Maxwell call the polarizing effect of electromotive force on a dielectric "electric displacement"? What does electric displacement suggest to him about the form of the electromagnetic field's energy? (227–228)

10. Why does Maxwell think that the properties of the electromagnetic field will make it possible for him to explain the induction of electric currents? (228)

11. How do Maxwell's general equations of the electromagnetic field provide him with strong reasons for thinking that "light itself . . . is an electromagnetic disturbance"? (229)

12. What does Maxwell mean when he says that "in speaking of the energy of the field," he wants to be understood literally? (230)

Discussion Questions

1. What does Maxwell mean when he says that ascertaining the magnitude and direction of the forces acting between electrical and magnetic bodies is a first step in "reducing these phenomena into scientific form"? (223) When confronted with the quantitative and qualitative characteristics of natural phenomena, how should a scientist decide which to take into account in developing a scientific explanation?

2. In what way can a scientific theory such as Weber's be "useful in leading to the coordination of phenomena," even though it is not the ultimate theory? (224) What reasons might Maxwell have for thinking that his own dynamical theory of the electromagnetic field comes closer to being an ultimate theory?

3. Why does Maxwell think that there must be a medium of some sort to support the operation of the electromagnetic field? (225–226) How does he think the "ethereal medium" and the electromagnetic field are related to each other? (228)

4. Why does Maxwell conceive of the electromagnetic field as "a complicated mechanism"? Must Maxwell's mechanical model be a literal representation of the physical structure and operation of the electromagnetic field for his theory to be valid? (228)

5. What is the "power of symbolical calculation" that Maxwell cites in referring to his general equations of the electromagnetic field? (229) How can equations such as these lead to greater insight about the unity underlying phenomena in the physical world?

6. What does Maxwell mean when he says that he is using words such as *electric momentum* and *electric elasticity* in an illustrative, not an explanatory, sense? (229–230) What are the strengths and weaknesses of scientists using language that makes analogies between what is known and what cannot yet be adequately explained?

Suggestions for Further Reading

By the author

Maxwell, James Clerk. *Matter and Motion*. New York: Dover Publications, 1991. Maxwell's concise and elegant survey of Newtonian dynamics, from the motion of simple particles to the analysis of complex systems, is a summary of classical physics, which would be unsettled in the twentieth century by relativity and quantum theory.

————. *Treatise on Electricity and Magnetism*. 2 vols. 3rd ed. New York: Dover Publications, 1954. In this treatise, from which the first two Maxwell selections in *What's the Matter?* are taken, Maxwell builds on the work of Faraday to lay the foundations of the science of electromagnetism, derives the general equations of field theory, and points the way to Einstein's special theory of relativity.

Simpson, Thomas K. *Maxwell on the Electromagnetic Field: A Guided Study*. New Brunswick, NJ: Rutgers University Press, 1997, 2001. This volume contains the paper that is included in *What's the Matter?* as well as two others that trace the development of Maxwell's speculations on the nature of the electromagnetic field. The outstanding commentaries and notes guide readers through Maxwell's reasoning; diagrams clarify difficult concepts.

About the author

Mahon, Basil. *The Man Who Changed Everything: The Life of James Clerk Maxwell*. Chichester, UK: John Wiley & Sons, 2003, 2004. This biography is both a thorough account of Maxwell's life and an explanation of the significance of his discoveries to modern science and technology.

About the topic

Arianrhod, Robyn. *Einstein's Heroes: Imagining the World Through the Language of Mathematics*. Oxford: Oxford University Press, 2005. The central theme of this book is how scientists—especially Maxwell—have used the language of mathematics to arrive at new insights into the nature of the physical world.

Einstein, Albert, and Leopold Infeld. *The Evolution of Physics: From Early Concepts to Relativity and Quanta*. New York: Simon & Schuster, 1938, copyright renewed 1966. Focusing on concepts rather than historical facts, this book provides one of the clearest explanations of the development of field theory and shows its direct relationship to Einstein's theory of relativity.

The measure of the value of a new hypothesis in physics is not its obviousness but its utility. If the hypothesis proves successful, one becomes used to it and it gradually becomes obvious of its own accord.

—Max Planck, "The Place of Modern Physics in the Mechanical View of Nature"

MAX PLANCK

Extending the Theories of Physics

In the late nineteenth century, when Max Planck (1858–1947) began his study of science, physicists were discovering that many new scientific problems could not be understood in terms of classical Newtonian physics. Experiments in electromagnetism and thermodynamics yielded results for which there were no adequate theoretical explanations. Scientists had not established whether matter was continuous and infinitely divisible, or composed of indivisible atoms. New techniques were needed to understand the behavior of the microscopic particles of gases, whose movements were too numerous to individually predict in terms of Newtonian mechanics. In addition, attempts to measure the speed of light in relation to the ether were calling into question the existence of Newton's absolute frame of reference for motion. Although scientific research was producing startling discoveries of such phenomena as x-rays, radioactivity, and the electron, explanations of these discoveries were lacking. Within a few years, the work of Max Planck and Albert Einstein provided scientists with the theoretical basis for understanding these discoveries and led to the two principle branches of modern physics, quantum theory and the theory of relativity.

Planck was born in Germany into a family that for many generations had produced distinguished officials devoted to the service of church and state. Planck's own character reflected this background and contributed to his outstanding ability as administrator of several important research institutes. He studied physics at the University of Munich and later at the University of Berlin, where he was appointed professor of theoretical physics in 1889. He taught and conducted research there until his retirement in 1928.

Planck's research concentrated on thermodynamics, the study of the relation of heat to other forms of energy. In the late 1890s, he succeeded in finding a way to mathematically formulate curves describing electromagnetic radiation of different frequencies given off by heated bodies. Previous attempts to do so using the principles of Newtonian mechanics and electrodynamics had resulted in predictions of immense amounts of high-frequency radiant energy that were never observed in experiments. Although Planck's formulas accurately predicted what actually happened, to make the mathematics work he had made the assumption that energy is emitted only in definite, discrete quantities, instead of varying continuously. This contradicted one of the fundamental assumptions of classical physics—that dynamical effects are continuous over an infinite range of intermediate values.

When Planck reported his results in 1900, he was not convinced that his assumption concerning energy packages, or *quanta*, in his mathematical formula for radiation reflected the actual structure of the physical world. In addition, to reach his solution he had made use of the techniques of statistical mechanics, something he had previously avoided doing because of the element of probability that they introduced into physics. Planck advocated the classical view that the goal of physics is an absolute, deterministic world picture in which phenomena can be explained in terms of clear mechanistic laws, even as he reluctantly accepted his revolutionary role in the development of quantum physics, with its reliance on principles of probability and indeterminacy. The fundamental number named Planck's constant in his honor assures his recognition as one of the founders of modern physics. Planck discovered this incredibly small number (6.626×10^{-34}), symbolized by h, which specifies the ratio of an electromagnetic quantum's energy (its discontinuous particle nature) to its frequency (its continuous wave nature). In 1905, Einstein used the idea of energy quanta to explain the behavior of light in photoelectric effects, confirming that Planck's assumption had a basis in physical reality.

Planck was a highly regarded teacher and received numerous awards, including the Nobel Prize in Physics in 1918. In 1930, he was appointed president of the Kaiser Wilhelm Society, renamed the Max Planck Society for the Advancement of Science after his death. During the 1930s, he personally confronted Adolf Hitler to protest the expulsion of Jews from German universities and chose to remain in Germany through World War II, hoping to preserve some of the intellectual integrity of German science. He suffered great hardships during the war, including the loss of his personal property and the execution of his son by the Nazis for taking part in an attempt to assassinate Hitler.

In the following essay, Planck considers how scientific theories evolve when the results of observation and experiment call into question underlying assumptions. In addition, he raises questions about what view of the world scientists must bring to their research in order to make progress.

Extending the
Theories of Physics

Experimental research in physics has not experienced, for a long time, such a stormy period, nor has its significance for human culture ever been so generally acknowledged as nowadays. Wireless waves, electrons, roentgen rays, and radioactive phenomena more or less arouse everybody's interest. If we consider only the wider question of how these new and brilliant discoveries have influenced and advanced our understanding of Nature and her laws, their importance does not appear, at first sight, to be commensurate with their brilliance.

Whoever tries to judge the state of present-day physical theories from a detached point of view may easily be led to the opinion that theoretical research is complicated to a certain extent by many new experimental discoveries, some of which were quite unforeseen. He will find that the present time is an unedifying period of aimless groping, in direct contrast to the clearness and certainty characteristic of the recent theoretical epoch, which may, therefore, with some justification, be called the classical epoch. Everywhere, old ideas, firmly rooted, are being displaced, generally accepted theorems are being cast aside and new hypotheses

This selection is titled "New Paths of Physical Knowledge" in A Survey of Physical Theory.

taking their place. Some of these hypotheses are so startling that they put a great strain on our comprehension and on our scientific ideas and do not appear to inspire confidence in the steady advance of science toward a fixed goal. Modern theoretical physics gives one the impression of an old and honored building that is falling into decay, with parts tottering one after the other, and its foundations threatening to give way.

No conception could be more erroneous than this. Great fundamental changes are, indeed, taking place in the structure of theoretical physics, but closer examination shows that this is not a case of destruction, but one of perfection and extension, that certain blocks of the building are only removed from their place in order to find a firmer and more suitable position elsewhere, and that the real fundamentals of the theory are today as fixed and immutable as ever they have been. After this more general consideration we will examine thoroughly the basis of these remarks.

The first impulse toward a revision and reconstruction of a physical theory is nearly always given by the discovery of one or more facts that cannot be fitted into the existing theory. Facts always form a central point about which the most important theories hinge. Nothing is more interesting to the true theorist than a fact that directly contradicts a theory generally accepted up to that time, for this is his particular work.

What is to be done in such a case? Only one thing is certain: the existing theory must be altered in such a way that it is made to agree with the newly discovered fact. But it is often a very difficult and complicated question to decide in what part of the theory the improvement has to be made. A theory is not formed from a single isolated fact but from a whole series of individual propositions combined together. It resembles a complicated organism, whose separate parts are so intimately connected that any interference in one part must, to some extent, affect other parts, often apparently quite remote, and it is not always easy to realize this fully. Thus, since each consequence of the theory is the result of the coordination of several propositions, any erroneous result deducted from the theory can generally be attributed to several of the propositions, and there are almost always numerous ways out of the difficulty. Usually, in the end, the question resolves itself into a conflict between two or three theorems, which were hitherto related in the theory, at least one of which theorems must be discarded on account of the new facts. The dispute often rages for years, and the final settlement means not only the exclusion of one of the theorems considered, but also, and this is especially important, quite naturally the corresponding strengthening and establishment of the remaining accepted propositions.

The most important and remarkable result of all such disputes arising in recent times is that the great general principles of physics have been established. There are the principle of conservation of energy, the principle of conservation of momentum, the principle of least action, and the laws of thermodynamics. These principles have, without exception, held the field and their force has increased appreciably in consequence. On the other hand, the theorems that failed to survive are ones that certainly served as apparent starting points for all theoretical developments, but only because they were thought to be so self-evident that it was usually considered unnecessary to mention them specifically, or they were completely forgotten. Briefly, it can be said that the latest developments of theoretical physics were vindicated through the triumph of the great principles of physics over certain deeply rooted assumptions and conceptions, which were accepted from habit.

A few such propositions may be mentioned in order to illustrate this. These had been accepted as self-evident foundations of their respective theories without any consideration, but in the light of new discoveries have been proved untenable or, at least, highly improbable, as opposed to the general principles of physics. I mentioned three: the invariability of the chemical atom, the mutual independence of space and time, and the continuity of all dynamical effects.

It is naturally not my intention to recount all the weighty arguments that have been directed against the *invariableness of the chemical atom*; I will only quote a single fact that has led to an inevitable conflict between a physical principle and this assumption, which had always hitherto been considered as self-evident. The fact is the continual development of heat from a radium compound, the physical principle is conservation of energy, and the conflict finally ended with the complete victory of this principle, though at first many wished to throw doubt on it.

A radium salt, enclosed in a lead chamber of sufficient thickness, continually develops heat at a calculated rate of about 135 calories per grain of radium per hour. Consequently, it always remains, like a furnace, at a higher temperature than its surroundings. The principle of conservation of energy states that the observed heat cannot be created out of nothing, but that there must be a corresponding change as the cause. In the case of a furnace, we have the continual burning; in the case of the radium compound, through lack of any other chemical phenomenon, a variation of the radium atom itself must be assumed. This hypothesis has established itself everywhere, although it appeared daring when looked at from the previously accepted point of view of chemical science.

Strictly considered, there is, indeed, a certain contradiction in the conception of a variable atom, since atoms were originally defined as the invariable ultimate particles of all matter. Accordingly, to be quite accurate, the term *atom* should be reserved for the really invariable elements, as, perhaps, electrons and hydrogen. But apart from the fact that perhaps it can never be established that an invariable element exists in an absolute sense, such an uncertainty of meaning of terms would lead to a terrible confusion in the literature. The present chemical atoms are no longer the atoms of Democritus, but they are accurately determinable numerically by means of another and much more rigid definition. Only these numbers are referred to when atomic change is mentioned, and a misunderstanding in the direction indicated appears quite impossible.

Until recently the *absolute independence of space and time* was considered no less self-evident than the invariableness of the atom. There was a definite physical meaning to the question of the simultaneity of two observations at different places, without any necessity to inquire who had taken the time measurement. Today it is quite the opposite. For a fact that up to now has been repeatedly verified by the most delicate optical and electro-dynamical experiments has brought that simple conception into conflict with the so-called principle of constant velocity of light, which came into favor through Maxwell and Lorentz, and which states that the velocity of propagation of light in empty space is independent of the motion of the waves. This fact is briefly, if not also clearly, called the relativity of all motion. If one accepts the relativity as being experimentally proved, one must abandon either the principle of constant velocity of light or the mutual independence of space and time.

Let us take a simple example. A time signal is sent out from a central station such as the Eiffel Tower by means of wireless telegraphy, as proposed in the projected international time service. Then all the surrounding stations, which are at the same distance from the central station, receive the signal at the same time and can adjust their clocks accordingly.

But such a method of adjusting time is inadmissible if one, mindful of the relativity of all motion, shifts his viewpoint from the earth to the sun, and thus regards the earth in motion. For, according to the principle of constant velocity of light, it is clear that those stations that, seen from the central station, lie in the direction of the earth's motion, will receive the signal later than those lying in the opposite direction, for the former move away from the oncoming light waves and must be overtaken by them, while the latter move to meet the waves. This, according to the principle of constant velocity of light, makes it quite impossible to determine time absolutely, i.e., independently of the movement of the observers. The two principles cannot exist side by side. So far, in the conflict, the principle of constant velocity of light has decidedly had the upper hand, and it is very probable that no change will come about, in spite of many ideas recently promulgated.

The third of the above-mentioned propositions deals with the *continuity of all dynamical effects*, formerly an undisputed hypothesis of all physical theories, which was condensed in Aristotle's well-known dogma: *natura non facit saltus.*[1] But even in this stronghold, always respected from ancient times, modern research has made an appreciable breach. In this case, recent discoveries have shown that the proposition is not in agreement with the principles of thermodynamics, and, unless appearances are deceptive, the days of its validity are numbered. Nature certainly seems to move in jerks, indeed of a very definite kind. To illustrate this more clearly, may I present a straightforward comparison.

Let us consider a sheet of water in which strong winds have produced high waves. After the wind has completely died down, the waves will continue for an appreciable time and move from one shore to the other. But a certain characteristic change will take place. The energy of the big, long waves will be transformed, to an ever-increasing extent, into the energy of small short waves, particularly when beating against the shore or some other rigid obstacle. This process will continue until finally the waves have become so small, and the movements so fine, that they become quite invisible to the eye. This is the well-known transformation of visible motion into heat, molar into molecular movements, ordered movements into disorder; for in the case of ordered movement, many neighboring

---

1. [Nature does not make jumps.]

molecules have the same velocity, while in disorderly movements, any particular molecule has its own special velocity and direction.

The process described here does not go on indefinitely, but is limited, naturally, by the size of the atom. The movement of a single atom, considered by itself, is always orderly, since all the individual parts of an atom move with a common velocity. The bigger the atom, the less the dissipation of energy that can take place. So far everything is clear, and the classical theory fits in perfectly.

Now let us consider another, quite analogous phenomenon, dealing not with water waves but with rays of light and heat. We here assume that rays emitted by a bright body are condensed into a closed space by suitable reflection and are there scattered by reflection from the walls. Here, again, there is a gradual transformation of radiant energy of long waves into shorter ones, of ordered waves into disorderly ones; the big, long waves correspond to the infrared rays, the small, short ones to the ultraviolet rays of the spectrum. According to the classical theory, one would expect all the energy to be concentrated ultimately at the ultraviolet end of the spectrum. In other words, that the infrared and visible rays are gradually lost and transformed into invisible and chemically active ultraviolet rays.

No trace of such a phenomenon can be discovered in nature. The transformation sooner or later reaches quite a definite, determinative end, and then the radiation remains completely stable.

Different attempts have been made to bring this fact into line with classical theory, but hitherto these attempts have always shown that the contradiction struck too deeply at the roots of the theory to leave it undisturbed. Nothing remains but to reconsider once more the foundations of the theory. And it has been once more substantiated that the principles of thermodynamics are unshakable. For the only way found hitherto that appears to promise a complete solution of the riddle is to start with the two laws of thermodynamics. It joins these, however, with a new peculiar hypothesis, the significance of which in the two cases mentioned above can be described as follows.

In the water waves, the dissipation of kinetic energy comes to an end on account of the fact that the atom retains its energy in a certain way, such that each atom represents a certain finite quantum of matter that can only move as a whole. Similarly, although the light and heat radiation is of a nonmaterial nature, certain phenomena must occur, which imply that radiation energy is retained in certain finite quanta, and the shorter the wavelength, and the quicker the oscillations, the more energy is retained.

Nothing can as yet be said with certainty of the dynamical representation of such quanta. Perhaps one could imagine quanta occurring in this manner, viz., that any source of radiation can only emit energy after the energy has reached a certain value, as, for example, a rubber tube, into which air is gradually pumped, suddenly bursts and discharges its contents when a certain definite quantity of air has been pumped in.

In all cases, the quantum hypothesis has given rise to this idea that in nature, changes occur that are not continuous but of an explosive nature. I need only mention that this idea has been brought into prominence by the discovery of, and closer research into, radioactive phenomena. The difficulties connected with exact investigations are lessened, since the results obtained on the quantum hypotheses agree better with observation than do those deduced from all previous theories.

But, further, if it is advantageous for a new hypothesis that it proves itself useful in spheres for which it was not intended, the quantum hypothesis has a great deal in its favor. I will here just refer to one point that is particularly striking. When air, hydrogen, and helium were liquefied, a rich field of experimental research in low temperatures was opened and has already yielded a series of new and very remarkable results.

To raise the temperature of a piece of copper by one degree, from -250° to -249°, the quantity of heat required is not the same as that necessary to raise it from 0° to 1°, but is about thirty times less. The lower the initial temperature of the copper, the less is the heat necessary, without any assignable limits. This fact not only contradicts our accepted ideas, but also is diametrically opposed to the demands of the classical ideas. For though man had learnt, more than a hundred years ago, to differentiate between temperature and quantity of heat, the kinetic theory of matter led to the deduction that the two quantities, though not exactly proportional, moved more or less parallel to one another.

The quantum hypothesis has fully explained this difficulty and, at the same time, has given us another result of great importance, namely, that the forces produced in a body by heat vibrations are of exactly the same type as those set up in elastic vibrations. With the help of the quantum hypothesis, the heat energy at different temperatures of a body containing atoms of only one sort can be calculated quantitatively from a knowledge of its elastic properties—the classical theory was very far from accomplishing this. A large number of further questions arise from this, questions that at first sight seem very strange, such as, for example, whether the oscillations of a tuning fork are absolutely continuous, or whether they follow the nature of quanta. Indeed, in sound waves, the energy quanta are extremely small on account of the relatively small frequency of the waves; in the case of A440,[2] for example, they are of the order of three quadrillionths of work units in absolute mechanical units. The ordinary theory of elasticity would, therefore, need just as little alteration on account of this as it needs on account of the circumstance that it looks on matter as completely continuous, whereas, strictly speaking, matter is of an atomic, that is, of a quantum nature. But the revolutionary nature of the new development must be evident to everybody, and though the form of the dynamical quanta may for the present remain rather mysterious, the facts available today leave no doubt as to their existence in some form or other. For that which can be measured, exists.

Thus, in the light of modern research, the physical world picture begins to show an ever-increasing connection between its separate parts and at the same time a certain definite form: the refinement of the parts appeared to have been missing from the earlier, less detailed view and must have remained concealed. But the question can always be repeated afresh: How far does this progress fundamentally satisfy our desire for knowledge? By refining our world picture, do we attain a clearer understanding of nature itself? Let us now consider briefly these important questions. Not that I shall say anything essentially new about this matter, with its manifold aspects, but because, at present, opinions are so divided on some things, and because all who take a deep interest in the real aims of science must take one side or the other.

Thirty-five years ago, Hermann von Helmholtz reached the conclusion that our perceptions provide not a representation of the external world, but at most only an indication thereof. For we have no grounds on which to make any sort of comparison between the actualities of external effects and those of the perceptions provoked by them. All ideas we form of the outer world are ultimately only reflections of our own perceptions.

2. [The A above middle C.]

Can we logically set up against our self-consciousness a "nature" independent of it? Are not all so-called natural laws really nothing more or less than expedient rules with which we associate the run of our perceptions as exactly and conveniently as possible? If that were so, it would follow that not only ordinary common sense but also exact natural research have been fundamentally at fault from the beginning; for it is impossible to deny that the whole of the present-day development of physical knowledge works toward as far-reaching a separation as possible of the phenomena in external nature from those in human consciousness.

The way out of this awkward difficulty is very soon evident if one continues the argument a step further. Let us assume that a physical world picture has been discovered that satisfies all claims that can be made upon it and that, therefore, can represent completely all natural laws discovered empirically. Then it can in no way be proved that such a picture in any way represents "actual" nature. However, there is a converse to this, and far too little emphasis is usually laid on it. Exactly similarly, the still more daring assertion cannot be disproved, that the assumed picture represents quite accurately actual nature in all points without exception. For, to disprove this, one must be able to speak of actual nature with certainty, which is acknowledged to be impossible.

Here yawns an enormous vacuum into which no science can penetrate; and the filling up of this vacuum is the work, not of pure, but of practical reason. It is the work of a healthy view of the world.

However difficult it may be to prove scientifically such a view of the world, one can build so well on it that it will stand unperturbed by any assaults, so long as it is consistent with itself and in agreement with the observed facts. But one must not imagine that advance is possible, even in the most exact of all natural sciences, without some view of the world, i.e., quite without some hypotheses not capable of proof. The theorem holds also in physics, that one cannot be happy without belief, at least belief in some sort of reality outside us. This undoubting belief points the way to the progressing creative power, it alone provides the necessary point of support in the aimless groping; and only it can uplift the spirit wearied by failure and urge it onward to fresh efforts. A research worker who is not guided in his work by any hypothesis, however prudently and provisionally formed, renounces from the beginning a deep understanding of his own results. Whoever rejects the belief in the reality of the atom and the electron, or in the electromagnetic nature of light waves, or in the identity of heat and motion, can most certainly never be convinced by a logical or empirical contradiction. But he must be careful how, from his point of view, he makes any advance in physical knowledge.

Indeed, belief alone is not enough. It is shown in the history of every science how easily it can lead to mistakes and deteriorate into narrow-mindedness and fanaticism. To remain a trustworthy guide, it must be continually verified by logic and experience, and to this end the only ultimate aid is conscientious and often wearisome and self-denying effort. He is no scientist who is not at least competent and willing to do the lowliest work, if necessary, whether in the laboratory or in the library, in the open air or at the desk. It is in such severe surroundings that the view of the world is ripened and purified. The significance and meaning of such a process can only be realized by those who have experienced it personally.

Content Questions

1. According to Planck, what prompts the need to revise a physical theory? (238)

2. Why is it a complicated question to decide which part of a theory must be revised? (238)

3. What is the difference, according to Planck, between the physical principles that have survived the revision of theories and those theorems that have failed to survive? (239)

4. Which principle of physics came into conflict with factual evidence questioning the invariableness of the chemical atom, and how did this principle resolve the conflict? (239–240)

5. What is Planck's explanation for why there is "a certain contradiction in the conception of a variable atom"? (240)

6. According to Planck's example, how is the principle of the constant velocity of light incompatible with the proposition of the absolute independence of space and time? (240–241)

7. What is the meaning of the proposition that all dynamical effects are continuous? How is this proposition the same as Aristotle's teaching that "nature does not make jumps"? (241)

8. In the example given by Planck, how is the diminishment of the wave action naturally limited by the size of the atom? (241–242)

9. In the analogous example involving rays of light and heat, what is the expected transformation that is not observed? (242)

10. What is the "new peculiar hypothesis" that is joined to the two laws of thermodynamics in order to explain the observed behavior of light and heat in Planck's example? (242–243)

11. What reasons does Planck give for the success of the quantum hypothesis? (243–244)

12. If sound waves followed the nature of quanta, why would the existing theory of elastic vibrations need little alteration to account for the oscillations of a tuning fork? (243–244)

13. For Helmholtz, what relation do the laws of science have to the physical world? (244)

14. What is Planck's argument against the view that a world picture representing all known natural laws cannot be proven to actually represent nature? (245)

15. What essential belief does Planck think a scientist must hold in order to make progress? (245–246)

Discussion Questions

1. What does Planck mean in saying that facts that contradict accepted theories are the "particular work" of the true theorist? (238)

2. In the light of new facts that bring an existing theory into question, how should a scientist decide which parts of the theory need to be improved? (238)

3. Can the principles of physics—the principle of conservation of energy, the laws of thermodynamics, the principle of least action, and others—be tested and improved in the same way as the theories of physics? (238–239)

4. Should scientists continually make an effort to uncover and question the hidden assumptions of established theories or should they do so only when conflicting facts force them to notice and examine these assumptions? (239)

5. What does Planck mean when he says that each of the three untenable propositions—concerning atoms, space and time, and continuous effects—was once accepted as "so self-evident"? (239) Is there any place for self-evident propositions in science?

6. Does discarding the assumption of the continuity of dynamical effects in light of new facts immediately lead to the quantum hypothesis or is there some other work scientists must do to form this hypothesis? (241–243)

7. In Planck's wave example, is the increase in entropy—the transformation of ordered movements into disorder—a continuous dynamical process or one that requires the quantum hypothesis for its complete explanation? (241–242)

8. In the experiment Planck describes, how does the "definite, determinative end" of the transformation of longer infrared and visible rays into shorter ultraviolet rays preclude an explanation in line with classical theory? How does joining the

quantum hypothesis to the two laws of thermodynamics offer a solution to this problem? (242)

9. Is Planck justified in assuming that "light and heat radiation is of a nonmaterial nature," while proposing that light and heat are retained "in certain finite quanta," like the atom in his wave example? (242–243)

10. What does Planck mean by the "dynamical representation of such quanta"? Does he think that the quantum hypothesis is deficient in not having this feature? (243)

11. Why does Planck emphasize that energy quanta in sound waves are extremely small? How is this small scale related to the long-held assumption that dynamical effects in nature are continuous? (244)

12. How do the facts about dynamical quanta available to Planck support his statement: "For that which can be measured, exists"? (244) Is this statement generally true?

13. What does Planck mean when he says that physical science "works toward as far-reaching a separation as possible of the phenomena in external nature from those in human consciousness"? If a physical world picture completely represents "all natural laws discovered empirically," does it follow that it also represents an actual reality apart from human consciousness? (245)

14. Is Planck correct in his conviction that without "belief in some sort of reality outside us," happiness and creative progress in science are not possible? (245)

15. Can someone be a conscientious scientist and at the same time hold beliefs about the meaning of the physical world that are not verifiable by logic and experience? (248–249)

Suggestions for Further Reading

By the author

Planck, Max. *Eight Lectures on Theoretical Physics*. Translated by A. P. Wills. Mineola, NY: Dover Publications, 1998. In 1909, ten years after his announcement of the quantum hypothesis, Planck delivered this series of lectures, in which he showed how the new theory, along with the field of statistical mechanics, was transforming the theoretical foundations of science.

————. *A Survey of Physical Theory.* New York: Dover Publications, 1993. In this collection of essays, from which the selection in *What's the Matter?* is taken, Planck explores the new directions in physics that his quantum theory initiated and speculates on whether the science of the future can preserve a unified picture of the physical world.

About the author

Heilbron, J. L. *Dilemmas of an Upright Man: Max Planck and the Fortunes of German Science.* Cambridge, MA: Harvard University Press, 2000. This biography traces Planck's rise to prominence and his struggles to preserve his ideals of science and culture through tumultuous intellectual and political times, including two world wars and the Nazi domination of his country.

About the topic

Gamow, George. *Thirty Years That Shook Physics: The Story of Quantum Theory.* Reprint. New York: Dover Publications, 1985. This lively and often humorous story of the first decades of the quantum revolution was written by a physicist personally acquainted with many of the scientists whose work he explains.

Kuhn, Thomas S. *The Structure of Scientific Revolutions.* 3rd ed. Chicago: University of Chicago Press, 1996. This highly influential book, the source of the idea of a paradigm shift, discusses how scientists move from doubt to acceptance of new theories, stressing social and psychological factors as much as compelling experimental evidence.

McCormmach, Russell. *Night Thoughts of a Classical Physicist.* Cambridge, MA: Harvard University Press, 1982, 1991. In this deeply moving work of fiction, set during World War I, an elderly German physicist reflects on the scientific and cultural changes that have unsettled his orderly world and recalls the great scientists, including Maxwell and Planck, who have inspired him.

Creating a new theory is not like destroying an old barn and erecting a skyscraper in its place. It is rather like climbing a mountain, gaining new and wider views, discovering unexpected connections between our starting point and its rich environment. But the point from which we started out still exists and can be seen, although it appears smaller and forms a tiny part of our broad view gained by the mastery of the obstacles on our adventurous way up.

—Albert Einstein and Leopold Infeld,
The Evolution of Physics

ALBERT EINSTEIN

The Special Theory of Relativity

*

The General Theory of Relativity

When Albert Einstein (1879–1955) began his scientific work in about 1900, the great achievements in physics during the previous century, particularly in understanding electromagnetism and thermodynamics, had also raised difficult new theoretical questions. These questions led scientists to rethink the fundamental concepts underlying their explanations of the physical world. Einstein's work was central to the two most significant new developments that resulted: the theory of relativity (often segmented into the special and general theories) and quantum theory. These theories became the mainstream ideas of modern physics. While many scientists contributed to the development of quantum theory, the theory of relativity was largely Einstein's creation.

Einstein was born in Germany and studied physics in Switzerland, where he worked as a technical examiner in the patent office in Bern while completing his doctorate. This job allowed him time to pursue his own scientific interests, and in 1905, five of his papers were published in a prestigious physics journal. Within a few years, the innovative solutions these papers proposed to current scientific problems attracted the attention of many eminent physicists, leading, in 1914, to Einstein's appointment to membership in the Prussian Academy of Sciences and to a professorship at the University of Berlin.

Each of Einstein's 1905 papers laid the foundation for a new branch of modern physics. In two of the papers, he used the recently formulated statistical analysis of probabilities in thermodynamics to establish the atomic structure of matter. In a third, he provided an explanation of the photoelectric effect, introducing the radically new idea that light sometimes behaves as if it consists of particle-like energy packets, or quanta. This paper's importance to the development of quantum theory was cited when Einstein received the 1921 Nobel Prize in Physics.

In the other two 1905 papers, Einstein addressed problems arising from discoveries in electromagnetism and introduced the ideas underlying the theory of relativity. Physicists had hypothesized a pervasive medium called the ether, absolutely at rest in space and time, to provide a mechanical model for the transmission of electromagnetic radiation waves, including light. The ether was also considered the reference frame with respect to which light's velocity is constant. However, repeated experiments found no evidence of the ether's existence. Furthermore, as Einstein explains in the following selection on special relativity, giving light an absolute frame of reference leads to an apparent incompatibility between the principle of relativity—which states that the laws of physics are the same for all observers moving relatively to each other at constant speeds—and the constant speed of light.

Einstein resolved these problems by disregarding the undetectable ether and extending the principle of relativity to the laws of electromagnetism through a profound analysis and redefinition of the meaning of space, time, and mass in physics. The resulting special theory of relativity ("special" because it is limited to objects in relative motion at constant speeds) had consequences far beyond the particular problems in electromagnetism that Einstein was considering. Einstein's theory limits Newton's laws of mechanics—long accepted as universal—to only those physical events occurring at a small fraction of the speed of light. The theory also demonstrates that in physics, space and time are not independent of each other (reflected in the new term *space-time*) nor are they independent of the frames of reference in which they are measured, leading to results that defy common sense but are logically and experimentally sound. Most significantly, the special theory of relativity introduces a new understanding of the way physical laws express invariant relationships among the changing events in the natural world that scientists observe from different reference frames, applying different methods of investigation. Since Einstein's intention in the theory was not to promote the idea that "everything is relative," an equally appropriate name for it might be the theory of invariance.

Einstein spent the next ten years generalizing the special theory of relativity to show that physical laws remain invariant for all observers, regardless of whether their relative motions are uniform or accelerated. Once he realized that the effects of acceleration and gravitational fields are equivalent, he was able to develop the general theory of relativity as an explanation of gravity fundamentally different from Newton's. Using complex mathematics, including non-Euclidean geometry, Einstein explained gravity not as a force, but rather as the result of the curvature of space-time, which according to his theory of relativity is determined by the distribution of mass in the universe. In 1919, three years after the general theory was published, its startling prediction that starlight is curved when passing close to the sun's enormous mass was confirmed by observations. As a result of the publicity that followed, Einstein's fame grew, and he became a public figure.

The theory of relativity has been essential to research in physics as scientists investigate new domains in which phenomena approach the speed of light or gravitational fields are unusually intense. The theory also gave rise to numerous predictions—including the existence of black holes and the expansion of the universe—and has been indispensable to the development of modern cosmology in the last half of the twentieth century.

See also Einstein, pages 301–303 and 497–498.

The Special Theory of Relativity

In the preface to Relativity: The Special and the General Theory, *Einstein says that he will present the main ideas of the theory of relativity "in the sequence and connection in which they actually originated." In the following selection, Einstein presents a series of thought experiments and a theoretical analysis of the concepts of space and time, calling into question the definitions of these concepts in classical physics. His counterintuitive conclusions raise questions about how theoretical reasoning in physics can lead scientists to new knowledge about the physical world that they observe and measure.*

1

Space and Time in Classical Mechanics

The purpose of mechanics is to describe how bodies change their position in space with "time." I should load my conscience with grave sins against the sacred spirit of lucidity were I to formulate the aims of mechanics in this way, without serious reflection and detailed explanations. Let us proceed to disclose these sins.

It is not clear what is to be understood here by "position" and "space." I stand at the window of a railway carriage that is traveling uniformly, and drop a stone on the embankment, without throwing it. Then, disregarding the influence of the air resistance, I see the stone descend in a straight line. A pedestrian who observes the misdeed from the footpath notices that the stone falls to earth in a parabolic curve. I now ask: Do the "positions" traversed by the stone lie "in reality" on a straight line or on a parabola? Moreover, what is meant here by motion "in space"? . . . In the first place we entirely shun the vague word *space*, of which, we must honestly acknowledge, we cannot form the slightest conception, and we replace it

This selection is taken from Relativity: The Special and the General Theory.

with "motion relative to a practically rigid body of reference." . . . If instead of "body of reference" we insert "system of coordinates," which is a useful idea for mathematical description, we are in a position to say: the stone traverses a straight line relative to a system of coordinates rigidly attached to the carriage, but relative to a system of coordinates rigidly attached to the ground (embankment) it describes a parabola. With the aid of this example it is clearly seen that there is no such thing as an independently existing trajectory (literally, "path-curve"), but only a trajectory relative to a particular body of reference.

In order to have a *complete* description of the motion, we must specify how the body alters its position *with time*; i.e., for every point on the trajectory it must be stated at what time the body is situated there. These data must be supplemented by such a definition of time that, in virtue of this definition, these time-values can be regarded essentially as magnitudes (results of measurements) capable of observation. If we take our stand on the ground of classical mechanics, we can satisfy this requirement for our illustration in the following manner. We imagine two clocks of identical construction; the man at the railway-carriage window is holding one of them, and the man on the footpath the other. Each of the observers determines the position on his own reference-body occupied by the stone at each tick of the clock he is holding in his hand. In this connection we have not taken account of the inaccuracy involved by the finiteness of the velocity of propagation of light. With this and with a second difficulty prevailing here we shall have to deal in detail later.

2

The Galilean System of Coordinates

As is well known, the fundamental law of the mechanics of Galilei-Newton, which is known as the law of inertia, can be stated thus: a body removed sufficiently far from other bodies continues in a state of rest or of uniform motion in a straight line. This law not only says something about the motion of the bodies, but it also indicates the reference-bodies or systems of coordinates, permissible in mechanics, which can be used in mechanical description. The visible fixed stars are bodies for which the law of inertia certainly holds to a high degree of approximation. Now if we use a system of coordinates that is rigidly attached to the earth, then, relative to this system, every fixed star describes a circle of immense radius in the course of an astronomical day, a result that is opposed to the statement of the law of inertia. So that if we adhere to this law we must refer these motions only to systems of coordinates relative to which the fixed stars do not move in a circle. A system of coordinates of which the state of motion is such that the law of inertia holds relative to it is called a Galilean system of coordinates. The laws of the mechanics of Galilei-Newton can be regarded as valid only for a Galilean system of coordinates.

3

The Principle of Relativity (in the Restricted Sense)

In order to attain the greatest possible clearness, let us return to our example of the railway carriage supposed to be traveling uniformly. We call its motion a uniform translation ("uniform" because it is of constant velocity and direction, "translation" because although the carriage changes its position relative to the embankment yet it does not rotate in so doing). Let us imagine a raven flying through the air in such a manner that its motion, as observed from the embankment, is uniform and in a straight line. If we were to observe the flying raven from the moving railway carriage, we should find that the motion of the raven would be one of different velocity and direction, but that it would still be uniform and in a straight line. Expressed in an abstract manner we may say: if a mass m is moving uniformly in a straight line with respect to a coordinate system K, then it will also be moving uniformly and in a straight line relative to a second coordinate system K', provided that the latter is executing a uniform translatory motion with respect to K. In accordance with the discussion contained in the preceding section, it follows that:

If K is a Galilean coordinate system, then every other coordinate system K' is a Galilean one, when, in relation to K, it is in a condition of uniform motion of translation. Relative to K' the mechanical laws of Galilei-Newton hold good exactly as they do with respect to K.

We advance a step farther in our generalization when we express the tenet thus: if, relative to K, K' is a uniformly moving coordinate system devoid of rotation, then natural phenomena run their course with respect to K' according to exactly the same general laws as with respect to K. This statement is called the principle of relativity (in the restricted sense).

As long as one was convinced that all natural phenomena were capable of representation with the help of classical mechanics, there was no need to doubt the validity of this principle of relativity. But in view of the more recent development of electrodynamics and optics, it became more and more evident that classical mechanics affords an insufficient foundation for the physical description of all natural phenomena. At this juncture the question of the validity of the principle of relativity became ripe for discussion, and it did not appear impossible that the answer to this question might be in the negative.

Nevertheless, there are two general facts that at the outset speak very much in favor of the validity of the principle of relativity. Even though classical mechanics does not supply us with a sufficiently broad basis for the theoretical presentation of all physical phenomena, still we must grant it a considerable measure of "truth," since it supplies us with the actual motions of the heavenly bodies with a delicacy of detail little short of wonderful. The principle of relativity must therefore apply with great accuracy in the domain of mechanics. But that a principle of such broad generality should hold with such exactness in one domain of phenomena, and yet should be invalid for another, is a priori not very probable.

We now proceed to the second argument, to which, moreover, we shall return later. If the principle of relativity (in the restricted sense) does not hold, then the Galilean coordinate systems K, K', K'', etc., which are moving uniformly relative to each other, will not be *equivalent* for the description of natural phenomena. In this case we should be constrained to believe that natural laws are capable of being formulated in a particularly simple manner, and of course only on condition that, from among all possible Galilean coordinate systems, we should have chosen *one* (K_0) of a particular state of motion as our body of reference. We should then be justified (because of its merits for the description of natural phenomena) in calling this system "absolutely at rest," and all other Galilean systems K "in motion." If, for instance, our embankment were the system K_0, then our railway carriage would be a system K, relative to which less simple laws would hold than with respect to K_0. This diminished simplicity would be due to the fact that the carriage K would be in motion (i.e., "really") with respect to K_0. In the general laws of nature that have been formulated with reference to K, the magnitude and direction of the velocity of the carriage would necessarily play a part. We should expect, for instance, that the note emitted by an organ pipe placed with its axis parallel to the direction of travel would be different from that emitted if the axis of the pipe were placed perpendicular to this direction. Now in virtue of its motion in an orbit round the sun, our earth is comparable with a railway carriage traveling with a velocity of about 30 kilometers per second. If the principle of relativity were not valid, we should therefore expect that the direction of motion of the earth at any moment would enter into the laws of nature, and also that physical systems in their behavior would be dependent on the orientation in space with respect to the earth. For owing to the alteration in direction of the velocity of revolution of the earth in the course of a year, the earth cannot be at rest relative to the hypothetical system K_0 throughout the whole year. However, the most careful observations have never revealed such anisotropic properties in terrestrial physical space, i.e., a physical nonequivalence of different directions. This is very powerful argument in favor of the principle of relativity.

4

The Theorem of the Addition of Velocities Employed in Classical Mechanics

Let us suppose our old friend the railway carriage to be traveling along the rails with a constant velocity v, and that a man traverses the length of the carriage in the direction of travel with a velocity w. How quickly or, in other words, with what velocity W does the man advance relative to the embankment during the process? The only possible answer seems to result from the following consideration: If the man were to stand still for a second, he would advance relative to the embankment through a distance v equal numerically to the velocity of the carriage. As a consequence of his walking, however, he traverses an additional distance w relative to the carriage, and hence also relative to the embankment, in this second, the distance *w* being numerically equal to the velocity with which he is walking. Thus in total he covers the distance $W = v + w$ relative to the embankment in the second considered. We shall see later that this result, which expresses the theorem of the addition of velocities employed in classical mechanics, cannot be maintained; in other words, the law that we have just written down does not hold in reality. For the time being, however, we shall assume its correctness.

5

The Apparent Incompatibility of the Law of Propagation of Light with the Principle of Relativity

There is hardly a simpler law in physics than that according to which light is propagated in empty space. Every child at school knows, or believes he knows, that this propagation takes place in straight lines with a velocity $c = 186,000$ mi./sec. . . . Based on observations of double stars, the Dutch astronomer De Sitter was also able to show that the velocity of the propagation of light cannot depend on the velocity of motion of the body emitting the light. The assumption that this velocity of propagation is dependent on the direction "in space" is in itself improbable.

In short, let us assume that the simple law of the constancy of the velocity of light *c* (in vacuum) is justifiably believed by the child at school. Who would imagine that this simple law has plunged the conscientiously thoughtful physicist into the greatest intellectual difficulties? Let us consider how these difficulties arise.

Of course we must refer the process of the propagation of light (and indeed every other process) to a rigid reference-body (coordinate system). As such a system let us again choose our embankment. We shall imagine the air above it to have been removed. If a ray of light be sent along the embankment, we see from the above that the tip of the ray will be transmitted with the velocity *c* relative to the embankment. Now let us suppose that our railway carriage is again traveling along the railway lines with the velocity *v*, and that its direction is the same as that of the ray of light, but its velocity of course much less. Let us inquire about the velocity of propagation of the ray of light relative to the carriage. It is obvious that we can here apply the consideration of the previous section, since the ray of light plays the part of the man walking along relatively to the carriage. The velocity W of the man relative to the embankment is here replaced by the velocity of light relative to the embankment. w is the required velocity of light with respect to the carriage, and we have

$$w = c - v.$$

The velocity of propagation of a ray of light relative to the carriage thus comes out smaller than c.

But this result comes into conflict with the principle of relativity set forth in section 3. For, like every other general law of nature, the law of the transmission of light in vacuo must, according to the principle of relativity, be the same for the railway carriage as reference-body as when the rails are the body of reference. But, from our above consideration, this would appear to be impossible. If every ray of light is propagated relative to the embankment with the velocity c, then for this reason it would appear that another law of propagation of light must necessarily hold with respect to the carriage—a result contradictory to the principle of relativity.

In view of this dilemma there appears to be nothing else for it than to abandon either the principle of relativity or the simple law of the propagation of light in vacuo. Those of you who have carefully followed the preceding discussion are almost sure to expect that we should retain the principle of relativity, which appeals so convincingly to the intellect because it is so natural and simple. The law of the propagation of light in vacuo would then have to be replaced by a more complicated law conformable to the principle of relativity. The development of theoretical physics shows, however, that we cannot pursue this course. The epoch-making theoretical investigations of H. A. Lorentz on the electrodynamical and optical phenomena connected with moving bodies show that experience in this domain leads conclusively to a theory of electromagnetic phenomena, of which the law of the constancy of the velocity of light in vacuo is a necessary consequence. Prominent theoretical physicists were therefore more inclined to reject the principle of relativity, in spite of the fact that no empirical data had been found that were contradictory to this principle.

At this juncture the theory of relativity entered the arena. As a result of an analysis of the physical conceptions of time and space, it became evident that *in reality there is not the least incompatibility between the principle of relativity and the law of propagation of light,* and that by systematically holding fast to both these laws a logically rigid theory could be arrived at. This theory has been called the *special theory of relativity* to distinguish it from the extended theory. In the following pages we shall present the fundamental ideas of the special theory of relativity.

6

On the Idea of Time in Physics

Lightning has struck the rails on our railway embankment at two places, *A* and *B*, far distant from each other. I make the additional assertion that these two lightning flashes occurred simultaneously. If I ask you whether there is sense in this statement, you will answer my question with a decided yes. But if I now approach you with the request to explain to me the sense of the statement more precisely, you find after some consideration that the answer to this question is not so easy as it appears at first sight.

After some time perhaps the following answer would occur to you: "The significance of the statement is clear in itself and needs no further explanation; of course it would require some consideration if I were to be commissioned to determine by observations whether in the actual case the two events took place simultaneously or not." I cannot be satisfied with this answer for the following reason. Supposing that as a result of ingenious considerations an able meteorologist were to discover that the lightning must always strike the places *A* and *B* simultaneously, then we should be faced with the task of testing whether or not this theoretical result is in accordance with the reality. We encounter the same difficulty with all physical statements in which the conception "simultaneous" plays a part. The concept does not exist for the physicist until he has the possibility of discovering whether or not it is fulfilled in an actual case. We thus require a definition of simultaneity such that this definition supplies us with the method by means of which, in the present case, he can decide by experiment whether or not both the lightning strokes occurred simultaneously. As long as this requirement is not satisfied, I allow myself to be deceived as a physicist (and of course the same applies if I am not a physicist), when I imagine that I am able to attach a meaning to the statement of simultaneity. (I would ask the reader not to proceed further until he is fully convinced on this point.)

After thinking the matter over for some time you then offer the following suggestion with which to test simultaneity. By measuring along the rails, the connecting line *AB* should be measured up and an observer placed at the midpoint *M* of the distance *AB*. This observer should be supplied with an arrangement (e.g., two mirrors inclined at 90°) that allows him visually to observe both places *A* and *B* at the same time. If the observer perceives the two flashes of lightning at the same time, then they are simultaneous.

I am very pleased with this suggestion, but for all that I cannot regard the matter as quite settled, because I feel constrained to raise the following objection: "Your definition would certainly be right, if only I knew that the light by means of which the observer at *M* perceives the lightning flashes travels along the length $A \rightarrow M$ with the same velocity as along the length $B \rightarrow M$. But an examination of this supposition would only be possible if we already had at our disposal the means of measuring time. It would thus appear as though we were moving here in a logical circle."

After further consideration you cast a somewhat disdainful glance at me—and rightly so—and you declare: "I maintain my previous definition nevertheless, because in reality it assumes absolutely nothing about light. There is only *one* demand to be made of the definition of simultaneity, namely, that in every real case it must supply us with an empirical decision as to whether or not the conception that has to be defined is fulfilled. That my definition satisfies this demand is indisputable. That light requires the same time to traverse the path $A \rightarrow M$ as for the path $B \rightarrow M$ is in reality neither a *supposition nor a hypothesis* about the physical nature of light, but a *stipulation* that I can make of my own free will in order to arrive at a definition of simultaneity."

It is clear that this definition can be used to give an exact meaning not only to *two* events, but to as many events as we care to choose, and independently of the positions of the scenes of the events with respect to the body of reference (here the railway embankment). We are thus led also to a definition of *time* in physics. For this purpose we suppose that clocks of identical construction are placed at the points *A*, *B*, and *C* of the railway line (coordinate system), and that they are set in such a manner that the positions of their pointers are simultaneously (in the above sense) the same. Under these conditions we understand by the "time" of an event the reading (position of the hands) of that one of these clocks which is in the immediate vicinity (in space) of the event. In this manner a time-value is associated with every event that is essentially capable of observation.

This stipulation contains a further physical hypothesis, the validity of which will hardly be doubted without empirical evidence to the contrary. It has been assumed that all these clocks go *at the same rate* if they are of identical construction. Stated more exactly: when two clocks arranged at rest in different places of a reference-body are set in such a manner that a *particular* position of the pointers of the one clock is *simultaneous* (in the above sense) with the *same* position of the pointers of the other clock, then identical "settings" are always simultaneous (in the sense of the above definition).

7

The Relativity of Simultaneity

Up to now our considerations have been referred to a particular body of reference, which we have styled a "railway embankment." We suppose a very long train traveling along the rails with the constant velocity v and in the direction indicated in figure 1. People traveling in this train will with advantage use the train as a rigid reference-body (coordinate system); they regard all events in reference to the train. Then every event that takes

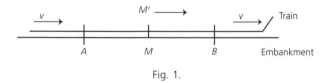

Fig. 1.

place along the line also takes place at a particular point of the train. Also the definition of simultaneity can be given relative to the train in exactly the same way as with respect to the embankment. As a natural conse-quence, however, the following question arises: Are two events (e.g., the two strokes of lightning A and B) that are simultaneous *with reference to the railway embankment* also simultaneous *relatively to the train?* We shall show directly that the answer must be in the negative.

When we say that the lightning strokes A and B are simultaneous with respect to the embankment, we mean that the rays of light emitted at the places A and B, where the lightning occurs, meet each other at the midpoint M of the length $A \rightarrow B$ of the embankment. But the events A and B also correspond to positions A and B on the train. Let M' be the midpoint of the distance $A \rightarrow B$ on the traveling train. Just when the flashes[1] of lightning occur, this point M' naturally coincides with the point M, but it moves toward the right in the diagram with the velocity v of the train. If an observer sitting in the position M' in the train did not possess this velocity, then he would remain permanently at M, and the light rays emitted by the flashes of lightning A and B would reach him simultaneously, i.e., they would meet just where he is situated. Now in reality (considered with reference to the railway embankment) he is hastening toward the beam of light coming from B, while he is riding on ahead of the beam of light coming from A. Hence the observer will see the beam of light emitted from B earlier than he will see that emitted from A. Observers who take the railway train as their reference-body must therefore come to the conclusion that the lightning flash B took place earlier than the lightning flash A. We thus arrive at the important result:

Events that are simultaneous with reference to the embankment are not simultaneous with respect to the train, and vice versa (relativity of simultaneity). Every reference-body (coordinate system) has its own particular time; unless we are told the reference-body to which the statement of time refers, there is no meaning in a statement of the time of an event.

Now before the advent of the theory of relativity it had always tacitly been assumed in physics that the statement of time had an absolute significance, i.e., that it is independent of the state of motion of the body of reference. But we have just seen that this assumption is incompatible with the most natural definition of simultaneity; if we discard this assumption, then the conflict between the law of the propagation of light in vacuo and the principle of relativity (developed in section 5) disappears.

---

1. As judged from the embankment.

We were led to that conflict by the considerations of section 4, which are now no longer tenable. In that section we concluded that the man in the carriage, who traverses the distance *w per second* relative to the carriage, traverses the same distance also with respect to the embankment *in each second* of time. But, according to the foregoing considerations, the time required by a particular occurrence with respect to the carriage must not be considered equal to the duration of the same occurrence as judged from the embankment (as reference-body). Hence it cannot be contended that the man in walking travels the distance *w* relative to the railway line in a time that is equal to one second as judged from the embankment.

Moreover, the considerations of section 4 are based on yet a second assumption, which, in the light of a strict consideration, appears to be arbitrary, although it was always tacitly made even before the introduction of the theory of relativity.

8

On the Relativity of the Conception of Distance

Let us consider two particular points on the train traveling along the embankment with the velocity *v*, and inquire as to their distance apart. We already know that it is necessary to have a body of reference for the measurement of a distance, with respect to which body the distance can be measured up. It is the simplest plan to use the train itself as reference-body (coordinate system). An observer in the train measures the interval by marking off his measuring rod in a straight line (e.g., along the floor of the carriage) as many times as is necessary to take him from the one marked point to the other. Then the number that tells us how often the rod has to be laid down is the required distance.

It is a different matter when the distance has to be judged from the railway line. Here the following method suggests itself. If we call *A'* and *B'* the two points on the train whose distance apart is required, then both of these points are moving with the velocity *v* along the embankment. In the first place we require to determine the points *A* and *B* of the embankment that are just being passed by the two points *A'* and *B'* at a particular time *t*— judged from the embankment. These points *A* and *B* of the embankment can be determined by applying the definition of time given in section 6. The distance between these points A and B is then measured by repeated application of the measuring rod along the embankment.

A priori it is by no means certain that this last measurement will supply us with the same result as the first. Thus the length of the train as measured from the embankment may be different from that obtained by measuring in the train itself. This circumstance leads us to a second objection that must be raised against the apparently obvious consideration of section 4. Namely, if the man in the carriage covers the distance w in a unit of time—*measured from the train*—then this distance—*as measured from the embankment*—is not necessarily also equal to w.

9

The Lorentz Transformation

The results of the last three sections show that the apparent incompatibility of the law of propagation of light with the principle of relativity (section 5) has been derived by means of a consideration that borrowed two unjustifiable hypotheses from classical mechanics; these are as follows:

(1) The time-interval (time) between two events is independent of the condition of motion of the body of reference.

(2) The space-interval (distance) between two points of a rigid body is independent of the condition of motion of the body of reference.

If we drop these hypotheses, then the dilemma of section 5 disappears, because the theorem of the addition of velocities derived in section 4 becomes invalid. The possibility presents itself that the law of the propagation of light in vacuo may be compatible with the principle of relativity, and the question arises: How have we to modify the considerations of section 4 in order to remove the apparent disagreement between these two fundamental results of experience? This question leads to a general one. In the discussion of section 4 we have to do with places and times relative both to the train and to the embankment. How are we to find the place and time of an event in relation to the train, when we know the place and time of the event with respect to the railway embankment? Is there a thinkable answer to this question of such a nature that the law of transmission of light in vacuo does not contradict the principle of relativity? In other words, can we conceive of a relation between place and time of the individual events relative to both reference-bodies, such that every ray of light possesses the velocity of transmission c relative to the embankment and relative to the train? This question leads to a quite definite positive answer, and to a perfectly definite transformation law for the space-time magnitudes of an event when changing over from one body of reference to another.

Before we deal with this, we shall introduce the following incidental consideration. Up to the present we have only considered events taking place along the embankment, which had mathematically to assume the function of a straight line. We can imagine this reference-body supplemented laterally and in a vertical direction by means of a framework of rods, so that an event that takes place anywhere can be localized with reference to this framework. Similarly, we can imagine the train traveling with the velocity v to be continued across the whole of space, so that every event, no matter how far off it may be, could also be localized with respect to the second framework. Without committing any fundamental error, we can disregard the fact that in reality these frameworks would continually interfere with each other, owing to the impenetrability of solid bodies. In every such framework, we imagine three surfaces perpendicular to each other marked out and designated as "coordinate planes" ("coordinate system"). A coordinate system K then corresponds to the embankment, and a coordinate system K' to the train. An event, wherever it may have taken place, would be fixed in space with respect to K by the three perpendiculars x, y, z on the coordinate planes, and with regard to time by a time-value t. Relative to K', *the same event* would be fixed in respect of space and time by corresponding values x', y', z', t', which of course are not identical with x, y, z, t. These magnitudes are to be regarded as results of physical measurements.

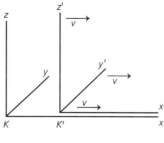

Fig. 2.

Obviously our problem can be exactly formulated in the following manner. What are the values x', y', z', t' of an event with respect to K', when the magnitudes x, y, z, t of the same event with respect to K are given? The relations must be so chosen that the law of the transmission of light in vacuo is satisfied for one and the same ray of light (and of course for every ray) with respect to K and K'. For the relative orientation in space of the coordinate systems indicated in the diagram (fig. 2), this problem is solved by means of the equations:

$$x' = \frac{x - vt}{\sqrt{1 - \frac{v^2}{c^2}}}$$

$$y' = y$$
$$z' = z$$

$$t' = \frac{t - \frac{v}{c^2} \cdot x}{\sqrt{1 - \frac{v^2}{c^2}}}$$

This system of equations is known as the Lorentz transformation.[2]

2. [Simple derivations of the Lorentz transformation can be found in many books on physics.]

If in place of the law of transmission of light we had taken as our basis the tacit assumptions of the older mechanics as to the absolute character of times and lengths, then instead of the above we should have obtained the following equations:

$$x' = x - vt$$
$$y' = y$$
$$z' = z$$
$$t' = t.$$

This system of equations is often termed the Galilei transformation. The Galilei transformation can be obtained from the Lorentz transformation by substituting an infinitely large value for the velocity of light c in the latter transformation.

Aided by the following illustration, we can readily see that, in accordance with the Lorentz transformation, the law of the transmission of light in vacuo is satisfied both for the reference-body K and for the reference-body K'. A light-signal is sent along the positive x-axis, and this light-stimulus advances in accordance with the equation

$$x = ct,$$

i.e., with the velocity c. According to the equations of the Lorentz transformation, this simple relation between x and t involves a relation between x' and t'. In point of fact, if we substitute for x the value ct in the first and fourth equations of the Lorentz transformation, we obtain:

$$x' = \frac{(c - v)t}{\sqrt{1 - \frac{v^2}{c^2}}}$$

$$t' = \frac{\left(1 - \frac{v}{c}\right)t}{\sqrt{1 - \frac{v^2}{c^2}}}$$

from which, by division, the expression

$$x' = ct'$$

immediately follows. If referred to the system K', the propagation of light takes place according to this equation. We thus see that the velocity of transmission relative to the reference-body K' is also equal to c. The same result is obtained for rays of light advancing in any other direction whatsoever. Of course this is not surprising, since the equations of the Lorentz transformation were derived conformably to this point of view.

10

The Behavior of Measuring Rods and Clocks in Motion

I place a meter-rod in the x'-axis of K' in such a manner that one end (the beginning) coincides with the point $x' = 0$, while the other end (the end of the rod) coincides with the point $x' = 1$. What is the length of the meter-rod relatively to the system K? In order to learn this, we need only ask where the beginning of the rod and the end of the rod lie with respect to K at a particular time t of the system K. By means of the first equation of the Lorentz transformation the values of these two points at the time $t = 0$ can be shown to be

$$x_{(\text{beginning of rod})} = 0 \sqrt{1 - \frac{v^2}{c^2}}$$

$$x_{(\text{end of rod})} = 1 \sqrt{1 - \frac{v^2}{c^2}},$$

the distance between the points being $\sqrt{1 - \frac{v^2}{c^2}}$. But the meter-rod is moving with the velocity v relative to K. It therefore follows that the length of a rigid meter-rod moving in the direction of its length with a velocity v is $\sqrt{1 - v^2/c^2}$ of a meter. The rigid rod is thus shorter when in motion than when at rest, and the more quickly it is moving, the shorter is the rod. For the velocity $v = c$ we should have $\sqrt{1 - v^2/c^2} = 0$, and for still greater velocities the square root becomes imaginary.[3] From this we conclude that in the theory of relativity the velocity c plays the part of a limiting velocity, which can neither be reached nor exceeded by any real body.

---

3. [In mathematics, the square root of a negative number is known as an imaginary number.]

Of course this feature of the velocity c as a limiting velocity also clearly follows from the equations of the Lorentz transformation, for these become meaningless if we choose values of v greater than c.

If, on the contrary, we had considered a meter-rod at rest in the x-axis with respect to K, then we should have found that the length of the rod as judged from K' would have been $\sqrt{1 - v^2/c^2}$; this is quite in accordance with the principle of relativity that forms the basis of our considerations.

A priori it is quite clear that we must be able to learn something about the physical behavior of measuring rods and clocks from the equations of transformation, for the magnitudes x, y, z, t are nothing more nor less than the results of measurements obtainable by means of measuring rods and clocks. If we had based our considerations on the Galilean transformation, we should not have obtained a contraction of the rod as a consequence of its motion.

Let us now consider a seconds-clock that is permanently situated at the origin $(x'=0)$ of K'. $t'= 0$ and $t'=1$ are two successive ticks of this clock. The first and fourth equations of the Lorentz transformation give for these two ticks:

$$t = 0$$

and

$$t = \frac{1}{\sqrt{1 - \frac{v^2}{c^2}}}$$

As judged from K, the clock is moving with the velocity v; as judged from this reference-body, the time that elapses between two strokes of the clock is not one second, but $\frac{1}{\sqrt{1 - \frac{v^2}{c^2}}}$ seconds, i.e., a somewhat larger time. As a consequence of its motion, the clock goes more slowly than when at rest. Here also the velocity c plays the part of an unattainable limiting velocity.

11

The Heuristic Value of the Theory of Relativity

Our train of thought in the foregoing pages can be epitomized in the following manner. Experience has led to the conviction that, on the one hand, the principle of relativity holds true and that on the other hand the velocity of transmission of light in vacuo has to be considered equal to a constant c. By uniting these two postulates, we obtained the law of transformation for the rectangular coordinates x, y, z and the time t of the events that constitute the processes of nature. In this connection we did not obtain the Galilei transformation, but, differing from classical mechanics, the *Lorentz transformation*.

The law of transmission of light, the acceptance of which is justified by our actual knowledge, played an important part in this process of thought. Once in possession of the Lorentz transformation, however, we can combine this with the principle of relativity and sum up the theory thus:

Every general law of nature must be so constituted that it is transformed into a law of exactly the same form when, instead of the space-time variables x, y, z, t of the original coordinate system K, we introduce new space-time variables x', y', z', t' of a coordinate system K'. In this connection the relation between the ordinary and the accented magnitudes is given by the Lorentz transformation. Or, in brief: general laws of nature are covariant with respect to Lorentz transformations.

This is a definite mathematical condition that the theory of relativity demands of a natural law, and in virtue of this, the theory becomes a valuable heuristic aid in the search for general laws of nature. If a general law of nature were to be found that did not satisfy this condition, then at least one of the two fundamental assumptions of the theory would have been disproved.

Content Questions

1. How does Einstein answer his own question about whether the positions of the falling stone "lie 'in reality' on a straight line or on a parabola"? (257–258)

2. What does Einstein mean by the "time-values" of the positions of the falling stone on its trajectory? What requirement does he say must be satisfied for the observers on the embankment and the train to be able to determine these time-values? (258)

3. How does the law of inertia indicate the systems of coordinates that are "permissible in mechanics"? Why does Einstein say that a system of coordinates rigidly attached to the earth is not Galilean? (258–259)

4. According to the principle of relativity, what behavior would scientists observe in natural phenomena in different coordinate systems moving uniformly in a straight line with respect to one another? (260)

5. If the principle of relativity did not hold, why would Galilean coordinate systems not be equivalent? (260–261)

6. Why is the invariance of the laws of nature observed on earth at different times of year a "very powerful argument in favor of the principle of relativity"? (261)

7. How can Einstein's equation for the addition of velocities, $W = v + w$, be rewritten to show the velocity of the walking man relative to the railway carriage? (262)

8. According to Einstein, what is the basis for the law governing light's propagation? What does it mean to say that "the velocity of the propagation of light cannot depend on the velocity of motion of the body emitting the light"? (262)

9. In Einstein's thought experiment, how does substituting the ray of light for the walking man lead to a result that "comes into conflict with the principle of relativity"? (263) If this result were valid, how would the law of light's propagation have to be revised?

10. What dilemma does the special theory of relativity solve? (263–264)

11. According to Einstein, what is necessary in order for a physicist to be able to attach meaning to a statement of simultaneity? (264–265)

12. What answer is given to Einstein's objection that the proposed definition of simultaneity makes assumptions about the physical nature of light? (265)

13. What is Einstein's definition of simultaneity? How does this definition lead to a definition of time in physics? (265–266)

14. Why does Einstein's definition of simultaneity require the observer on the train to conclude that "the lightning flash *B* took place earlier than the lightning flash *A*"? (266–267)

15. Why does Einstein's thought experiment about the lightning flashes lead to the conclusion that "every reference-body (coordinate system) has its own particular time"? (267)

16. What assumptions about time are "no longer tenable" in light of the recognition of the relativity of simultaneity? How do those assumptions lead to the apparent conflict between the law of light's propagation and the principle of relativity? (268)

17. Why does Einstein stipulate that, in order to judge the distance between points *A'* and *B'* relative to the embankment, we must first determine points *A* and *B* of the embankment "at a particular time"? How does "applying the definition of time given in section 6" allow us to determine points *A* and *B*? (268–269)

18. Why does Einstein conclude that "it is by no means certain" that the measurement of the length of the train from the embankment will give the same result as "that obtained by measuring in the train itself"? (269)

19. What assumptions about the measurement of distance in the thought experiment in section 4 no longer hold in light of the relativity of distance? (269)

20. Why is the theorem of the addition of velocities invalidated by dropping the hypotheses that time- and space-intervals are independent of the motion of the body of reference? How does this result make the dilemma in section 5 disappear? (269)

21. What does Einstein mean by "a perfectly definite transformation law for the space-time magnitudes of an event"? (270)

22. For the coordinate systems *K*, corresponding to the embankment, and *K'*, corresponding to the train, why do the Lorentz equations show that $y' = y$ and $z' = z$? (271)

23. What does the system of equations known as the Lorentz transformation allow us to know about the same event relative to different coordinate systems? Why does the factor c appear in these equations and not in the Galilei transformation equations? (271–272)

24. What happens to the size of the fractions $\frac{v^2}{c^2}$ and $\frac{v}{c^2}$ in the Lorentz equations if larger and larger values are substituted for c? Why does substituting an "infinitely large value" for c change the Lorentz equations into the Galilei equations? (271–272)

25. What does the fact that $c = \frac{x}{t} = \frac{x'}{t'}$ demonstrate about the Lorentz transformation equations? (272)

26. What happens to the size of the fraction $\frac{v^2}{c^2}$ as the value of v increases? Why does the length of the rod, as measured relative to system K, approach zero as the value of v approaches c? (273–274)

27. Why does Einstein say that finding the length of the rod to be the same whether judged from system K or K' "is quite in accordance with the principle of relativity that forms the basis of our considerations"? (274)

28. What does the mathematical expression for the time that elapses between two strokes of a moving clock reveal about the length of a second, as judged from K, when the value of v approaches c? (274)

29. How does the factor $\sqrt{1 - \frac{v^2}{c^2}}$ show why the shortening of measuring rods and the slowing of clocks in motion, as described by the theory of relativity, are not ordinarily noticed? Why didn't the Galilei transformation describe the same effects? (273–274)

30. What does Einstein mean when he says that "general laws of nature are covariant with respect to Lorentz transformations"? (275)

Discussion Questions

1. What does Einstein mean by "the sacred spirit of lucidity," which he says he would sin against if he did not seriously reflect on the definitions of key concepts in mechanics? (257)

2. Why does Einstein think that "we cannot form the slightest conception" of the word *space*? What justifies his replacement of space with the idea of "motion relative to a practically rigid body of reference"? (257–258)

3. Can the principle of relativity be scientifically proven, or do physicists postulate it in order to formulate general laws of nature? (260–261)

4. What does Einstein mean when he says that the principle of relativity is "natural and simple"? (263)

5. What is the difference between the *principle* of relativity and Einstein's *theory* of relativity? (263–264)

6. In speaking of the idea of simultaneity, what does Einstein mean when he says that "the concept does not exist for the physicist until he has the possibility of discovering whether or not it is fulfilled in an actual case"? Why does Einstein ask the reader "not to proceed further until he is fully convinced on this point"? (264–265)

7. How can one arrive at Einstein's definition of simultaneity by stipulating, as a matter of "free will," that light requires the same time to traverse the two paths to the observer's position? Why does Einstein say that this stipulation is "neither a *supposition nor a hypothesis* about the physical nature of light"? (265)

8. Why does Einstein base his definition of time on a physical hypothesis about the way that clocks operate? (265–266) In physics, can the definition of time be separated from the definition of how time is measured?

9. What allows Einstein to discard the assumption that time has "an absolute significance, i.e., that it is independent of the state of motion of the body of reference"? (267) How do scientists determine when it is legitimate to discard previously accepted fundamental assumptions about the nature of the physical world?

10. What does Einstein mean by an "event" in physics? What does it mean to refer to the same event relative to different coordinate systems? (269–271)

11. According to the theory of relativity, why is it that "c plays the part of a limiting velocity"? (273)

12. How is it possible to "learn something about the physical behavior of measuring rods and clocks from the equations of transformation"? (274) In physics, how can the theoretical knowledge provided by mathematics be as certain as the knowledge derived from observations and experiments?

13. What does it mean to say that a general law of nature retains the same form when transformed according to the Lorentz equations? (275)

14. According to Einstein, how can the theory of relativity be "a valuable heuristic aid in the search for general laws of nature"? Does the discovery of new general laws of nature that conform to the "definite mathematical condition" of covariance with respect to Lorentz transformations prove that the theory of relativity is true? (275)

15. Are the relativity of time and the relativity of distance statements about the physical world itself, or about how the physical world is measured? How does Einstein think that physics should regard this distinction?

Suggestions for Further Reading

By the author

Einstein, Albert. *Autobiographical Notes*. Translated and edited by Paul Arthur Schilpp. La Salle, IL: Open Court Publishing Company, 1979, 1996. In this brief book, Einstein provides an account of what he says is most important for others to know about him: the origin and development of his scientific ideas.

————. *Einstein's Miraculous Year: Five Papers That Changed the Face of Physics.* Edited by John Stachel. Princeton, NJ: Princeton University Press, 1998, 2005. The complete texts of Einstein's five 1905 groundbreaking papers, including the one in which he introduced his idea of special relativity, are accompanied by introductory notes that discuss the reasons for their great significance.

————. *Relativity: The Special and the General Theory.* Translated by Robert W. Lawson. New York: Pi Press, 2005. This edition of Einstein's own explanation of relativity for general readers, from which the selections in *What's the Matter?* are taken, contains illuminating commentaries by leading physicist Robert Geroch.

Einstein, Albert, and Leopold Infeld. *The Evolution of Physics: From Early Concepts to Relativity and Quanta.* New York: Simon & Schuster, 1938, copyright renewed 1966. By focusing entirely on the concepts of physics, this history of modern science since Galileo provides one of the best ways to understand the ideas behind the theory of relativity.

About the topic

Born, Max. *Einstein's Theory of Relativity.* Rev. ed. New York: Dover Publications, 1962. This detailed account of relativity by an eminent physicist, beginning with a review of classical physics, is for those willing to tackle some high school–level mathematics in order to gain a rewarding understanding of Einstein's ideas.

Epstein, Lewis Carroll. *Relativity Visualized.* San Francisco: Insight Press, 1992. Taking an approach similar to that of Einstein himself, the author of this well-illustrated book leads the reader through a series of thought experiments designed to give a nonmathematical understanding of the concepts of relativity.

Hoffmann, Banesh. *Relativity and Its Roots.* New York: Scientific American Books, 1983; Mineola, NY: Dover Publications, 1999. Written by one of Einstein's colleagues and biographers, this entertaining and nontechnical explanation of relativity emphasizes the continuity of its development from the work of Kepler, Galileo, Newton, Faraday, and Maxwell.

Lightman, Alan. *Einstein's Dreams.* New York: Pantheon, 1993; New York: Vintage Contemporaries, 2004. This series of thirty brief, poetic stories describes alternative worlds, each with its own self-consistent physical laws. The setting is Einstein's own dreaming mind during the night before he submitted his 1905 paper on special relativity for publication.

The General Theory
of Relativity

In this selection, Einstein uses questions and thought experiments to help us see why the equivalence of accelerated motion and gravity is the basis for generalizing the theory of relativity to include all systems of reference, whatever their state of motion. The general theory of relativity is highly complex, with far-reaching implications for understanding the nature of space, time, and gravity. The principle of equivalence is fundamental to this vast topic. Addressing the questions that Einstein raises about this principle will provide a strong foundation for further exploration of the general theory of relativity.

1

Special and General Principle of Relativity

The basal principle, which was the pivot of all our previous considerations,[1] was the *special* principle of relativity, i.e., the principle of the physical relativity of all *uniform* motion. Let us once more analyze its meaning carefully.

It was at all times clear that, from the point of view of the idea it conveys to us, every motion must be considered only as a relative motion. Returning to the illustration we have frequently used of the embankment and the railway carriage, we can express the fact of the motion here taking place in the following two forms, both of which are equally justifiable:

    (a) The carriage is in motion relative to the embankment.
    (b) The embankment is in motion relative to the carriage.

In (a) the embankment, in (b) the carriage, serves as the body of reference in our statement of the motion taking place. If it is simply a question

1. [See "The Special Theory of Relativity," section 5, pages 262–264.]

This selection is taken from Relativity: The Special and the General Theory.

of detecting or of describing the motion involved, it is in principle imma-terial to what reference-body we refer the motion. As already mentioned, this is self-evident, but it must not be confused with the much more comprehensive statement called the principle of relativity, which we have taken as the basis of our investigations.

The principle we have made use of not only maintains that we may equally well choose the carriage or the embankment as our reference-body for the description of any event (for this, too, is self-evident). Our prin-ciple rather asserts what follows: if we formulate the general laws of nature as they are obtained from experience, by making use of

(a) the embankment as reference-body,
(b) the railway carriage as reference-body,

then these general laws of nature (e.g., the laws of mechanics or the law of the propagation of light in vacuo) have exactly the same form in both cases. This can also be expressed as follows: for the *physical* description of natural processes, neither of the reference-bodies K, K' is unique (literally, "specially marked out") as compared with the other. Unlike the first, this latter statement need not of necessity hold a priori; it is not contained in the conceptions of "motion" and "reference-body" and derivable from them; only *experience* can decide as to its correctness or incorrectness.

Up to the present, however, we have by no means maintained the equivalence of *all* bodies of reference K in connection with the formulation of natural laws. Our course was more on the following lines. In the first place, we started out from the assumption that there exists a reference-body K, whose condition of motion is such that the Galilean law holds with respect to it: a particle left to itself and sufficiently far removed from all other particles moves uniformly in a straight line. With reference to K (Galilean reference-body) the laws of nature were to be as simple as possible. But in addition to K, all bodies of reference K' should be given preference in this sense, and they should be exactly equivalent to K for the formulation of natural laws, provided that they are in a state of *uniform rec-tilinear and nonrotary motion* with respect to K; all these bodies of reference are to be regarded as Galilean reference-bodies. The validity of the prin-ciple of relativity was assumed only for these reference-bodies, but not for others (e.g., those possessing motion of a different kind). In this sense we speak of the *special* principle of relativity, or special theory of relativity.

In contrast to this we wish to understand by the *general* principle of relativity the following statement: all bodies of reference *K, K'*, etc., are equivalent for the description of natural phenomena (formulation of the general laws of nature), whatever may be their state of motion. . . .

Since the introduction of the special principle of relativity has been justified, every intellect that strives after generalization must feel the temptation to venture the step toward the general principle of relativity. But a simple and apparently quite reliable consideration seems to suggest that, for the present at any rate, there is little hope of success in such an attempt. Let us imagine ourselves transferred to our old friend the railway carriage, which is traveling at a uniform rate. As long as it is moving uniformly, the occupant of the carriage is not sensible of its motion, and it is for this reason that he can without reluctance interpret the facts of the case as indicating that the carriage is at rest, but the embankment in motion. Moreover, according to the special principle of relativity, this interpretation is quite justified also from a physical point of view.

If the motion of the carriage is now changed into a nonuniform motion, as for instance by a powerful application of the brakes, then the occupant of the carriage experiences a correspondingly powerful jerk forward. The retarded motion is manifested in the mechanical behavior of bodies relative to the person in the railway carriage. The mechanical behavior is different from that of the case previously considered, and for this reason it would appear to be impossible that the same mechanical laws hold relatively to the nonuniformly moving carriage, as hold with reference to the carriage when at rest or in uniform motion. At all events it is clear that the Galilean law does not hold with respect to the nonuniformly moving carriage. Because of this, we feel compelled at the present juncture to grant a kind of absolute physical reality to nonuniform motion, in opposition to the general principle of relativity. But in what follows we shall soon see that this conclusion cannot be maintained.

2

The Gravitational Field

"If we pick up a stone and then let it go, why does it fall to the ground?" The usual answer to this question is: "Because it is attracted by the earth." Modern physics formulates the answer rather differently, for the following reason. As a result of the more careful study of electromagnetic phenomena, we have come to regard action at a distance as a process impossible without the intervention of some intermediary medium. If, for instance, a magnet attracts a piece of iron, we cannot be content to regard this as meaning that the magnet acts directly on the iron through the intermediate empty space, but we are constrained to imagine—after the manner of Faraday—that the magnet always calls into being something physically real in the space around it, that something being what we call a magnetic field. In its turn this magnetic field operates on the piece of iron, so that the latter strives to move toward the magnet. We shall not discuss here the justification for this incidental conception, which is indeed a somewhat arbitrary one. We shall only mention that with its aid electromagnetic phenomena can be theoretically represented much more satisfactorily than without it, and this applies particularly to the transmission of electromagnetic waves. The effects of gravitation also are regarded in an analogous manner.

The action of the earth on the stone takes place indirectly. The earth produces in its surroundings a gravitational field, which acts on the stone and produces its motion of fall. As we know from experience, the intensity of the action on a body diminishes according to a quite definite law, as we proceed farther and farther away from the earth. From our point of view this means that the law governing the properties of the gravitational field in space must be a perfectly definite one, in order to represent correctly the diminution of gravitational action with the distance from operative bodies. It is something like this: the body (e.g., the earth) produces a field in its immediate neighborhood directly; the intensity and direction of the field at points farther removed from the body are thence determined by the law that governs the properties in space of the gravitational fields themselves.

In contrast to electric and magnetic fields, the gravitational field exhibits a most remarkable property, which is of fundamental importance for what follows. Bodies that are moving under the sole influence of a gravitational field receive an acceleration, *which does not in the least depend either on the material or on the physical state of the body.* For instance, a piece of lead and a piece of wood fall in exactly the same manner in a gravitational field (in vacuo), when they start off from rest or with the same initial velocity. This law, which holds most accurately, can be expressed in a different form in the light of the following consideration.

According to Newton's law of motion, we have

$$\text{(Force)} = \text{(inertial mass)} \times \text{(acceleration)},$$

where the inertial mass is a characteristic constant of the accelerated body. If now gravitation is the cause of the acceleration, we then have

$$\text{(Force)} = \text{(gravitational mass)} \times \text{(intensity of the gravitational field)},$$

where the gravitational mass is likewise a characteristic constant for the body. From these two relations follows:

$$\text{(acceleration)} = \frac{\text{(gravitational mass)}}{\text{(inertial mass)}} \times \text{(intensity of the gravitational field)}.$$

If now, as we find from experience, the acceleration is to be independent of the nature and the condition of the body and always the same for a given gravitational field, then the ratio of the gravitational to the inertial mass must likewise be the same for all bodies. By a suitable choice of units we can thus make this ratio equal to unity. We then have the following law: the *gravitational* mass of a body is equal to its *inertial* mass.

It is true that this important law had hitherto been recorded in mechanics, but it had not been *interpreted*. A satisfactory interpretation can be obtained only if we recognize the following fact: *the same quality of a body manifests itself according to circumstances as "inertia" or as "weight"* (literally, "heaviness"). In the following section we shall show to what extent this is actually the case, and how this question is connected with the general postulate of relativity.

3

The Equality of Inertial and Gravitational Mass as an Argument for the General Postulate of Relativity

We imagine a large portion of empty space, so far removed from stars and other appreciable masses that we have before us approximately the conditions required by the fundamental law of Galilei. It is then possible to choose a Galilean reference-body for this part of space (world), relative to which points at rest remain at rest and points in motion continue permanently in uniform rectilinear motion. As reference-body let us imagine a spacious chest resembling a room with an observer inside who is equipped with apparatus. Gravitation naturally does not exist for this observer. He must fasten himself with strings to the floor, otherwise the slightest impact against the floor will cause him to rise slowly toward the ceiling of the room.

To the middle of the lid of the chest is fixed externally a hook with rope attached, and now a being (what kind of a being is immaterial to us) begins pulling at this with a constant force. The chest together with the observer then begin to move "upward" with a uniformly accelerated motion. In course of time their velocity will reach unheard-of values— provided that we are viewing all this from another reference-body that is not being pulled with a rope.

But how does the man in the chest regard the process? The acceleration of the chest will be transmitted to him by the reaction of the floor of the chest. He must therefore take up this pressure by means of his legs if he does not wish to be laid out full length on the floor. He is then standing in the chest in exactly the same way as anyone stands in a room of a house on our earth. If he releases a body that he previously had in his hand, the acceleration of the chest will no longer be transmitted to this body, and for this reason the body will approach the floor of the chest with an accelerated relative motion. The observer will further convince himself that *the acceleration of the body toward the floor of the chest is always of the same magnitude, whatever kind of body he may happen to use for the experiment.*

Relying on his knowledge of the gravitational field (as it was discussed in the preceding section), the man in the chest will thus come to the conclusion that he and the chest are in a gravitational field that is constant with regard to time. Of course he will be puzzled for a moment as to why the chest does not fall in this gravitational field. Just then, however, he discovers the hook in the middle of the lid of the chest and the rope that is attached to it, and he consequently comes to the conclusion that the chest is suspended at rest in the gravitational field.

Ought we to smile at the man and say that he errs in his conclusion? I do not believe we ought to if we wish to remain consistent; rather, we must admit that his mode of grasping the situation violates neither reason nor known mechanical laws. Even though it is being accelerated with respect to the Galilean space first considered, we can nevertheless regard the chest as being at rest. Thus we have good grounds for extending the principle of relativity to include bodies of reference that are accelerated with respect to each other, and as a result we have gained a powerful argument for a generalized postulate of relativity.

We must note carefully that the possibility of this mode of interpretation rests on the fundamental property of the gravitational field of giving all bodies the same acceleration, or—what comes to the same thing—on the law of the equality of inertial and gravitational mass. If this natural law did not exist, the man in the accelerated chest would not be able to interpret the behavior of the bodies around him on the supposition of a gravitational field, and he would not be justified on the grounds of experience in supposing his reference-body to be "at rest."

Suppose that the man in the chest fixes a rope to the inner side of the lid, and that he attaches a body to the free end of the rope. The result of this will be to stretch the rope so that it will hang "vertically" downward. If we ask for an opinion of the cause of tension in the rope, the man in the chest will say, "The suspended body experiences a downward force in the gravitational field, and this is neutralized by the tension of the rope; what determines the magnitude of the tension of the rope is the *gravitational mass* of the suspended body." On the other hand, an observer who is poised freely in space will interpret the condition of things thus: "The rope must perforce take part in the accelerated motion of the chest, and it transmits this motion to the body attached to it. The tension of the rope is just large enough to effect the acceleration of the body. That which determines the magnitude of the tension of the rope is the *inertial mass* of the body." Guided by this example, we see that our extension of the principle of relativity implies the *necessity* of the law of the equality of inertial and gravitational mass. Thus we have obtained a physical interpretation of this law.

From our consideration of the accelerated chest we see that a general theory of relativity must yield important results on the laws of gravitation. In point of fact, the systematic pursuit of the general idea of relativity has supplied the laws satisfied by the gravitational field. Before proceeding further, however, I must warn the reader against a misconception suggested by these considerations. A gravitational field exists for the man in the chest, despite the fact that there was no such field for the coordinate system first chosen. Now we might easily suppose that the existence of a gravitational field is always only an *apparent* one. We might also think that, regardless of the kind of gravitational field that may be present, we could always choose another reference-body such that *no* gravitational field exists with reference to it. This is by no means true for all gravitational fields, but only for those of quite special form. It is, for instance, impossible to choose a body of reference such that, as judged from it, the gravitational field of the earth (in its entirety) vanishes.

We can now appreciate why that argument is not convincing, which we brought forward against the general principle of relativity at the end of section 1. It is certainly true that the observer in the railway carriage experiences a jerk forward as a result of the application of the brake, and that he recognizes in this the nonuniformity of motion (retardation) of the carriage. But he is compelled by nobody to refer this jerk to a "real" acceleration (retardation) of the carriage. He might also interpret his experience thus: "My body of reference (the carriage) remains permanently at rest. With reference to it, however, there exists (during the period of application of the brakes) a gravitational field that is directed forward and that is variable with respect to time. Under the influence of this field, the embankment together with the earth moves nonuniformly in such a manner that their original velocity in the backward direction is continuously reduced."

4

In What Respects Are the Foundations of Classical Mechanics and of the Special Theory of Relativity Unsatisfactory?

We have already stated several times that classical mechanics starts out from the following law: material particles sufficiently far removed from other material particles continue to move uniformly in a straight line or continue in a state of rest. We have also repeatedly emphasized that this fundamental law can only be valid for bodies of reference K that possess certain unique states of motion, and that are in uniform translational motion relative to each other. Relative to other reference-bodies K, the law is not valid. Both in classical mechanics and in the special theory of relativity we therefore differentiate between reference-bodies K relative to which the recognized laws of nature can be said to hold, and reference-bodies K relative to which these laws do not hold.

But no person whose mode of thought is logical can rest satisfied with this condition of things. He asks, "How does it come that certain reference-bodies (or their states of motion) are given priority over other reference-bodies (or their states of motion)?" *What is the reason for this preference?* In order to show clearly what I mean by this question, I shall make use of a comparison.

I am standing in front of a gas range. Standing alongside each other on the range are two pans so much alike that one may be mistaken for the other. Both are half full of water. I notice that steam is being emitted continuously from one pan, but not from the other. I am surprised at this, even if I have never seen either a gas range or a pan before. But if I now notice a luminous something of bluish color under the first pan but not under the other, I cease to be astonished, even if I have never before seen a gas flame. For I can only say that this bluish something will cause the emission of the steam, or at least *possibly* it may do so. If, however, I notice the bluish something in neither case, and if I observe that one continuously emits steam while the other does not, then I shall remain astonished and dissatisfied until I have discovered some circumstance to which I can attribute the different behavior of the two pans.

Analogously, I seek in vain for a real something in classical mechanics (or in the special theory of relativity) to which I can attribute the different

291

behavior of bodies considered with respect to the reference-systems K and K'. Newton saw this objection and attempted to invalidate it, but without success. But E. Mach recognized it most clearly of all, and because of this objection he claimed that mechanics must be placed on a new basis. It can only be gotten rid of by means of a physics that is conformable to the general principle of relativity, since the equations of such a theory hold for every body of reference, whatever may be its state of motion.

5

A Few Inferences from the General Principle of Relativity

The considerations of section 3 show that the general principle of relativity puts us in a position to derive properties of the gravitational field in a purely theoretical manner. Let us suppose, for instance, that we know the space-time "course" for any natural process whatsoever, as regards the manner in which it takes place in the Galilean domain relative to a Galilean body of reference K. By means of purely theoretical operations (i.e., simply by calculation) we are then able to find how this known natural process appears, as seen from a reference-body K' that is accelerated relatively to K. But since a gravitational field exists with respect to this new body of reference K', our consideration also teaches us how the gravitational field influences the process studied.

For example, we learn that a body that is in a state of uniform rectilinear motion with respect to K (in accordance with the law of Galilei) is executing an accelerated and, in general, curvilinear motion with respect to the accelerated reference-body K' (chest). This acceleration or curvature corresponds to the influence on the moving body of the gravitational field prevailing relatively to K'. It is known that a gravitational field influences the movement of bodies in this way, so that our consideration supplies us with nothing essentially new.

However, we obtain a new result of fundamental importance when we carry out the analogous consideration for a ray of light. With respect to the Galilean reference-body K, such a ray of light is transmitted rectilinearly with the velocity c. It can easily be shown that the path of the same ray of light is no longer a straight line when we consider it with reference to the accelerated chest (reference-body K').[2] From this we conclude that, *in general, rays of light are propagated curvilinearly in gravitational fields.* In two respects this result is of great importance.

In the first place, it can be compared with the reality. Although a detailed examination of the question shows that the curvature of light rays required by the general theory of relativity is only exceedingly small for the gravitational fields at our disposal in practice, its estimated magnitude for light rays passing the sun at grazing incidence is nevertheless 1.7 seconds of arc. This ought to manifest itself in the following way. As seen from the earth, certain fixed stars appear to be in the neighborhood of the sun, and are thus capable of observation during a total eclipse of the sun. At such times, these stars ought to appear to be displaced outward from the sun by an amount indicated above, as compared with their apparent position in the sky when the sun is situated at another part of the heavens. The examination of the correctness or otherwise of this deduction is a problem of the greatest importance, the early solution of which is to be expected of astronomers.[3]

In the second place our result shows that, according to the general theory of relativity, the law of the constancy of the velocity of light in vacuo, which constitutes one of the two fundamental assumptions in the special theory of relativity and to which we have already frequently referred, cannot claim any unlimited validity. A curvature of rays of light can only take place when the velocity of propagation of light varies with position. Now we might think that as a consequence of this, the special theory of relativity—and, with it, the whole theory of relativity—would be laid in the dust. But in reality this is not the case. We can only conclude that the special theory of relativity cannot claim an unlimited domain of validity; its results hold only so long as we are able to disregard the influences of gravitational fields on the phenomena (e.g., of light).

2. [That is, a ray of light traveling from one side to the opposite side of the upward accelerated chest would appear to curve. This is because the chest moves upward while the light is traveling across it and strikes the opposite side at a lower point than it would if the chest were at rest.]

3. By means of the star photographs of two expeditions equipped by a Joint Committee of the Royal and Royal Astronomical Societies, the existence of the deflection of light demanded by theory was first confirmed during the solar eclipse of May 29, 1919.

Since it has often been contended by opponents of the theory of relativity that the special theory of relativity is overthrown by the general theory of relativity, it is perhaps advisable to make the facts of the case clearer by means of an appropriate comparison. Before the development of electrodynamics, the laws of electrostatics were looked upon as the laws of electricity. At the present time we know that electric fields can be derived correctly from electrostatic considerations only for the case, which is never strictly realized, in which the electrical masses are quite at rest relatively to each other, and to the coordinate system. Should we be justified in saying that for this reason electrostatics is overthrown by the field equations of Maxwell in electrodynamics? Not in the least. Electrostatics is contained in electrodynamics as a limiting case; the laws of the latter lead directly to those of the former for the case in which the fields are invariable with regard to time. No fairer destiny could be allotted to any physical theory than that it should of itself point out the way to the introduction of a more comprehensive theory, in which it lives on as a limiting case.

In the example of the transmission of light just dealt with, we have seen that the general theory of relativity enables us to derive theoretically the influence of a gravitational field on the course of natural processes, the laws of which are already known when a gravitational field is absent. But the most attractive problem, to the solution of which the general theory of relativity supplies the key, concerns the investigation of the laws satisfied by the gravitational field itself. Let us consider this for a moment.

We are acquainted with space-time domains that behave (approximately) in a Galilean fashion under suitable choice of reference-body, i.e., domains in which gravitational fields are absent. If we now refer such a domain to a reference-body K' possessing any kind of motion, then relative to K' there exists a gravitational field that is variable with respect to space and time.[4] The character of this field will of course depend on the motion chosen for K'. According to the general theory of relativity, the general law of the gravitational field must be satisfied for all gravitational fields obtainable in this way. Even though by no means all gravitational fields can be produced in this way, we may yet entertain the hope that the general law of gravitation will be derivable from such gravitational fields of a special kind. This hope has been realized in the most beautiful manner.

4. This follows from a generalization of the discussion in section 3.

Content Questions

1. According to Einstein, why is the "principle of the physical relativity of all *uniform* motion" self-evident, while the "much more comprehensive statement called the principle of relativity" is not? (283–284)

2. In the special theory of relativity, under what conditions are different bodies of reference exactly equivalent? What conditions would be necessary for the general principle of relativity to be valid? (284–285)

3. In Einstein's example of the braking railway carriage, why would the passenger think that the laws of the "mechanical behavior of bodies" relative to a nonuniformly moving carriage are different from those relative to a carriage in uniform motion or at rest? (285)

4. Why does Einstein say that granting "a kind of absolute physical reality to nonuniform motion" would be "in opposition to the general principle of relativity"? (285)

5. According to Einstein, how does modern physics explain why a stone falls to the ground when it is picked up and dropped? What does Einstein mean by "the properties in space of the gravitational fields themselves"? (286)

6. In the special theory of relativity, what characteristic of bodies emphasized by the concepts of inertial mass and gravitational mass is not taken into consideration? (287)

7. How does the law that "the *gravitational* mass of a body is equal to its *inertial* mass" follow from the fact that the acceleration of a body in a given gravitational field does not depend on the body's composition or physical state? (287)

8. In Einstein's thought experiment, why is it that "gravitation naturally does not exist" for the man in the chest? (288)

9. Why does Einstein stipulate that the chest is pulled upward "with a uniformly accelerated motion"? Why does he say that the object released by the observer will approach the floor with an "accelerated relative motion"? (288)

10. Why does the man in the chest conclude that he is at rest in a gravitational field? (288–289)

11. How does regarding the chest as being at rest provide "good grounds for extending the principle of relativity to include bodies of reference that are accelerated with respect to each other"? (289)

12. Why does Einstein perform the thought experiment in which the man in the chest suspends an object from a rope? Why does the man in the chest interpret the tension on the rope differently from the observer outside the chest? (289–290)

13. How does the thought experiment of the man in the chest allow the railway passenger to interpret the jerk he feels when the train's brakes are applied as the effect of a gravitational field? Why does the possibility of this interpretation show that the original argument against the general principle of relativity "is not convincing"? (290)

14. Why does Einstein find it unsatisfactory that classical mechanics and the special theory of relativity give priority to some reference bodies over others? (291)

15. In Einstein's analogy of the pans of water on the gas range, why does he specify that the pans are "so much alike that one may be mistaken for the other"? Why would he be "astonished and dissatisfied" if he observed one of the pans emitting steam but saw no flame under either of them? (291)

16. Why does a gravitational field exist with respect to the "new body of reference K'"? Why does Einstein say that the curvilinear motion of a body accelerated with respect to K' "corresponds to the influence on the moving body of the gravitational field"? (292)

17. Why does Einstein consider the conclusion that "*rays of light are propagated curvilinearly in gravitational fields*" to be "a new result"? (292–293)

18. In Einstein's proposed observation of light rays from stars during an eclipse, why would the stars "appear to be displaced outward from the sun"? (293)

19. According to Einstein, why doesn't the result of the general theory of relativity— that light rays curve under the influence of gravitational fields—invalidate the special theory of relativity? (293)

20. What new knowledge about gravitation does Einstein think can be gained from the general theory of relativity? (294)

Discussion Questions

1. Why does Einstein base his investigations on "the much more comprehensive statement called the principle of relativity"? In what way is this statement a principle, since Einstein says that its correctness must still be decided by "*experience*"? (284)

2. What does Einstein mean when he says that the law stating that the gravitational mass of a body is equal to its inertial mass "had hitherto been recorded in mechanics, but it had not been *interpreted*"? (287) If a natural law is already known, what do scientists gain by interpreting it?

3. Even though the man in the chest concludes that he is in a gravitational field when he is in fact being uniformly accelerated upward, why does Einstein say that "his mode of grasping the situation violates neither reason nor known mechanical laws"? (289) Is there any experiment that the man could perform to determine whether he is in a gravitational field or being uniformly accelerated?

4. Why is Einstein justified in saying that the extension of the principle of relativity "implies the *necessity*" of the law of the equality of inertial and gravitational mass? What does Einstein mean by a "physical interpretation of this law"? (289–290)

5. According to the general theory of relativity, what is the difference between an "*apparent*" gravitational field and a gravitational field such as the earth's? Why is Einstein confident that the general law of gravitation can be derived from considering apparent gravitational fields? (290)

6. As a scientist carrying out investigations of the physical world, why would Einstein use thought experiments such as that of the man in the accelerated chest? (288–290) In order to be established as scientifically valid, do the logically sound conclusions of thought experiments have to be confirmed by physical experiments and observations?

7. In Einstein's analogy of the pans of water on the gas range, what does he mean by "some circumstance" to which the different behavior of the pans could be attributed? Why does Einstein say that he is seeking a "real something," rather than a cause, to explain why recognized laws of nature hold only for "certain reference-bodies (or their states of motion)" and not others? (291)

8. What does Einstein mean when he says that the properties of the gravitational field can be derived "in a purely theoretical manner"? (292) In their investigations, how can scientists use both theoretical deductions and experimental observations to form a picture of the physical world?

9. What does it mean to say that a physical theory "lives on as a limiting case" of a more comprehensive theory? (294) Does classical mechanics live on in this way within the special and general theories of relativity?

10. Why does Einstein focus his attention on gravity in explaining how the general principle of relativity might be established?

Suggestions for Further Reading

By the author
Einstein, Albert. *Relativity: The Special and the General Theory.* Translated by Robert W. Lawson. New York: Pi Press, 2005. One of the strengths of this book, Einstein's own introduction to relativity for general readers from which the selections in *What's the Matter?* are taken, is that it clearly communicates the way in which the special and general theories form a continuous whole.

About the author
Pais, Abraham. *"Subtle Is the Lord . . .": The Science and the Life of Albert Einstein.* Oxford: Oxford University Press, 1982, 2005. Of all the biographies of Einstein, this one, by a fellow physicist and acquaintance, most fully captures both the events of Einstein's life and the substance of his scientific achievements.

About the topic
Fritzsch, Harald. *The Curvature of Spacetime, Newton, Einstein, and Gravitation.* Translated by Karin Heusch. New York: Columbia University Press, 2002, 2004. Through fictitious dialogues between Einstein and Newton, general relativity is explored and contrasted with the older worldview of classical physics.

Geroch, Robert. *General Relativity from A to B.* Chicago: University of Chicago Press, 1978, 1981. This nonmathematical, descriptive introduction to general relativity clearly presents such key concepts as the geometry of space-time and time intervals.

Thorne, Kip S. *Black Holes and Time Warps: Einstein's Outrageous Legacy.* New York: W. W. Norton & Company, 1994, 1995. This lively and detailed discussion of developments in theoretical physics and astrophysics shows how general relativity has continued to provide scientists with the most fruitful model of the universe, while leading to the prediction of a range of hardly imaginable phenomena such as wormholes.

Wheeler, John Archibald. *A Journey into Gravity and Spacetime.* New York: Scientific American Library, 1990; New York: W. H. Freeman and Company, 1999. Written by one of the leading physicists of the twentieth century, this beautifully illustrated introduction to general relativity rewards close attention to its masterful explanations.

Zee, A. *Einstein's Universe: Gravity at Work and Play.* Oxford: Oxford University Press, 2001. This is one of the clearest and most entertaining explanations of how general relativity has altered our understanding of the way in which gravity operates.

A theory is the more impressive the greater the simplicity of its premises, the more different kinds of things it relates, and the more extended its area of applicability.

—Albert Einstein, *Autobiographical Notes*

ALBERT EINSTEIN

$$E = mc^2$$

The equation $E = mc^2$ has come to symbolize everything from a brilliant scientist's extraordinary ability to uncover the secrets of the universe to the horrors unleashed by the development of nuclear weapons. However, this wide array of associations obscures the equation's significance as the precise formulation of one of modern physics' most important principles: the equivalence of energy and mass.

Albert Einstein (1879–1955) was primarily a theoretical rather than an experimental physicist. His discoveries resulted from his profound analysis and redefinition, often in mathematical terms, of the basic concepts that scientists use to explain physical events: space, time, energy, mass, motion, and force. Einstein recognized that a scientific theory's value lies in its ability to adequately represent observable and measurable physical phenomena. At the same time, he believed that the principles underlying scientific theories are "free inventions of the human intellect," having their source in the physicist's intuition and creative imagination. The brevity of the equation $E = mc^2$ reflects Einstein's conviction that it should be possible to express fundamental insights about the physical world in simple terms.

In 1905, when he was twenty-six, Einstein published a paper laying the foundations of the theory of relativity by postulating that the speed of light is constant in empty space and that the laws of physics are the same for all observers moving relatively to one another at constant velocities. Although each of these principles was already widely known from experiments, Einstein's creative insight was that they could serve together as the axioms of his new theory. He then logically deduced that measurements of space and time depend on the relative motion of observers, leading to new laws of motion radically different from those of Newtonian physics. Several months later, Einstein published a brief paper entitled, "Does the Inertia of a Body Depend on Its Energy Content?" In a few pages, he demonstrated mathematically that the equivalence of mass and energy is a direct consequence of the postulate of light's constant velocity. Since physicists had previously considered mass and energy to be fundamentally different from each other, the startling theoretical discovery of their equivalence led Einstein to write to a friend, "The argument is amusing and seductive; but for all I know, the Lord might be laughing over it and leading me around by the nose."

To see how the equivalence of mass and energy follows from Einstein's theory of relativity, it is necessary to consider what happens to an object's mass as it is accelerated. Before the theory of relativity, scientists thought that when a force acts continuously on an object, the object will keep accelerating without limit, while the mass of the object will remain constant. Einstein theoretically demonstrated that from the postulate of light's constant velocity, it follows that a moving object's velocity can never be measured as equaling or exceeding that of light. Therefore, the kinetic energy that an object acquires as it is acted on by force becomes less and less effective in making the object accelerate. To account for this increase in the object's inertial resistance to acceleration, Einstein concluded that the object's kinetic energy is converted into increased mass. When an object approaches the velocity of light as a limit, its rate of acceleration becomes infinitely slow and its mass becomes infinitely large. The equation $E = mc^2$ states the conversion relationship between energy and mass, emphasizing that even a small portion of the inertial mass of an object is equivalent to vast amounts of energy, since the speed of light, c, is an immense number.

Einstein's affirmative answer to the question in his paper's title led physicists to a greatly extended statement of the law of the conservation of energy. Mass was now understood to be one aspect of the energy that must be taken into consideration in calculating any physical system's total energy. Although in most physical changes the amount of converted energy or mass is too small to detect, in the decades following Einstein's discovery, scientists experimentally confirmed his theory in reactions involving radioactive substances where the amount of energy converted from mass is very large and can be measured. Both peaceful and military applications of the principle quickly followed.

Einstein's discovery of the equivalence of mass and energy was one of the most important developments since the time of Galileo and Newton in scientists' ongoing search for theories that unify physical concepts previously thought to be separate. Einstein spent the last decades of his career in an unrelenting but unsuccessful attempt to bring together the two most significant streams of thought in twentieth-century physics—the theory of relativity and quantum theory—into one unified theory.

The following selection was published in the magazine *Science Illustrated* in 1946, the year after the only nuclear bombs ever used in warfare were dropped by the United States on the Japanese cities of Hiroshima and Nagasaki. In his explanation of the origin of $E = mc^2$, Einstein asks us to consider how physicists acquire greater theoretical power to explain the physical world by discovering fundamental relationships among mass, energy, and the forces of nature. He also raises urgent questions about the practical consequences of this increased power and our responsibilities in using it wisely.

See also Einstein, pages 253–255 and 497–498.

$$E = mc^2$$

In order to understand the law of the equivalence of mass and energy, we must go back to two conservation or "balance" principles which, independent of each other, held a high place in pre-relativity physics. These were the principle of the conservation of energy and the principle of the conservation of mass. The first of these, advanced by Leibnitz as long ago as the seventeenth century, was developed in the nineteenth century essentially as a corollary of a principle of mechanics.

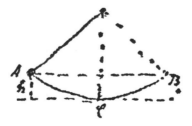

Drawing from Dr. Einstein's manuscript

Consider, for example, a pendulum whose mass swings back and forth between the points *A* and *B*. At these points the mass *m* is higher by the amount *h* than it is at *C*, the lowest point of the path (see drawing). At *C*, on the other hand, the lifting height has disappeared and instead of it the

305

mass has a velocity v. It is as though the lifting height could be converted entirely into velocity, and vice versa. The exact relation would be expressed as $mgh = (1/2)mv^2$, with g representing the acceleration of gravity.[1] What is interesting here is that this relation is independent of both the length of the pendulum and the form of the path through which the mass moves.

The significance is that something remains constant throughout the process, and that something is energy. At A and at B it is an energy of position, or "potential" energy; at C it is an energy of motion, or "kinetic" energy. If this conception is correct, then the sum $mgh + (1/2)mv^2$ must have the same value for any position of the pendulum, if h is understood to represent the height above C, and v the velocity at that point in the pendulum's path. And such is found to be actually the case. The generalization of this principle gives us the law of the conservation of mechanical energy. But what happens when friction stops the pendulum?

The answer to that was found in the study of heat phenomena. This study, based on the assumption that heat is an indestructible substance that flows from a warmer to a cooler object, seemed to give us a principle of the "conservation of heat." On the other hand, from time immemorial it has been known that heat could be produced by friction, as in the fire-making drills of the Indians. The physicists were for long unable to account for this kind of heat "production." Their difficulties were overcome only when it was successfully established that, for any given amount of heat produced by friction, an exactly proportional amount of energy had to be expended. Thus did we arrive at a principle of the "equivalence of work and heat." With our pendulum, for example, mechanical energy is gradually converted by friction into heat.

In such fashion the principles of the conservation of mechanical and thermal energies were merged into one. The physicists were thereupon persuaded that the conservation principle could be further extended to take in chemical and electromagnetic processes—in short, could be applied to all fields. It appeared that in our physical system there was a sum total of energies that remained constant through all changes that might occur.

---

1. [*mgh*: the conventional expression for potential energy—sometimes called the energy of position—in a gravitational field; $(1/2)mv^2$: the conventional expression for kinetic energy, the energy of motion.]

Now for the principle of the conservation of mass. Mass is defined by the resistance that a body opposes to its acceleration (inert mass). It is also measured by the weight of the body (heavy mass). That these two radically different definitions lead to the same value for the mass of a body is, in itself, an astonishing fact. According to the principle—namely, that masses remain unchanged under any physical or chemical changes—the mass appeared to be the essential (because unvarying) quality of matter. Heating, melting, vaporization, or combining into chemical compounds would not change the total mass.

Physicists accepted this principle up to a few decades ago. But it proved inadequate in the face of the special theory of relativity. It was therefore merged with the energy principle—just as, about sixty years before, the principle of the conservation of mechanical energy had been combined with the principle of the conservation of heat. We might say that the principle of the conservation of energy, having previously swallowed up that of the conservation of heat, now proceeded to swallow that of the conservation of mass—and holds the field alone.

It is customary to express the equivalence of mass and energy (though somewhat inexactly) by the formula $E = mc^2$, in which c represents the velocity of light, about 186,000 miles per second. E is the energy that is contained in a stationary body; m is its mass. The energy that belongs to the mass m is equal to this mass, multiplied by the square of the enormous speed of light—which is to say, a vast amount of energy for every unit of mass.

But if every gram of material contains this tremendous energy, why did it go so long unnoticed? The answer is simple enough: so long as none of the energy is given off externally, it cannot be observed. It is as though a man who is fabulously rich should never spend or give away a cent; no one could tell how rich he was.

Now we can reverse the relation and say that an increase of E in the amount of energy must be accompanied by an increase of E/c^2 in the mass. I can easily supply energy to the mass—for instance, if I heat it by 10 degrees. So why not measure the mass increase, or weight increase, connected with this change? The trouble here is that in the mass increase the enormous factor c^2 occurs in the denominator of the fraction. In such a case the increase is too small to be measured directly, even with the most sensitive balance.

For a mass increase to be measurable, the change of energy per mass unit must be enormously large. We know of only one sphere in which such amounts of energy per mass unit are released: namely, radioactive disintegration. Schematically, the process goes like this: An atom of the mass M splits into two atoms of the mass M' and M'', which separate with tremendous kinetic energy. If we imagine these two masses as brought to rest—that is, if we take this energy of motion from them—then, considered together, they are essentially poorer in energy than was the original atom. According to the equivalence principle, the mass sum $M' + M''$ of the disintegration products must also be somewhat smaller than the original mass M of the disintegrating atom—in contradiction to the old principle of the conservation of mass. The relative difference of the two is on the order of one-tenth of one percent.

Now, we cannot actually weigh the atoms individually. However, there are indirect methods for measuring their weights exactly. We can likewise determine the kinetic energies that are transferred to the disintegration products M' and M''. Thus it has become possible to test and confirm the equivalence formula. Also, the law permits us to calculate in advance, from precisely determined atom weights, just how much energy will be released with any atom disintegration we have in mind. The law says nothing, of course, as to whether—or how—the disintegration reaction can be brought about.

What takes place can be illustrated with the help of our rich man. The atom M is a rich miser who, during his life, gives away no money (energy). But in his will he bequeaths his fortune to his sons M' and M'', on condition that they give to the community a small amount, less than one thousandth of the whole estate (energy or mass). The sons together have somewhat less than the father had (the mass sum $M' + M''$ is somewhat smaller than the mass M of the radioactive atom). But the part given to the community, though relatively small, is still so enormously large (considered as kinetic energy) that it brings with it a great threat of evil. Averting that threat has become the most urgent problem of our time.

Content Questions

1. How does Einstein's example of the pendulum demonstrate the law of the conservation of mechanical energy? What does it mean to say that mechanical energy is conserved? (305–306)

2. According to the law of the conservation of mechanical energy, what are the relative values of mgh (potential energy) and $(1/2)mv^2$ (kinetic energy) when the pendulum is halfway between either A and C or B and C in the diagram? (305–306)

3. How could the stopping of a pendulum by friction demonstrate the "equivalence of work and heat"? When scientists recognized this equivalence, how were conservation principles affected? (306)

4. What does Einstein mean when he says, "It appeared that in our physical system there was a sum total of energies that remained constant through all changes that might occur"? (306)

5. What does it mean to say that the two definitions of mass lead to "the same value for the mass of a body"? (307)

6. Why did scientists formulate a principle of the conservation of mass rather than a principle of the conservation of matter? (307)

7. Why does Einstein say that, following the discovery of the special theory of relativity, the principle of the conservation of energy "holds the field alone"? (307)

8. What makes it certain that E always represents "a vast amount of energy for every unit of mass"? (307)

9. How would the formula $E = mc^2$ be written if it were reversed to show an increase in mass resulting from an increase in energy? How does this reversed formula show that the increase in mass that occurs when energy is increased is usually "too small to be measured directly"? (307)

10. Even though the atoms that experience radioactive decay are very small and have relatively little mass, why is their change in mass measurable? (308)

11. According to the formula $E = mc^2$, what is the source of the "tremendous kinetic energy" released when an atom of mass M separates into atoms of mass M' and M''? (308)

12. How does $E = mc^2$ show that "the mass sum $M' + M''$ of the disintegration products must also be somewhat smaller than the original mass M of the disintegrating atom"? How is this result "in contradiction to the old principle of the conservation of mass"? (308)

13. How could scientists use the formula $E = mc^2$ to calculate in advance how much energy would be released from "any atom disintegration we have in mind"? (308)

14. In Einstein's story about the miser's bequest, what does the rich man's fortune represent? Why does Einstein emphasize that the portion to be given to the community is "relatively small" compared to the entire fortune? (308)

15. Why would an enormously large amount of kinetic energy be a "great threat" to the community? (308)

Discussion Questions

1. Why would physicists look for conservation principles, such as those for mechanical energy, thermal energy, and mass? (305–307)

2. Why does Einstein point out that in the example of the pendulum, the relation $mgh = (1/2)mv^2$ is "independent of both the length of the pendulum and the form of the path through which the mass moves"? (306)

3. In physics, what does it mean to say that heat and work, or mass and energy, are equivalent to each other? Is this relation of equivalence the same as saying that they are identical? (306–307)

4. What does Einstein mean when he says that the two definitions of mass are "radically different" from each other? Why does he call it "an astonishing fact" that these definitions lead to the same value for the mass of a body? (307)

5. After the principle of the conservation of energy "swallowed up" the principles of the conservation of heat and the conservation of mass, were the conservation principles of heat and mass still valid? (307)

6. In order to measure the change of energy per mass unit for atom M, why does Einstein stipulate that the two atoms it splits into—M' and M''—should be imagined as being brought to rest? If the energy being measured is not "energy of motion," what kind of energy is it? (308)

7. Why does Einstein point out that the law of the equivalence of mass and energy "says nothing, of course, as to whether—or how—the [radioactive] disintegration reaction can be brought about"? (308)

8. Why does Einstein add the story of the miser's bequest to his explanation of the meaning of the equation that he discovered? Why does he say that the bequest brings "a great threat of evil," and that "averting that threat has become the most urgent problem of our time"? (308)

Suggestions for Further Reading

By the author

Einstein, Albert. *Ideas and Opinions.* Reprint. New translations and revisions by Sonja Bargmann. New York: Modern Library, 1994. This anthology of Einstein's shorter writings, from which the selection in *What's the Matter?* is taken, includes several brief explanations of the basic ideas of his theory of relativity.

About the author

Hoffmann, Banesh. *Albert Einstein, Creator and Rebel.* In collaboration with Helen Dukas. New York: Viking Press, 1972; reprint, New York: Plume Books, 1988. The author of this biography was a colleague of Einstein's and conveys a deep understanding of Einstein's independent-minded approach to scientific investigation.

About the topic

Bodanis, David. *E = mc²: A Biography of the World's Most Famous Equation.* New York: Walker, 2000; New York: Berkley Publishing, 2001. After explaining the meaning of each of the equation's symbols, this book traces the history of its immense significance for scientific research and its consequences in the development of atomic weapons.

Lightman, Alan. *Great Ideas in Physics: The Conservation of Energy, the Second Law of Thermodynamics, the Theory of Relativity, and Quantum Mechanics.* 3rd ed. New York: McGraw-Hill, 2000. The chapter on the theory of relativity provides a clear derivation of the equation $E = mc^2$ as well as an interesting discussion of Einstein's approach to creating scientific theories.

Rigden, John S. *Einstein 1905: The Standard of Greatness.* Cambridge, MA: Harvard University Press, 2005. In this history of Einstein's most productive year, the significance of each of his five groundbreaking papers is discussed, including the one in which he first formulated $E = mc^2$ almost as an afterthought to the theory of relativity.

Schwinger, Julian. *Einstein's Legacy: The Unity of Space and Time.* New York: Scientific American Library, 1986; Mineola, NY: Dover Publications, 2002. This outstanding survey of Einstein's work by an eminent physicist includes a detailed explanation of $E = mc^2$, showing its connection to the conservation of energy law.

For the modern physicist, only the so-called "observables" (i.e., principally, observable properties) have any significance, and all modern physics is based on their mutual relation. The things which cannot be observed are good only for idle thinking— you have no restrictions in inventing them, and no possibility of checking their existence, or of making any use of them.

—George Gamow, *Mr. Tompkins in Paperback*

GEORGE GAMOW

Quantum Uncertainty

From the beginning of the twentieth century, quantum theory and the theory of relativity set the direction for all subsequent theoretical and experimental work in physics. Both led to new ways of thinking about the physical world, but each has a very different relationship to classical physics, which had been dominant for more than two hundred years since the time of Newton. Though the theory of relativity profoundly altered the classical understanding of time, space, and motion, it shares with classical physics the conviction that there are exact scientific laws that allow us to understand the physical world with complete certainty. Rather than replace the principles of classical physics, the theory of relativity incorporates them into a larger theoretical structure. In contrast, quantum theory introduces ideas about the physical world and the nature of scientific explanation and observation that are fundamentally incompatible with classical physics.

Classical physics assumes that physical events are completely determinate and predictable. Provided that all the initial conditions of a system of bodies are simultaneously known—their positions, their velocities, the forces acting on them—the entire future of the system can also be known. Uncertainty in observations and predictions is attributed to technical limitations in the accuracy of measuring devices and the skill of investigators in using them. As long as scientific observations are confined to the scale of objects not vastly smaller than human observers, classical physics provides adequate explanations of the physical world.

On the other hand, quantum physics asserts that there is inherent uncertainty in our ability to simultaneously know the positions and velocities of a system of bodies, therefore limiting our ability to predict the system's future. In quantum physics, this uncertainty comes from the nature of the physical world itself and from our interactions with it when we make observations. Consequently, quantum physics raises many interesting questions concerning the limitations of science in being able to reveal an objective, physical world existing independently of human beings. Because quantum effects are apparent only at infinitesimally small scales, it is commonly assumed that quantum uncertainty applies only to the behavior of objects at the sub-atomic level. In fact, quantum uncertainty applies to the physical world at all scales and therefore represents a complete break with the worldview of classical physics.

Scientists developed quantum theory between 1900 and 1930 as a way to make sense of experimental results that could not be explained in terms of classical physics. Many of these experiments involved new investigations of the microscopic structure of matter, where familiar assumptions about the physical world did not seem to apply. The creation of early quantum physics was largely the work of eight men: Max Planck, Albert Einstein, Niels Bohr, Max Born, Werner Heisenberg, Erwin Schrödinger, Louis de Broglie, and Paul Dirac. These scientists were aware of one another's ideas and engaged in the kind of collaborative dialogue that is one of the most important characteristics of successful scientific communities.

George Gamow (1904–1968) was one of the younger scientists to make important contributions to early quantum theory. He was born in Russia and in the late 1920s went to study at the University of Göttingen in Germany, which Born and Heisenberg had made one of the leading centers of quantum theory research. His explanation of nuclear radioactivity as a quantum-mechanical phenomenon caught the attention of Niels Bohr, who invited him to the Institute of Theoretical Physics in Copenhagen. There, Gamow developed a model of atomic nuclei that is the basis for theories of nuclear fission and fusion. Gamow was one of the first scientists to speculate on the connection between nuclear processes and the evolution of the universe and was responsible for formulating the big bang theory.

The following selection is from *The NEW World of Mr. Tompkins*, one of Gamow's many science books for general readers. It provides an overview of the essential features of quantum theory from the perspective of Gamow's fictional character, Mr. Tompkins, as he listens to a physics lecture. Gamow's effective use of thought experiments and imaginative storytelling to explain quantum theory raises a question: What kinds of analogies and metaphors can contemporary scientists use to help visualize ideas about the physical world? This question becomes particularly important as theories of modern physics move further away from the world we ordinarily perceive and as scientists abandon physical models in favor of abstract mathematical formulations.

Quantum Uncertainty

The audience for the professor's next lecture was not quite as large as it had been at the beginning of the series; some had clearly not stayed the course. But it was still sizeable. As Mr. Tompkins sat there waiting, he recalled [his friend's] remark about the difficulties of learning quantum theory; [Mr. Tompkins] anxiously wondered how he would manage. But he was determined to master it, if he could. He even held out hopes that where quantum physics was concerned, it might prove to be *his* turn to tutor *her*!

The professor entered . . .[1]

Ladies and gentlemen:

In my two previous lectures I tried to show you how the discovery of the upper limit for all physical velocities brought us to a complete reconstruction of nineteenth-century ideas about space and time.

This development of the critical analysis of the foundations of physics did not, however, stop at this stage; still more striking discoveries and conclusions were in store. I am referring to the branch of physics known as *quantum theory*. This is not so much concerned with the properties of

1. [Ellipses are from the author unless bracketed.]

This selection is taken from chapter 8, "Quantum Snooker," of The NEW World of Mr. Tompkins.

space and time themselves, as with the mutual interactions and motions of material objects taking place in space and time.

In classical physics it was always accepted as self-evident that the interaction between any two physical bodies could be made as small as required by the conditions of the experiment, and practically reduced to zero whenever necessary. For example, suppose the aim is to investigate the heat developed in a certain process, and one is concerned that the introduction of a thermometer would take away a certain amount of the heat, and thus introduce a disturbance. The experimenter was confident that by using a smaller thermometer (or a very tiny thermocouple), this disturbance could be reduced to a point below the limits of needed accuracy.

The conviction that any physical process can, in principle, be observed with any required degree of precision, without disturbing it by the observation, was so strong that nobody troubled to formulate such a proposition explicitly. However, new empirical facts accumulated since the beginning of the twentieth century steadily brought physicists to the conclusion that the situation is really much more complicated. In fact, *there exists in nature a certain lower limit of interaction which can never be reduced.* This natural limit of accuracy is negligibly small for most kinds of processes we are normally familiar with in ordinary life. They do, however, become highly significant when it comes to the interactions taking place in such tiny mechanical systems as atoms and molecules.

In the year 1900, the German physicist Max Planck was thinking about the conditions of equilibrium between matter and radiation. He came to a surprising conclusion: No such equilibrium was possible if the interaction between the matter and radiation took place continuously, as had always been supposed. Instead, he proposed that the energy was transferred between matter and radiation *in a sequence of separate "shocks."* A particular amount of energy was transferred in each of these elementary acts of interaction. In order to get the desired equilibrium, and to achieve agreement with the experimental facts, it was necessary to introduce a simple mathematical relation which stated that the amount of energy transferred in each shock was proportional to the frequency of the radiation responsible for the transfer of energy.

Thus, denoting the coefficient of proportionality by the symbol h, Planck was led to accept that the minimal portion, or *quantum*, of energy transferred was given by the expression

$$E = hf \qquad (1)$$

where f stands for the frequency of the radiation. The constant h has the numerical value 6.6×10^{-34} Joule second, and is usually called *Planck's constant*. (I take it you are all familiar with the notation that 10^{-34} means:

$$1/10,000,000,000,000,000,000,000,000,000,000,000$$

where that is supposed to be 34 zeros on the denominator.) Note that Planck's constant has a very small value, and it is this that is responsible for the fact that quantum phenomena are usually not observed in our everyday life.

A further development of Planck's ideas was due to Einstein. He concluded that not only is radiation emitted as "packages of energy," but these packages subsequently transfer energy to matter in the same localized way as particles do. In other words, each package remains intact—it does not disperse its energy over a wide region, as was previously assumed. These packages of energy are referred to as "quanta of light," or *photons*.

Insofar as photons are moving, they should possess, apart from their energy hf, a certain momentum also. According to relativistic mechanics, this should be equal to their energy divided by the velocity of light, c. Remembering that the frequency of light is related to its wavelength, λ, by the relation $f = c/\lambda$, we can write for the momentum of a photon:

$$p = hf/c = h/\lambda \qquad (2)$$

Thus, a photon's momentum decreases with wavelength.

One of the best experimental proofs of the correctness of the idea of light quanta, and the energy and momentum ascribed to them, was given by the investigation of the American physicist Arthur Compton. Studying the interactions between light and electrons, he arrived at the result that electrons set in motion by the action of a ray of light behaved exactly as if they had been struck by a particle with the energy and momentum given by equations (1) and (2). The photons themselves, after colliding with the electrons, were also shown to suffer certain changes (in their frequency), in excellent agreement with the prediction of the theory.

Thus, we can say that, as far as the interaction with matter is concerned, the quantum property of electromagnetic radiation, such as light, is a well-established experimental fact.

A further development of the quantum ideas was due to the Danish physicist Niels Bohr. In 1913, he was first to express the idea that *the internal motion of any mechanical system may possess only a discrete set of possible energy values.* As a result, that internal motion can change its state only by finite steps, the transition being accompanied by the radiation, or absorption, of a discrete amount of energy (the energy difference between the two allowed energy states). This idea was prompted by the observation that when atomic electrons emit radiation, the resulting spectrum is not continuous but consists of certain frequencies only—a "line spectrum." In other words, in accordance with equation (1), the emitted radiation has only certain energy values. This could be understood if Bohr's hypothesis concerning the allowed energy states of the emitter were correct—in this case, the energy states of the electrons in the atom.

The mathematical rules defining the possible states of mechanical systems are more complicated than in the case of radiation and we will not enter here into their formulation. Suffice it to say that, when describing the motion of a particle such as an electron, there are circumstances where it becomes necessary to ascribe to it the properties of a *wave*. The necessity for doing this was first indicated by the French physicist Louis de Broglie, on the basis of his theoretical studies of the structure of the atom. He recognized that whenever a wave finds itself in a confined space, such as a sound wave within an organ pipe, or the vibrations of a violin string, only certain frequencies or wavelengths are permitted to it. These waves have to "fit" the dimensions of the confining space, giving rise to what we call *standing waves*. De Broglie argued that if the electrons in an atom had a wave associated with them, then because the waves were confined (to the vicinity of the atomic nucleus), their wavelength would only be able to take on the discrete values permitted to standing waves. Furthermore, if this proposed wavelength were related to the electron's momentum by an equation similar to equation (2) for light, i.e.,

$$p_{particle} = h/\lambda \qquad (3)$$

then that would entail the momentum (and hence the energy) of the electron being able to take on only certain permitted values. This would of course provide a neat explanation of the discrete energy levels of electrons in atoms, and the consequent line spectrum nature of their emitted radiation.

In the following years the wave properties of the motion of material particles were firmly established by numerous experiments. They showed such phenomena as the *diffraction* of a beam of electrons passing through a small opening, and *interference phenomena* taking place even for such comparatively large and complex particles as molecules. The observed wave properties of material particles were, of course, absolutely incomprehensible from the point of view of classical conceptions of motion. De Broglie himself was forced to a rather unnatural point of view: that the particles are "accompanied" by certain waves which, so to speak, "direct" their motion.

Due to the extremely small value of the constant, *h*, the wavelengths of material particles are exceedingly small—even for the lightest fundamental particle, the electron. Whenever the wavelength of radiation is small compared with the dimensions of apertures it might be going through, the diffraction effects are tiny and the radiation to all intents and purposes passes through in an undeviated manner. That is why a football passing through the gap between the goal posts does not undergo any visible change of direction due to diffraction. The wave nature of particles is of importance only for motions taking place in such small regions as the inside of atoms and molecules. Here they play a crucial part in our knowledge of the internal structure of matter.

One of the most direct proofs of the existence of the sequence of discrete states of these tiny mechanical systems was given by the experiments of James Franck and Gustav Hertz. They bombarded atoms with electrons of varying energy, and noticed that definite changes in the state of the atom took place only when the energy of the bombarding electrons reached certain discrete values. If the energy of the electrons was brought below a certain limit, no effect whatsoever was observed in the atoms. This was because the amount of energy carried by each electron was not sufficient to raise the atom from the first allowed quantum state into the second.

So how are we to view these new ideas in relation to classical mechanics?

The fundamental concept concerning motion in classical theory is that a particle, at any given moment, occupies a certain position in space and possesses a definite velocity characterizing its positional changes with time along its trajectory. These fundamental notions of position, velocity, and trajectory, on which the entire edifice of classical mechanics is built, are formed (as are all our other notions) from observation of the phenomena around us. As we saw earlier with the classical notions of space and time, we must expect that they might be in need of radical modification as soon as our experience extends into new and previously unexplored regions.

If I ask you why you believe that a moving particle occupies at any given moment a certain position, and that over the course of time it will describe a definite line called the trajectory, you will probably answer: "Because I see it this way, when I observe its motion." But let us analyze this method of forming the classical notion of the trajectory and see if it really will lead to a definite result. For this purpose we imagine a physicist supplied with sensitive apparatus, trying to pursue the motion of a little material body thrown from the wall of her laboratory. She decides to make her observation by "seeing" how the body moves. Of course, to see the moving body, she must illuminate it. Knowing that light in general produces a pressure on the body, and so might disturb its motion, she decides to use short-flash illumination only at the moments when she makes the observation. For her first trial she wants to observe only ten points on the trajectory and thus she chooses her flashlight source so weak that the integral effect of light pressure during ten successive illuminations should be within the accuracy she needs. Thus, flashing her light ten times during the fall of the body, she obtains, with the desired accuracy, ten points on the trajectory.

Now she wants to improve on the experiment and get a more precise fix on the trajectory—one hundred points this time. She knows that a hundred successive illuminations will disturb the motion too much and therefore, preparing for the second set of observations, chooses her flashlight ten times less intense. For the third set of observations, desiring to have one thousand points, she makes the flashlight a hundred times fainter than originally. Proceeding in this way, and constantly decreasing the intensity of her illumination, she can obtain as many points on the trajectory as she wants, without increasing the possible error above the limit she had chosen at the beginning. This highly idealized, but in principle quite possible, procedure represents the strictly logical way to construct the motion of a trajectory by "looking at the moving body." As you can see, from the point of view of classical physics, all of this is perfectly possible.

But now let us see what happens if we introduce the quantum limitations and take into account the fact that the action of any radiation can be transferred only in the form of photons. We have seen that our observer was constantly reducing the amount of light illuminating the moving body. But now we have to recognize that she will find it impossible to continue to do this once she has come down to a level of illumination equivalent to one photon per flash. Either all or none of the photon will be reflected from the moving body; one cannot have a fraction of a photon.

Now, the experimenter might argue that, in accordance with equation (2), the effect of a collision with a photon would be less if the wavelength were larger. Consequently she resolves to increase the number of observations by making compensatory increases in the wavelength of the light used. But here she meets with another difficulty. It is well known that when using light of a certain wavelength, one cannot see details smaller than the wavelength used. (One cannot paint a Persian miniature using a housepainter's brush!) Thus, by using longer and longer waves, she will spoil the estimate of each single point and soon will come to the stage where each estimate will be uncertain by an amount comparable to the size of her laboratory and more. Thus she will be forced finally to a compromise between the large number of observed points and the uncertainty of each estimate. Thus she will never be able to arrive at an exact trajectory as a mathematical line such as that obtained by her classical colleagues. Her best result will be a rather broad, washed-out band.

The method discussed here is an optical method; we could try another possibility, using a mechanical method. For this purpose our experimenter can devise some tiny mechanical recording devices, say little bells on springs, which would register the passage of material bodies if such a body passes close to them. She can spread a large number of such bells through the space through which the moving body is expected to pass and, after the particle's passage, the "ringing of bells" will indicate its track. In classical physics one can make the bells as small and sensitive as one likes, and in the limiting case of an infinite number of infinitely small bells, the notion of a trajectory can be formed again with any desired precision. However, the quantum limitations for mechanical systems will spoil the situation again. The clappers of the bells are in the confined space of the bell itself. They will therefore have only certain discrete energy states allowed to them. If the bells are too small, the amount of momentum they need to take from the moving body in order to get the clapper to ring will be large, and, as a result, the motion of the particle will undergo a correspondingly large disturbance. If, on the other hand, the bells are large, little disturbance will be caused, but the uncertainty of each position will be large. The final trajectory deduced will again be a spread-out band!

These considerations might lead you to seek yet some other practical method for determining the trajectory—perhaps a more elaborate and complicated one. But let me point out that what we have been discussing here has not been so much the analysis of two particular experimental techniques, but an idealization of the most *general* question of physical measurement. Any scheme of measurement whatsoever will necessarily be reducible to the elements described in these two methods, and will finally yield the same result: exact position and trajectory have no place in a world subject to quantum laws . . .

It was at this point in the lecture that Mr. Tompkins gave up his battle to keep his leaden eyes open. His head drooped, suddenly to jerk up as he tried to force himself to keep awake; it drooped once more, another slight jerk, another droop . . .

Having ordered a pint from the bar, Mr. Tompkins was about to find himself a seat when his attention was taken by the click of snooker balls. He remembered that there was a snooker table in the back room of this pub, so he thought he would go and take a look. The room was filled with men in shirtsleeves, drinking and chatting animatedly as they waited their turn to play. Mr. Tompkins approached the table and started to watch the game.

There was something very strange about it! A player put a ball on the table and hit it with the cue. Watching the rolling ball, Mr. Tompkins noticed to his great surprise that the ball began to "spread out." This was the only expression he could find for the odd behavior of the ball which, as it moved, seemed to become more and more washed out, losing its sharp contours. It looked as if not one ball was rolling across the table but a great number of balls, all partially penetrating into each other. Mr. Tompkins had often observed analogous phenomena before, but not on the strength of less than one drink. He could not understand why it was happening now.

"Hmm," he thought, "I wonder how this 'fuzzy' ball is going to hit another one."

The player who had hit the ball was evidently an expert; the moving ball hit the other head-on just as it was meant to; there was a loud sound of impact just like the collision between two ordinary balls. Then both the ball that had been moving and the one that had been stationary (Mr. Tompkins could not positively say which was which) sped off "in all different directions at once." Very peculiar. There were no longer two balls looking only somewhat fuzzy, but instead it seemed that innumerable balls, all of them very vague and fuzzy, were rushing about within an angle of 180° round the direction of the original impact. It resembled a wave spreading from the point of collision, with a maximum flow of balls in the direction of the original impact.

"That's a nice example of probability waves they've got there," said a familiar voice behind him. Mr. Tompkins swung round to find the professor at his shoulder.

"Oh, it's you," he said. "Good. Perhaps you could explain what's going on here."

"Certainly. The landlord seems to have got himself some balls suffering from 'quantum-elephantism'—if I may so express myself. All objects in nature, of course, are subject to quantum laws. But Planck's constant (the quantity governing the scale of the quantum effects) is very, very small—at least it is normally. But for these balls here, the constant seems much larger—about ONE, I reckon. Which is actually quite useful; here you can see everything happening with your very own eyes. Normally you can only infer this sort of behavior using very sensitive and sophisticated methods of observation."

The professor became thoughtful. "I must say I would dearly love to know how the landlord got hold of these balls. Strictly speaking, they can't exist in our world. Planck's constant is the same for all objects."

"Maybe he imported them from some other world," suggested Mr. Tompkins. "But tell me, why do the balls spread out like this?"

"Oh, that's all to do with the fact that their position on the table is not quite definite. You cannot indicate the position of a ball exactly; the best you can say is that the ball is 'mostly here' but 'partially somewhere else.'"

"It actually, *physically* is in all these different places at once?" asked Mr. Tompkins incredulously.

The professor hesitated. "Maybe, maybe not. That's certainly how some people would say it was. Others would say that it is our *knowledge* of the ball's position that's uncertain. The interpretation of quantum physics has always been a subject for debate. There's no consensus even now."

Mr. Tompkins continued to gaze in wonder at the fuzzy snooker balls. "This is all very unusual," he murmured.

"On the contrary," insisted the professor, "it is absolutely usual—in the sense that it happens all the time, to every material object in the universe. It's simply that h is so very small. Our ordinary methods of observation are too crude; they mask this underlying type of indeterminacy. And it's this that misleads people into thinking that position and velocity are in themselves definite quantities. They recognize that in purely practical terms you're never going to be able to *determine* what those values of position and velocity are—not to *infinite* precision—but this they put down to nothing more than the clumsiness of their measuring techniques. But in truth, both quantities are *fundamentally* indefinite to some extent.

"Actually it is possible to alter the *balance* of uncertainties. For example, you might want to concentrate on improving the accuracy of your determination of position. OK, you can do that, but the price you have to pay is an increase in the uncertainty of the velocity. Alternatively you can go for precision of velocity, but then you have to sacrifice precision of position. Planck's constant governs the relation between these two uncertainties."

"I'm not altogether sure . . . ," began Mr. Tompkins.

"Oh, it's quite simple, really," continued the professor. "Look here, I am going to put definite limits on the position of this ball."

The fuzzy-looking ball he spoke of was lazily rolling over the table. He reached across and trapped it inside the wooden triangle the players use for setting up the balls at the start of a game. Immediately the ball seemed to go berserk. The whole of the inside of the triangle became filled up with a blur of ivory.

"You see!" said the professor. "I have now defined the position of the ball to the extent of the dimensions of the triangle. Previously all we could say for certain was that it was on the table—somewhere. But look what it's done to the velocity. The uncertainty in the velocity has shot up."

"Can't you stop it rushing about like that?" asked Mr. Tompkins.

"No—it's physically impossible. Any object in an enclosed space has to possess a certain motion—we physicists call it *zero-point motion*. It's impossible for it to stay still. If it *did* stay still then we would know for certain what its velocity was; it would be zero. But we are not allowed to know the velocity if we have a pretty good fix on its position—as we do here with the ball confined to lie within the boundaries of the triangle."

While Mr. Tompkins was watching the ball dashing to and fro in its enclosure—like a tiger in a cage—something very odd happened. The ball got out! It was now on the *outside* of the triangle, rolling toward a distant corner of the table. But how? It wasn't that it jumped over the wall of the triangle; instead it had sort of "leaked" through the barrier.

"Hah!" exclaimed the professor excitedly. "Did you see that? One of the most interesting consequences of quantum theory: it is impossible to hold anything inside an enclosure indefinitely—provided there is enough energy for the object to run away once it has crossed the barrier. Sooner or later the object will 'leak through' and get away."

"Good grief!" declared Mr. Tompkins. "Then I'll never go to the zoo again." His vivid imagination immediately conjured up a picture of lions and tigers "leaking through" the walls of their cages. Then his thoughts took a somewhat different turn: what if his car leaked out of its locked garage? He had a mental image of it passing through the garage wall, like the proverbial ghost of the middle ages, and careering off down the street. He wondered whether his car insurance covered such eventualities.

He mentioned this to the professor, and asked, "How long would I have to wait for that to happen?"

After making some rapid calculations in his head, the professor came back with: "It will take about 1,000,000,000 . . . 000,000 years."

Even though Mr. Tompkins was accustomed to large numbers in the bank's account, he lost count of the number of naughts in the professor's answer. It was, however, a reassuringly long period of time—enough for him not to be unduly worried.

"But tell me," he said. "In the ordinary world—in the absence of balls like these—how can such things be observed if it takes so long to happen?"

"Good question. There's no point hanging around hoping to see ordinary, everyday objects perform these feats. No, the point is the effects of the quantum laws only really become noticeable when you're dealing with very small masses such as atoms or electrons. For such tiny particles, the quantum effects are so large that ordinary mechanics becomes quite inapplicable. A collision between two atoms, say, would look exactly like a collision between two of these 'quantum-elephantistic' balls. Not only that, but the motion of electrons within an atom resembles very closely the zero-point motion of the ball when it was inside the wooden triangle."

"And do the electrons escape from their atoms very often?" asked Mr. Tompkins.

"No, no," responded the professor hurriedly. "No, that doesn't happen at all. You must remember what I said about the object having enough energy to get away once it has leaked through the barrier. An electron is held in an atom by the force of attraction between the negative electric charge it carries and the positive charge on the protons in the nucleus. The electron does not have enough energy to escape this pull, so it cannot get away. No, if you want to see leakage, then I suggest examining the nucleus of the atom. To some extent a nucleus can behave as though it's made up of alpha particles."

"Alpha particle?"

"That's the name given historically to the nucleus of a helium atom. It consists of two neutrons and two protons. It is exceptionally tightly bound; the four particles can 'fit together' in a very efficient manner. Anyway, as I was saying, because alpha particles are so tightly bound, heavy nuclei can in some circumstances behave as though they were a collection of alpha particles—rather than individual neutrons and protons. Although the alphas are moving about within the overall volume of the nucleus, they are constrained to stay within that volume by the short-range attractive forces that bind nuclear particles together. At least, they stay together normally, but every so often, one of the alphas escapes. It gets out beyond the range of the attractive nuclear force that had been constraining it. In fact, now it is subject only to the long-range repulsive force between its positive electric charge and that on the rest of the nucleus it has left behind. So now the alpha is propelled away. It's a form of *radioactive nuclear decay*. So, as you see, this is quite analogous to your car in its garage—only the alpha escapes more quickly!"

At this point, Mr. Tompkins felt a strange sensation in his arm. It had begun to shake. He heard a woman's hushed voice saying, "Shh!"

He awoke to find a lady sitting next to him on the lecture theater bench. She was gently tapping him on the arm. She smiled sympathetically and whispered, "You were beginning to snore."

Mr. Tompkins pulled himself together and silently mouthed the words "thank you" to her. He wondered how much of the lecture he had missed. Perhaps even in his sleep he had been unconsciously tuned in. He remembered hearing a report once of someone who was supposed to have learned a foreign language by going to sleep with headphones on. Anyway, the professor was still in full flow . . .

Let us now return to our experimenter and try to get the mathematical form for the limitations imposed by quantum conditions. We have already seen that whatever method of observation is used, there is always a conflict between the estimate of position and that of velocity of the moving object. In the optical method, the collision between the object and the photon from the illuminating source will, because of the law of conservation of momentum, introduce an uncertainty in the momentum of the particle comparable with the momentum of the photon used. Thus, using equation (3), we can write for the uncertainty of momentum of the particle

$$\Delta p_{\text{particle}} \cong h/\lambda \tag{4}$$

Remembering that the uncertainty of position of the particle is given by the wavelength (i.e., $\Delta q \cong \lambda$) we deduce:

$$\Delta p_{\text{particle}} \times \Delta q_{\text{particle}} \cong h \tag{5}$$

In the mechanical method of observation using the bells, the momentum of the moving particle will be made uncertain by the amount taken by the bell clapper. Because the clapper is confined within the bell, its momentum must be such as to correspond with a wavelength comparable to the dimensions of the bell, l. Thus, using equation (3), $\Delta p_{\text{particle}} \cong h/l$. Recalling that in this case the uncertainty of position is given by the size of the bell (i.e., $\Delta q \cong l$), we come again to the same equation (5). This universal relationship between the two uncertainties, involving as it does Planck's constant, was first formulated by the German physicist Werner Heisenberg. Hence, equation (5) is known as the *Heisenberg uncertainty relationship*. From this it becomes immediately clear that the better one defines the position, the more indefinite the momentum (or velocity) becomes, and vice versa. Remembering that momentum is the product of the mass of the moving particle and its velocity, we can write

$$\Delta v_{particle} \times \Delta q_{particle} \cong h/m_{particle} \tag{6}$$

For bodies that we usually handle, these uncertainties are exceedingly small. For a light particle of dust, with a mass of 0.000,000,1 g, both position and velocity can be measured with an accuracy of 0.000,000,01%! However, for an electron (with a mass of 10^{-30} kg), the product $\Delta v \Delta q$ should be of the order of 10^{-4} m^2/s. Inside an atom, the velocity of an electron should be less than 10^6 m/s, otherwise it will escape. So its velocity needs to be defined to a precision within that limiting velocity. Using equation (5), this gives 10^{-10} m for the uncertainty of position, i.e., we would expect that this would represent the total dimensions of an atom. And indeed, that is what we find to be the case in practice. Here we begin to glimpse the power and usefulness of Heisenberg's uncertainty relationship. Merely from a knowledge of the strength of the forces within the atom (and hence the maximum velocities allowed to the electrons), we are able to arrive at an estimate of the size of atoms!

In this lecture I have tried to show you a picture of the radical change that our classical ideas of motion have had to undergo. The elegant and sharply defined classical notions are gone, and you might well be wondering how physicists manage to keep afloat on this ocean of uncertainty. It cannot be a function of an introductory lecture like this to provide you with the full mathematical rigor of quantum mechanics. But for those of you interested, let me give you the flavor of it.

It is clear that if we cannot in general define the position of a material particle by a mathematical point, and its trajectory by a mathematical line, we have to use other mathematical methods of description. This in fact entails the use of continuous functions. Such functions will allow us to define the "density of presence" of the object as it "spreads out" in space.

I should perhaps warn you against the erroneous idea that the function describing the "density of presence" has a physical reality in our ordinary three-dimensional space. [. . .] The quantum mechanical *wave function* [. . .] only *describes* the motion, and helps us to predict the relative probabilities of various possible outcomes of our next observation of the object. For example, suppose we have an electron beam being diffracted as it passes through slits in a barrier, before finally striking a distant screen where its arrival is recorded. The wave function for this physical setup will allow us to calculate the relative probabilities for the electrons arriving at different locations on the screen—their arrival being in the form of localized quanta or particles.

The Austrian physicist Erwin Schrödinger was the first to write the equation defining the behavior of the wave function, Ψ, of a material particle. I am not going to enter here into the mathematical derivation of his fundamental equation, but I will draw your attention to the requirements that lead to it, the most important of these being a very unusual one: the equation must be written in such a way that the function describing the motion of material particles should show all the characteristics of a *wave*.

Thus, the behavior of our Ψ function is not analogous to (let us say) the passage of heat through a wall heated on one side, but rather to the movement of a mechanical deformation (a sound wave) through the same wall. Mathematically, it requires a definite, rather restricted form of equation. This fundamental condition, together with the additional requirement that our equations should go over into the equations of classical mechanics when applied to particles of large mass for which quantum effects should become negligible, practically reduces the problem of finding the equation to a purely mathematical exercise.

If you are interested in how the equation looks in its final form, here it is:

$$\nabla^2\Psi + \frac{4\pi m i}{h}\Psi - \frac{8\pi^2 m}{h}U\Psi = 0 \qquad (7)$$

In this equation, the particles have mass, m, and the function U represents the potential of the forces acting on the particles. The equation gives the solution for the motion of the particles, given the particular distribution of forces. The application of *Schrödinger's wave equation* has allowed physicists to develop the most complete and logically consistent picture of all phenomena taking place in the subatomic world. [. . .]

I am particularly sorry that time does not permit me to describe to you the further progress of quantum theory in its relation to the theory of relativity. This development, due mainly to the work of the British physicist Paul Dirac, brings in a number of very interesting points and has also led to some extremely important experimental discoveries. I may be able to return at some other time to these problems, but here for the present I must stop.

Content Questions

1. How did quantum theory alter the idea in classical physics that, for any experiment involving the interaction of physical bodies, observations can be made to any required degree of precision? (318)

2. In the formulation of the relation of energy to frequency, why does Planck's constant (*h*) assure that quantum effects are not observable in everyday life? (319)

3. What did Einstein add to Planck's idea of the quantum in order to theoretically predict the behavior of light? How did Compton's experimental observation of electrons set in motion by light verify Einstein's predictions? (319)

4. How did de Broglie's theory that the waves associated with electrons have discrete values support Bohr's explanation of line spectra in atomic radiation? Why did de Broglie describe the waves as accompanying and directing particles? (320–321)

5. According to classical physics, what is meant by the trajectory of a moving body? Why does Gamow think that the classical notion of trajectory might need to be modified? (321–322)

6. Why does the experimenter in the professor's example keep decreasing the intensity of the source of illumination in order to get a more accurate fix on the moving body's trajectory? In terms of classical physics, why is it important that the experimenter be able to decrease the illumination without limit? (322–323)

7. How does the experimenter try to compensate for the quantum limitations imposed by the photon? Why does this attempt fail to provide an exact trajectory such as the one theoretically possible in classical physics? (323)

8. What is the quantum limitation in the mechanical method for finding a moving body's trajectory? How does this limitation correspond to Planck's and de Broglie's idea of quantum energy levels? (323–324)

9. In the failure of the mechanical method to provide an exact trajectory, what is the relationship between uncertainty about the moving body's momentum and uncertainty about its position? (323–324)

10. What reason does the professor give for presenting only two methods—the optical and the mechanical—for attempting to accurately determine a trajectory? (324)

11. In Mr. Tompkins's dream, how must Planck's constant (*h*) be different from its actual value in order for him to be able to directly observe quantum effects? (325)

12. In the mathematical form for the limitation imposed by quantum conditions $\Delta p_{particle} \times \Delta q_{particle} \cong h$, if the uncertainty in momentum Δp decreases, what must happen to the uncertainty in position Δq? (329)

13. How does knowing the limiting velocity for an electron, combined with Heisenberg's uncertainty relationship, allow us to estimate the size of atoms? (330)

14. In place of the certainties of classical physics, what mathematical methods does quantum mechanics use to describe and predict the motion of objects such as electrons? (330–331)

15. How is the Schrödinger equation related to the equations of classical mechanics? (331)

Discussion Questions

1. In classical physics, why didn't scientists explicitly formulate their conviction that they could reduce without limit disturbances that resulted from the making of observations? Was their conviction scientifically justifiable? (318)

2. How is a natural limit to scientific accuracy different from a practical limit, which is imposed by the methods and experimental equipment that are available for making observations? (318)

3. What does it mean for a physical process to be continuous, as opposed to proceeding "*in a sequence of separate 'shocks'*"? Is continuousness experimentally observable? (318)

4. Why does the professor say that Planck introduced a simple mathematical relation "to achieve agreement with the experimental facts"? (318–319) Does a mathematical formula used in this way, such as Planck's equation $E = hf$, explain experimental facts or just describe a necessary relationship among them?

5. How could de Broglie's speculative idea of the wave properties of particles be useful in giving explanations of experimental results if the idea was incomprehensible from the point of view of the prevailing classical concepts of motion? (320–321)

6. Does the optical method for determining the classical notion of a trajectory lead to a definite result? Why does the professor emphasize that each time the experimenter increases the number of observations, she does so with a desired level of accuracy in mind? (322–323)

7. What is the difference between the sources of uncertainty in the mechanical method for determining a trajectory and the sources of uncertainty in the optical method? (322–324)

8. How are the examples of optical and mechanical methods for determining trajectories idealizations of "the most *general* question of physical measurement?" (324)

9. If we were able to see quantum effects directly at the scale of familiar objects, as Mr. Tompkins does in his dream, would that make them more comprehensible? (325–327)

10. What does the professor mean when he says that position and velocity are "*fundamentally* indefinite"? (326)

11. In what sense can the professor say that a mathematical expression, Planck's constant (h), "governs" the relation between the uncertainty of position and velocity? (326)

12. What change would Mr. Tompkins observe in the billiard ball's motion if the wooden triangle defining the ball's position were enlarged? Would the change observed by him have to do with a physical change in the ball or a change in his knowledge of the ball? (326–327)

13. Why is Mr. Tompkins upset when he sees the billiard ball "leak" out of the wooden triangle? How does this leakage imply that in the subatomic domain, the ordinary principles of mechanics do not apply? (327–328)

14. How does Heisenberg's uncertainty relationship limit what physics is able to discover about the world? (329–330)

15. Why does the professor warn Mr. Tompkins against the erroneous idea that the Schrödinger equation "has a physical reality in our ordinary three-dimensional space"? (330–331)

Suggestions for Further Reading

By the author

Gamow, George. *Mr. Tompkins in Paperback*. Cambridge: Cambridge University Press, 1993. This edition is a reprint of the original version of Gamow's classic, first published in 1940. Although some of the scientific information is slightly out of date, it has its own unique humor worth experiencing.

———. *Thirty Years That Shook Physics*: *The Story of Quantum Theory*. Reprint. New York: Dover Publications, 1985. Gamow tells the story of the period from 1900 to 1930 when quantum theory unsettled the foundations of classical physics through the work of Planck, Bohr, Heisenberg, and others, many of whom were Gamow's teachers and colleagues.

Gamow, George, and Russell Stannard. *The NEW World of Mr. Tompkins*. Cambridge: Cambridge University Press, 1999, 2001. In this updated version of Gamow's classic, from which the selection in *What's the Matter?* is taken, Mr. Tompkins's lively imagination takes readers on a series of adventures from the outer reaches of the cosmos to the microscopic quantum world.

About the topic

Al-Khalili, Jim. *Quantum: A Guide for the Perplexed*. London: Weidenfeld & Nicolson, 2003, 2004. This outstanding survey by a scientist who is also a popular public lecturer captures the ongoing excitement of research and speculation in quantum physics and features beautifully designed graphics.

Gribbin, John. *Q Is for Quantum: An Encyclopedia of Particle Physics*. Edited by Mary Gribbin. New York: Free Press, 1988; New York: Touchstone, 2000. This is the kind of well-written reference book that is interesting to read, not merely to consult. Besides presenting extended definitions of terms and discussions of concepts, it includes short biographies of many of the scientists who shaped modern physics.

Hoffmann, Banesh. *The Strange Story of the Quantum*. 2nd ed. New York: Dover Publications, 1959. This is one of the clearest overall explanations (appropriate for general readers) of the basic concepts of quantum theory. Hoffmann makes use of imaginative analogies and examples to show why quantum theory is so unsettling to commonsense ideas about the world.

It is only through refined measurements and careful experimentation that we can have a wider vision. And then we see unexpected things: we see things that are far from what we would guess—far from what we could have imagined. Our imagination is stretched to the utmost, not, as in fiction, to imagine things that are not really there, but just to comprehend those things that *are* there.

—Richard Feynman,
The Character of Physical Law

RICHARD FEYNMAN

Quantum Behavior

The experimental evidence for the phenomenon of wave-particle duality was one
of the most unsettling aspects of the subatomic realm that physicists had to come
to terms with as they struggled to develop quantum theory in the early twentieth
century. Although quantum theory has continued to make possible extraordinarily
precise predictions and provide guidance for research in physics, the profound questions raised by wave-particle duality remain unresolved. The idea that an electron or
light sometimes behaves as a particle and sometimes as a wave, depending on the
circumstances in which it is experimentally observed, represents the fundamental
break of quantum theory from classical physics.

In classical physics, all phenomena can be explained by means of particles *and*
waves, which are considered essentially different, each with their own distinctive
characteristics. Particles of any size—whether grains of sand or planets—are objects
with definite positions in space and properties such as mass, momentum, and volume. Waves are spread-out disturbances in a medium, such as water or air, with
characteristics of wavelength, frequency, and height (also called amplitude). When
particles come into contact with one another, the forces that arise can cause the
particles to move in different directions while still remaining distinct objects. When
waves meet, unlike particles, they interfere with each other and blend to form a
composite wave, with the result depending on whether or not the peaks and troughs
of the original waves coincide, which is referred to as being in or out of phase. For
classical physics, particles have the status of solid things in the physical world, while
waves are usually considered patterns of motion and displacement in a medium and
they continue to travel due to the properties of the medium.

Between 1900 and 1905, as a result of their attempts to explain experiments
that could not be understood in terms of classical physics, Max Planck and Albert
Einstein proposed several new ideas that brought into question the clear-cut distinction between waves and particles. Planck's quantum hypothesis attributed particle-like
characteristics to radiation, previously thought to consist of waves. Einstein proposed

that light behaves as if it consists of minute particles, later named photons. Also, Einstein's special theory of relativity showed that it was not necessary for electromagnetic waves to have the hypothetical medium of the ether for their propagation, giving waves the status of distinct things, comparable to particles. In the 1920s, the physicist Louis de Broglie proposed the idea that if wavelike phenomena such as light sometimes exhibit particle-like characteristics, particles of matter should sometimes exhibit wavelike characteristics. His equation, $\rho = h/\lambda$, states that the momentum (ρ) of a particle is inversely proportional to the particle's wavelength (λ); that is, the greater the wavelength, the less the momentum, raising the question of what it could mean to say that a particle has wavelength. All of these hypotheses of Planck, Einstein, and de Broglie have been repeatedly confirmed by experiments.

Richard Feynman (1918–1988) was one of the outstanding physicists in the first generation that followed the founders of quantum theory. By the time he began his career, the fundamental principles had been formulated, and quantum mechanics—to which Feynman made immense contributions—had been accepted as the basis of research in all fields of physics. In the early 1960s, when he was at the California Institute of Technology, Feynman was persuaded to develop a freshman physics course. The following selection is from his classroom lectures, *The Feynman Lectures on Physics*.

The experiments with electrons that Feynman describes are new versions of the double-slit experiment that Thomas Young conducted in the early 1800s, in which Young found evidence that light consists of waves producing interference patterns. Feynman uses thought experiments to demonstrate what he calls the *"only* mystery" of quantum mechanics, but in the years following this lecture, actual experiments have clearly shown many times the behavior of electrons that he describes. When a physicist of Feynman's stature repeatedly claims, as he does in the following selection, that he can describe but not explain quantum behavior, he is raising important questions about the nature of scientific knowledge. In demonstrating that scientists' methods of observation seem to influence whether electrons' behavior is particle-like or wavelike, Feynman challenges us to consider whether scientists can continue to maintain the ideal of providing an unambiguous, objective picture of the physical world.

See also Feynman, pages 13–14.

Quantum Behavior

Quantum mechanics" is the description of the behavior of matter in all its details and, in particular, of the happenings on an atomic scale. Things on a very small scale behave like nothing that you have any direct experience about. They do not behave like waves, they do not behave like particles, they do not behave like clouds, or billiard balls, or weights on springs, or like anything that you have ever seen.

Newton thought that light was made up of particles, but then it was discovered that it behaves like a wave. Later, however (in the beginning of the twentieth century), it was found that light did indeed sometimes behave like a particle. Historically, the electron, for example, was thought to behave like a particle, and then it was found that in many respects it behaved like a wave. So it really behaves like neither. Now we have given up. We say: "It is like *neither*."

There is one lucky break, however—electrons behave just like light. The quantum behavior of atomic objects (electrons, protons, neutrons, photons, and so on) is the same for all; they are all "particle waves," or whatever you want to call them. So what we learn about the properties of electrons (which we shall use for our examples) will apply also to all "particles," including photons of light.

This selection is taken from chapter 6, "Quantum Behavior," of Six Easy Pieces.

The gradual accumulation of information about atomic and small-scale behavior during the first quarter of the twentieth century, which gave some indications about how small things do behave, produced an increasing confusion that was finally resolved in 1926 and 1927 by Schrödinger, Heisenberg, and Born.[1] They finally obtained a consistent description of the behavior of matter on a small scale. We take up the main features of that description in this chapter.

Because atomic behavior is so unlike ordinary experience, it is very difficult to get used to and it appears peculiar and mysterious to everyone, both to the novice and to the experienced physicist. Even the experts do not understand it the way they would like to, and it is perfectly reasonable that they should not, because all of direct, human experience and of human intuition applies to large objects. We know how large objects will act, but things on a small scale just do not act that way. So we have to learn about them in a sort of abstract or imaginative fashion and not by connection with our direct experience.

In this chapter we shall tackle immediately the basic element of the mysterious behavior in its most strange form. We choose to examine a phenomenon that is impossible, *absolutely* impossible, to explain in any classical way, and that has in it the heart of quantum mechanics. In reality, it contains the *only* mystery. We cannot explain the mystery in the sense of "explaining" how it works. We will *tell* you how it works. In telling you how it works we will have told you about the basic peculiarities of all quantum mechanics.

An Experiment with Bullets

To try to understand the quantum behavior of electrons, we shall compare and contrast their behavior, in a particular experimental setup, with the more familiar behavior of particles like bullets, and with the behavior of waves like water waves. We consider first the behavior of bullets in the experimental setup shown diagrammatically in figure 1. We have a machine gun that shoots a stream of bullets. It is not a very good gun, in that it sprays the bullets (randomly) over a fairly large angular spread, as

1. [Erwin Schrödinger (1887–1961), Austrian physicist; Werner Heisenberg (1901–1976), German physicist; Max Born (1882–1970), German physicist.]

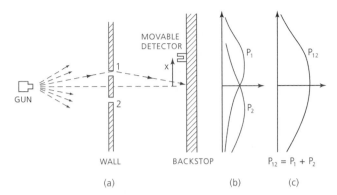

Fig. 1. Interference experiment with bullets.

indicated in the figure. In front of the gun we have a wall (made of armor plate) that has in it two holes just about big enough to let a bullet through. Beyond the wall is a backstop (say a thick wall of wood) that will "absorb" the bullets when they hit it. In front of the wall we have an object that we shall call a "detector" of bullets. It might be a box containing sand. Any bullet that enters the detector will be stopped and accumulated. When we wish, we can empty the box and count the number of bullets that have been caught. The detector can be moved back and forth (in what we will call the x-direction). With this apparatus, we can find out experimentally the answer to the question: "What is the probability that a bullet that passes through the holes in the wall will arrive at the backstop at the distance x from the center?" First, you should realize that we should talk about probability because we cannot say definitely where any particular bullet will go. A bullet that happens to hit one of the holes may bounce off the edges of the hole and may end up anywhere at all. By "probability" we mean the chance that the bullet will arrive at the detector, which we can measure by counting the number that arrive at the detector in a certain time and then taking the ratio of this number to the *total* number that hit the backstop during that time. Or, if we assume that the gun always shoots at the same rate during the measurements, the probability we want is just proportional to the number that reach the detector in some standard time interval.

For our present purposes we would like to imagine a somewhat idealized experiment in which the bullets are not real bullets but *indestructible* bullets—they cannot break in half. In our experiment we find that bullets always arrive in lumps, and when we find something in the detector, it is always one whole bullet. If the rate at which the machine gun fires is made very low, we find that at any given moment either nothing arrives, or one and only one—exactly one—bullet arrives at the backstop. Also, the size of the lump certainly does not depend on the rate of firing of the gun. We shall say: "Bullets *always* arrive in identical lumps." What we measure with our detector is the probability of arrival of a lump. And we measure the probability as a function of x. The result of such measurements with this apparatus (we have not yet done the experiment, so we are really imagining the result) is plotted in the graph drawn in part (c) of figure 1. In the graph we plot the probability to the right and x vertically, so that the x-scale fits the diagram of the apparatus. We call the probability P_{12} because the bullets may have come either through hole 1 or through hole 2. You will not be surprised that P_{12} is large near the middle of the graph but gets small if x is very large. You may wonder, however, why P_{12} has its maximum value at $x = 0$. We can understand this fact if we do our experiment again after covering up hole 2, and once more while covering up hole 1. When hole 2 is covered, bullets can pass only through hole 1, and we get the curve marked P_1 in part (b) of the figure. As you would expect, the maximum of P_1 occurs at the value of x that is on a straight line with the gun and hole 1. When hole 1 is closed, we get the symmetric curve P_2 drawn in the figure. P_2 is the probability distribution for bullets that pass through hole 2. Comparing parts (b) and (c) of figure 1, we find the important result that

$$P_{12} = P_1 + P_2.$$

The probabilities just add together. The effect with both holes open is the sum of the effects with each hole open alone. We shall call this result an observation of "no interference," for a reason that you will see later. So much for bullets. They come in lumps, and their probability of arrival shows no interference.

An Experiment with Waves

Now we wish to consider an experiment with water waves. The apparatus is shown diagrammatically in figure 2. We have a shallow trough of water. A small object labeled the "wave source" is jiggled up and down by a

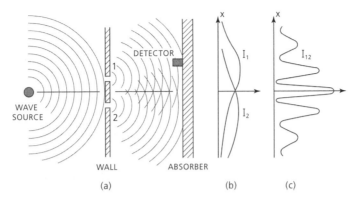

Fig. 2. Interference experiment with water waves.

motor and makes circular waves. To the right of the source we have again a wall with two holes, and beyond that is a second wall, which, to keep things simple, is an "absorber," so that there is no reflection of the waves that arrive there. This can be done by building a gradual sand "beach." In front of the beach we place a detector that can be moved back and forth in the x-direction, as before. The detector is now a device that measures the "intensity" of the wave motion. . . .

With our wave apparatus, the first thing to notice is that the intensity can have *any* size. If the source just moves a very small amount, then there is just a little bit of wave motion at the detector. When there is more motion at the source, there is more intensity at the detector. The intensity of the wave can have any value at all. We would *not* say that there was any "lumpiness" in the wave intensity.

Now let us measure the wave intensity for various values of x (keeping the wave source operating always in the same way). We get the interesting-looking curve marked I_{12} in part (c) of the figure.

[We] observe that the original wave is diffracted at the holes, and new circular waves spread out from each hole. If we cover one hole at a time and measure the intensity distribution at the absorber, we find the rather simple intensity curves shown in part (b) of the figure. I_1 is the intensity of the wave from hole 1 (which we find by measuring when hole 2 is blocked off) and I_2 is the intensity of the wave from hole 2 (seen when hole 1 is blocked).

The intensity I_{12} observed when both holes are open is certainly *not* the sum of I_1 and I_2. We say that there is "interference" of the two waves. At some places (where the curve I_{12} has its maxima) the waves are "in phase" and the wave peaks add together to give a large amplitude and, therefore, a large intensity. We say that the two waves are "interfering constructively" at such places. There will be such constructive interference wherever the distance from the detector to one hole is a whole number of wavelengths larger (or shorter) than the distance from the detector to the other hole.

At those places where the two waves arrive at the detector with a phase difference of π (where they are "out of phase") the resulting wave motion at the detector will be the difference of the two amplitudes. The waves "interfere destructively," and we get a low value for the wave intensity. We expect such low values wherever the distance between hole 1 and the detector is different from the distance between hole 2 and the detector by an odd number of half-wavelengths. The low values of I_{12} in figure 2 correspond to the places where the two waves interfere destructively.

. . . So much for water waves. The intensity can have any value, and it shows interference.

An Experiment with Electrons

Now we imagine a similar experiment with electrons. It is shown diagrammatically in figure 3. We make an electron gun, which consists of a tungsten wire heated by an electric current and surrounded by a metal box with a hole in it. . . . In front of the gun is again a wall (just a thin metal plate) with two holes in it. Beyond the wall is another plate, which will serve as a "backstop." In front of the backstop we place a movable detector. The detector might be a Geiger counter or, perhaps better, an electron multiplier, which is connected to a loudspeaker.

We should say right away that you should not try to set up this experiment (as you could have done with the two we have already described). This experiment has never been done in just this way. The trouble is that the apparatus would have to be made on an impossibly small scale to show the effects we are interested in. We are doing a "thought experiment," which we have chosen because it is easy to think about. We know the results that *would* be obtained because there *are* many experiments

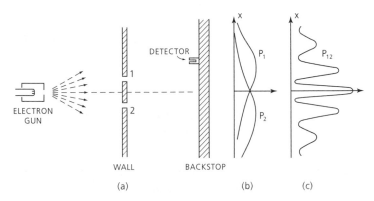

Fig. 3. Interference experiment with electrons.

that have been done, in which the scale and the proportions have been chosen to show the effects we shall describe.

The first thing we notice with our electron experiment is that we hear sharp "clicks" from the detector (that is, from the loudspeaker). And all clicks are the same. There are *no* "half-clicks."

We would also notice that the clicks come very erratically. Something like: click . . . . . click-click . . . click . . . . click . . . . click-click . . . . . . click . . . , etc., just as you have, no doubt, heard a Geiger counter operating. If we count the clicks that arrive in a sufficiently long time—say for many minutes—and then count again for another equal period, we find that the two numbers are very nearly the same. So we can speak of the *average rate* at which the clicks are heard (so-and-so-many clicks per minute on the average).

As we move the detector around, the *rate* at which the clicks appear is faster or slower, but the size (loudness) of each click is always the same. If we lower the temperature of the wire in the gun, the rate of clicking slows down, but still each click sounds the same. We would notice also that if we put two separate detectors at the backstop, one *or* the other would click, but never both at once. (Except that once in a while, if there were two clicks very close together in time, our ear might not sense the separation.) We conclude, therefore, that whatever arrives at the backstop arrives in "lumps." All the "lumps" are the same size: only whole "lumps" arrive, and they arrive one at a time at the backstop. We shall say: "Electrons always arrive in identical 'lumps.' "

Just as for our experiment with bullets, we can now proceed to find experimentally the answer to the question: "What is the relative probability that an electron 'lump' will arrive at the backstop at various distances x from the center?" As before, we obtain the relative probability by observing the rate of clicks, holding the operation of the gun constant. The probability that "lumps" will arrive at a particular x is proportional to the average rate of clicks at that x.

The result of our experiment is the interesting curve marked P_{12} in part (c) of figure 3. Yes! That is the way electrons go.

The Interference of Electron Waves

Now let us try to analyze the curve of figure 3 to see whether we can understand the behavior of the electrons. The first thing we would say is that since they come in lumps, each lump, which we may as well call an electron, has come either through hole 1 or through hole 2. Let us write this in the form of a "proposition":

> Proposition A: Each electron *either* goes through hole 1 *or* it goes through hole 2.

Assuming Proposition A, all electrons that arrive at the backstop can be divided into two classes: (1) those that come through hole 1, and (2) those that come through hole 2. So our observed curve must be the sum of the effects of the electrons that come through hole 1 and the electrons that come through hole 2. Let us check this idea by experiment. First, we will make a measurement for those electrons that come through hole 1. We block off hole 2 and make our counts of the clicks from the detector. From the clicking rate, we get P_1. The result of the measurement is shown by the curve marked P_1 in part (b) of figure 3. The result seems quite reasonable. In a similar way, we measure P_2, the probability distribution for the electrons that come through hole 2. The result of this measurement is also drawn in the figure.

The result P_{12} obtained with *both* holes open is clearly not the sum of P_1 and P_2, the probabilities for each hole alone. In analogy with our water-wave experiment, we say: "There is interference."

For electrons: $P_{12} \neq P_1 + P_2$.

How can such an interference come about? Perhaps we should say: "Well, that means, presumably, that it is *not true* that the lumps go either through hole 1 or hole 2, because if they did, the probabilities should add. Perhaps they go in a more complicated way. They split in half and . . . " But no! They cannot, they always arrive in lumps . . . "Well, perhaps some of them go through 1, and then they go around through 2, and then around a few more times, or by some other complicated path . . . then by closing hole 2, we changed the chance that an electron that *started out* through hole 1 would finally get to the backstop . . . " But notice! There are some points at which very few electrons arrive when *both* holes are open, but that receive many electrons if we close one hole, so *closing* one hole *increased* the number from the other. Notice, however, that at the center of the pattern, P_{12} is more than twice as large as $P_1 + P_2$. It is as though closing one hole *decreased* the number of electrons that come through the other hole. It seems hard to explain *both* effects by proposing that the electrons travel in complicated paths.

It is all quite mysterious. And the more you look at it the more mysterious it seems. Many ideas have been concocted to try to explain the curve for P_{12} in terms of individual electrons going around in complicated ways through the holes. None of them has succeeded. None of them can get the right curve for P_{12} in terms of P_1 and P_2. . . .

We conclude the following: the electrons arrive in lumps, like particles, and the probability of arrival of these lumps is distributed like the distribution of intensity of a wave. It is in this sense that an electron behaves "sometimes like a particle and sometimes like a wave." . . .

. . . There are a large number of subtleties involved in the fact that nature does work this way. We would like to illustrate some of these subtleties for you now. First, since the number that arrives at a particular point is *not* equal to the number that arrives through 1 plus the number that arrives through 2, as we would have concluded from Proposition A, undoubtedly we should conclude that *Proposition A is false*. It is *not* true that the electrons go *either* through hole 1 or hole 2. But that conclusion can be tested by another experiment.

Watching the Electrons

We shall now try the following experiment. To our electron apparatus we add a very strong light source, placed behind the wall and between the two holes, as shown in figure 4. We know that electric charges scatter light. So when an electron passes, however it does pass, on its way to the detector, it will scatter some light to our eye, and we can *see* where the electron goes. If, for instance, an electron were to take the path via hole 2 that is sketched in figure 4, we should see a flash of light coming from the vicinity of the place marked *A* in the figure. If an electron passes through hole 1 we would expect to see a flash from the vicinity of the upper hole. If it should happen that we get light from both places at the same time, because the electron divides in half . . . Let us just do the experiment!

Here is what we see: *every* time that we hear a click from our electron detector (at the backstop), we *also see* a flash of light *either* near hole 1 *or* near hole 2, but *never* both at once! And we observe the same result no matter where we put the detector. From this observation we conclude that when we look at the electrons we find that the electrons go either through one hole or the other. Experimentally, Proposition A is necessarily true.

What, then, is wrong with our argument *against* Proposition A? Why isn't P_{12} just equal to $P_1 + P_2$? Back to the experiment! Let us keep track of the electrons and find out what they are doing. For each position (*x*-location) of the detector we will count the electrons that arrive and *also* keep track of which hole they went through, by watching for the flashes. We can keep track of things this way: whenever we hear a click, we will put a count in column 1 if we see the flash near hole 1, and if we see the flash near hole 2, we will record a count in column 2. Every electron that arrives is recorded in one of two classes: those that come through 1 and those that come through 2. From the number recorded in column 1 we get the probability P'_1 that an electron will arrive at the detector via hole 1; and from the number recorded in column 2 we get P'_2, the probability that an electron will arrive at the detector via hole 2. If we now repeat such a measurement for many values of *x*, we get the curves for P'_1 and P'_2 shown in part (b) of figure 4.

Well, that is not too surprising! We get for P'_1 something quite similar to what we got before for P_1 by blocking off hole 2; and P'_2 is similar to what we got by blocking hole 1. So there is *not* any complicated business

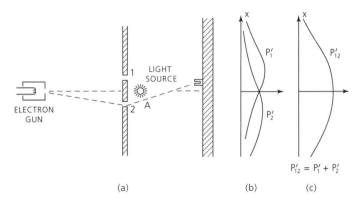

Fig. 4. A different electron experiment.

like going through both holes. When we watch them, the electrons come through just as we would expect them to come through. Whether the holes are closed or open, those that we see come through hole 1 are distributed in the same way whether hole 2 is open or closed.

But wait! What do we have *now* for the *total* probability, the probability that an electron will arrive at the detector by any route? We already have that information. We just pretend that we never looked at the light flashes, and we lump together the detector clicks that we have separated into the two columns. We *must* just *add* the numbers. For the probability that an electron will arrive at the backstop by passing through *either* hole, we do find $P'_{12} = P_1 + P_2$. That is, although we succeeded in watching which hole our electrons come through, we no longer get the old interference curve P_{12}, but a new one, P'_{12}, showing no interference! If we turn out the light, P_{12} is restored.

We must conclude that *when we look at the electrons* the distribution of them on the screen is different than when we do not look. Perhaps it is turning on our light source that disturbs things? It must be that the electrons are very delicate, and the light, when it scatters off the electrons, gives them a jolt that changes their motion. We know that the electric field of the light acting on a charge will exert a force on it. So perhaps we *should* expect the motion to be changed. Anyway, the light exerts a big influence on the electrons. By trying to "watch" the electrons we have changed their motions. That is, the jolt given to the electron when the photon is scattered by it is such as to change the electron's motion enough so that if it *might* have gone to where P_{12} was at a maximum it will instead land where P_{12} was a minimum; that is why we no longer see the wavy interference effects.

You may be thinking: "Don't use such a bright source! Turn the brightness down! The light waves will then be weaker and will not disturb the electrons so much. Surely, by making the light dimmer and dimmer, eventually the wave will be weak enough that it will have a negligible effect." Okay. Let's try it. The first thing we observe is that the flashes of light scattered from the electrons as they pass by do *not* get weaker. *It is always the same-sized flash.* The only thing that happens as the light is made dimmer is that sometimes we hear a click from the detector but see *no flash at all.* The electron has gone by without being "seen." What we are observing is that light *also* acts like electrons; we *knew* that it was "wavy," but now we find that it is also "lumpy." It always arrives—or is scattered—in lumps that we call *photons.* As we turn down the *intensity* of the light source we do not change the *size* of the photons, only the *rate* at which they are emitted. *That* explains why, when our source is dim, some electrons get by without being seen. There did not happen to be a photon around at the time the electron went through.

This is all a little discouraging. If it is true that whenever we "see" the electron we see the same-sized flash, then those electrons we see are *always* the disturbed ones. Let us try the experiment with a dim light anyway. Now whenever we hear a click in the detector we will keep a count in three columns: in column 1 those electrons seen by hole 1, in column 2 those electrons seen by hole 2, and in column 3 those electrons not seen at all. When we work up our data (computing the probabilities) we find these results: those "seen by hole 1" have a distribution like P_1'; those "seen by hole 2" have a distribution like P_2' (so that those "seen by either hole 1 or 2" have a distribution like P_{12}'); and those "not seen at all" have a "wavy" distribution just like P_{12} of figure 3! *If the electrons are not seen, we have interference!*

That is understandable. When we do not see the electron, no photon disturbs it, and when we do see it, a photon has disturbed it. There is always the same amount of disturbance because the light photons all produce the same-sized effects and the effect of the photons being scattered is enough to smear out any interference effect.

Is there not *some* way we can see the electrons without disturbing them? We learned in an earlier chapter that the momentum carried by a photon is inversely proportional to its wavelength ($p = h/\lambda$). Certainly the jolt given to the electron when the photon is scattered toward our eye depends on the momentum that photon carries. Aha! If we want to disturb the electrons only slightly we should not have lowered the *intensity* of the light, we should have lowered its *frequency* (the same as increasing its wavelength). Let us use light of a redder color. We could even use infrared light, or radiowaves (like radar), and "see" where the electron went with the help of some equipment that can "see" light of these longer wavelengths. If we use "gentler" light perhaps we can avoid disturbing the electrons so much.

Let us try the experiment with longer waves. We shall keep repeating our experiment, each time with light of a longer wavelength. At first, nothing seems to change. The results are the same. Then a terrible thing happens. . . . Due to the *wave nature* of the light, there is a limitation on how close two spots can be and still be seen as two separate spots. This distance is of the order of the wavelength of light. So now, when we make the wavelength longer than the distance between our holes, we see a *big* fuzzy flash when the light is scattered by the electrons. We can no longer tell which hole the electron went through! We just know it went somewhere! And it is just with light of this color that we find that the jolts given to the electron are small enough so that P'_{12} begins to look like P_{12}—that we begin to get some interference effect. And it is only for wavelengths much longer than the separation of the two holes (when we have no chance at all of telling where the electron went) that the disturbance due to the light gets sufficiently small that we again get the curve P_{12} shown in figure 3.

In our experiment we find that it is impossible to arrange the light in such a way that one can tell which hole the electron went through, and at the same time not disturb the pattern. It was suggested by Heisenberg that the then-new laws of nature could only be consistent if there were some basic limitation on our experimental capabilities not previously recognized. He proposed, as a general principle, his *uncertainty principle*, which we can state in terms of our experiment as follows: "It is impossible to design an apparatus to determine which hole the electron passes through, that will not at the same time disturb the electrons enough to destroy the interference pattern." If an apparatus is capable of determining which hole the electron goes through, it *cannot* be so delicate that it does not disturb the pattern in an essential way. No one has ever found (or even thought of) a way around the uncertainty principle. So we must assume that it describes a basic characteristic of nature.

The complete theory of quantum mechanics that we now use to describe atoms, and, in fact, all matter, depends on the correctness of the uncertainty principle. Since quantum mechanics is such a successful theory, our belief in the uncertainty principle is reinforced. But if a way to "beat" the uncertainty principle were ever discovered, quantum mechanics would give inconsistent results and would have to be discarded as a valid theory of nature.

"Well," you say, "what about Proposition A? It is true, or is it *not* true, that the electron either goes through hole 1 or it goes through hole 2?" The only answer that can be given is that we have found from experiment that there is a certain special way that we have to think in order that we do not get into inconsistencies. What we must say (to avoid making wrong predictions) is the following: If one looks at the holes, or, more accurately, if one has a piece of apparatus that is capable of determining whether the electrons go through hole 1 or hole 2, then one *can* say that it goes either through hole 1 or hole 2. *But*, when one does *not* try to tell which way the electron goes, when there is nothing in the experiment to disturb the electrons, then one may *not* say that an electron goes either through hole 1 or hole 2. If one does say that, and starts to make any deductions from the statement, he will make errors in the analysis. This is the logical tightrope on which we must walk if we wish to describe nature successfully. . . .

First Principles of Quantum Mechanics

. . . One might still like to ask: "How does it work? What is the machinery behind the law?" No one has found any machinery behind the law. No one can "explain" any more than we have just "explained." No one will give you any deeper representation of the situation. We have no ideas about a more basic mechanism from which these results can be deduced.

We would like to emphasize a very important difference between classical and quantum mechanics. We have been talking about the probability that an electron will arrive in a given circumstance. We have implied that in our experimental arrangement (or even in the best possible one) it would be impossible to predict exactly what would happen. We can only predict the odds! This would mean, if it were true, that physics has given up on the problem of trying to predict exactly what will happen in a definite circumstance. Yes! Physics *has* given up. *We do not know how to predict what would happen in a given circumstance,* and we believe now that it is impossible, that the only thing that can be predicted is the probability of different events. It must be recognized that this is a retrenchment in our earlier ideal of understanding nature. It may be a backward step, but no one has seen a way to avoid it.

We make now a few remarks on a suggestion that has sometimes been made to try to avoid the description we have given: "Perhaps the electron has some kind of internal works—some inner variables—that we do not yet know about. Perhaps that is why we cannot predict what will happen. If we could look more closely at the electron we could be able to tell where it would end up." So far as we know, that is impossible. We would still be in difficulty. Suppose we were to assume that inside the electron there is some kind of machinery that determines where it is going to end up. That machine must *also* determine which hole it is going to go through on its way. But we must not forget that what is inside the electron should not be dependent on what *we* do, and in particular upon whether we open or close one of the holes. So if an electron, before it starts, has already made up its mind (a) which hole it is going to use, and (b) where it is going to land, we should find P_1 for those electrons that have chosen hole 1, P_2 for those that have chosen hole 2, *and necessarily* the sum $P_1 + P_2$ for those that arrive through the two holes. There seems to be no way around this. But we have verified experimentally that that is not the case. And no one has figured a way out of this puzzle. So at the present time we must limit ourselves to computing probabilities. We say "at the present time," but we suspect very strongly that it is something that will be with us forever—that it is impossible to beat that puzzle—that this is the way nature really *is*.

Content Questions

1. Why does Feynman use the term "particle waves" to contrast atomic behavior with ordinary experience? What is he referring to as "ordinary experience"? (339–340)

2. In the experiment with bullets, why are the positions of the bullets that are registered by the detector described in terms of probabilities? (341)

3. Why is it important to imagine that the bullets are indestructible and cannot break into fragments? (341–342)

4. In the probability curve P_{12}, why is the maximum value at $x = 0$? (342)

5. In the experiment with waves, what is the effect of the two holes in the wall, indicated in figure 2? (343–344)

6. What characteristic of waves makes their behavior different from that of "lumpy" bullets? In the description of the interaction of waves, what is meant by "interference"? (343–344)

7. How does the probability curve for wave intensity with both holes open, I_{12} (figure 2), imply that, unlike bullets, waves are not "lumpy"? (343)

8. In the experiment with electrons, what prediction about the shape of the probability curves might be made from the fact that the detector does not register "half-clicks"? (345)

9. How does the probability curve P_{12} seem to contradict Proposition A, which states, "Each electron *either* goes through hole 1 *or* it goes through hole 2"? (345–346)

10. Why do the maximum and minimum points on the probability curve P_{12} make it difficult to explain the apparent interference pattern "by proposing that the electrons travel in complicated paths" through both holes? (347)

11. How does the conclusion that an electron behaves "sometimes like a particle and sometimes like a wave" lead to the further conclusion that Proposition A is false? (347)

12. In order to test the conclusion that Proposition A is false, why is it important to try the experiment of watching electrons by noticing both light flashes and clicks of the detector while keeping both holes open? (348–349)

13. How are the probability curves for the electron-watching experiment (figure 4) related to the probability curves for the experiment with bullets (figure 1)? How are they related to the probability curves for the experiments with waves and electrons (figures 2 and 3) when one of the holes is blocked? (349)

14. According to Feynman's explanation, why is the interference pattern displayed in probability curve P_{12} (figure 3) restored when the light is turned out? (350)

15. How does the phenomenon that there are sometimes detector clicks without light flashes when the intensity of the light source is decreased lead to the conclusion that light is not only "wavy" but also "lumpy"? How does the idea that light is "lumpy" help explain why the interference pattern for electrons appears when the electrons are not disturbed by photons? (350)

16. Why would light with longer wavelengths disturb electrons less? What is the "terrible thing" that Feynman says happens when this kind of light is used in the electron experiment? (351)

17. What is the "basic limitation on our experimental capabilities" stated by the uncertainty principle? (351)

18. What answer does Feynman propose to the question of whether or not Proposition A is true? (352)

19. According to Feynman, what is the difference between classical and quantum mechanics in how they would predict the behavior of electrons in the experiments? (352–353)

20. Why does Feynman reject the proposal that the peculiarities of quantum behavior could be explained away by "some inner variables" of the electron that have not yet been discovered? (353)

Discussion Questions

1. How can knowledge of quantum behavior, acquired "in a sort of abstract or imaginative fashion and not by connection with our direct experience," tell us about the nature of physical reality? (340) In making scientific investigations, what counts as "direct experience"?

2. What does Feynman mean when he says that the phenomenon that he is going to examine "has in it the heart of quantum mechanics"? What is this phenomenon and how does it contain "the *only* mystery" of quantum mechanics? (340)

3. In the experiment with bullets, what conditions determine where a particular bullet will hit the backstop and be registered by the detector? If we had complete knowledge of these conditions, would it still be necessary to describe the final positions of the bullets in terms of probabilities? (341)

4. In the wave experiment, what conditions determine the wave intensity registered by the detector at any particular location on the *x*-axis? Would it be possible to precisely predict the result of actions by the wave source if we had complete knowledge of these conditions? (342–343)

5. What does Feynman mean when he says that a thought experiment is "easy to think about"? (344) How can thought experiments help scientists develop explanations of natural phenomena?

6. On what basis does Feynman formulate Proposition A? In trying to explain quantum behavior, why is it important to try to determine whether Proposition A is true or false by testing it against experimental results? (346)

7. If "turning on our light source" inevitably affects what we can observe about the behavior of atomic objects such as electrons, does quantum mechanics describe an objective physical world existing independently of observers? (349, 351–352)

8. How do the experimental limitations proposed by the uncertainty principle make it impossible to precisely predict the path of an electron in terms of its position and momentum? How do these limitations distinguish quantum behavior from the behavior of such things as bullets and water waves? (351–352)

9. What is the "basic characteristic of nature" described by the uncertainty principle? (352)

10. What is the "special way that we have to think" in order to answer the question of whether the electron goes through hole 1 or hole 2? Does this special way of thinking address the question of what the electron really does? (352)

11. What does Feynman mean by "the logical tightrope on which we must walk if we wish to describe nature successfully"? (352)

12. Why does Feynman suggest that, in giving up trying to predict with absolute certainty *"what would happen in a given circumstance,"* quantum mechanics may represent a backward step in science's earlier ideal of understanding nature? (353) Why would some scientists consider that quantum mechanics' prediction of events in terms of probabilities falls short of this ideal?

Suggestions for Further Reading

By the author

Feynman, Richard P. *QED: The Strange Theory of Light and Matter.* Princeton, NJ: Princeton University Press, 1985, 1988. In these lectures on quantum electrodynamics (QED), the field that he helped to establish, Feynman shows how quantum theory can explain the interaction of light and electrons.

————. *Six Easy Pieces: Essentials of Physics, Explained by Its Most Brilliant Teacher.* Reading, MA: Addison-Wesley, 1995; reprint, New York: Perseus Books Group, 1996. This book, from which the selection in *What's the Matter?* is taken, consists of six chapters from Feynman's landmark *Lectures on Physics.* These chapters discuss Feynman's views on the relation of physics to other sciences and, with a minimum of formal mathematics, outline the basic principles of the conservation of energy, gravitation, and quantum behavior.

About the topic

Gribbin, John. *In Search of Schrödinger's Cat: Quantum Physics and Reality.* New York: Bantam Books, 1984. This introduction to quantum theory for general readers covers both the history of its development as well as its most speculative consequences.

Lightman, Alan. *Great Ideas in Physics: The Conservation of Energy, the Second Law of Thermodynamics, the Theory of Relativity, and Quantum Mechanics.* 3rd ed. New York: McGraw-Hill, 2000. The chapter on quantum mechanics is particularly helpful in explaining both the mathematics and the philosophical implications of the uncertainty principle.

Pagels, Heinz R. *The Cosmic Code: Quantum Physics As the Language of Nature.* New York: Simon & Schuster, 1982; reprint, New York: Bantam Books, 1984. The first half of this survey contains one of the clearest explanations of the break between classical physics, represented by Einstein, and quantum physics, represented by Niels Bohr.

Rae, Alastair I. M. *Quantum Physics: Illusion or Reality?* 2nd ed. Cambridge: Cambridge University Press, 2004. After outlining experiments that display quantum behavior, this book discusses various interpretations that have been offered to explain that behavior.

If the physicist did not demand a theory to explain his results and could be content, say, with a description of the lines appearing on photographic plates, everything would be simple. . . . Difficulties arise only in the attempt to classify and synthesize the results, to establish the relation of cause and effect between them— in short, to construct a theory.

—Werner Heisenberg,
The Physical Principles of the Quantum Theory

WERNER HEISENBERG

The Copenhagen Interpretation of Quantum Theory

In 1913, the Danish physicist Niels Bohr proposed a model of the atom that was partly based on the quantum hypothesis that electrons absorb and emit energy in fixed amounts, called *quanta*. Because Bohr's model was successful in explaining experimental results, physicists came to accept the new and controversial quantum hypothesis as a useful concept for solving problems involving quantum phenomena. However, by the 1920s, atomic science was a piecemeal array of numerous hypotheses and computational techniques that lacked a unifying theory to provide the explanations, interpretations, and mathematical tools essential to scientific progress.

After Bohr won the Nobel Prize in Physics in 1922, his Institute for Theoretical Physics in Copenhagen became a leading research center, attracting scientists from many countries, among them the German physicist Werner Heisenberg (1901–1976), who went to Copenhagen to pursue his interest in quantum theory under Bohr's guidance. In 1925, Heisenberg formulated a mathematical model for quantum mechanics, an entirely new version of the science of mechanics that applies to subatomic phenomena; it was recognized as a foundation for a coherent quantum theory. Almost simultaneously, the Austrian physicist Erwin Schrödinger formulated quantum theory in terms of a wave equation, something more familiar to scientists than Heisenberg's mathematics. Schrödinger intended his equation to describe a physical model for atomic phenomena, which Heisenberg's highly abstract mathematics could not do. However, the German physicist Max Born interpreted the Schrödinger equation as representing statistical probabilities for the occurrence of quantum events rather than representing an actual physical model. Most physicists, including Heisenberg, accepted this interpretation, thereby establishing the importance for quantum theory of mathematical models based on probabilities, unsupported by physical models that could be visualized.

In 1927, Heisenberg proposed that when one is simultaneously determining experimental values for pairs of variables, such as position and velocity or energy and time, it is not possible to reduce the amount of uncertainty for the values to zero. This uncertainty principle, one of the foundations of quantum theory, was summed up by Heisenberg when he wrote, "We *cannot* know, as a matter of principle, the present in all its details." His statement marked the complete break of quantum physics from classical physics, which assumes that present conditions can be known with complete certainty and that the future can be predicted fully. In 1932, Heisenberg was awarded the Nobel Prize in Physics. Bohr and Heisenberg remained friends and colleagues until the Nazi era, when Heisenberg's decision to remain in Germany to work on military research projects led to a permanent break in their relationship. After World War II, Heisenberg became the director of the Max Planck Institute for Physics and Astrophysics in Göttingen, and then in Munich, and actively promoted the peaceful use of atomic power.

In the following selection, Heisenberg discusses the main features of the Copenhagen interpretation of quantum theory, so-called because it developed out of conversations between Bohr and his students at his institute in the 1920s. The Copenhagen interpretation is a set of loosely stated principles that reflect a philosophical stance toward many of the unsettling aspects of quantum theory. Quantum theory had become an accumulation of peculiar experimental observations, mathematical tools (such as those formulated by Heisenberg and Schrödinger), and a few fundamental principles, including Heisenberg's uncertainty principle. Many aspects of quantum theory—including the wave-particle duality of subatomic entities, the reliance on mathematical probabilities to describe physical reality, and the limitations to measuring basic physical properties with absolute certainty—were contrary to both common sense and previously held convictions of classical physics. At the same time, quantum theory yielded highly accurate predictions. The Copenhagen interpretation was proposed to suggest new ways of thinking about what happens when scientists conduct experiments in the realm of quantum events. Because Bohr and Heisenberg made a strong case for it at scientific conferences in the late 1920s, its ideas were widely adopted. However, Albert Einstein was never able to accept its insistence on the fundamental element of chance underlying physical reality, and other scientists have proposed significant alternative interpretations.

Heisenberg's essay raises many profound questions about the role of the observer in scientific investigations and the relation of the realm of quantum events to that of the vastly larger devices used to make scientific measurements. In addition, he discusses the limitations of language in describing quantum events and the use of contradictory pictures of quantum phenomena in a complementary way to understand physical reality.

The Copenhagen Interpretation of Quantum Theory

The Copenhagen interpretation of quantum theory starts from a paradox. Any experiment in physics, whether it refers to the phenomena of daily life or to atomic events, is to be described in the terms of classical physics. The concepts of classical physics form the language by which we describe the arrangement of our experiments and state the results. We cannot and should not replace these concepts with any others. Still the application of these concepts is limited by the relations of uncertainty. We must keep in mind this limited range of applicability of the classical concepts while using them, but we cannot and should not try to improve them.

For a better understanding of this paradox it is useful to compare the procedure for the theoretical interpretation of an experiment in classical physics and in quantum theory. In Newton's mechanics, for instance, we may start by measuring the position and the velocity of the planet whose motion we are going to study. The result of the observation is translated into mathematics by deriving numbers for the coordinates and the momenta of the planet from the observation. Then the equations of motion are used to derive from these values of the coordinates and momenta at a given time the values of these coordinates or any other properties of the system at a later time, and in this way the astronomer can predict the properties of the system at a later time. He can, for instance, predict the exact time for an eclipse of the moon.

In quantum theory the procedure is slightly different. We could, for instance, be interested in the motion of an electron through a cloud chamber and could determine by some kind of observation the initial position and velocity of the electron. But this determination will not be accurate; it will at least contain the inaccuracies following from the uncertainty relations and will probably contain still larger errors due to the difficulty of the experiment. It is the first of these inaccuracies that allows us to translate the result of the observation into the mathematical scheme of quantum theory. A probability function is written down that represents the experimental situation at the time of the measurement, including even the possible errors of the measurement.

This probability function represents a mixture of two things, partly a fact and partly our knowledge of a fact. It represents a fact insofar as it assigns at the initial time the probability unity (i.e., complete certainty) to the initial situation: the electron moving with the observed velocity at the observed position; "observed" means observed within the accuracy of the experiment. It represents our knowledge insofar as another observer could perhaps know the position of the electron more accurately. The error in the experiment does—at least to some extent—not represent a property of the electron but a deficiency in our knowledge of the electron. Also this deficiency of knowledge is expressed in the probability function.

In classical physics one should, in a careful investigation, also consider the error of the observation. As a result one would get a probability distribution for the initial values of the coordinates and velocities and therefore something very similar to the probability function in quantum mechanics. Only the necessary uncertainty due to the uncertainty relations is lacking in classical physics.

When the probability function in quantum theory has been determined at the initial time from the observation, one can from the laws of quantum theory calculate the probability function at any later time and can thereby determine the probability for a measurement giving a specified value of the measured quantity. We can, for instance, predict the probability for finding the electron at a later time at a given point in the cloud chamber. It should be emphasized, however, that the probability function does not in itself represent a course of events in the course of time. It represents a tendency for events and our knowledge of events. The probability function can be connected with reality only if one essential condition is fulfilled: if a new measurement is made to determine a certain property of the system. Only then does the probability function allow us to calculate the probable result of the new measurement. The result of the measurement again will be stated in terms of classical physics.

Therefore, the theoretical interpretation of an experiment requires three distinct steps: (1) the translation of the initial experimental situation into a probability function; (2) the following up of this function in the course of time; and (3) the statement of a new measurement to be made of the system, the result of which can then be calculated from the probability function. For the first step the fulfillment of the uncertainty relations is a necessary condition. The second step cannot be described in terms of the classical concepts; there is no description of what happens to the system between the initial observation and the next measurement. It is only in the third step that we change over again from the "possible" to the "actual."

Let us illustrate these three steps in a simple ideal experiment. It has been said that the atom consists of a nucleus and electrons moving around the nucleus; it has also been stated that the concept of an electronic orbit is doubtful. One could argue that it should at least in principle be possible to observe the electron in its orbit. One should simply look at the atom through a microscope of a very high resolving power; then one would see the electron moving in its orbit. Such a high resolving power could . . . not be obtained by a microscope using ordinary light, since the inaccuracy of the measurement of the position can never be smaller than the wavelength of the light. But a microscope using γ-rays with a wavelength smaller than the size of the atom would do. Such a microscope has not yet been constructed, but that should not prevent us from discussing the ideal experiment.

Is the first step, the translation of the result of the observation into a probability function, possible? It is possible only if the uncertainty relation is fulfilled after the observation. The position of the electron will be known with an accuracy given by the wavelength of the γ-ray. The electron may have been practically at rest before the observation. But in the act of observation at least one light quantum of the γ-ray must have passed the microscope and must first have been deflected by the electron. Therefore, the electron has been pushed by the light quantum, it has changed its momentum and its velocity, and one can show that the uncertainty of this change is just big enough to guarantee the validity of the uncertainty relations. Therefore, there is no difficulty with the first step.

At the same time one can easily see that there is no way of observing the orbit of the electron around the nucleus. The second step shows a wave packet moving not around the nucleus but away from the atom, because the first light quantum will have knocked the electron out from the atom. The momentum of light quantum of the γ-ray is much bigger than the original momentum of the electron if the wavelength of the γ-ray is much smaller than the size of the atom. Therefore, the first light quantum is sufficient to knock the electron out of the atom and one can never observe more than one point in the orbit of the electron; therefore, there is no orbit in the ordinary sense. The next observation—the third step—will show the electron on its path from the atom. Quite generally there is no way of describing what happens between two consecutive observations. It is of course tempting to say that the electron must have been somewhere between the two observations and that therefore the electron must have described some kind of path or orbit even if it may be impossible to know which path. This would be a reasonable argument in classical physics. But in quantum theory it would be a misuse of the language that, as we will see later, cannot be justified. We can leave it open for the moment, whether this warning is a statement about the way in which we should talk about atomic events or a statement about the events themselves, whether it refers to epistemology or to ontology. In any case we have to be very cautious about the wording of any statement concerning the behavior of atomic particles.

Actually we need not speak of particles at all. For many experiments it is more convenient to speak of matter waves; for instance, of stationary matter waves around the atomic nucleus. Such a description would directly contradict the other description if one does not pay attention to the limitations given by the uncertainty relations. Through the limitations the contradiction is avoided. The use of "matter waves" is convenient, for example, when dealing with the radiation emitted by the atom. By means of its frequencies and intensities, the radiation gives information about the oscillating charge distribution in the atom, and there the wave picture comes much nearer to the truth than the particle picture. Therefore, Bohr[1] advocated the use of both pictures, which he called "complementary" to each other. The two pictures are of course mutually exclusive, because a certain thing cannot at the same time be a particle (i.e., substance confined to a very small volume) and a wave (i.e., a field spread out over a large space), but the two complement each other. By playing with both pictures, by going from the one picture to the other and back again, we finally get the right impression of the strange kind of reality behind our atomic experiments. Bohr uses the concept of "complementarity" at several places in the interpretation of quantum theory. The knowledge of the position of a particle is complementary to the knowledge of its velocity or momentum. If we know the one with high accuracy we cannot know the other with high accuracy; still we must know both for determining the behavior of the system. The space-time description of the atomic events is complementary to their deterministic description. The probability function obeys an equation of motion as the coordinates did in Newtonian mechanics; its change in the course of time is completely determined by the quantum mechanical equation, but it does not allow a description in space and time. The observation, on the other hand, enforces the description in space and time but breaks the determined continuity of the probability function by changing our knowledge of the system.

Generally the dualism between two different descriptions of the same reality is no longer a difficulty since we know from the mathematical formulation of the theory that contradictions cannot arise. The dualism between the two complementary pictures—waves and particles—is also clearly brought out in the flexibility of the mathematical scheme. The formalism is normally written to resemble Newtonian mechanics, with equations of motion for the coordinates and the momenta of the particles. But by a simple transformation it can be rewritten to resemble a wave equation for an ordinary three-dimensional matter wave. Therefore, this possibility of playing with different complementary pictures has its analogy in the different transformations of the mathematical scheme; it does not lead to any difficulties in the Copenhagen interpretation of quantum theory.

A real difficulty in the understanding of this interpretation arises, however, when one asks the famous question: But what happens "really"

1. [Niels Bohr (1885–1962), Danish physicist.]

in an atomic event? It has been said before that the mechanism and the results of an observation can always be stated in terms of the classical concepts. But what one deduces from an observation is a probability function, a mathematical expression that combines statements about possibilities or tendencies with statements about our knowledge of facts. So we cannot completely objectify the result of an observation; we cannot describe what "happens" between this observation and the next. This looks as if we had introduced an element of subjectivism into the theory, as if we meant to say that what happens depends on our way of observing it or on the fact that we observe it. Before discussing this problem of subjectivism it is necessary to explain quite clearly why one would get into hopeless difficulties if one tried to describe what happens between two consecutive observations.

For this purpose it is convenient to discuss the following ideal experiment: We assume that a small source of monochromatic light radiates toward a black screen with two small holes in it. The diameter of the holes may be not much bigger than the wavelength of the light, but their distance will be very much bigger. At some distance behind the screen a photographic plate registers the incident light. If one describes this experiment in terms of the wave picture, one says that the primary wave penetrates through the two holes; there will be secondary spherical waves starting from the holes that interfere with one another, and the interference will produce a pattern of varying intensity on the photographic plate.

The blackening of the photographic plate is a quantum process, a chemical reaction produced by single light quanta. Therefore, it must also be possible to describe the experiment in terms of light quanta. If it would be permissible to say what happens to the single light quantum between its emission from the light source and its absorption in the photographic plate, one could argue as follows: The single light quantum can come through the first hole or through the second one. If it goes through the first hole and is scattered there, its probability for being absorbed at a certain point of the photographic plate cannot depend upon whether the second hole is closed or open. The probability distribution on the plate will be the same as if only the first hole was open. If the experiment is repeated many times and one takes together all cases in which the light quantum has gone through the first hole, the blackening of the plate due to these cases will correspond to this probability distribution. If one considers only those light quanta that go through the second hole, the blackening should correspond to a probability distribution derived from the assumption that only the second hole is open. The total blackening, therefore, should just be the sum of the blackenings in the two cases; in other words, there should be no interference pattern. But we know this is not correct, and the experiment will show the interference pattern. Therefore, the statement that any light quantum must have gone *either* through the first *or* through the second hole is problematic and leads to contradictions. This example shows clearly that the concept of the probability function does not allow a description of what happens between two observations. Any attempt to find such a description would lead to contradictions; this must mean that the term *happens* is restricted to the observation.

Now, this is a very strange result, since it seems to indicate that the observation plays a decisive role in the event and that the reality varies, depending upon whether we observe it or not. To make this point clearer we have to analyze the process of observation more closely.

To begin with, it is important to remember that in natural science we are not interested in the universe as a whole, including ourselves, but we direct our attention to some part of the universe and make that the object of our studies. In atomic physics this part is usually a very small object, an atomic particle or a group of such particles, sometimes much larger—the size does not matter; but it is important that a large part of the universe, including ourselves, does *not* belong to the object.

Now, the theoretical interpretation of an experiment starts with the two steps that have been discussed. In the first step we have to describe the arrangement of the experiment, eventually combined with a first observation, in terms of classical physics and translate this description into a probability function. This probability function follows the laws of quantum theory, and its change in the course of time, which is continuous, can be calculated from the initial conditions; this is the second step. The probability function combines objective and subjective elements. It contains statements about possibilities or better tendencies (*potentia* in Aristotelian philosophy), and these statements are completely objective, they do not depend on any observer; and it contains statements about our knowledge of the system that of course are subjective insofar as they may be different for different observers. In ideal cases the subjective element in the probability function may be practically negligible as compared with the objective one. The physicists then speak of a *pure case*.

When we now come to the next observation, the result of which should be predicted from the theory, it is very important to realize that our object has to be in contact with the other part of the world, namely, the experimental arrangement, the measuring rod, etc., before or at least at the moment of observation. This means that the equation of motion for the probability function does now contain the influence of the interaction with the measuring device. This influence introduces a new element of uncertainty, since the measuring device is necessarily described in the terms of classical physics; such a description contains all the uncertainties concerning the microscopic structure of the device that we know from thermodynamics, and since the device is connected with the rest of the world, it contains in fact the uncertainties of the microscopic structure of the whole world. These uncertainties may be called objective insofar as they are simply a consequence of the description in the terms of classical physics and do not depend on any observer. They may be called subjective insofar as they refer to our incomplete knowledge of the world.

After this interaction has taken place, the probability function contains the objective element of tendency and the subjective element of incomplete knowledge, even if it has been a pure case before. It is for this reason that the result of the observation cannot generally be predicted with certainty; what can be predicted is the probability of a certain result of the observation, and this statement about the probability can be checked by repeating the experiment many times. The probability function—unlike the common procedure in Newtonian mechanics—does not describe a certain event but, at least during the process of observation, a whole ensemble of possible events.

The observation itself changes the probability function discontinuously; it selects of all possible events the actual one that has taken place. Since through the observation our knowledge of the system has changed discontinuously, its mathematical representation also has undergone the discontinuous change and we speak of a *quantum jump*. When the old adage "Natura non facit saltus"[2] is used as a basis for criticism of quantum theory, we can reply that certainly our knowledge can change suddenly and that this fact justifies the use of the term *quantum jump*.

---

2. ["Nature does not make jumps."]

Therefore, the transition from the "possible" to the "actual" takes place during the act of observation. If we want to describe what happens in an atomic event, we have to realize that the word *happens* can apply only to the observation, not to the state of affairs between two observations. It applies to the physical, not the psychical act of observation, and we may say that the transition from the possible to the actual takes place as soon as the interaction of the object with the measuring device, and thereby with the rest of the world, has come into play; it is not connected with the act of registration of the result by the mind of the observer. The discontinuous change in the probability function, however, takes place with the act of registration, because it is the discontinuous change of our knowledge in the instant of registration that has its image in the discontinuous change of the probability function.

To what extent, then, have we finally come to an objective description of the world, especially of the atomic world? In classical physics, science started from the belief—or should one say from the illusion?—that we could describe the world, or at least parts of the world, without any reference to ourselves. This is actually possible to a large extent. We know that the city of London exists whether we see it or not. It may be said that classical physics is just that idealization in which we can speak about parts of the world without any reference to ourselves. Its success has led to the general ideal of an objective description of the world. Objectivity has become the first criterion for the value of any scientific result. Does the Copenhagen interpretation of quantum theory still comply with this ideal? One may perhaps say that quantum theory corresponds to this ideal as far as possible. Certainly quantum theory does not contain genuine subjective features, it does not introduce the mind of the physicist as a part of the atomic event. But it starts from the division of the world into the "object" and the rest of the world, and from the fact that at least for the rest of the world we use the classical concepts in our description. This division is arbitrary and historically a direct consequence of our scientific method; the use of the classical concepts is finally a consequence of the general human way of thinking. But this is already a reference to ourselves and insofar our description is not completely objective.

It has been stated in the beginning that the Copenhagen interpretation of quantum theory starts with a paradox. It starts from the fact that we describe our experiments in the terms of classical physics and at the same time from the knowledge that these concepts do not fit nature accurately. The tension between these two starting points is the root of the statistical character of quantum theory. Therefore, it has sometimes been suggested that one should depart from the classical concepts altogether and that a radical change in the concepts used for describing the experiments might possibly lead back to a nonstatistical, completely objective description of nature.

This suggestion, however, rests upon a misunderstanding. The concepts of classical physics are just a refinement of the concepts of daily life and are an essential part of the language that forms the basis of all natural science. Our actual situation in science is such that we *do* use the classical concepts for the description of the experiments, and it was the problem of quantum theory to find theoretical interpretation of the experiments on this basis. There is no use in discussing what could be done if we were other beings than we are. At this point we have to realize, as von Weizsäcker has put it, that "nature is earlier than man, but man is earlier than natural science." The first part of the sentence justifies classical physics, with its ideal of complete objectivity. The second part tells us why we cannot escape the paradox of quantum theory, namely, the necessity of using the classical concepts.

We have to add some comments on the actual procedure in the quantum-theoretical interpretation of atomic events. It has been said that we always start with a division of the world into an object, which we are going to study, and the rest of the world, and that this division is to some extent arbitrary. It should indeed not make any difference in the final result if we, e.g., add some part of the measuring device or the whole device to the object and apply the laws of quantum theory to this more complicated object. It can be shown that such an alteration of the theoretical treatment would not alter the predictions concerning a given experiment. This follows mathematically from the fact that the laws of quantum theory are for the phenomena in which Planck's constant can be considered as a very small quantity, approximately identical with the classical laws. But it would be a mistake to believe that this application of the quantum-theoretical laws to the measuring device could help to avoid the fundamental paradox of quantum theory.

The measuring device deserves this name only if it is in close contact with the rest of the world, if there is an interaction between the device and the observer. Therefore, the uncertainty with respect to the microscopic behavior of the world will enter into the quantum-theoretical system here just as well as in the first interpretation. If the measuring device could be isolated from the rest of the world, it would be neither a measuring device nor could it be described in the terms of classical physics at all.

With regard to this situation Bohr has emphasized that it is more realistic to state that the division into the object and the rest of the world is not arbitrary. Our actual situation in research work in atomic physics is usually this: we wish to understand a certain phenomenon, we wish to recognize how this phenomenon follows from the general laws of nature. Therefore, that part of matter or radiation that takes part in the phenomenon is the natural "object" in the theoretical treatment and should be separated in this respect from the tools used to study the phenomenon. This again emphasizes a subjective element in the description of atomic events, since the measuring device has been constructed by the observer, and we have to remember that what we observe is not nature in itself but nature exposed to our method of questioning. Our scientific work in physics consists in asking questions about nature in the language that we possess and trying to get an answer from experiment by the means that are at our disposal. In this way quantum theory reminds us, as Bohr has put it, of the old wisdom that when searching for harmony in life one must never forget that in the drama of existence we are ourselves both players and spectators. It is understandable that in our scientific relation to nature our own activity becomes very important when we have to deal with parts of nature into which we can penetrate only by using the most elaborate tools.

Content Questions

1. What paradox is the starting point of the Copenhagen interpretation of quantum theory? (363)

2. How does the procedure for interpreting an experiment according to quantum theory differ from the procedure according to classical physics? (363–364)

3. What does Heisenberg mean when he says that the "probability function represents a mixture of two things, partly a fact and partly our knowledge of a fact"? (364)

4. What inaccuracy in the procedure for determining the initial position and velocity of an electron does not enter into the procedure for determining the initial position and velocity of a planet? (364)

5. After the initial observation of an electron's position, what information does the probability function give about the electron's future position? What does the probability function allow us to do after making a new measurement? (364–365)

6. In Heisenberg's microscope experiment, why does he use gamma rays instead of ordinary light? What effect does the wavelength of gamma rays have on the accuracy of the experiment? (365–366)

7. In the microscope experiment, why is there no way to describe what happens between two consecutive observations? (366)

8. According to Heisenberg and Bohr, how do the mutually exclusive pictures of electrons as particles and as waves complement each other? (366–367)

9. What contradiction results from stating that in the two-hole experiment a light quantum must have gone through either the first hole or the second hole? (368–369)

10. What do physicists mean by a *pure case*? In making an experimental observation, how does the interaction of the measuring device with the object of investigation alter a pure case? (369)

11. What does Heisenberg mean by a *quantum jump*? How does this event result from the influence on the probability function of an observation being made? (370)

12. According to Heisenberg, what happens during an observation that results in the transition from the "possible" to the "actual"? What occurs when the mind of the observer registers the result of the observation? (371)

13. What does the Copenhagen interpretation introduce into science that is a departure from classical physics' criterion of complete objectivity? (371)

14. Why does Heisenberg say that the suggestion to depart from the concepts of classical physics used to describe quantum experiments "rests upon a misunderstanding"? (372)

15. Why can't adding the classical measuring device to the atomic object of study and then applying the laws of quantum theory to "this more complicated object" avoid the fundamental paradox of quantum theory? (372)

Discussion Questions

1. What does it mean to describe a physics experiment "in the terms of classical physics"? Why would an experiment, either in classical physics or quantum theory, need a "theoretical interpretation"? (363)

2. In speaking of the kinds of inaccuracies in an experiment with electrons, why does Heisenberg call the uncertainty due to the uncertainty relations "necessary"? (364) In physics, is there a difference between inaccuracy and uncertainty?

3. Why is making a new measurement the "essential condition" for connecting the probability function to reality? Why is it necessary to fulfill this condition in order to calculate the result of the new measurement? (365)

4. In his microscope experiment, what does Heisenberg mean when he says that "there is no orbit in the ordinary sense"? Why is it not reasonable in quantum theory to say that the electron must have been somewhere between two consecutive observations? (366)

5. According to Heisenberg, why do we have to be "very cautious about the wording of any statement concerning the behavior of atomic particles"? (366) How are the verbal statements made about observations and experiments as important as measurements and calculations?

6. How can the use of "matter waves" for convenience when dealing with atomic radiation come "much nearer to the truth than the particle picture"? (366–367) Does a theoretical picture that is convenient work the same as one that is true?

7. What is the "right impression of the strange kind of reality behind our atomic experiments" that Heisenberg says we can get by going back and forth between the wave and particle pictures? (367)

8. Why is Heisenberg convinced that the flexible mathematical formulation of quantum theory shows that the dualism of complementary wave and particle pictures "does not lead to any difficulties in the Copenhagen interpretation"? (367)

9. How does the concept of the probability function preclude a description of what happens between two observations in the two-hole experiment? (368–369)

10. In natural science, what does it mean for a measuring device to be in contact with an object of study? What does Heisenberg mean when he says that the measuring device itself is "connected with the rest of the world"? (370)

11. How is a probability distribution in Newtonian mechanics different from the "ensemble of possible events" provided by a probability function in quantum theory? (370)

12. Why does Heisenberg suggest that it was an illusion for classical physics to believe that it could describe the world objectively, "without any reference to ourselves"? (371) How does the Copenhagen interpretation attempt to avoid this illusion?

13. How does Weizsäcker's statement that "man is earlier than natural science" affirm the necessity of using the classical concepts in describing experiments? (372)

14. According to Heisenberg and the Copenhagen interpretation, how should scientists decide where to make the division between their object of study and the rest of the world? Why does Bohr think that this division is not arbitrary? (372–373)

15. Is Heisenberg correct in saying that "what we observe is not nature in itself but nature exposed to our method of questioning"? (373) Can scientists keep the conviction that they are investigating an objective world without the belief that they are making observations of nature itself?

Suggestions for Further Reading

By the author

Heisenberg, Werner. *Encounters with Einstein: And Other Essays on People, Places, and Particles.* Princeton, NJ: Princeton University Press, 1989. In this collection of writings from his last years, Heisenberg reflects on the reasons for the directions taken by modern science and its impact on contemporary society.

———. *Physics and Philosophy: The Revolution in Modern Science.* Amherst, NY: Prometheus Books, 1999. The essays in this collection, from which the selection in *What's the Matter?* is taken, discuss the underlying philosophical ideas of the Copenhagen interpretation of quantum theory and their significance for modern science and culture.

About the author

Cassidy, David C. *Uncertainty: The Life and Science of Werner Heisenberg.* New York: W. H. Freeman and Company, 1991. Along with providing a detailed history of Heisenberg's scientific achievements, this biography explores the controversy surrounding the part he played in Germany's attempt to build atomic weapons during World War II.

About the topic

Bolles, Edmund Blair. *Einstein Defiant: Genius Versus Genius in the Quantum Revolution.* Washington, D.C.: Joseph Henry Press, 2004. This history depicts Einstein's lifelong refusal to accept the probabilistic world of quantum theory that put him at odds with Niels Bohr and the mainstream of twentieth-century physics.

Frayn, Michael. *Copenhagen.* New York: Anchor Books, 2000. Based on a meeting between Heisenberg and Niels Bohr during World War II, this play speculates on what they discussed and its implications for Germany's effort to build atomic weapons. The dramatic structure is a clever and moving portrayal of the uncertainty principle applied to human interactions.

Pais, Abraham. *Niels Bohr's Times.* Oxford: Oxford University Press, 1991. This biography of one of the founders of modern physics thoroughly covers his scientific accomplishments in atomic theory and quantum physics and provides a complete portrait of his personal life and his importance as a teacher and public figure.

It is not instinctive for a scientist to adopt an attitude that leads to asking about a fundamental theoretical proposition the question, "Is it reasonable?" . . . For the scientist the natural question to ask takes the different form, "What makes you think that might be the case?" This is an altogether more open form of inquiry.

—John Polkinghorne, *Exploring Reality: The Intertwining of Science and Religion*

JOHN POLKINGHORNE

Quantum Perplexity and Debate

Following the proposal by Max Planck and Albert Einstein in the early twentieth century that particles absorb and emit energy in discrete packages, or quanta, scientists struggled to come to terms with the unsettling new field of quantum theory. Planck and Einstein had proposed the quantum hypothesis to solve problems with experimental results in thermodynamics and the photoelectric effect that had resisted explanation in terms of classical physics. The idea that dynamic processes in nature are continuous and divisible without limit had been an underlying assumption of physical science from the time of Aristotle. Since quantum theory introduced ideas that contradicted this assumption, scientists reluctantly adopted the theory only because it was successful in accounting for phenomena in the rapidly developing study of atomic structure. Continuing to the present day, quantum theory has provided the foundation for investigating the structure of matter and has revolutionized numerous fields, including chemistry, electrodynamics, molecular biology, and cosmology. The effectiveness of quantum mechanics in helping scientists to conduct experiments in the domain of subatomic particles and to solve theoretical and practical problems is unquestionable. Entire industries are based on products that use quantum technology, including computer chips, lasers, and MRI scanners. Although quantum theory has had great success, many scientists and philosophers continue to ask searching questions concerning what the theory tells us about the nature of the physical world.

John Polkinghorne (1930–) has had a distinguished career both as a physicist and as a theologian. He studied physics at Trinity College, Cambridge, where one of his teachers was Paul Dirac, a pioneer in quantum mechanics. In 1979, Polkinghorne was ordained a priest of the Church of England, and he has written many books that explore the difficult question of God's relation to a world governed by scientific law. In the following selection, Polkinghorne investigates several interpretations of quantum theory—alternatives to the widely accepted Copenhagen interpretation—that attempt to explain the theory's central dilemma: the relation of the domain of quantum effects to the more familiar domain of Newtonian mechanics.

By the 1920s, it was apparent that subatomic events do not conform to the assumptions and laws of classical physics. The discontinuity of quantum effects profoundly alters what can be known about the movement of subatomic things such as electrons, since there is no way to understand the idea of a continuous path in their jump from one quantum energy level to another. Furthermore, for different experiments it is convenient to consider electrons as either particles or waves, which leads to the question of whether they are really one or the other. At a deeper level, quantum theory calls into question belief in the continuity of the chain of cause and effect. Polkinghorne focuses on this last problem through an event called the collapse of the wave packet, related to a fundamental equation formulated by Erwin Schrödinger in 1926, which treats subatomic things as wavelike. The equation allows physicists to define a range of probable values for an electron's momentum and position by means of a mathematical concept called a wave packet. The wave packet represents a wavelike electron and can be imagined as a package of waves of various wavelengths confined to a small region in space approximately the size of an equivalent particle-like electron. When scientists make measurements of an electron, the wave packet, which contains many probable values for the electron's characteristics, is said to collapse into the one value determined by the measuring instruments. Polkinghorne raises a critical question about this event when he asks, "What fixes the result of a particular experiment when the theory is only able to assign probabilities for a variety of possible outcomes?"

The question Polkinghorne investigates concerns one of the fundamental convictions of physics: that its goal is to provide greater understanding of an objective physical world that is unified by the same natural laws applying to all domains, whether cosmic, human, or subatomic in scale. The dilemma of what causes the wave packet's collapse raises doubt about how this unity of domains is possible. Some physicists dismiss questions such as these as irrelevant to the practice of physics, especially in light of quantum theory's success as a set of procedures for conducting research. Polkinghorne places these questions at the center of physics and invites us to think about the need for interpretations of quantum theory that can lead to greater understanding about the world.

Quantum Perplexity and Debate

The Schrödinger equation is as nice a differential equation as any classical physicist could wish to see. All is smoothness and continuity. It is only when we try to extract some information by means of a measurement that the traumatic discontinuity of the collapse of the wave packet takes place. Here is the unique point at which the fitful indeterminacy of quantum theory makes itself felt. Here, in consequence, is the source of perplexity and debate.

Measurement involves an intervention by our everyday world into the quantum world. Our macroscopic world is precise; it is the domain of classical Newtonian physics. The microscopic quantum world is imprecise; it is the domain of Heisenberg uncertainty. How do these two worlds interlock? In particular, how does it come about that the imprecise quantum world yields a precise answer when it is experimentally interrogated? What fixes the result of a particular experiment when the theory is only able to assign probabilities for a variety of possible outcomes?

Because we do not have direct access to the microworld, any measurement involves a chain of amplification by which the state of affairs on the

This selection is taken from chapter 6, "Fixing It," of The Quantum World.

very small scale is made to manifest a corresponding signal in the every-day world of the laboratory. In the time-honored language of thought experiments, the pointer moves across the scale to a mark saying "here." Let us consider such a chain of consequence, spanning small to large.

Suppose we are trying to determine the spin of an electron along a particular direction, to find out whether it is "up" or "down." The standard technique is to use a Stern-Gerlach experiment. The electron is made to pass through a magnetic field which deflects it in different directions according to the different orientations of the spin. If the spin is "up," the electron goes off one way, if it is "down," the electron goes off the other way. We can place some detecting devices, photographic plates or Geiger counters, say, which will register whether the electron has arrived at A or B. If we analyze such an experiment, what we obtain is a chain of correlations:

> If the electron's spin is "up," then it will be deflected to A, and then the Geiger counter at A will click

> *or*

> if the electron's spin is "down," then it will be deflected to B, and then the Geiger counter at B will click.

We can extend the chain to take into account the presence of an observer who "then hears the counter at A(B) click."

You see what is happening? The buck of decision is being passed down the chain of consequence. At no stage do we say *now* this happens (the counter at A actually clicks) but always *then* this happens (if . . . then the counter at A clicks). All that is being asserted is a correlation. Yet we know that the matter does get settled somehow. Experiments actually yield results. The question is, where along the chain does the collapse of the wave packet take place? Where do we shrug off the "I will if you will" tale of correlation and reach an actual decision about what has occurred on this occasion?

The need to settle this point is emphasized by the stories of two of the cast list in quantum mechanical folklore: Schrödinger's cat and Wigner's friend.

The unfortunate animal in question is incarcerated in a closed box which also contains a radioactive atom with a 50-50 chance of decaying in the next hour, emitting a γ-ray in the process. If this emission takes place, it triggers the breaking of a vial of poison gas, which instantaneously kills the cat. At the end of the hour, before I lift off the lid of the box, the orthodox principles of quantum theory bid me consider the cat to be in a state which is an evenhanded superposition of the states "alive" and "dead." On opening the box the wave packet collapses and I find either a cooling corpse or a frisking feline. It is scarcely necessary to emphasize the absurdity of the proposition that this state of affairs, whichever it is, has been brought about by my action in lifting the lid. It must surely be the case that the cat is competent to act as observer of its own survival or demise and does not need me to settle the issue for it. Along the chain of consequence, from atomic decay to my act of observation, things must have got fixed at least by the time that the cat's experience entered into it.

Wigner's friend serves to make a similar point. He is observing the electron being deflected by the magnetic field in the Stern-Gerlach experiment and listening to the Geiger counters to see whether it is the one at A or the one at B which clicks. Wigner knows a priori that the probabilities of these two events are equal. The electron beam is unpolarized (as we say), so that it is an evenhanded superposition of "up" and "down." On a particular occasion, Wigner asks his friend which counter clicked. The friend replies that it was A. For Wigner the electron's wave packet then collapses into the state in which the spin is definitely "up." Yet this state of affairs has surely not been brought about by Wigner's intervention. If he asks his friend "What did you hear before I asked you?" his friend will reply with some impatience "I told you before, the counter at A clicked." Wigner has to take his friend's claim to experience as seriously as we take Wigner's. At least by the time that the friend heard the click it must have been settled on that occasion that the electron's spin was "up."

Schrödinger's cat and Wigner's friend are links in the chain from microscopic object to my knowing the result of a measurement made upon that object. The reasonable interpretation of their experience seems to demand that by the time the chain had reached them the actual result of the observation had become fixed. The cat knows whether it is dead; Wigner's friend knows what he heard. In other words, the intervention of consciousness in either a developed form (Wigner's friend) or at a more rudimentary level (Schrödinger's cat) seems to provide the latest link in the chain at which the matter could be settled. Of course, it might be the case that it had been settled long before that.

Four different ways have been suggested in which one might seek a resolution of the problem of the collapse of the wave packet. None of them is free from difficulty.

The first one tries to cut the chain. It says that the wave function is not a description of a physical system but simply a description of my knowledge of it. It does not worry where that knowledge comes from. There is, of course, no problem about a state of knowledge suffering a sharp change. I have no idea which football club won the FA Cup in 1981. Consulting a reference book "collapses my soccer information wave packet" into the unique state "Tottenham Hotspur." I do not need to agonize about that sort of discontinuity of experience. It is clear enough what has happened. I was ignorant and then I was enlightened. The change is in my mind.

It sounds seductively simple to say that it is all in the mind. Bishop Berkeley, in the eighteenth century, encouraged us to contemplate just such a step. He would, however, be an ill-chosen ally for quantum mechanics, for a retreat into the idealist castle would be a highly injudicious move. It would have the effect of demoting physics to a branch of psychology. The subject cannot allow itself to suffer such a fate. The knowledge with which it deals originates outside us; the concept of nature standing over against us is not lightly to be abandoned. Without it the point of physics would be lost, the authentic experience of discovery denied. . . .

We must, therefore, take seriously the chain of correlated consequence linking electron to observer. The second possibility is to say that things get fixed along that chain once the objects with which we have to deal have become "large." In essence this is the answer of what is called the Copenhagen interpretation. Bohr[1] and his friends hammered out an approach to the understanding of quantum theory which hardened into a rigid orthodoxy prescribed for the faithful. An important part of their creed was the existence of classical measuring instruments. The pointers and other registration devices incorporated in these pieces of apparatus act with Newtonian dependability. There is no doubt at all whether the reading says "up" or "down." The Copenhagen school therefore says that it is at this stage that results get fixed and knowledge is established. The conscious observer can then take note if he wishes to do so. To be sure it

1. [Niels Bohr (1885–1962), Danish physicist.]

384

is a little difficult to be certain how big "large" has to be before this behavior sets in—indeed it was emphasized by Bohr and his friends that the line could be drawn at different places along the chain—but somewhere this classical behavior had to set in to make measurement possible.

The proposal has a certain attraction. If we go into a laboratory we shall find it littered with devices of just this character, capable of affording an unambiguous answer to an experimental inquiry. The problem is to understand how this undoubted fact finds a consistent place within quantum theory. . . . As we go along the chain of correlated consequences to larger and larger systems, the links in the chain become tighter and tighter, less and less subject to quantum mechanical "creakiness." It does not explain how the intervention of these (nearly) classical systems *chooses* one chain rather than another as the physical occurrence on a particular occasion. By assigning such a determining role to classical instruments, Bohr divided the world into two, the uncertain quantum world and the objectifying world of measuring instruments. . . . It is far from clear how these two worlds could be juxtaposed without subverting and contradicting the very quantum theory they were invented to explain. . . .

The third suggestion seizes on the role of the conscious observer to provide the resolution of our difficulty. Here, at the end of the chain, is the intervention of an agency of a manifestly different character from all that has preceded it. It may be hard to tell "large" from "small," or to bring classical and quantum objects into consistent association, but it seems far less perplexing to find a difference between the mental and the physical and so to attribute a special property to the interface of consciousness at which they meet each other. Consciousness does have a unique character about it, a character which we know from direct experience and which we can reasonably attribute by analogy to other human beings and, perhaps, to cats. We said that this was the last stage before which any unfixedness could be tolerated. Maybe it is the actual point at which things are settled. It will not surprise you to learn that Eugene Wigner has been a leading proponent of this view. It is not so drastic a solution as our first all-in-the-mind theory, which attributes to the wave function a significance purely in terms of human knowledge, for this third view takes the external world much more seriously as the origin of the chain of correlated consequence. . . .

Nevertheless there is something very unattractive about this particular suggestion. It is astonishingly anthropocentric or, at best, biocentric. Are we to suppose that in the thousands of millions of years before conscious life emerged in the world—and still today in those extensive parts of the universe where no conscious life has yet developed—no wave packet has ever collapsed, no atom for certain decayed? That quantum mechanics as we know it is a biologically induced phenomenon? That photographic plates stored away uninspected at the end of an experiment only acquire a definite image when someone opens the drawer to have a look at them? It takes a bit of swallowing.

The dilemma of those who evoke consciousness as the basis of phenomena was succinctly stated by Ronnie Knox in his limerick on idealism:

> There once was a man who said, "God
> Must think it exceedingly odd
> If he finds that this tree
> Continues to be
> When there's no one about in the Quad."

An anonymous author provided an answer along lines approved by Bishop Berkeley:

> Dear Sir, Your astonishment's odd;
> I am always about in the Quad.
> And that's why the tree
> Will continue to be,
> Since observed by Yours faithfully, God.

Such a riposte would not, however, be available to a defender of the interpretation of quantum mechanical measurement presently under consideration, supposing him to wish to avail himself of it. Divine reduction of wave packets would be an overkill, since it would operate everywhere and always, forcing the electron each time to go through a definite slit. The point about measurement is that it only occurs spasmodically. (This observation is in accord with the classic theological understanding of creation, which sees God as the ground and support of all that is [in our terms, the guarantor of the Schrödinger equation] but not as an object among objects [no collapser of wave packets].)

It might seem that we have now exhausted all possible ways of trying to comprehend quantum mechanical measurement. There remains, however, one further suggestion which easily exceeds all others in its bizarre quality. This is the many-worlds interpretation proposed in 1957 by Hugh Everett III. It arose in the context of the thinking of people whose job it is to think big. They were cosmologists wrestling to apply quantum mechanics to Einstein's general theory of relativity, for which the natural system for consideration is the universe itself. Here is a case where talk of classical measuring apparatus, or the role of an external observer, is simply squeezed out. There is no room for their separate existence in the all-embracing picture of the cosmos. The quantum mechanical formalism itself is left as the sole source of insight. A daring proposal was made to reconcile the continuity of the Schrödinger equation with the discontinuity of empirical experience. It was supposed that, in every circumstance in which there is a choice of experimental outcome, in fact each possibility is realized. The world at that instant splits up into many worlds, in each of which one of the possible results of the measurement is the one that actually occurs. Thus for Schrödinger's cat there is one world in which it lives and another world in which it dies. These worlds are, so to speak, alongside each other but incapable of communicating with each other in any way. This latter point is supposed to explain our feeling that we experience a continuity of existence for ourselves. The cat who lives is unaware of the cat who dies. All the time I am being repeatedly cloned as copies of myself multiply to pursue their separate lives in the many worlds into which my world is continually splitting. Each of these alter egos is unaware of the others, so that he is untroubled by his derivation from the common ancestor he unwittingly shares with the many other Polkinghornes who branched off in the course of some quantum mechanical act of measurement.

It is enough to make poor William of Ockham[2] turn in his grave. Entities are being multiplied with incredible profusion. Such prodigality makes little appeal to professional scientists, whose instincts are to seek for a tight and economic understanding of the world. Very few of them indeed have espoused the Everett interpretation. It has, however, been more popular with what one might call the "gee-whiz" school of science

2. [William of Ockham (1284?–1347?), English philosopher who employed the principle in logic that become known as *Ockham's razor*.]

popularizers, always out to stun the public with the weirdness of what they have to offer. "Are you on an aircraft about to crash?" they ask. "Don't worry, there are other worlds in which the quantum fluctuations have gone along a different path which will prevent the crash. Those carbon copies of yourself which inhabit those worlds will live on." Personally I should find that cold comfort. Reality is not to be trifled with and sliced up in this way.

It is a curious tale. All over the world measurements are continually being made on quantum mechanical systems. The theory triumphantly predicts, within its probabilistic limits, what their outcomes will be. It is all a great success. Yet we do not understand what is going on. Does the fixity on a particular occasion set in as a purely mental act of knowledge? At a transition from small to large physical systems? At the interface of matter and mind that we call consciousness? In one of the many subsequent worlds into which the universe has divided itself? Of the suggestions that we have canvassed, the one that seems to be the most promising is that which points to the emergence of classical measuring instruments from a quantum mechanical substrate, even if the mode and consistency of this happening is harder to comprehend than Copenhagen orthodoxy is willing to recognize.

It is puzzle with a familiar ring to it. Our knowledge of the world is organized into subjects which form a hierarchy, graded by the degree of complexity of the systems which they treat as basic. At the bottom is physics, the most reductionist of all; above it there is biology; then psychology and anthropology; sociology; and (some of us would wish to add) theology. At each level in this hierarchy we find both a dependence on those subjects which lie below and also a claim to a degree of autonomy for the concepts which are specific to that level. How these claims and dependencies are reconciled, how the views of the different disciplines fit consistently together to give a total picture of the one world of experience is a problem both vast and baffling. As someone who is both a physicist and a priest I am aware of some of the puzzles involved in teasing out the relation of the scientific and religious views of the world. To take another example, there are many biologists who, despite the acknowledged successes of molecular biology, do not believe that their subject is just a complex corollary to physics. My instinct is to believe that those who defend the autonomy of their particular "level" are right to do so, but I also think that our present state of knowledge is insufficient to permit us to understand satisfactorily how this level autonomy comes about. We no more understand how biology emerges from physics than we understand how classical measuring apparatus emerges from quantum mechanics. But it is at least interesting that there seems to be this level shift problem embedded within physics itself.

Content Questions

1. What scientific activity results in the discontinuity of the wave packet's collapse? (381)

2. Which characteristics of the domains of Newtonian physics and quantum theory raise questions about how these worlds interlock when a measurement fixes the result of an experiment? (381)

3. How is the Stern-Gerlach experiment an example of a "chain of amplification," giving scientists access to the microworld of quantum behavior? (381–382)

4. What is the difference between the statement of a "chain of correlations" and the statement of the actual outcome of an experiment? (382)

5. In the story of Schrödinger's cat, why does the claim that opening the box determines whether the cat is alive or dead lead to an absurdity? (382–383)

6. Why is it important that Schrödinger's cat and Wigner's friend are *conscious* links in the chain from the microscopic object to the scientist who finally learns the result of the experiments? (382–383)

7. Why does Polkinghorne say that to claim the wave function is just a description of one's knowledge of it "would have the effect of demoting physics to a branch of psychology"? (384)

8. In the Copenhagen interpretation, what problem arises in drawing a line between the quantum world and the world of "large" classical measuring instruments? (384–385)

9. According to Polkinghorne, what does the Copenhagen interpretation fail to explain about the chain of correlated consequences leading from the quantum microworld to measurements made by classical instruments? (385)

10. In the third suggestion for resolving the problem of the wave packet's collapse, why is the intervention of consciousness "less perplexing" than the intervention of measuring instruments in the Copenhagen interpretation? (385)

11. Why does Polkinghorne call the third suggestion for resolving the problem of the wave packet's collapse "astonishingly anthropocentric or, at best, biocentric"? (386)

12. Why does Polkinghorne say that the idea of divine reduction of wave packets is incompatible with the idea of quantum mechanical measurement? (386)

13. How does the many-worlds interpretation explain what happens when one of the possible experimental results predicted by Schrödinger's equation becomes fixed by a measurement? (387)

14. What leads Polkinghorne to call his account of alternative quantum theory interpretations "a curious tale"? (388)

15. According to Polkinghorne, what is the "level shift problem" in the hierarchy of subjects into which we organize our knowledge of the world? (388–389)

Discussion Questions

1. Why does Polkinghorne call the discontinuity of the wave packet's collapse "traumatic"? Why is the collapse the source of perplexity and debate about the meaning of quantum theory? (381)

2. What does Polkinghorne mean when he states that measurement involves an "intervention by our everyday world into the quantum world"? (381) Are all scientific measurements interventions of some kind?

3. What is a "chain of correlations"? Is it different from a sequence of causes and effects? (382)

4. Why is there a need to settle the question of where the collapse of the wave packet takes place? (382)

5. Why can't the condition of Schrödinger's cat or Wigner's friend's observation settle the matter of where the collapse of the wave packet occurred? What leads Polkinghorne to say that it could have been settled long before the intervention of consciousness? (382–383)

6. Is Polkinghorne correct in saying that the point of physics would be lost without the conviction that it deals with knowledge originating outside us? Is this conviction an adequate reason for him to reject the suggestion that the "wave function is not a description of a physical system but simply a description of my knowledge of it"? (384)

7. What justifies the Copenhagen interpretation in assigning a determining role to classical measuring instruments? (384–385)

8. In the third suggestion for resolving the problem of the wave packet's collapse, is the intervention of consciousness as convincing as the intervention of classical measuring instruments in the Copenhagen interpretation? (385)

9. Why does Polkinghorne find the third suggestion for resolving the problem of the wave packet's collapse "very unattractive"? Is there a scientific basis for his rejection of quantum mechanics as a "biologically induced phenomenon"? (385–386)

10. Is the many-worlds interpretation scientifically verifiable? (387–388)

11. If quantum theory is so successful in making predictions, why does the theory need an interpretation for us to "understand what is going on"? (388)

12. Why does Polkinghorne think that the most promising of the suggestions for understanding the wave packet's collapse is the one that "points to the emergence of classical measuring instruments from a quantum mechanical substrate"? (388)

13. What does Polkinghorne mean in saying that physics is the most reductionist of all the subjects by which our knowledge of the world is organized? (388)

14. In the hierarchy of knowledge that Polkinghorne describes, how could biology simultaneously depend on physics and be autonomous? (388–389)

15. Is Polkinghorne right in wanting to add theology to the hierarchy of knowledge that he describes? (388)

Suggestions for Further Reading

By the author

Polkinghorne, John C. *The Quantum World*. New York: Longman, 1984; Princeton, NJ: Princeton University Press, 1989. In this basic survey, from which the selection in *What's the Matter?* is taken, Polkinghorne, a working physicist who is also a priest and writer on theology, discusses the disagreements over what quantum theory says about the nature of the physical world.

————. *Science and Theology: An Introduction.* Minneapolis, MN: Fortress Press, 1998. Following a survey of the historical relationship between science and religion, Polkinghorne discusses an array of questions that both science and religion address and shows the potential of contemporary science to illuminate theological issues.

About the topic

Bohm, David. *Wholeness and the Implicate Order.* New York: Routledge, 2002. Parting company with the widely accepted Copenhagen interpretation of quantum theory, this eminent physicist makes a case for an alternative understanding of reality that unites the physical world and consciousness into an unbroken whole.

Gribbin, John. *Schrödinger's Kittens and the Search for Reality: Solving the Quantum Mysteries.* Boston: Little, Brown, 1995; New York: Back Bay Books, 1996. This sequel to the author's *In Search of Schrödinger's Cat* explores quantum theory in the light of ongoing developments in particle physics.

Herbert, Nick. *Quantum Reality: Beyond the New Physics.* Garden City, NY: Anchor Press/Doubleday, 1985; New York: Anchor Books, 1987. This book discusses why the interpretation of quantum physics provokes such strong controversy.

Pesic, Peter. *Seeing Double: Shared Identities in Physics, Philosophy, and Literature.* Cambridge, MA: MIT Press, 2002, 2003. This book begins with the question: How can we understand that human individuality rests on a quantum world of identical, anonymous particles? The exploration of this question leaves behind the usual boundaries between science and other disciplines, drawing on literature, philosophy, and history.

To me, the most satisfying thing that has come out of these speculations about the very early universe is the possible parallel between the history of the universe and its logical structure. . . . That which we now do by mathematics was done in the very early universe by heat—physical phenomena directly exhibited the essential simplicity of nature. But no one was there to see it.

—Steven Weinberg, *The First Three Minutes*

STEVEN WEINBERG

The Origin of the Universe

The first efforts to explain how the earth and heavens came to be were myths like
the one at the beginning of the following selection from *The First Three Minutes*
(1977) by the theoretical physicist Steven Weinberg (1933–). Whether expressed
through myths or scientific theories, cosmology—the attempt to explain the structure and origin of the universe—is one of the fundamental ways in which humans
try to make sense of the physical world. In the twentieth century, cosmology under-
went profound changes because of increasingly refined techniques in astronomy and
discoveries in particle physics. Scientists joined knowledge of the large-scale structure
of stars and galaxies with knowledge of the subatomic structure of matter, pointing
the way toward a theory of the origin and future of the universe. As Weinberg writes
in *The First Three Minutes*, "It is in the early universe, especially the first hundredth
of a second, that the problems of the theory of elementary particles come together
with the problems of cosmology." The history of how the universe evolved is also the
history of how matter evolved, and this represents one of the most important unifi-
cations of different areas of study in modern physics.

    Weinberg's work builds on the observations, theories, and predictions of many
twentieth-century scientists. In the 1920s, the astronomer Edwin Hubble observed
that light from distant galaxies was shifted toward the red end of the spectrum,
something that would occur if these galaxies were receding into space at great velocities. He considered this strong evidence that the universe is expanding, rather than
remaining in a steady state, and his discovery raised the question of when and how
such expansion could have begun. The cosmologist Georges Lemaître offered the
hypothesis that the explosion of an extremely dense and hot primordial atom could
explain the origin of an expanding and cooling universe in which cosmic density is
decreasing. This way of envisioning the formation of the universe suggested that the
study of cosmic evolution involved an understanding of the thermonuclear explosion
that initiated it. The nuclear physicist George Gamow realized that if the universe is
expanding as the result of an explosion, or "big bang," there should be residue of

this event in the form of microwave radiation uniformly distributed throughout space. When this cosmic background radiation was detected by communications satellites in 1964, proponents of the big bang had strong evidence that their theory was correct.

Weinberg's distinguished career in science reflects the powerful links between cosmology and particle physics, fields to which he has made major contributions. Much of his research has focused on the attempt to find a comprehensive theory of the four fundamental forces of nature—gravity, the electromagnetic force, the strong force, and the weak force—which are thought to have been unified until an instant after the big bang. In 1979, Weinberg was awarded the Nobel Prize in Physics, with Abdus Salam and Sheldon Glashow, for the theory of how the electromagnetic and weak forces are the same at extremely high energy levels, as was the case immediately following the big bang. Weinberg, Salam, and Glashow showed that the existence of these two forces represents what physicists call a *broken symmetry*, the result of a primordial event in which the original unity of forces was shattered. As Weinberg explains in *The Whole Shebang* (1997) by Timothy Ferris, "There was a time in the very early universe . . . when the symmetry hadn't yet been broken and the forces were all the same—not only mathematically the same, at some deep level having to do with the field equations, but *actually* the same." Broken symmetries are among the clues that allow physicists to reconstruct conditions at the beginning of the universe. Through particle accelerators that replicate the initial high-energy environment, scientists can in effect go back in time and observe how atoms and their components behaved just after the original explosion. Experimental and theoretical work has revealed that not only matter, but all the components we think of as constituting physical reality—including forces, space, and time—have an origin.

In the following selection, Weinberg raises questions about what kinds of theoretical models are conducive to scientific progress and what it means for a scientist to keep an open mind about highly speculative theories. He also asks us to consider how human beings can find meaning in a universe that, according to the science of cosmology, has evolved from "an unspeakably unfamiliar early condition, and faces a future extinction of endless cold or intolerable heat."

See also Weinberg, pages 413–414.

The Origin of the Universe

The origin of the universe is explained in the *Younger Edda*, a collection of Norse myths compiled around 1220 by the Icelandic magnate Snorri Sturleson. In the beginning, says the *Edda*, there was nothing at all. "Earth was not found, nor Heaven above, a Yawning-gap there was, but grass nowhere." To the north and south of nothing lay regions of frost and fire, Niflheim and Muspelheim. The heat from Muspelheim melted some of the frost from Niflheim, and from the liquid drops there grew a giant, Ymer. What did Ymer eat? It seems there was also a cow, Audhumla. And what did *she* eat? Well, there was also some salt. And so on.

I must not offend religious sensibilities, even Viking religious sensibilities, but I think it is fair to say that this is not a very satisfying picture of the origin of the universe. Even leaving aside all objections to hearsay evidence, the story raises as many problems as it answers, and each answer requires a new complication in the initial conditions.

We are not able merely to smile at the *Edda*, and forswear all cosmogonical speculation—the urge to trace the history of the universe back to its beginnings is irresistible. From the start of modern science in the sixteenth and seventeenth centuries, physicists and astronomers have returned again and again to the problem of the origin of the universe.

This selection is taken from chapter 1, "Introduction: The Giant and the Cow," chapter 5, "The First Three Minutes," and chapter 8, "Epilogue: The Prospect Ahead," of The First Three Minutes.

However, an aura of the disreputable always surrounded such research. I remember that during the time that I was a student and then began my own research (on other problems) in the 1950s, the study of the early universe was widely regarded as not the sort of thing to which a respectable scientist would devote his time. Nor was this judgment unreasonable. Throughout most of the history of modern physics and astronomy, there simply has not existed an adequate observational and theoretical foundation on which to build a history of the early universe.

Now, in just the past decade, all this has changed. A theory of the early universe has become so widely accepted that astronomers often call it the *standard model*.[1] It is more or less the same as what is sometimes called the *big bang* theory, but supplemented with a much more specific recipe for the contents of the universe. . . .

. . . It may be useful to start with a summary of the history of the early universe, as presently understood in the standard model. . . .

In the beginning, there was an explosion. Not an explosion like those familiar on earth, starting from a definite center and spreading out to engulf more and more of the circumambient air, but an explosion that occurred simultaneously everywhere, filling all space from the beginning, with every particle of matter rushing apart from every other particle. "All space" in this context may mean either all of an infinite universe, or all of a finite universe that curves back on itself like the surface of a sphere. Neither possibility is easy to comprehend, but this will not get in our way; it matters hardly at all in the early universe whether space is finite or infinite.

At about one-hundredth of a second, the earliest time about which we can speak with any confidence, the temperature of the universe was about a hundred thousand million (10^{11}) degrees Celsius. This is much hotter than in the center of even the hottest star, so hot, in fact, that none of the components of ordinary matter—molecules, or atoms, or even the nuclei of atoms—could have held together. Instead, the matter rushing apart in this explosion consisted of various types of the so-called elementary particles, which are the subject of modern high-energy nuclear physics.

. . . One type of particle that was present in large numbers is the electron, the negatively charged particle that flows through wires in electric

1. [*standard model:* this theory is different from the Standard Model of particle physics, a descriptive theory of the elementary particles of matter and their interactions.]

currents and makes up the outer parts of all atoms and molecules in the present universe. Another type of particle that was abundant at early times is the positron, a positively charged particle with precisely the same mass as the electron. In the present universe, positrons are found only in high-energy laboratories, in some kinds of radioactivity, and in violent astronomical phenomena like cosmic rays and supernovas, but in the early universe the number of positrons was almost exactly equal to the number of electrons. In addition to electrons and positrons, there were roughly similar numbers of various kinds of neutrinos, ghostly particles with no mass or electric charge whatever. Finally, the universe was filled with light. This does not have to be treated separately from the particles—the quantum theory tells us that light consists of particles of zero mass and zero electrical charge known as photon. (Each time an atom in the filament of a light bulb changes from a state of higher energy to one of lower energy, one photon is emitted. There are so many photons coming out of a light bulb that they seem to blend together in a continuous stream of light, but a photoelectric cell can count individual photons, one by one.) Every photon carries a definite amount of energy and momentum depending on the wavelength of the light. To describe the light that filled the early universe, we can say that the number and average energy of the photons was about the same as for electrons or positrons or neutrinos.

The particles—electrons, positrons, neutrinos, photons—were continually being created out of pure energy, and then after short lives being annihilated again. Their number therefore was not preordained, but fixed instead by a balance between processes of creation and annihilation. From this balance we can infer that the density of this cosmic soup at a temperature of a hundred thousand million degrees was about four thousand million (4×10^9) times that of water. There was also a small contamination of heavier particles, protons and neutrons, which in the present world form the constituents of atomic nuclei. (Protons are positively charged; neutrons are slightly heavier and electrically neutral.) The proportions were roughly one proton and one neutron for every thousand million electrons or positrons or neutrinos or photons. This number—a thousand million photons per nuclear particle—is the crucial quantity that had to be taken from observation in order to work out the standard model of the universe. The discovery of the cosmic radiation background . . . was in effect a measurement of this number.

As the explosion continued the temperature dropped, reaching thirty thousand million (3×10^{10}) degrees Celsius after about one-tenth of a second; ten thousand million degrees after about one second; and three thousand million degrees after about fourteen seconds. This was cool enough so that the electrons and positrons began to annihilate faster than they could be re-created out of the photons and neutrinos. The energy released in this annihilation of matter temporarily slowed the rate at which the universe cooled, but the temperature continued to drop, finally reaching one thousand million degrees at the end of the first three minutes. It was then cool enough for the protons and neutrons to begin to form into complex nuclei, starting with the nucleus of heavy hydrogen (or deuterium), which consists of one proton and one neutron. The density was still high enough (a little less than that of water) so that these light nuclei were able rapidly to assemble themselves into the most stable light nucleus, that of helium, consisting of two protons and two neutrons.

At the end of the first three minutes the contents of the universe were mostly in the form of light, neutrinos, and antineutrinos. There was still a small amount of nuclear material, now consisting of about 73 percent hydrogen and 27 percent helium, and an equally small number of electrons left over from the era of electron-positron annihilation. This matter continued to rush apart, becoming steadily cooler and less dense. Much later, after a few hundred thousand years, it would become cool enough for electrons to join with nuclei to form atoms of hydrogen and helium. The resulting gas would begin under the influence of gravitation to form clumps, which would ultimately condense to form the galaxies and stars of the present universe. However, the ingredients with which the stars would begin their life would be just those prepared in the first three minutes.

The standard model sketched above is not the most satisfying theory imaginable of the origin of the universe. Just as in the *Younger Edda*, there is an embarrassing vagueness about the very beginning, the first hundredth of a second or so. Also, there is the unwelcome necessity of fixing initial conditions, especially the initial thousand-million-to-one ratio of photons to nuclear particles. We would prefer a greater sense of logical inevitability in the theory.

For example, one alternative theory that seems philosophically far more attractive is the so-called steady state model. In this theory, proposed in the late 1940s by Herman Bondi, Thomas Gold, and (in a somewhat different formulation) Fred Hoyle, the universe has always been just about the same as it is now. As it expands, new matter is continually created to fill up the gaps between the galaxies. Potentially, all questions about why the universe is the way it is can be answered in this theory by showing that it is the way it is because that is the only way it can stay the same. The problem of the early universe is banished; there was no early universe.

How then did we come to the standard model? And how has it supplanted other theories, like the steady state model? It is a tribute to the essential objectivity of modern astrophysics that this consensus has been brought about, not by shifts in philosophical preference or by the influence of astrophysical mandarins, but by the pressure of empirical data.

. . . The two great clues, furnished by astronomical observation, that have led us to the standard model [are] the discoveries of the recession of distant galaxies and of a weak radio static filling the universe. . . .

Can we really be sure of the standard model? Will new discoveries overthrow it and replace the present standard model with some other cosmogony, or even revive the steady state model? Perhaps. I cannot deny a feeling of unreality in writing about the first three minutes as if we really know what we are talking about.

However, even if it is eventually supplanted, the standard model will have played a role of great value in the history of cosmology. It is now respectable (though only in the last decade or so) to test theoretical ideas in physics or astrophysics by working out their consequences in the context of the standard model. It is also common practice to use the standard model as a theoretical basis for justifying programs of astronomical observation. Thus, the standard model provides an essential common language that allows theorists and observers to appreciate what each other are doing. If some day the standard model is replaced by a better theory, it will probably be because of observations or calculations that drew their motivation from the standard model. . . .

In following this account of the first three minutes, the reader may feel that he can detect a note of scientific overconfidence. He might be right. However, I do not believe that scientific progress is always best advanced by keeping an altogether open mind. It is often necessary to forget one's doubts and to follow the consequences of one's assumptions wherever they may lead—the great thing is not to be free of theoretical prejudices, but to have the right theoretical prejudices. And always, the test of any theoretical preconception is in where it leads. The standard model of the early universe has scored some successes, and it provides a coherent theoretical framework for future experimental programs. This does not mean that it is true, but it does mean that it deserves to be taken seriously.

Nevertheless, there *is* one great uncertainty that hangs like a dark cloud over the standard model. Underlying all the calculations described is the *cosmological principle*, the assumption that the universe is homogeneous and isotropic. (By "homogeneous" we mean that the universe looks the same to any observer who is carried along by the general expansion of the universe, wherever that observer may be located; by "isotropic" we mean that the universe looks the same in all directions to such an observer.) We know from direct observation that the cosmic microwave radiation background is highly isotropic about us, and from this we infer that the universe has been highly isotropic and homogeneous ever since the radiation went out of equilibrium with matter, at a temperature of about 3,000 K. However, we have no evidence that the cosmological principle was valid at earlier times.

It is possible that the universe was initially highly inhomogeneous and anisotropic, but has subsequently been smoothed out by the frictional forces exerted by the parts of the expanding universe on each other. Such a "mixmaster" model has been particularly advocated by Charles Misner of the University of Maryland. It is even possible that the heat generated by the frictional homogenization and isotropization of the universe is responsible for the enormous 1,000 million-to-one present ratio of photons to nuclear particles. However, to the best of my knowledge, no one can say why the universe should have any specific initial degree of inhomogeneity or anisotropy, and no one knows how to calculate the heat produced by its smoothing out.

In my opinion, the appropriate response to such uncertainties is not (as some cosmologists might like) to scrap the standard model, but rather to take it very seriously and to work out its consequences thoroughly, if only in the hope of turning up a contradiction with observation. It is not even clear that a large initial anisotropy and inhomogeneity would have much effect on the story presented. It might be that the universe was smoothed out in the first few seconds; in that case the cosmological production of helium and deuterium could be calculated as if the cosmological principle were always valid. Even if the anisotropy and inhomogeneity of the universe persisted beyond the era of helium synthesis, the helium and deuterium production in any uniformly expanding clump would depend only on the expansion rate within that clump, and might not be very different from the production calculated in the standard model. It might even be that the whole universe that we can see when we look all the way back to the time of nucleosynthesis is but a homogeneous and isotropic clump within a larger inhomogeneous and anisotropic universe.

The uncertainty surrounding the cosmological principle becomes really important when we look back to the very beginning or forward to the final end of the universe. . . . However, it must always be admitted that our simple cosmological models may only describe a small part of the universe, or a limited portion of its history.

~ ~ ~

The universe will certainly go on expanding for a while. As to its fate after that, the standard model gives an equivocal prophecy: it all depends on whether the cosmic density is less or greater than a certain critical value.

If the cosmic density is *less* than the critical density, then the universe is of infinite extent and will go on expanding forever. Our descendants, if we have any then, will see thermonuclear reactions slowly come to an end in all the stars, leaving behind various sorts of cinder: black dwarf stars, neutron stars, perhaps black holes. Planets may continue in orbit, slowing down a little as they radiate gravitational waves but never coming to rest in any finite time. The cosmic backgrounds of radiation and neutrinos will continue to fall in temperature in inverse proportion to the size of the universe, but they will not be missed; even now we can barely detect the 3 K microwave radiation background.

On the other hand, if the cosmic density is *greater* than the critical value, then the universe is finite and its expansion will eventually cease, giving way to an accelerating contraction. If, for instance, the cosmic density is twice its critical value, and if the presently popular value of the Hubble constant (15 kilometers per second per million light years) is correct, then the universe is now 10,000 million years old; it will go on expanding for another 50,000 million years, and then begin to contract. The contraction is just the expansion run backward: after 50,000 million years the universe would have regained its present size, and after another 10,000 million years it would approach a singular state of infinite density.

During at least the early part of the contracting phase, astronomers (if there are any) will be able to amuse themselves by observing both red shifts and blue shifts. Light from nearby galaxies would have been emitted at a time when the universe was larger than it is when the light is observed, so when it is observed this light will appear to be shifted toward the short wavelength end of the spectrum, i.e., toward the blue. On the other hand, the light from extremely distant objects would have been emitted at a time when the universe was still in the early stages of its expansion, when the universe was even smaller than it is when the light is observed, so when it is observed this light will appear to be shifted toward the long wavelength end of the spectrum, i.e., toward the red.

The temperature of the cosmic backgrounds of photons and neutrinos will fall and then rise as the universe expands and then contracts, always in inverse proportion to the size of the universe. If the cosmic density now is twice its critical value, then our calculations show that the universe at its maximum dilation will be just twice as large as at present, so the microwave background temperature will then be just one-half its present value of 3 K, or about 1.5 K. Then, as the universe begins to contract, the temperature will start to rise.

At first no alarms will sound—for thousands of millions of years the radiation background will be so cool that it would take a great effort to detect it at all. However, when the universe has recontracted to one-hundredth its present size, the radiation background will begin to domi-nate the sky: the night sky will be as warm (300 K) as our present sky at day. Seventy million years later the universe will have contracted another tenfold, and our heirs and assigns (if any) will find the sky intolerably bright. Molecules in planetary and stellar atmospheres and in interstellar space will begin to dissociate into their constituent atoms, and the atoms will break up into free electrons and atomic nuclei. After another 700,000 years, the cosmic temperature will be at ten million degrees; then stars and planets themselves will dissolve into a cosmic soup of radiation, electrons, and nuclei. The temperature will rise to ten thousand million degrees in another twenty-two days. The nuclei will then begin to break up into their constituent protons and neutrons, undoing all the work of both stellar and cosmological nucleosynthesis. Soon after that, electrons and positrons will be created in great numbers in photon-photon collisions, and the cosmic background of neutrinos and antineutrinos will regain thermal communion with the rest of the universe.

Can we really carry this sad story all the way to its end, to a state of infinite temperature and density? Does time really have a stop some three minutes after the temperature reaches a thousand million degrees? Obviously, we cannot be sure. . . . The whole universe must be described in the language of quantum mechanics at temperatures above 100 million million million million million degrees (10^{32} K), and no one has any idea what happens then. Also, if the universe is not really isotropic and homogeneous, then our whole story may have lost its validity long before we would have to face the problems of quantum cosmology.

From these uncertainties some cosmologists derive a sort of hope. It may be that the universe will experience a kind of cosmic "bounce," and begin to reexpand. In the *Edda*, after the final battle of the gods and giants at Ragnorak, the earth is destroyed by fire and water, but the waters recede, the sons of Thor come up from hell carrying their father's hammer, and the whole world begins once more. But if the universe does reexpand, its expansion will again slow to halt and be followed by another contraction, ending in another cosmic Ragnorak, followed by another bounce, and so on forever.

If this is our future, it presumably also is our past. The present expanding universe would be only the phase following the last contraction and bounce. . . . Looking farther back, we can imagine an endless cycle of expansion and contraction stretching into the infinite past, with no beginning whatever.

Some cosmologists are philosophically attracted to the oscillating model, especially because, like the steady state model, it nicely avoids the problem of Genesis. It does, however, face one severe theoretical difficulty. In each cycle the ratio of photons to nuclear particles (or, more precisely, the entropy per nuclear particle) is slightly increased by a kind of friction (known as *bulk viscosity*) as the universe expands and contracts. As far as we know, the universe would then start each new cycle with a new, slightly larger ratio of photons to nuclear particles. Right now this ratio is large, but not infinite, so it is hard to see how the universe could have previously experienced an infinite number of cycles.

However all these problems may be resolved, and whichever cosmological model proves correct, there is not much of comfort in any of this. It is almost irresistible for humans to believe that we have some special relation to the universe, that human life is not just a more-or-less farcical outcome of a chain of accidents reaching back to the first three minutes, but that we were somehow built in from the beginning. As I write this I happen to be in an airplane at 30,000 feet, flying over Wyoming en route home from San Francisco to Boston. Below, the earth looks very soft and comfortable—fluffy clouds here and there, snow turning pink as the sun sets, roads stretching straight across the country from one town to another. It is very hard to realize that all this is just a tiny part of an overwhelmingly hostile universe. It is even harder to realize that this present universe has evolved from an unspeakably unfamiliar early condition, and faces a future extinction of endless cold or intolerable heat. The more the universe seems comprehensible, the more it also seems pointless.

But if there is no solace in the fruits of our research, there is at least some consolation in the research itself. Men and women are not content to comfort themselves with tales of gods and giants, or to confine their thoughts to the daily affairs of life; they also build telescopes and satellites and accelerators, and sit at their desks for endless hours working out the meaning of the data they gather. The effort to understand the universe is one of the very few things that lifts human life a little above the level of farce, and gives it some of the grace of tragedy.

Content Questions

1. What is the standard model of the origin of the universe? How was the explosion that began the universe different from explosions we are familiar with on earth? (398)

2. What conditions of the universe at one-hundredth of a second determined that only elementary particles could exist? (398)

3. What process determined the number of particles in the early universe? What was the proportion of heavier particles to elementary particles, and why was this ratio crucial to working out the standard model? (398–399)

4. How did the material at the end of the first three minutes compare to material at the first one-hundredth of a second? (400)

5. Why were hydrogen and helium the first nuclei to form? (400)

6. In what way do both the Norse creation myth and the standard model lack "logical inevitability"? (400)

7. How does the steady state model account for current conditions in the universe? (400–401)

8. Even though the steady state model is "philosophically far more attractive," why do most scientists accept the standard model? (400–401)

9. What has the "essential common language" of the standard model enabled scientists to do? (401)

10. What assumptions about the universe does the cosmological principle make? Why does Weinberg say that uncertainty about the cosmological principle "hangs like a dark cloud over the standard model"? (402)

11. How might the standard model retain accuracy as a picture of the universe even if it were established that the universe was initially inhomogeneous and anisotropic? (402–403)

12. What is critical density, and how will it determine whether the universe expands forever or eventually contracts? (403–404)

13. Why would the contracting universe produce red shifts and blue shifts in its early stages? (404)

14. In the contracting universe, what process leads the cosmic background of neutrinos and antineutrinos to regain "thermal communion" with the rest of the universe? (404–405)

15. Why does the ratio of photons to neutron particles pose a "severe theoretical difficulty" to the oscillating model of the universe? (405–406)

Discussion Questions

1. Why does Weinberg begin his discussion of scientific cosmology by retelling a Norse creation myth? (397)

2. Why is the study of elementary particles essential to providing evidence for cosmological theories? (398–400)

3. Why does Weinberg call the fixing of initial conditions in the standard model an "unwelcome necessity"? What would it mean for the standard model to have "a greater sense of logical inevitability"? (400)

4. In what way does the "pressure of empirical data" drive the acceptance or rejection of scientific theories? Against what is the pressure of empirical data exerted? (401)

5. What is a theoretical model in science and how does it provide a basis for justifying programs of observation? (401)

6. What does Weinberg mean when he says, "I do not believe that scientific progress is always best advanced by keeping an altogether open mind"? (401)

7. What is the difference between the standard model providing "a coherent theoretical framework" and its being true? As long as a model has "scored some successes" should a scientist care whether or not it is true? (402)

8. Why are uncertainties in the standard model reasons "to take it very seriously and to work out its consequences thoroughly"? (402)

9. Why might theories that avoid "the problem of Genesis" be philosophically attractive to cosmologists? (405)

10. Should scientists be wary of theories that are philosophically attractive? (405)

11. What does Weinberg mean when he says, "The more the universe seems comprehensible, the more it also seems pointless"? (406)

12. Do you agree with Weinberg that trying to understand the universe scientifically "lifts human life a little above the level of farce, and gives it some of the grace of tragedy"? (406)

Suggestions for Further Reading

By the author

Weinberg, Steven. *The First Three Minutes: A Modern View of the Origin of the Universe.* Updated ed. New York: Basic Books, 1993. This detailed account of the beginning of the universe, from which the selection in *What's the Matter?* is taken, tells the story of how scientists discovered the evidence that led to the widely accepted standard model of cosmology.

About the topic

Barrow, John D. *The Origin of the Universe.* New York: Basic Books, 1994, 1997. One of the most important researchers on the cutting edge of cosmology reports on how speculations about the behavior of matter at the origin of the universe can help us to understand its current observed structure.

Davies, P. C. W. *The Last Three Minutes: Conjectures About the Ultimate Fate of the Universe.* New York: Basic Books, 1994, 1997. This entertaining overview of theoretical speculation about the end of the universe ranges from the possibility of its dispersion into an infinite void to its collapse and compression in an event referred to as the "Big Crunch."

Guth, Alan H. *The Inflationary Universe: The Quest for a New Theory of Cosmic Origins.* Reading, MA: Addison-Wesley, 1997; New York: Perseus Books Group, 1998. The author, who developed the concept of the inflationary universe, explains the evidence for his theory that at its origin the universe expanded rapidly before settling down to a more gradual rate of growth.

Rees, Martin J. *Before the Beginning: Our Universe and Others*. Reading, MA: Addison-Wesley, 1997; New York: Perseus Books Group, 1998. In addition to outlining the experimental and theoretical work of modern cosmologists, the author explains the reasons for his startling theory that an infinite number of unobservable universes exist, each with its own physical laws.

Silk, Joseph. *On the Shores of the Unknown: A Short History of the Universe*. Cambridge: Cambridge University Press, 2005. This summary of the current theories and controversies of cosmology by a leading astrophysicist also provides an excellent account of the methods that scientists use to explore events extremely distant in time and space.

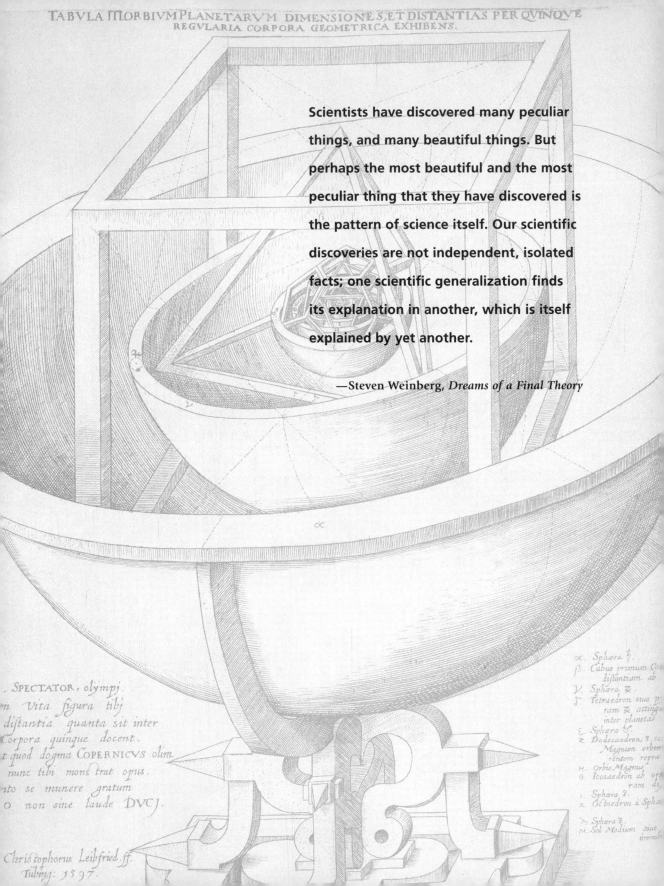

Scientists have discovered many peculiar things, and many beautiful things. But perhaps the most beautiful and the most peculiar thing that they have discovered is the pattern of science itself. Our scientific discoveries are not independent, isolated facts; one scientific generalization finds its explanation in another, which is itself explained by yet another.

—Steven Weinberg, *Dreams of a Final Theory*

STEVEN WEINBERG

Beautiful Theories:
Symmetry and Mathematics

Scientists sometimes describe theories that successfully explain the physical world
as "beautiful," a word more commonly used to describe works of art. In the following
selection, the theoretical physicist Steven Weinberg (1933–) investigates the nature of
beauty in a physical theory—beauty that is sometimes as important as well-established
quantitative data when judging a theory's validity.

 Beauty in a scientific theory is no easier to define than beauty in a work of art.
As Weinberg points out, a theory is considered beautiful not merely because of the
aesthetic pleasure it gives, but also because it possesses identifiable characteristics
that account for one's sense of its beauty. There is a range of opinion about what
these characteristics might be. For many scientists, the characteristics that make a
theory beautiful are closely related to its ability to provide an explanation, supported
by experimental evidence, of some aspect of the physical world. Because theories
in physics are developed and formulated in the language of mathematics, Weinberg
asks us to compare what physicists and mathematicians mean when they call their
own theories beautiful.

 The use of mathematical models to explain the physical world has a long history. Centuries before modern experimental science, the ancient Greek philosopher
Pythagoras saw the universe in terms of patterns of numbers, while Plato imagined
that the underlying structure of the world consists of perfect geometrical shapes.
For both, the beauty of mathematical forms played a large part in convincing them
of the truth of their explanations. In seventeenth-century Europe, scientists such as
Galileo, Johannes Kepler, and Isaac Newton started to use the abstract simplifications
of physical phenomena that mathematics can provide in order to uncover hidden
relationships in the natural world. Their theoretical work with mathematics, along
with a more rigorous approach to conducting experiments, marked the beginning of
modern physics. Newton's masterwork, *Philosophiae Naturalis Principia Mathematica*
(*The Mathematical Principles of Natural Philosophy,* 1687), consists almost entirely of

mathematical proofs; it defines the laws of force and establishes the principle that gravity acts everywhere in the universe. Since then, most theories in physics have been mathematically formulated.

Mathematics is routinely used as a practical tool in experimental physics to make measurements and perform calculations. It allows scientists to quantify their observations and to keep to a minimum the number of concepts—such as time, length, and mass—that they need to consider in order to better understand how the physical world operates. Theoretical physicists, on the other hand, are primarily interested in the complex ideas of pure mathematics that not only help them organize their current knowledge, but also allow them to speculate about new areas of investigation.

In the twentieth century, the mathematical concept that has become central to theoretical physics is symmetry, one of the qualities often regarded as beautiful in art. The work of the mathematician Amelie Noether was important in establishing theoretical guidelines for identifying symmetry in physics. Her theorem states that if the form of the equations describing the behavior of a physical system does not change when the system changes, then there is some physical quantity conserved—for example, energy, mass, momentum, or a yet undiscovered quantity. When a physical quantity is conserved there is symmetry.

Some physicists have claimed that understanding nature is equivalent to understanding its symmetries. Weinberg himself has stated, in Timothy Ferris's book *The Whole Shebang* (1997), "The task of the physicist is to see through the appearances down to the underlying, very simple, symmetric reality." As modern physicists search for a final theory explaining all known elementary particles of matter and their interactions, they rely more and more on mathematical models such as the symmetries of group theory to suggest new lines of investigation.

In "Beautiful Theories: Symmetry and Mathematics," Weinberg raises the fundamental question about the relation of physics and mathematics, asking why the abstract creations of pure mathematics have an uncanny ability to describe and explain the nature of the physical world.

See also Weinberg, pages 395–396.

Beautiful Theories: Symmetry and Mathematics

Some of the talk about the importance of beauty in science has been little more than gushing. I do not propose to use this chapter just to say more nice things about beauty. Rather, I want to focus more closely on the nature of beauty in physical theories, on why our sense of beauty is sometimes a useful guide and sometimes not, and on how the usefulness of our sense of beauty is a sign of our progress toward a final theory.

A physicist who says that a theory is beautiful does not mean quite the same thing that would be meant in saying that a particular painting or a piece of music or poetry is beautiful. It is not merely a personal expression of aesthetic pleasure; it is much closer to what a horse trainer means when he looks at a racehorse and says that it is a beautiful horse. The horse trainer is of course expressing a personal opinion, but it is an opinion about an objective fact: that, on the basis of judgments that the trainer could not easily put into words, this is the kind of horse that wins races.

Of course, different horse trainers may judge a horse differently. That is what makes horseracing. But the horse trainer's aesthetic sense is a means

This selection is taken from chapter 6, "Beautiful Theories," of Dreams of a Final Theory.

to an objective end—the end of selecting horses that win races. The physicist's sense of beauty is also supposed to serve a purpose—it is supposed to help the physicist select ideas that help us to explain nature. Physicists, just as horse trainers, may be right or wrong in their judgments, but they are not merely enjoying themselves. They often *are* enjoying themselves, but that is not the whole purpose of their aesthetic judgments.

This comparison raises more questions than it answers. First, what *is* a beautiful theory? What are the characteristics of physical theories that give us a sense of beauty? A more difficult question: Why does the physicist's sense of beauty work, when it does work? . . . Something as personal and subjective as our sense of beauty helps us not only to invent physical theories but even to judge the validity of theories. Why are we blessed with such aesthetic insight? The effort to answer the question raises another question that is even more difficult, although perhaps it sounds trivial: What is it that the physicist wants to accomplish?

What is a beautiful theory? The curator of a large American art museum once became indignant at my use of the word "beauty" in connection with physics. He said that in his line of work professionals have stopped using this word because they realize how impossible it is to define. Long ago the physicist and mathematician Henri Poincaré admitted that "it may be very hard to define mathematical beauty, but that is just as true of beauty of all kinds."

I will not try to define beauty, any more than I would try to define love or fear. You do not define these things; you know them when you feel them. Later, after the fact, you may sometimes be able to say a little to describe them, as I will try to do here.

By the beauty of a physical theory, I certainly do not mean merely the mechanical beauty of its symbols on the printed page. The metaphysical poet Thomas Traherne took pains that his poems should make pretty patterns on the page, but this is no part of the business of physics. I should also distinguish the sort of beauty I am talking about here from the quality that mathematicians and physicists sometimes call elegance. An elegant proof or calculation is one that achieves a powerful result with a minimum of irrelevant complication. It is not important for the beauty of a theory that its equations should have elegant solutions. The equations of general relativity are notoriously difficult to solve except in the simplest situations, but this does not detract from the beauty of the theory itself.

Einstein has been quoted as saying that scientists should leave elegance to tailors.

Simplicity is part of what I mean by beauty, but it is a simplicity of ideas, not simplicity of a mechanical sort that can be measured by counting equations or symbols. Both Einstein's and Newton's theories of gravitation involve equations that tell us the gravitational forces produced by any given amount of matter. In Newton's theory there are three of these equations (corresponding to the three dimensions of space); in Einstein's theory there are fourteen. In itself, this cannot be counted as an aesthetic advantage of Newton's theory over Einstein's. And in fact it is Einstein's theory that is more beautiful, in part because of the simplicity of his central idea about the equivalence of gravitation and inertia. That is a judgment on which scientists have generally agreed, and it was largely responsible for the early acceptance of Einstein's theory.

There is another quality besides simplicity that can make a physical theory beautiful—it is the sense of inevitability that the theory may give us. In listening to a piece of music or hearing a sonnet, one sometimes feels an intense aesthetic pleasure at the sense that nothing in the work could be changed, that there is not one note or one word that you would want to have different. In Raphael's *Holy Family* the placement of every figure on the canvas is perfect. This may not be of all paintings in the world your favorite, but as you look at that painting, there is nothing that you would want Raphael to have done differently. The same is partly true (it is never more than partly true) of general relativity. Once you know the general physical principles adopted by Einstein, you understand that there is no other significantly different theory of gravitation to which Einstein could have been led. As Einstein said of general relativity, "The chief attraction of the theory lies in its logical completeness. If a single one of the conclusions drawn from it proves wrong, it must be given up; to modify it without destroying the whole structure seems to be impossible."

This is less true of Newton's theory of gravitation. Newton could have supposed that the gravitational force decreases with the inverse cube of distance rather than the inverse square if that is what the astronomical data had demanded, but Einstein could not have incorporated an inverse-cube law in his theory without scrapping its conceptual basis. Thus Einstein's fourteen equations have an inevitability and hence beauty that Newton's three equations lack. I think that this is what Einstein meant when he referred to the side of the equations that involve the gravitational field in his general theory of relativity as beautiful, as if made of marble, in contrast with the other side of the equations, referring to matter, which he said were still ugly, as if made of mere wood. The way that the gravitational field enters Einstein's equations is almost inevitable, but nothing in general relativity explained why matter takes the form it does.

The same sense of inevitability can be found (again, only in part) in our modern Standard Model of the strong and electroweak forces that act on elementary particles. There is one common feature that gives both general relativity and the Standard Model most of their sense of inevitability and simplicity: they obey *principles of symmetry.*

A symmetry principle is simply a statement that something looks the same from certain different points of view. Of all such symmetries, the simplest is the approximate bilateral symmetry of the human face. Because there is little difference between the two sides of your face, it looks the same whether viewed directly or when left and right are reversed, as when you look in a mirror. It is almost a cliché of filmmaking to let the audience realize suddenly that the actor's face they have been watching has been seen in a mirror; the surprise would be spoiled if people had two eyes on the same side of the face like flounders, and always on the same side.

Some things have more extensive symmetries than the human face. A cube looks the same when viewed from six different directions, all at right angles to each other, as well as when left and right are reversed. Perfect crystals look the same not only when viewed from various different directions but also when we shift our positions within the crystal by certain amounts in various directions. A sphere looks the same from any direction. Empty space looks the same from all directions and all positions.

Symmetries like these have amused and intrigued artists and scientists for millennia but did not really play a central role in science. We know many things about salt, and the fact that it is a cubic crystal and therefore looks the same from six different points of view does not rank among the most important. Certainly bilateral symmetry is not the most interesting thing about a human face. The symmetries that are really important in nature are not the symmetries of *things*, but the symmetries of *laws*.

A symmetry of the laws of nature is a statement that when we make certain changes in the point of view from which we observe natural phenomena, the laws of nature we discover do not change. Such symmetries are often called principles of *invariance*. For instance, the laws of nature that we discover take the same form however our laboratories are oriented; it makes no difference whether we measure directions relative to north or northeast or upward or any other direction. This was not so obvious to ancient or medieval natural philosophers; in everyday life there certainly seems to be a difference between up and down and horizontal directions. Only with the birth of modern science in the seventeenth century did it become clear that down seems different from up or north only because below us there happens to be a large mass, the earth, and not (as Aristotle thought) because the natural place of heavy or light things is downward or upward. Note that this symmetry does not say that up is the same as down; observers who measure distances upward or downward from the earth's surface report different description of events such as the fall of an apple, but they discover the same laws, such as the law that apples are attracted by large masses like the earth.

The laws of nature also take the same form wherever our laboratories are located; it makes no difference to our results whether we do our experiments in Texas or Switzerland or on some planet on the other side of the galaxy. The laws of nature take the same form however we set our clocks; it makes no difference whether we date events from the Hegira or the birth of Christ or the beginning of the universe. This does not mean that nothing changes with time or that Texas is just the same as Switzerland, only that the laws discovered at different times and in different places are the same. If it were not for these symmetries the work of science would have to be redone in every new laboratory and in every passing moment.

Any symmetry principle is at the same time a principle of simplicity. If the laws of nature did distinguish among directions like up or down or north, then we would have to put something into our equations to keep track of the orientation of our laboratories, and they would be correspondingly less simple. Indeed, the very notation that is used by mathematicians and physicists to make our equations look as simple and compact as possible has built into it an assumption that all directions in space are equivalent. . . .

There are symmetries of space-time that are less obvious than these simple translations or rotations. The laws of nature also appear to take the same form to observers moving at different constant velocities; it makes no difference whether we do our experiments here in the solar system, whizzing around the center of the galaxy at hundreds of kilometers per second, or in a distant galaxy rushing away from our own at tens of thousands of kilometers per second. This last symmetry principle is sometimes called the principle of relativity. . . . Einstein explicitly designed his version of the principle of relativity to be consistent with an experimental fact, that the speed of light seems the same however the observer is moving. In this sense the emphasis on symmetry as a question of physics in Einstein's 1905 paper on special relativity marks the beginning of the modern attitude to symmetry principles.

In the context of prequantum physics Einstein's special theory of relativity fit in well with a dualistic view of nature: there are particles, like the electrons, protons, and neutrons in ordinary atoms, and there are fields, like the gravitational or the electromagnetic field. The advent of quantum mechanics led to a much more unified view. Quantum mechanically, the energy and momentum of a field like the electromagnetic field comes in bundles known as photons that behave exactly like particles, though like particles that happen to have no mass. Similarly, the energy and momentum in the gravitational field come in bundles called gravitons, that also behave like particles of zero mass. In a large-scale field of force like the sun's gravitational field we do not notice individual gravitons, essentially because there are so many of them.

In 1929 Werner Heisenberg and Wolfgang Pauli . . . explained in a pair of papers how massive particles like the electron could also be understood as bundles of energy and momenta in different sorts of fields, such as the electron field. Just as the electromagnetic force between two electrons is due in quantum mechanics to the exchange of photons, the force between photons and electrons is due to the exchange of electrons. The distinction between matter and force largely disappears; any particle can play the role of a test body on which forces act and by its exchange can produce other forces. Today it is generally accepted that the only way to combine the principles of special relativity and quantum mechanics is through the quantum theory of fields or something very like it. This is precisely the sort of logical rigidity that gives a really fundamental theory its beauty: quantum mechanics and special relativity are nearly incompatible, and their reconciliation in quantum field theory imposes powerful restrictions on the ways that particles can interact with one another.

All the symmetries mentioned so far only limit the kinds of force and matter that a theory may contain—they do not in themselves *require* the existence of any particular type of matter or force. Symmetry principles have moved to a new level of importance in the [twentieth century] and especially in the last few decades: there are symmetry principles that dictate the very existence of all the known forces of nature.

In general relativity the underlying principle of symmetry states that *all* frames of reference are equivalent: the laws of nature look the same not only to observers moving at any constant speed but to all observers, whatever the acceleration or rotation of their laboratories. Suppose we move our physical apparatus from the quiet of a university laboratory, and do our experiments on a steadily rotating merry-go-round. Instead of measuring directions relative to north, we would measure them with respect to the horses fixed to the rotating platform. At first sight the laws of nature will appear quite different. Observers on a rotating merry-go-round observe a centrifugal force that seems to pull loose objects to the outside of the merry-go-round. If they are born and grown up on the merry-go-round and do not know that they are on a rotating platform, they describe nature in terms of laws of mechanics that incorporate this centrifugal force, laws that appear quite different from those discovered by the rest of us.

The fact that the laws of nature seem to distinguish between stationary and rotating frames of reference bothered Isaac Newton and continued to trouble physicists in the following centuries. In the 1880s the Viennese physicist and philosopher Ernst Mach pointed the way toward a possible reinterpretation. Mach emphasized that there was something else besides centrifugal force that distinguishes the rotating merry-go-round and more conventional laboratories. From the point of view of an astronomer on the merry-go-round, the sun, stars, galaxies—indeed, the bulk of the matter of the universe—seems to be revolving around the zenith. You or I would say that this is because the merry-go-round is rotating, but an astronomer who grew up on the merry-go-round and naturally uses *it* as his frame of reference would insist that it is the rest of the universe that is spinning around him. Mach asked whether there was any way that this great apparent circulation of matter could be held responsible for centrifugal force. If so, then the laws of nature discovered on the merry-go-round might actually be the same as those found in more conventional laboratories;

the apparent difference would simply arise from the different enviroment seen by observers in their different laboratories.

Mach's hint was picked up by Einstein and made concrete in his general theory of relativity. In general relativity there is indeed an influence exerted by the distant stars that creates the phenomenon of centrifugal force in a spinning merry-go-round: it is the force of gravity. Of course nothing like this happens in Newton's theory of gravitation, which deals only with a simple attraction between all masses. General relativity is more complicated; the circulation of the matter of the universe around the zenith seen by observers on the merry-go-round produces a field somewhat like the magnetic field produced by the circulation of electricity in the coils of an electromagnet. It is this "gravitomagnetic" field that in the merry-go-round frame of reference produces the effects that in more conventional frames of reference are attributed to centrifugal force. The equations of general relativity, unlike those of Newtonian mechanics, are precisely the same in the merry-go-round laboratory and conventional laboratories; the difference between what is observed in these laboratories is entirely due to their different environment—a universe that revolves around the zenith or one that does not. But, if gravitation did not exist, this reinterpretation of centrifugal force would be impossible, and the centrifugal force felt on a merry-go-round would allow us to distinguish between the merry-go-round and more conventional laboratories and would thus rule out any possible equivalence between laboratories that are rotating and those that are not. *Thus the symmetry among different frames of reference requires the existence of gravitation.*

The symmetry underlying the electroweak theory is a little more esoteric. It does not have to do with changes in our point of view in space and time but rather with changes in our point of view about the identity of the different types of elementary particle. Just as it is possible for a particle to be in a quantum-mechanical state in which it is neither definitely here nor there, or spinning neither definitely clockwise nor counterclockwise, so also through the wonders of quantum mechanics it is possible to have a particle in a state in which it is neither definitely an electron nor definitely a neutrino until we measure some property that would distinguish the two, like the electric charge. In the electroweak theory the form of the laws of nature is unchanged if we replace electrons and neutrinos everywhere in our equations with such mixed states that are neither electrons nor neutrinos. Because various other types of particles interact with electrons and neutrinos, it is necessary at the same time to mix up families of these other particle types, such as up quarks with down quarks, as well as the photons with its siblings, the positively and negatively charged *W* particles and the neutral *Z* particles. This is the symmetry that connects the electromagnetic forces, which are produced by an exchange of photons, with the weak nuclear forces that are produced by the exchange of the *W* and *Z* particles. The photon and the *W* and *Z* particles appear in the electroweak theory as bundles of the energy of four fields, fields that are required by this symmetry of the electroweak theory in much the same way that the gravitational field is required by the symmetries of general relativity.

Symmetries of the sort underlying the electroweak theory are called *internal symmetries*, because we can think of them as having to do with the intrinsic nature of the particles, rather than their position or motion. Internal symmetries are less familiar than those that act on ordinary space and time, such as those governing general relativity. You can think of each particle as carrying a little dial, with a pointer that points in directions marked "electron" or "neutrino" or "photon" or "*W*" or anywhere in between. The internal symmetry says that the laws of nature take the same form if we rotate the markings on these dials in certain ways.

Furthermore, for the sort of symmetry that governs the electroweak forces, we can rotate the dials differently for particles at different times or positions. This is much like the symmetry underlying general relativity, which allows us to rotate our laboratory not only by some fixed angle but also by an amount that increases with time, by placing it on a merry-go-round. The invariance of the laws of nature under a group of such position-dependent and time-dependent internal symmetry transformations is called a *local* symmetry (because the effect of the symmetry transformations depends on location in space and time) or a *gauge* symmetry (for reasons that are purely historical). It is the local symmetry between different frames of reference in space and time that makes gravitation necessary, and in much the same way it is a second local symmetry between electrons and neutrinos (and between up quarks and down quarks and so on) that makes the existence of the photon, *W*, and *Z* fields necessary. . . .

I have been referring to principles of symmetry as giving theories a kind of rigidity. You might think that this is a drawback, that the physicist wants to develop theories that are capable of describing a wide variety of phenomena and therefore would like to discover theories that are as flexible as possible—theories that make sense under a wide variety of possible circumstances. That is true in many areas of science, but it is not true in this kind of fundamental physics. We are on the track of something universal—something that governs physical phenomena throughout the universe—something that we call the laws of nature. We do not want to discover a theory that is capable of describing all imaginable kinds of force among the particles of nature. Rather, we hope for a theory that rigidly will allow us to describe only those forces—gravitational, electroweak, and strong—that actually as it happens do exist. This kind of rigidity in our physical theories is part of what we recognize as beauty. . . .

The beauty that we find in physical theories like general relativity or the Standard Model is very like the beauty conferred on some works of art by the sense of inevitability that they give us—the sense that one would not want to change a note or a brush stroke or a line. But just as in our appreciation of music or painting or poetry, this sense of inevitability is a matter of taste and experience and cannot be reduced to formula.

Every other year the Lawrence Berkeley Laboratory publishes a little booklet that lists the properties of the elementary particles as known to that date. If I say that the fundamental principle governing nature is that the elementary particles have the properties listed in this booklet, then it is certainly true that the known properties of the elementary particles follow inevitably from this fundamental principle. This principle even has predictive power—every new electron or proton created in our laboratories will be found to have the mass and charge already listed in the booklet. But the principle itself is so ugly that no one would feel that anything had been accomplished. Its ugliness lies in its lack of simplicity and inevitability—the booklet contains thousands of numbers, any one of which could be changed without making nonsense of the rest of the information. There is no logical formula that establishes a sharp dividing line between a beautiful explanatory theory and a mere list of data, but we know the difference when we see it—we demand a simplicity and rigidity in our principles before we are willing to take them seriously. Thus not only is our aesthetic judgment a means to the end of finding scientific explanations and judging their validity—*it is part of what we mean by an explanation.*

Other scientists sometimes poke fun at elementary particle physicists because there are now so many so-called elementary particles that we have to carry the Berkeley booklet around with us to remind us of all the particles that have been discovered. But the mere number of particles is not important. As Abdus Salam has said, it is not particles or forces with which nature is sparing, but principles. The important thing is to have a set of simple and economical principles that explain why the particles are what they are. It *is* disturbing that we do not yet have a complete theory of the sort we want. But when we do, it will not matter very much how many kinds of particle or force it describes, as long as it does so beautifully, as an inevitable consequence of simple principles.

The kind of beauty that we find in physical theories is of a very limited sort. It is, as far as I have been able to capture it in words, the beauty of simplicity and inevitability—the beauty of perfect structure, the beauty of everything fitting together, of nothing being changeable, of logical rigidity. It is a beauty that is spare and classic, the sort we find in the Greek tragedies. But this is not the only kind of beauty that we find in the arts. A play of Shakespeare does not have this beauty, at any rate not to the extent that some of his sonnets have. Often the director of a Shakespeare play chooses to leave out whole speeches. In the Olivier film version of *Hamlet*, Hamlet never says, "Oh what a rogue and peasant slave am I!" And yet the performance works, because Shakespeare's plays are not spare, perfect structures like general relativity or *Oedipus Rex*; they are big messy compositions whose messiness mirrors the complexity of life. That is part of the beauty of his plays, a beauty that to my taste is of a higher order than the beauty of a play of Sophocles or the beauty of general relativity for that matter. Some of the greatest moments in Shakespeare are those in which he deliberately abandons the model of Greek tragedy and introduces an extraneous comic proletarian—a doorkeeper or gardener or fig seller or gravedigger—just before his major characters encounter their fates. Certainly the beauty of theoretical physics would be a very bad exemplar for the arts, but such as it is it gives us pleasure and guidance.

There is another respect in which it seems to me that theoretical physics is a bad model for the arts. Our theories are very esoteric—necessarily so, because we are forced to develop these theories using a language, the language of mathematics, that has not become part of the general equipment of the educated public. Physicists generally do not like the fact that our theories are so esoteric. On the other hand, I have occasionally heard artists talk proudly about their work being accessible only to a band of cognoscenti and justify this attitude by quoting the example of physical theories like general relativity that also can be understood only by initiates. Artists, like physicists, may not always be able to make themselves understood by the general public, but esotericism for its own sake is just silly.

Although we seek theories that are beautiful because of a rigidity imposed on them by simple underlying principles, creating a theory is not simply a matter of deducing it mathematically from a set of preordained principles. Our principles are often invented as we go along, sometimes precisely because they lead to the kind of rigidity we hope for. I have no doubt that one of the reasons that Einstein was so pleased with his idea about the equivalence of gravitation and inertia was that this principle led to only one fairly rigid theory of gravitation and not to an infinite variety of possible theories of gravitation. Deducing the consequences of a given set of well-formulated physical principles can be difficult or easy, but it is the sort of thing that physicists learn to do in graduate school and that they generally enjoy doing. The creation of *new* physical principles is agony and apparently cannot be taught. . . .

It is precisely in the application of pure mathematics to physics that the effectiveness of aesthetic judgments is most amazing. It has become a commonplace that mathematicians are driven in their work by the wish to construct formalisms that are conceptually beautiful. The English mathematician G. H. Hardy explained that "mathematical patterns like those of the painters or the poets must be beautiful. The ideas, like the colors or the words, must fit together in a harmonious way. Beauty is the first test. There is no permanent place for ugly mathematics." And yet mathematical structures that confessedly are developed by mathematicians because they seek a sort of beauty are often found later to be extraordinarily valuable by the physicist.

For illustration, let us return to the example of non-Euclidean geometry and general relativity. After Euclid, mathematicians tried for two millennia to learn whether the different assumptions underlying Euclid's geometry were logically independent of each other. If the postulates were not independent, if some of them could be deduced from the others, then the unnecessary postulates could be dropped, yielding a more economical and hence more beautiful formulation of geometry. This effort came to a head in the early years of the nineteenth century, when "the prince of geometers" Karl Friedrich Gauss and others developed a non-Euclidean geometry for a sort of curved space that satisfied all Euclid's postulates except the fifth. This showed that Euclid's fifth postulate is indeed logically independent of the other postulates. The new geometry was developed in order to settle a historic question about the foundations of geometry, not at all because anyone thought it applied to the real world.

Non-Euclidean geometry was then extended by one of the greatest of all mathematicians, Georg Friedrich Bernhard Riemann, to a general theory of curved spaces of two or three or any number of dimensions. Mathematicians continued to work on Riemannian geometry because it was so beautiful, without any idea of physical applications. Its beauty was again largely the beauty of inevitability. Once you start thinking about curved spaces, you are led almost inevitably to the introduction of the mathematical quantities (metrics, affine connections, curvature tensors, and so on) that are the ingredients of Riemannian geometry. When Einstein started to develop general relativity, he realized that one way of expressing his ideas about the symmetry that relates different frames of reference was to ascribe gravitation to the curvature of space-time. He asked a friend, Marcel Grossman, whether there existed any mathematical theory of curved spaces—not merely of curved two-dimensional surfaces in ordinary Euclidean three-dimensional space, but of curved three-dimensional spaces, or even curved four-dimensional space-times. Grossman gave Einstein the good news that there did in fact exist such a mathematical formalism, the one developed by Riemann and others, and taught him this mathematics, which Einstein then incorporated into general relativity. The mathematics was there waiting for Einstein to make use of, although I believe that Gauss and Riemann and the other differential geometers of the nineteenth century had no idea that their work would ever have any application to physical theories of gravitation.

An even stranger example is provided by the history of internal symmetry principles. In physics, internal symmetry principles typically impose a kind of family structure on the menu of possible particles. The first known example of such a family was provided by the two types of particle that make up ordinary atomic nuclei, the proton and neutron. Protons and neutrons have very nearly the same mass, so, once the neutron was discovered by James Chadwick in 1932, it was natural to suppose that the strong nuclear forces (which contribute to the neutron and proton masses) should respect a simple symmetry: the equations governing these forces should preserve their form if everywhere in these equations the roles of neutrons and protons are reversed. This would tell us among other things that the strong nuclear force is the same between two neutrons as between two protons but would tell us nothing about the force between a proton and a neutron. It was therefore somewhat a surprise when experiments in 1936 revealed that the nuclear force between two protons is about the same as the force between a proton and a neutron. This observation gave rise to the idea of a symmetry that goes beyond mere interchanges of protons and neutrons, a symmetry under continuous transformations that change protons and neutrons into particles that are proton-neutron mixtures, with arbitrary probabilities of being a proton or a neutron.

These symmetry transformations act on the particle label that distinguishes protons and neutrons in a way that is mathematically the same as the way that ordinary rotations in three dimensions act on the spins of particles like protons or neutrons or electrons. With this example in mind, until the 1960s many physicists tacitly assumed that the internal symmetry transformations that leave the laws of nature unchanged had to take the form of rotations in some internal space of two, three, or more dimensions, like the rotations of protons and neutrons into one another. The textbooks on the application of symmetry principles to physics then available (including the classic books of Hermann Weyl and Eugene Wigner) barely gave any hint that there were other mathematical possibilities. It was not until a host of new particles was discovered in cosmic rays and then at accelerators like the Bevatron in Berkeley in the late 1950s that a wider view of the possibilities of internal symmetries was forced on the world of theoretical physics. These particles seemed to fall into families that were more extensive than the simple proton-neutron pair of twins. For instance, the neutron and proton were found to bear a strong family likeness to six other particles known as hyperons, of the same spin and similar mass. What sort of internal symmetry could give rise to such extended kinship groups?

Around 1960 physicists studying this question began to turn for help to the literature of mathematics. It came to them as a delightful surprise that mathematicians had in a sense already cataloged all possible symmetries. The complete set of transformations that leaves anything unchanged, whether a specific object or the laws of nature, forms a mathematical structure known as a *group*, and the general mathematics of symmetry transformations is known as *group theory*. Each group is characterized by abstract mathematical rules that do not depend on what it is that is being transformed, just as the rules of arithmetic do not depend on what it is we are adding or multiplying. The menu of the types of families that are allowed by any particular symmetry of the laws of nature is completely dictated by the mathematical structure of the symmetry group.

Those groups of transformations that act continuously, like rotations in ordinary space or the mixing of electrons and neutrinos in the electroweak theory, are called *Lie groups*, after the Norwegian mathematician Sophus Lie. The French mathematician Élie Cartan had in his 1894 thesis given a list of all the "simple" Lie groups, from which all others could be built up by combining their transformations. In 1960 Gell-Mann[1] and the Israeli physicist Yuval Ne'eman independently found that one of these simple Lie groups (known as SU(3)) was just right to impose a family structure on the crowd of elementary particles much like what had been found experimentally. Gell-Mann borrowed a term from Buddhism and called this symmetry principle the eightfold way, because the better-known particles fell into families with eight members, like the neutron, proton, and their six siblings. Not all families were then complete; a new particle was needed to complete a family of ten particles that are similar to neutrons and protons and hyperons but have three times higher spin. It was one of the great successes of the new SU(3) symmetry that this predicted particle was subsequently discovered in 1964 at Brookhaven and turned out to have the mass estimated by Gell-Mann.

Yet this group theory that turned out to be so relevant to physics had been invented by mathematicians for reasons that were strictly internal to mathematics. . . . Neither . . . Lie nor Cartan had any idea of the sort of application that group theory would have in physics.

It is very strange that mathematicians are led by their sense of mathematical beauty to develop formal structures that physicists only later find useful, even where the mathematician had no such goal in mind. A well-known essay by the physicist Eugene Wigner refers to this phenomenon as "The Unreasonable Effectiveness of Mathematics." Physicists generally

---

1. [Murray Gell-Mann (1929–), American physicist.]

find the ability of mathematicians to anticipate the mathematics needed in the theories of physicists quite uncanny. It is as if Neil Armstrong in 1969 when he first set foot on the surface of the moon had found in the lunar dust footsteps of Jules Verne.

Where then *does* a physicist get a sense of beauty that helps not only in discovering theories of the real world, but even in judging the validity of physical theories, sometimes in the teeth of contrary experimental evidence? And how does a mathematician's sense of beauty lead to structures that are valuable decades or centuries later to physicists, even though the mathematician may have no interest in physical applications?

There seem to me to be three plausible explanations, two of them applicable throughout much of science and the third limited to the most fundamental areas of physics. The first explanation is that the universe itself acts on us a random, inefficient, and yet in the long run effective, teaching machine. Just as through an infinite series of accidental events, atoms of carbon and nitrogen and oxygen and hydrogen joined together to form primitive forms of life that later evolved into protozoa and fishes and people, in the same manner our way of looking at the universe has gradually evolved through a natural selection of ideas. Through countless false starts, we have gotten it beaten into us that nature is a certain way, and we have grown to look at that way that nature is as beautiful.

I suppose this would be everyone's explanation of why the horse trainer's sense of beauty helps when it does help in judging which horse can win races. The racehorse trainer has been at the track for many years—has experienced many horses winning or losing—and has come to associate, without being able to express it explicitly, certain visual cues with the expectation of a winning horse.

One of the things that makes the history of science so endlessly fascinating is to follow the slow education of our species in the sort of beauty to expect in nature. I once went back to the original literature of the 1930s on the earliest internal symmetry principle in nuclear physics, the symmetry that I mentioned earlier between neutrons and protons, to try to find the one research article that first presented this symmetry principle the way it would be presented today, as a fundamental fact about nuclear physics that stands on its own, independent of any detailed theory of nuclear forces. I could find no such article. It seems that in the 1930s it was simply not good form to write papers based on symmetry principles. What was good form was to write papers about nuclear forces. If the forces turned out to have a certain symmetry, so much the better, for, if you knew the proton-neutron force, you did not have to guess the proton-proton force. But the symmetry principle itself was not regarded, as far as I can tell, as a feature that would legitimize a theory—that would make the theory beautiful. Symmetry principles were regarded as mathematical tricks; the real business of physicists was to work out the dynamical details of the forces we observe.

We feel differently today. If experimenters were to discover some new particles that formed families of some sort or other like the proton-neutron doublet, then the mail would instantly be filled with hundreds of preprints of theoretical articles speculating about the sort of symmetry that under-lies this family structure, and, if a new kind of force were discovered, we would all start speculating about the symmetry that dictates the existence of that force. Evidently we have been changed by the universe acting as a teaching machine and imposing on us a sense of beauty with which our species was not born. . . .

The second of the reasons why we expect successful scientific theories to be beautiful is simply that scientists tend to choose problems that are likely to have beautiful solutions. The same may even apply to our friend the racehorse trainer. He trains horses to win races; he has learned to rec-ognize which horses are likely to win and he call these horses beautiful; but, if you take him aside and promise not to repeat what he says, he may confess to you that the reason he went into the business of training horses to win races in the first place was because the horses that he trains are such beautiful animals.

A good example in physics is provided by the phenomenon of smooth phase transitions, like the spontaneous disappearance of magnetism when an iron permanent magnet is heated above a temperature of 770°C, the temperature known as the Curie point. Because this is a smooth transition, the magnetization of a piece of iron goes to zero gradually as the tempera-ture approaches the Curie point. The surprising thing about such phase transitions is the *way* that the magnetization goes to zero. Estimates of vari-ous energies in a magnet had led physicists to expect that, when the tem-perature is only slightly below the Curie point, the magnetization would be simply proportional to the square root of the difference between the Curie point and the temperature. Instead it was observed experimentally that the magnetization is proportional to the 0.37 power of this difference. That is, the dependence of the magnetization on the temperature is somewhere between proportional to the square root (the 0.5 power) and the cube root (the 0.33 power) of the difference between the Curie point and the temperature.

Powers like this 0.37 are called *critical exponents*, sometimes with the adjective "nonclassical" or "anomalous," because they are not what had been expected. Other quantities were observed to behave in similar ways in this and other phase transitions, in some cases with precisely the same critical exponents. This is not an intrinsically glamorous phenomenon, like black holes or the expansion of the universe. Nevertheless, some of the brightest theoretical physicists in the world worked on the problem of the critical exponents, until the problem was eventually solved in 1972 by Kenneth Wilson and Michael Fisher, both then at Cornell. Yet it might have been thought that the precise calculation of the Curie point itself was a problem of greater practical importance. Why should leaders of condensed matter theory give the problem of the critical exponents so much greater priority?

I think that the problem of critical exponents attracted so much attention because physicists judged that it would be likely to have a beautiful solution. The clues that suggested that the solution would be beautiful were above all the universality of the phenomenon, the fact that the same critical exponents would crop up in very different problems, and also the fact that physicists have become used to finding that the most essential properties of physical phenomena are often expressed in terms of laws that relate physical quantities to powers of other quantities, such as the inverse-square law of gravitation. As it turned out, the theory of critical exponents has a simplicity and inevitability that makes it one of the most beautiful in all of physics. In contrast, the problem of calculating the precise temperatures of phase transitions is a messy one whose solution involves complicated details of the iron or other substance that undergoes the phase transition, and for this reason it is studied either because of its practical importance or in want of anything better to do. . . .

Sometimes when our sense of beauty lets us down, it is because we have overestimated the fundamental character of what we are trying to explain. A famous example is the work of the young Johannes Kepler on the sizes of the orbits of planets.

Kepler was aware of one of the most beautiful conclusions of Greek mathematics, concerning what are called the Platonic solids. These are three-dimensional objects with plane boundaries, for which every vertex and every face and every line are exactly like every other vertex, face, and line. An obvious example is the cube. The Greeks discovered that there are all together only five of these Platonic solids: the cube, the triangular pyramid, the twelve-sided dodecahedron, the eight-sided octahedron, and the twenty-sided icosahedron. . . . The Platonic solids furnish a prime example of mathematical beauty; this discovery has the same sort of beauty as the Cartan catalog of all possible continuous symmetry principles.

Kepler in his *Mysterium cosmographicum* proposed that the existence of only five Platonic solids explained why there were (apart from Earth) just five planets: Mercury, Venus, Mars, Jupiter, and Saturn. (Uranus, Neptune, and Pluto were not discovered until later.) To each one of these five planets Kepler associated one of the Platonic solids, and he made the guess that the radius of each planet's orbit was in proportion to the radius of the corresponding Platonic solid when the solids are nested within each other in the right order. Kepler wrote that he had worked over the irregularities of planetary motion "until they were at last accommodated to the laws of nature."

To a scientist today it may seem a scandal that one of the founders of modern science should invent such a fanciful model of the solar system. This is not only because Kepler's scheme did not fit observations of the solar system (though it did not), but much more because we know that this is not the sort of speculation that is appropriate to the solar system. But Kepler was not a fool. The kind of speculative reasoning he applied to the solar system is very similar to the sort of theorizing that elementary particle physicists do today; we do not associate anything with the Platonic solids, but we do believe for instance in a correspondence between different possible kinds of force and different members of the Cartan catalog of all possible symmetries. Where Kepler went wrong was not in using this sort of guesswork, but in supposing (as most philosophers before him had supposed) that the planets are important.

Of course, the planets are important in some ways. We live on one of them. But their existence is not incorporated into the laws of nature at any fundamental level. We now understand that the planets and their orbits are the results of a sequence of historical accidents and that, although physical theory can tell us which orbits are stable and which would be chaotic, there is no reason to expect any relations among the sizes of their orbits that would be mathematically simple and beautiful.

It is when we study truly fundamental problems that we expect to find beautiful answers. We believe that, if we ask why the world is the way it is and then ask why that answer is the way it is, at the end of this chain of explanations we shall find a few simple principles of compelling beauty. We think this in part because our historical experience teaches us that as we look beneath the surface of things, we find more and more beauty. Plato and the neo-Platonists taught that the beauty we see in nature is a reflection of the beauty of the ultimate, the *nous*. For us, too, the beauty of present theories is an anticipation, a premonition, of the beauty of the final theory. And in any case, we would not accept any theory as final unless it were beautiful.

Although we do not yet have a sure sense of where in our work we should rely on our sense of beauty, still in elementary particle physics aesthetic judgments seem to be working increasingly well. I take this as evidence that we are moving in the right direction, and perhaps not so far from our goal.

Content Questions

1. According to Weinberg, how is a physicist's sense that a theory is beautiful different from a person's sense that a work of art is beautiful? Why does Weinberg think that a horse trainer's judgment of the beauty of horses is like a physicist's judgment of the beauty of theories? (415–416)

2. How does Weinberg's idea of elegance in mathematics differ from his idea of beauty in scientific theories? (416–417)

3. What characteristics of Einstein's theory of gravitation lead Weinberg to judge it more beautiful than Newton's? (417–418)

4. Why are the symmetries of laws in nature also called "principles of *invariance*"? How do these principles impart simplicity to scientific theories? (418–419)

5. How is the principle of relativity also a principle of the symmetry of space-time? (419–420)

6. Why does Weinberg say that in the general theory of relativity *"the symmetry among different frames of reference requires the existence of gravitation"*? (422)

7. What are internal symmetries? How do they differ from the more familiar symmetries of space and time in physics? (423)

8. How is the local symmetry that governs the electroweak forces similar to the local symmetry that makes gravitation necessary in the general theory of relativity? How is local symmetry different from internal symmetry? (423)

9. Why is a "kind of rigidity in our physical theories" part of what physicists recognize as beauty? (423–424)

10. According to Weinberg, why is a "set of simple and economical principles" necessary to the beauty of a theory of elementary particles? (425)

11. According to Weinberg, what are the qualities that impart beauty to pure mathematics? (426)

12. How does the mathematical theory of groups help physicists extend their understanding of the internal symmetries of particles? Why do physicists generally find it "uncanny" that a mathematical idea such as group theory can predict the existence of undiscovered particles? (428–430)

13. Why does Weinberg think that the physicist's and the horse trainer's sense of beauty could be the result of the universe acting as a "teaching machine"? (430–431)

14. What factors made it likely that the solution to the problem of critical exponents would be beautiful? How does this example help explain how scientists acquire their sense of beauty? (431–432)

15. How was Kepler's application of a beautiful mathematical model to a scientific problem similar to what modern scientists do when they look for symmetries in nature? According to Weinberg, why did Kepler's sense of beauty let him down when he tried to apply the Platonic solids to the problem of determining the planets' orbits? (432–434)

Discussion Questions

1. How can a physicist's sense of beauty in scientific theories be more than a subjective opinion? (415–416) How can aesthetic judgment be "a means to the end of finding scientific explanations and judging their validity"? (424)

2. What does Weinberg mean when he says that the kind of simplicity that imparts beauty to theories is "a simplicity of ideas, not simplicity of a mechanical sort"? Why is this simplicity of ideas necessary for a scientist to judge a theory beautiful? (417)

3. What characteristics give a scientific theory a "sense of inevitability"? (417) Why is inevitability part of what makes theories beautiful? (424)

4. Why does Weinberg assert that "the symmetries that are really important in nature are not the symmetries of *things*, but the symmetries of *laws*"? (418)

5. What do physicists mean when they say that the laws of nature "take the same form" when natural phenomena are observed from different points of view? How does symmetry assure that the laws will keep the same form? (418–419)

6. What does Weinberg mean when he says that some symmetry principles "dictate the very existence of all the known forces of nature"? (421)

7. According to Weinberg's description of the general theory of relativity, how does an "underlying principle of symmetry" establish the theory? How is establishing a theory in this way different from doing so through experimentation and observation? (421–422)

8. What does it mean to change our point of view about "the identity of the different types of elementary particle" when thinking about *internal symmetries*? (422–423)

9. Why isn't a list of well-established scientific data as valuable for explaining the nature of the physical world as theories that possess the characteristics of simplicity, inevitability, and rigidity? (424–425)

10. If Weinberg is correct in saying that the creation of new physical principles "apparently cannot be taught," how do these principles come to be? Why does Weinberg refer to the activity that brings about these principles as creation, rather than discovery? (426)

11. What does Weinberg mean by "pure mathematics"? Why would scientists think that mathematical theories, created without any thought of their application to physics, could help them understand anything about the physical world? (426–427)

12. Why would a scientist rely on a sense of beauty to judge the validity of physical theories, even "in the teeth of contrary experimental evidence"? (430) Are there circumstances in which experimental evidence might be a less certain guide than a sense of beauty?

13. In Weinberg's example of the universe as a "teaching machine," what does he mean by "a natural selection of ideas"? Why does Weinberg say that this machine imposes on us "a sense of beauty with which our species was not born"? (430–431)

14. Why would scientists consider the solution to the problem of calculating precise temperatures for phase transitions less beautiful than the theoretical solution to the problem of critical exponents? (432)

15. What does Weinberg mean by "truly fundamental problems" in physics? When should physicists rely on their sense of beauty in their work on fundamental problems? (434)

Suggestions for Further Reading

By the author

Weinberg, Steven. *Dreams of a Final Theory: The Scientist's Search for the Ultimate Laws of Nature.* New York: Pantheon Books, 1992; New York: Vintage, 1994. This collection of essays, from which the selection in *What's the Matter?* is taken, centers on how a universal theory uniting all the laws of nature might be found and how it would be mathematically, philosophically, and aesthetically satisfying.

About the topic

Close, Frank. *Lucifer's Legacy: The Meaning of Asymmetry.* Oxford: Oxford University Press, 2000, 2001. The author, a leading particle physicist, presents a wide-ranging survey of asymmetries in nature—from the molecular level to the universe at large—and speculates that these imbalances are not only essential for life but the necessary consequence of the big bang.

Crease, Robert P. *The Prism and the Pendulum: The Ten Most Beautiful Experiments in Science.* New York: Random House, 2003, 2004. Focusing on groundbreaking experiments from ancient times to the twentieth century, this book shows how scientists are motivated by considerations of beauty as much as truth in their work.

Icke, Vincent. *The Force of Symmetry.* Cambridge: Cambridge University Press, 1995. This introduction to the significance of symmetry in physics provides a thorough explanation of how this concept has guided work in quantum theory, relativity, and the highly successful Standard Model of subatomic particles.

Kline, Morris. *Mathematics and the Search for Knowledge.* New York: Oxford University Press, 1985, 1986. A leading historian of mathematics examines why the abstract science of mathematics is the most powerful instrument for investigating the physical universe.

Zee, A. *Fearful Symmetry: The Search for Beauty in Modern Physics.* Princeton, NJ: Princeton University Press, 1999. Though thoroughly grounded in scientific facts and details, this highly entertaining survey focuses on the aesthetic motivations that animate twentieth-century physics and the intellectual framework in which fundamental physics operates.

Our goal is not to *know everything* about the universe but rather to understand how the universe works and why it is the way it is. Learning that there are things we cannot know is actually part of that understanding, and in no way does it imply that we cannot understand how the universe works and why it is the way it is.

—Gordon Kane, *Supersymmetry*

GORDON KANE

Why Physics Is the
Easiest Science: Effective Theories

Frequently, nonscientists dismiss the claim that a scientific theory provides certain knowledge of the world by saying, "It's just a theory," as if it is only an unproven, hypothetical statement. However, scientists consider a theory to be a well-established body of knowledge that can be relied on with great confidence, one that represents a highly accurate explanation of some aspects of the world. They believe that a sound scientific theory correlates facts and experimental observations in a clear, logical form, often in mathematical terms; that it explains previously existing problems; and that it allows them to make quantitative predictions that can be tested. At the same time, scientists recognize that a successful theory will suggest new paths of investigation that may significantly modify and extend the theory itself, even replacing some of its basic assumptions

One reason that the study of physics has progressed—especially since the time of Galileo and Newton—has been the conviction of scientists that the physical world can best be explained through scientific theories rather than through dogmatic teachings or collections of data. In physics, the aim of theories has been to reduce the explanation of the immense variety of phenomena in the physical world to the simplest underlying principles. Taking this highly successful reductionist approach, physicists have been able to unify explanations of phenomena that at first appeared quite different. For example, Isaac Newton demonstrated that the same laws explain the motion of earthly and celestial objects, and Maxwell's theory of electromagnetism not only unified electrical and magnetic phenomena, but also explained light and optics in the same terms. In the twentieth century, both Einstein's theory of relativity and quantum theory extended the scientific understanding of the physical world to scales of distance and size vastly larger as well as much smaller than those considered in the theories of classical physics. Physicists have since applied this extension of scale to their search for a primary theory—one unifying all explanations of the physical world—in the new realms revealed by astrophysics, relativistic cosmology, and especially particle physics.

At the beginning of the twenty-first century, the Standard Model of particle physics provides the most thorough description so far of the underlying principles of the physical world. It does so in terms of elementary particles that account for matter as well as the electromagnetic, strong, and weak forces of nature. Its predictions have been repeatedly verified over several decades of intensive experimental research.

Gordon Kane (1937–) is the Victor Weisskopf Collegiate Professor of Physics at the University of Michigan, and is a leading researcher and writer in particle physics. His research centers on extending the Standard Model of particle physics. In much of his work, Kane emphasizes the concept of *supersymmetry*, which, if verified experimentally, could hold the key to a primary theory unifying the particles associated with matter and those associated with forces. As Kane explains in his book *Supersymmetry* (2000), it is

> a surprising and subtle idea—the idea that the equations representing the basic laws of nature don't change if certain particles in the equations are interchanged with one another. Just as a square on a piece of paper looks the same if you rotate it by 90 degrees, the equations that physicists have found to describe nature often do not change when certain operations are performed on them. When that happens, the equations are said to have symmetry. Supersymmetry is such a proposed symmetry—the "super" is included in its name because [it] is more surprising and more hidden from everyday view than previously discovered symmetries.

In addition, Kane has been a strong advocate for government funding of research in particle physics. Besides the inherent value of expanding our knowledge of the universe, such research carries implications for many aspects of modern technology, including medicine, electronics, and nuclear power. It requires experimental devices that produce extremely high levels of energy and are capable of detecting traces of effects that occur at infinitesimal scales far beyond our ability to observe them directly. Thus, research in particle physics is extraordinarily expensive, and Kane encourages citizens to commit to the value of this research by supporting government funding for it.

In the following selection, taken from *Supersymmetry*, Kane asks us to consider how the method of effective theories helps scientists understand the interrelation of different segments of the physical world and gain insight into both how and why the world operates as it does.

Why Physics Is the Easiest Science: Effective Theories

If we had to understand the whole physical universe at once in order to understand any part of it, we would never have made any progress. Suppose that the properties of atoms depended on their history, or on whether they were in stars or people or labs—we might not understand them yet. In many areas of biology and ecology and other fields, systems are influenced by many factors, and of course the behavior of people is dominated by our interactions with others. In these areas progress comes more slowly. The physical world, on the other hand, can be studied in segments that hardly affect one another, as I will explain in this chapter. If our goal is learning how things work, a segmented approach is very fruitful. That is one of several reasons why physics began earlier in history than other sciences, and why it has made considerable progress: it really is the easiest science. (Other reasons include the relative ease with which experimenters can change one quantity at a time, holding others fixed; the relative ease of improving experiments when the implications are unclear; and the high likelihood that results are

This selection is taken from chapter 3, "Why Physics Is the Easiest Science—Effective Theories," of Supersymmetry.

described by simple mathematics, a property that enables investigators to deduce testable predictions.)

Once we understand all the segments, we can connect and unify them, a unification based on real understanding of how the parts of the world behave rather than on philosophical speculation. The history of physics could be written as a process of tackling the separate areas once the technology and available understanding allow them to be studied, followed by the continual unification of segments into a larger whole. Today one can argue that in physics, we are finally working at the boundaries of this process, where research focuses on unifying all of the interactions and particles—this is an exciting time intellectually. In recent years physicists have understood this approach better and have made it more explicit and formal. The jargon for the modern way of thinking of theories and their relations is the method of "effective theories." . . . Sometimes this approach has been called a reductionist one. But the word *reductionist* has different meanings and implications for different people, so I won't use it here. For physicists, *reductionist* implies simultaneously separating areas to study them *and* integrating them as they become understood.

Organizing Effective Theories by Distance Scales

Probably the best way to organize effective theories is in terms of the typical size of structures studied by a particular effective theory, which we speak of as the distance scale of normal phenomena described by that theory. Imagine starting by thinking about the universe at very large distances, so large that our sun and all stars look like small objects from such distances. This is the effective theory of cosmology, where stars cluster in galaxies because of their gravitational attraction, and galaxies are attracted to each other and form clusters of galaxies. Because of gravitational attraction, everything is moving on a background of the expanding universe. The only force that matters is gravity. We can use simple Newtonian rules to describe motion—deviations due to effects described by quantum theory are tiny and can be ignored. We can study how stars and planets and galaxies form, their typical sizes, how they distribute themselves around the universe, and so on. It doesn't matter whether the particles that make up stars and planets are composed of quarks or not, nor does it matter how many forces there are at the small distances inside a nucleus.

The large-scale universe is insensitive to what its contents are except for their mass and energy. Because of this indifference, cosmology can make progress regardless of whether we understand how stars work, whether protons are made of quarks, and so on. We can learn from astronomy data that there is dark matter. At the same time, if the dark matter is composed of particles, we cannot learn from astronomy or cosmology what kind of particles they are, because cosmology is largely insensitive to the properties that distinguish one particle from another, such as their masses and what charges they carry.

Next consider smaller distances, about the size of stars. We can study how stars form, how they get their energy supply, how long they will shine—that is, we can work out an effective theory of stars. While doing that, we can ignore whether the stars are in galaxies and whether there are top quarks or people. Let's go to a smaller distance, say people size, and consider the physics. Gravity keeps us on the planet, but otherwise it is the electromagnetic force that matters. All of our senses come from mechanical and chemical effects based on the electromagnetic force. Sight consists of photons interacting with electrons in our eyes, followed by electrical signals traveling to our brains. Touch begins with pressure affecting cells in the skin, leading to electrical signals propagating to the brain. Hearing starts with air molecules hitting molecules in the eardrum, interacting via electromagnetic forces. Friction, essential for us to stay in place or to move, is due to electromagnetic forces between atoms. We don't need to know about the weak or strong forces, or about the galaxy, to study people-sized physics. The energy that the sun supplies to the earth provides all of our food and essentially all of our energy, mostly from stored solar energy, but otherwise how the sun works does not matter. Here is a case where phenomena from one effective theory provide input to another in a very specific way—the earth can be viewed as a closed system except for the input of solar energy. From the point of view of the effective theory of the planet earth, how the sun generates its energy is irrelevant.

Now consider atomic size. Here we'll be able to see even better how powerful the effective theory idea is. To be able to use the basic equations that govern atoms, we have to input some information, essentially a few properties of the electron (its mass and electric charge and spin) and the same properties for each of the naturally occurring nuclei, if we want to describe the whole periodic table of the elements. A description of atoms doesn't need to take account of whether stars or galaxies or people exist, whether the nucleus is made of protons and neutrons, or whether protons are made of quarks.

Before we go to even smaller distances, this is a good place to stop and consider some of the implications of this way of thinking. When we have a tentative theory of atoms, we want to test its predictions and determine whether it explains phenomena we already know. The predictions for the lifetimes of atoms, for the energies of photons emitted by atoms, for the sizes of atoms, and so on depend on pieces of input information—on the masses and charges and spins of the electron and the nuclei. Every effective theory has some input parameters such as these. Without input information about the electron and nuclei, we could solve the equations but not evaluate the results numerically, so we could not test the theory, make any useful predictions, or tell whether we had the right theory. For example, the radius of the hydrogen atom is $h^2/m_e e^2$ (h is Planck's constant, m_e is the electron's mass, and e is the magnitude of the electric charge of the electron). If we measure the size of the hydrogen atom, we still can't check whether the theory is working unless we know (by measurement or calculation) the mass and charge of the electron and Planck's constant (all three were measured nearly a century ago).

Now we can emphasize an important aspect of effective theories. When we study the effective theory of the nucleus, we want to be able to calculate the masses and spins and charges of the nuclei—those parameters are results derived in the effective theory at that level. But for the next higher level, the atom, those parameters are the input. They can be input if they are measured, whether or not they are understood in the effective theory of nuclei. Similarly, the electron is a fundamental particle whose mass and electric charge will, it is hoped, be calculable someday in a fundamental theory such as string theory, but for the effective theory of atomic physics it does not matter whether they are calculable or understood, if they have been measured. We have known the numerical value of the mass of the electron since the beginning of the twentieth century, but we do not understand why it has that value. The value of the electron's mass can be input into every effective theory that depends on the electron. Every effective theory so far has some input that is for it a given, not something to be questioned; for the effective theory of atoms, the mass of the electron is such a given.

If a theory has inputs, it is an effective theory. From this point of view, the goal of particle physics is to learn the ultimate theory at the smallest distances, recognizing it as the theory for which no parameters have to be input to calculate its predictions. For the ultimate theory, it is not satisfactory to input the electron mass; rather, it is necessary to be able to calculate that mass from basic principles and to explain why it has the value it does.

Every effective theory is based on others: it is effective theories all the way down, until the ultimate one. Each effective theory has certain structures that bind together at its level—stars, atoms, nuclei, protons. As viewed from the effective theory of stars, stars are made of nuclei and electrons bound by the gravitational force, but for the effective theory of cosmology, they are just inputs characterized by a mass and brightness. For the effective theory of nuclei, nuclei are bound states of neutrons and protons, but for the effective theory of atoms, they are merely pointlike inputs. All systems and structure are inputs at one level of effective theories but are something to be derived and explained by the effective theory at a smaller distance. In a sense, a given effective theory can be explained in terms of shorter-distance theories and the input from them. Dirac[1] said that his equation that unified special relativity and quantum theory for the interactions of electrons and nuclei explained all of chemistry, and in a sense he was right. His equation, plus the input parameters describing electrons and nuclei, in principle explained all chemical processes. In another sense, however, he was not right, because in practice one could never start from the Dirac equation and calculate the properties of molecules, or figure out their structure, or determine how to construct new molecules with certain desired properties—the questions are just too complicated to solve. For example, Dirac could not have deduced that water is wet from his equation. For each effective theory, new regularities are found, and properties arise that are not predictable *in practice*. These are often called emergent properties. Life is an emergent property too. Physics tells us everything that molecules can do and cannot do. In particular, physics can tell us that life will not emerge on some planets if circumstances are too adverse, but it cannot guarantee that life *will* emerge on a planet where conditions are favorable, even though the emergence of life may be very likely.

1. [Paul Dirac (1902–1984), British theoretical physicist.]

Another way to view effective theories is in terms of types of understanding. At its own level, an effective theory provides a "how understanding," a description of how things work. But for the effective theory above it, at larger distances, the smaller-distance effective theory explains all or some of the input parameters, thus providing a "why understanding." For example, nuclear physics describes the properties of nuclei, using the proton and its electric charge, spin, mass, and magnetic properties as given, unexplained input. But the Standard Model provides the explanation, making it possible to calculate all those properties of the proton in terms of quarks bound by gluons.

Yet another perspective appears if we observe that in general, all areas of science are intrinsically open-ended: chemistry, the physics of materials, geology, biology, and so on. There is no end to the number of possible systems and variations that can be studied. But particle physics and cosmology are different. If the fundamental laws that govern the universe are found and understood, that's it—these two fields (that are merging into one) will end.

Having examined some implications of effective theories, let's return to the progression to smaller distances. We can go from atoms through the effective theory of nuclei, protons, and neutrons to quarks and leptons. Another important point is that each effective theory works well at its level, but it breaks down as we go to smaller distances and find new kinds of structure. When we went inside protons we found quarks, so we could not make a theory of protons unless we understood quarks and their interactions as well.

To go deeper into matter, it will help to keep track of the distance scales numerically. Because we will cover a huge range of distances, we need to use powers of 10—remember that each step in the power is a factor of 10 in the result: 10^{-1}\$ is a dime, 10^{-2}\$ is a penny, and 10^{3}\$ is one thousand dollars. There are two scales that are useful for us to keep track of: meters, which are a typical human size, and another length called the Planck length, after Max Planck, who first introduced it soon after he took the initial step toward the quantum theory in 1899. The Planck length is extremely small; we'll understand it better later in this chapter. People are typically a meter or two in size. All of our analysis will be very approximate, so we won't worry about whether we speak of the height or width or radius of a system. We'll keep track of powers of 10 but not worry about distinguishing between things that might differ by a factor of 2 or so in size. People are about 10^{35} Planck lengths (1 followed by 35 zeros) tall, 1 or 2 meters. Atoms are about 10^{-10} meter (one ten-billionth of a meter), about 10^{25} Planck lengths, in radius. Protons are about 100,000 times smaller than atoms, 10^{-15} meter or 10^{20} Planck lengths. Most particle physicists currently expect that quarks, leptons, photons, W and Z [bosons], and gluons will ultimately be understood as having a stringlike extension if we could view them at a distance scale of about 1 Planck length, or 10^{-35} (a decimal point followed by 34 zeros and a 1) meter—they should seem pointlike until we can study them at that scale.

In the language of this chapter, we can think of the Standard Model . . . as the effective theory of quarks and leptons interacting on a scale of about 10^{-17} meter, or 10^{18} Planck lengths, about 100 times smaller than protons and neutrons. Sometimes we call this the collider scale, because it is associated with the typical energies at which the experimental collider facilities operate.

The goal of particle physics is an ultimate theory of the natural world. What should we call it? People have called it a *theory of everything*, but that name is somewhat misleading; it really is not a theory of weather, stars, psychology, and everything at once. It has been called the *final theory*; that is a good name, but when I first read it I misinterpreted it to mean the last in a succession of theories that replaced each other, as though all the theories on the way to the final one should be discarded. In fact, all the effective theories coexist simultaneously, and all are part of our description of nature. Therefore, I would like to choose a somewhat different name. I find I like calling it the *primary theory*, a term that suggests the theory one arrives at after going through a sequence of effective theories at smaller and smaller distances. As we will see more clearly in a few paragraphs, the primary theory should be the description of nature at a distance scale of about 1 Planck length, or about 10^{-35} meter. . . .

The Physics of the Planck Scale

Whenever we describe a segment of nature, we have to talk about the actual quantities that are calculated or predicted or explained in units—meters, seconds, kilograms, or other appropriate units. In Carl Sagan's novel *Contact*, a signal from an extraterrestrial intelligence has been detected, with instructions on how to build a Machine to facilitate communication. There is a conversation between a scientist and an administrator.

> "Don't ask why we need two tons of erbium. Nobody has the faintest idea."
>
> "I wasn't going to ask that. I want to know how they told you how much a ton is."
>
> "They counted it out for us in Planck masses. A Planck mass is—"
>
> "Never mind, never mind. It's something that physicists all over the universe know about, right? And I've never heard of it."

For every effective theory there is a natural system of units, one where the description of phenomena is simple and not clumsy. It would be silly to measure room sizes in Planck lengths just because the primary theory is best talked about in those units. Consider the units for atoms more closely. The radius of an atom can be expressed in terms of the properties of the electron plus Planck's constant h, which sets the scale of all quanta. h is the fundamental, universal constant of quantum theory. Denoting the electric charge of the electron by e, and the mass of the electron by m_e, we find that the radius (r) of the hydrogen atom, the simplest atom, is equal to h^2/e^2m_e. The size of the atom is fully determined by these inputs. Nothing else matters. The nucleus, for example, is just a tiny object at the center. Once we know r, we can express the sizes of all atoms in terms of r; we don't need to use the input of h or the electron properties anymore. r is the natural size unit for atoms. Atoms with different numbers of electrons will have somewhat different sizes, with radii such as $1.2r$ or $2.4r$, but all will be some number that is not too big or small times r. r is expressed in terms of parameters that are givens for atomic physics—maybe e and m_e can be calculated someday in string theory, but they cannot be understood in atomic physics.

We can learn a great deal from this kind of analysis. For example, this expression for the size of an atom has major implications. It tells us that the size of atoms is essentially a universal quantity. Given the basic quantities (Planck's constant and the mass and charge of the electron), the size of all atoms of all kinds, anywhere in the universe, is determined. Because mountains and plants and animals are all made of atoms, their sizes are approximately determined by the size of atoms and the electromagnetic and gravitational forces. Combining atoms into genes and cells to evolve an organism that can manipulate and deal with the world requires a large number of cells and sets a minimum size for the organism. Having a brain with enough neurons to make enough connections to make decisions about the world requires a brain of a certain minimum size, because the atoms cannot be made smaller than the size determined by the radius r. Nothing the size of a butterfly, anywhere in the universe, will ever be able to think.

Suppose now that we have just discovered the primary theory. To present the results, we have to express the predictions and explanations in appropriate units. What units should we use? We expect the natural units for the primary theory to be very universal ones, not dependent on whether the universe has people or stars. There is only one known way to make universal units. There are only three universal constants in nature common to all aspects of nature—to all interactions and all particles. They are Planck's constant h; the speed of light (denoted by c), which is constant under all conditions; and Newton's constant G, which measures the strength of the gravitational force. Because Einstein proved that energy and mass are convertible into one another, and gravitation is a force proportional to the amount of energy a system has, everything in the universe feels the gravitational force. In fact, using these three quantities—h, c, and G, it is possible to construct combinations that have the units of length, time, and energy. We expect all the quantities that enter into the primary theory or are solutions of the equations of the primary theory to be expressible in terms of the units constructed from h, c, and G. (For the interested reader, the result for the Planck length is $(hG/c^3)^{1/2}$, which is about equal to 10^{-35} meter, as we said before. For completeness, the Planck time is $(hG/c^5)^{1/2}$, which is about 10^{-44} second, and the Planck mass is $(hc/G)^{1/2}$, which is about 10^{-8} kilogram.) The Planck distance and time are extremely small, whereas the Planck mass (or, equivalently, energy) is very large for a particle. . . .

The Planck length and time can also be interpreted as the smallest length and time that we can make sense of in a world described by quantum theory and having a universal gravitational force. The arguments that teach us that are interesting and not too complicated, but to explain them we have to recall the definition of a black hole. Basically, the idea of a black hole is simple. Imagine being on a planet and launching a rocket. If you give the rocket enough speed, it can escape the gravitational attraction of the planet and travel into outer space. If you increase the mass of the planet, you have to increase the speed the rocket requires to escape. If you increase the mass so much that the required speed exceeds the speed of light, then the rocket can't escape because nothing can go faster than light. The rocket (and everything) is trapped. Light also feels gravitational forces, so beams of light are trapped too. Because gravitational forces increase with decreasing distance, if you pack some mass into a sphere of smaller radius, it is harder to escape from it, so the condition for having a black hole depends on both the amount of mass and the size of the sphere you pack the mass into.

Now the fascinating thing is that if we put an object having the Planck energy in a region with a radius of the Planck length, we satisfy the conditions to have a black hole! We cannot separate such a region into parts, or get information out from a measurement, so we cannot define space to a greater precision than the Planck length! Because distance is speed × time, and speed can be at most the speed of light, and there is a minimum distance we can define, there is also a minimum time we can define—that comes out to be the Planck time. We saw above that the Planck scale provides the natural units for expressing the primary theory when the units are constructed from the fundamental constants h, c, and G. Now we see a second reason for expecting the Planck scale to be the distance scale for the primary theory: there does not appear to be a way, even in principle, to make sense of smaller distances or times. The times when events occur cannot be specified, or even put in order, more precisely than the Planck time.

There is a third interesting argument that gives the same answer. The gravitational force between two objects is proportional to their energies and grows as the distance between them decreases. Consider, for example, two protons. Normally, the repulsive electrical force between them is much larger than the attractive gravitational force. But if the energies of the protons are increased to the Planck energy, then the gravitational force between them becomes about equal to the electrical force between them. All the forces become about the same strength at the Planck scale, rather than being widely different in strength, as they are in our everyday world. Thus we might expect the gravitational force to unify with the others at the Planck scale, just as one might hope for in the primary theory.

The arguments of this chapter have led in several ways to the idea that it makes sense to analyze the physical world with effective theories organized by the distance scale to which they apply and to move toward a primary theory that unifies the forces and particles and is valid at the smallest scale that makes sense, the Planck scale. Of course these arguments do not prove that is how nature works; we will not know that until we achieve such a description. The Planck scale is very small, but not beyond our imagination. Some readers may recall the delightful *Powers of Ten* book and movie by the designers Charles and Ray Eames, in which the universe was looked at in snapshots each ten times smaller than the previous one, starting with the largest cosmological distances. When the Eameses did this work, shortly before the Standard Model was discovered, they could not meaningfully go to smaller distances than the proton. Today the Standard Model takes us nearly 3 powers of 10 smaller than the proton. From the universe down to the Standard Model domain is about 46 powers of 10, and from the Standard Model to the Planck scale is only about 16 more powers of 10. Looked at that way, perhaps it does not seem so far. . . .

The Human Scales

Since the time of Copernicus, who taught us that the earth is not at the center of the universe, we have learned that if we want to understand the world, we have to go beyond how the world seems to be and ask for evidence of how it is. We have learned that matter in the heavens and matter on earth obey the same natural laws, that we are made of the same atoms as the earth and the stars, that we and all organisms on earth evolved from cells, that we have unconscious minds that affect our behavior, and that our star is only one of a hundred billion stars in our galaxy. We have learned that the rules that govern nature (quantum theory and special relativity) are not apparent in our everyday classical world, and that the laws of nature have symmetries that are hidden from us but important (such as the particle interchange symmetry of the Standard Model). Perhaps even the number of space dimensions of the world will be larger than the three we are aware of. To understand the universe, we must recognize that additional hidden aspects of nature may arise at scales far different from the human scale, and we must learn how to uncover them.

Content Questions

1. According to Kane, why does progress in biology and ecology come more slowly than in physics? (443–444)

2. What is the "modern way of thinking of theories and their relations" that Kane refers to as the "method of 'effective theories'"? (444)

3. How do distance scales help organize effective theories? (444–446)

4. In an effective theory of cosmology, why are the Newtonian laws of motion sufficient for explaining the formation of stars, planets, and galaxies? Why is it possible to make progress in cosmology regardless of whether we understand how stars work or whether protons are made of quarks? (444–445)

5. How do the input parameters of Planck's constant and the mass and charge of the electron allow a theory of atoms to be checked? (446)

6. In effective theories, what is the difference between being able to measure and being able to calculate the electron's mass and charge? What does Kane mean when he says that an input is a given? (446–447)

7. How is an ultimate theory, such as string theory, different from an effective theory? (447)

8. According to Kane, why are some of the properties of an effective theory not explained by other effective theories at smaller distance scales? (447)

9. How can the same effective theory provide, in Kane's terms, both a "how understanding" and a "why understanding"? (448)

10. What did the Standard Model have to accomplish in order to provide an explanation for the properties of the proton? (448)

11. Why does Kane prefer to call the ultimate theory of the natural world the "*primary theory*"? (449)

12. Why is the radius (r) of the hydrogen atom the natural size unit for atoms? How do the terms in which r is expressed tell us that the size of atoms is a universal quantity? (450–451)

13. Why would we expect the natural units for the primary theory to be universal ones? (451)

14. Why can't space and time be defined to a greater precision than the Planck scale? (452)

15. What reasons are there for thinking that the Planck scale is the distance scale for the primary theory? (452–453)

Discussion Questions

1. Why does Kane call physics "the easiest science" when it is often considered the most difficult? (443)

2. What does Kane mean by "segments" of the physical world? (444) When physicists study the natural world, how do they decide how to segment it?

3. Why do effective theories depend on input parameters? (445–447) How can a scientist determine the appropriate input parameters for a particular effective theory, such as the one that explains the behavior of atoms?

4. In his description of the ultimate theory that is the goal of particle physics, what does Kane mean by the "basic principles" that would be used to make calculations? (447)

5. What are "emergent properties"? Why are they "not predictable *in practice*"? (447)

6. Is a scientific explanation adequate if it doesn't provide both a "how understanding" and a "why understanding"? (448)

7. How do particle physics and cosmology differ from sciences such as biology and chemistry that Kane says are "intrinsically open-ended"? What does it mean to say that particle physics and cosmology will end if they are successful in discovering and understanding the fundamental laws that govern the universe? (448)

8. Why wouldn't the discovery of the primary theory make it necessary to discard any of the sequence of effective theories that Kane says "coexist simultaneously"? (449)

9. Is the knowledge that "atoms cannot be made smaller than the size determined by the radius *r*" sufficient to assert that "nothing the size of a butterfly, anywhere in the universe, will ever be able to think"? (450–451)

10. What is the "one known way to make universal units"? (451)

11. Why does Kane say that the Planck scale is "the smallest scale that makes sense"? Why does he make a point of saying that this scale is "not beyond our imagination"? (453)

12. What does Kane mean by "the human scale"? (453) Does this scale have any characteristics that distinguish it from the distance scales of effective theories?

Suggestions for Further Reading

By the author

Kane, Gordon. *The Particle Garden: Our Universe As Understood by Particle Physicists.* Reading, MA: Addison-Wesley, 1995, 1996. This outstanding history of particle physics clearly explains its fundamental concepts and experimental methods and speculates on how this field of research can be extended in the search for a unified theory of the physical world.

————. *Supersymmetry: Unveiling the Ultimate Laws of Nature.* Cambridge, MA: Perseus Books Group, 2000, 2001. This book for general readers, from which the selection in *What's the Matter?* is taken, explains the fundamental principles of the Standard Model of particle physics and why its extension through supersymmetry points the way to a primary theory unifying all the laws of physics.

About the topic

Barrow, John D. *Theories of Everything: The Quest for Ultimate Explanation.* Oxford: Clarendon Press, 1991. This survey of the ways in which scientists are attempting to find a theory of the physical world that can encompass all known laws and phenomena is particularly good in describing the differing approaches of physicists and mathematicians to the problem.

Close, Frank, Michael Marten, and Christine Sutton. *The Particle Odyssey: A Journey to the Heart of Matter.* Oxford: Oxford University Press, 2002, 2004. This history of particle physics, from its origins in the discovery of x-rays in 1895 to the latest frontiers of research, is richly illustrated with color photographs of subatomic events that complement the explanations in the text.

Davies, P. C. W., and Julian Brown, eds. *Superstrings: A Theory of Everything?* Cambridge: Cambridge University Press, 1988, 1992. The first part of this book summarizes the directions taken by modern physics and provides a good foundation for understanding the emergence of string theory. The second part consists of stimulating interviews with nine leading physicists who have been involved in the development of string theory.

Weinberg, Steven. *Dreams of a Final Theory: The Scientist's Search for the Ultimate Laws of Nature.* New York: Pantheon Books, 1992; New York: Vintage, 1994. This collection of essays by a leading modern physicist centers on how a universal theory uniting all the laws of nature might be found and how it would be mathematically, philosophically, and aesthetically satisfying.

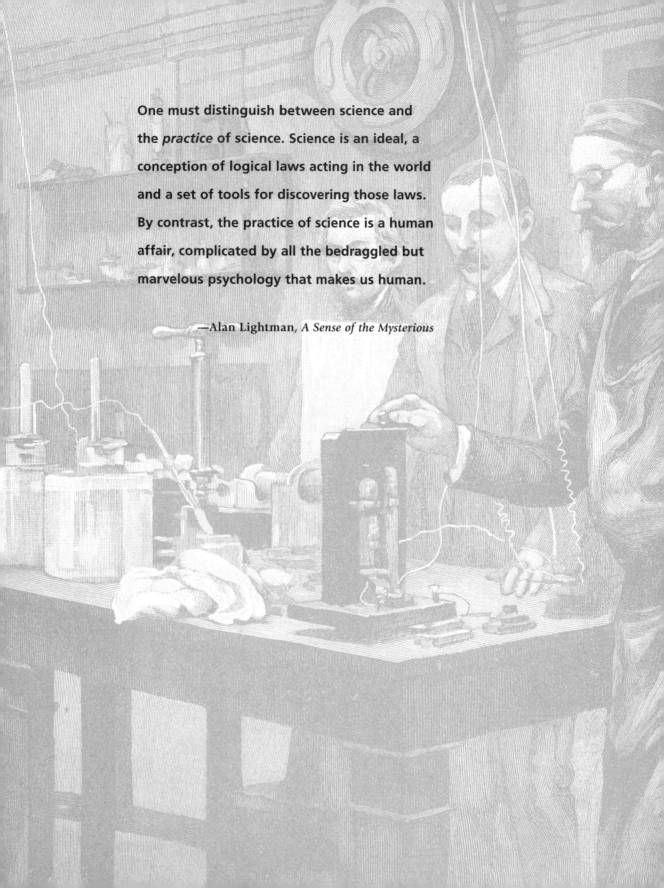

One must distinguish between science and the *practice* of science. Science is an ideal, a conception of logical laws acting in the world and a set of tools for discovering those laws. By contrast, the practice of science is a human affair, complicated by all the bedraggled but marvelous psychology that makes us human.

—Alan Lightman, *A Sense of the Mysterious*

ALAN LIGHTMAN

Metaphor in Science

When scientists investigate the physical world, they make use of a wide range of intellectual skills—they form hypotheses, design and carry out experiments, gather quantitative data, reason inductively, and work with complex mathematics. Common conceptions of scientific work tend to emphasize the application of these skills, and in fact, the day-to-day activity of many scientists does involve meticulous experimentation, observation, measurement, and analysis of accumulated data. But scientists are ultimately concerned with interpreting their findings, seeking answers to questions about the meaning of their experimental results, and devising new questions to investigate. To pursue these aims, they develop models and theories that explain their various findings in terms of unifying principles.

When scientists attempt to explain phenomena in the physical world, they begin with what can be observed both directly and through measuring devices. However, theories and models allow scientists to think about causes that lie beyond these sense perceptions and to imaginatively transcend our limited ability to perceive extremes of size, distance, and time. For example, to create a model of an event 14 billion years in the past, the big bang theory of the universe's origin brings together knowledge about light signals gathered from distant galaxies and measurements of the traces made by subatomic particles on highly sensitive devices. Even though theories and models must be rigorously grounded in well-established knowledge about how the physical world operates, they are also the result of scientists' creativity and speculative imagination, which often leaps far ahead of what can be derived from facts alone.

Metaphors are a central feature of the theories and models that scientists create. A metaphor helps explain the underlying and unseen causes of physical phenomena through comparison with something familiar that can readily be pictured. As both a scientist and a writer, Alan Lightman (1948–) is ideally suited to explore how the human imagination uses metaphor to make sense of the world. In his book *A Sense of the Mysterious* (2005), Lightman writes, "Ever since I was a young boy, my passions have been divided between science and art. I was fortunate to make a life in both, as a physicist and a novelist, and even to find creative sympathies between the two, but I have had to live with a constant tension in myself and a continual rumbling in my gut." This tension represents Lightman's attraction both to the certainties of science and mathematics, and to the power of poetry and fiction to explore the "ambiguities and complexities of the human mind."

When he was an undergraduate at Princeton, Lightman realized that he was more suited to theoretical than to experimental physics. He did graduate work at the California Institute of Technology, where one of his thesis committee members was Richard Feynman. After receiving his PhD in 1974, Lightman conducted research in astrophysics and taught at Cornell and Harvard, and in 1981, he began publishing essays about what he refers to as "the human side of science." Since then, he has written several highly regarded novels and science books, and his essays have appeared in numerous magazines. Lightman's two great professional interests, science and literature, came together in 1989, when he was appointed professor of both physics and writing at the Massachusetts Institute of Technology. At MIT, Lightman helped to institute a requirement that all undergraduates take a writing or speaking course during each of their four years, emphasizing the need for science students to have well-developed language skills along with technical expertise.

In the following selection, taken from *A Sense of the Mysterious,* Lightman investigates how metaphor enters into scientific explanations through the nature of language itself, as a "critical part of our reasoning and discovery." Drawing on examples from the work of many of the writers in *What's the Matter?* he urges scientists to be cautious in their use of metaphors to help depict the physical world, particularly as the objects of modern physics become more and more removed from our sensory experience.

Metaphor in Science

I remember the day, during my first course in cosmology, when the professor was trying to explain how the universe could be expanding outward in all directions, but without any center of the expansion. To his credit, the teacher had covered the blackboard with equations, but we students still couldn't picture the situation. How could something explode uniformly in all directions without a middle of the explosion? Then the professor said to pretend that space is two-dimensional and that the stars and galaxies are dots on the surface of an expanding balloon. From the point of view of any one dot, the other dots are moving away from it in all directions, yet no dot is the center. This powerful metaphor, first introduced by Arthur Eddington in 1931, has helped students of cosmology ever since, in every country and every language where the subject is taught. It works for anyone who has seen a balloon inflated.

Metaphor is critical to science. Metaphor in science serves not just as a pedagogical device, like the cosmic balloon, but also as an aid to scientific discovery. In doing science, even though words and equations are used with the intention of having precise meanings, it is almost impossible not to reason by physical analogy, not to form mental pictures, not to imagine balls bouncing and pendulums swinging. Metaphor is part of the process of science. I will illustrate this point with some examples from physics.

461

In an essay on light and color in 1672, published in *Philosophical Transactions of the Royal Society*, Isaac Newton describes his first experiments with a prism. He darkened his chamber, made a small hole in his "window-shuts," and let a ray of sunlight enter a prism and spread out into colors on the opposite wall. He then interprets this phenomenon in terms of a theory of light:

> Then I began to suspect whether the rays, after their trajection through
> the prism, did not move in curved lines, and according to their more or
> less curvity tend to divers parts of the wall. And it increased my suspicion,
> when I remembered that I had often seen a tennis ball struck with an
> oblique racket describe such a curved line. . . . For the same reason, if
> the rays of light should possibly be globular bodies, and by their oblique
> passage out of one medium into another, acquire a circulating motion,
> they ought to feel the greater resistance from the ambient ether on that side
> where the motions conspire, and hence be continually bowed to the other.

This passage is particularly revealing because it is a diary of Newton's personal thoughts in trying to understand the nature of light. Although Newton subsequently rejected the idea that light rays can curve through space, he continued to develop his corpuscular theory of light. In Query 29 of the *Opticks* (1704), Newton writes that rays of light are "bodies of different sizes, the least of which may take violet, the weakest and darkest of the colours and the most easily diverted by refracting surfaces." The largest and strongest light corpuscles carry red, the color least bent by a prism. Newton's mechanical worldview, of which light was only a part, held sway for two centuries.

A hundred years after Newton's *Opticks*, the physician and physicist Thomas Young allowed sunlight from his window to fall on a screen with two small holes in it. He then observed the alternating pattern of light and dark striking the opposite wall. From these patterns, Young proposed, in a paper entitled "Interference of Light" (1807), that light consisted of "waves" rather than particles:

> Supposing the light of any given colour to consist of undulations of a
> given breadth, or of a given frequency, it follows that these undulations
> must be liable to those effects which we have already examined in the
> case of the waves of water, and the pulses of sound.

Young goes on to describe clearly the interference of two sets of circular waves moving outward from the two holes in his screen—a process of positive and negative reinforcement that would produce just the pattern of light seen on the wall. One cannot imagine how Young would have interpreted his observations without having seen overlapping ripples in a pond.

The great nineteenth-century physicist James Clerk Maxwell used an elaborate mechanical model, actually a sustained metaphor, to fathom the workings of electricity and magnetism. By analogy with fluids, Maxwell envisioned a magnetic field to be made out of closely spaced little whirl-pools, which he called vortices. To solve the problem of what happens when two of these neighboring whirlpools touch and try to slow each other down, Maxwell mentally inserted between each pair of vortices a system of electric particles that would act as ball bearings. Designed for the purpose of reducing friction, the electric particles were also responsi-ble for carrying electric current. The mechanical metaphors here are strik-ing. In his paper "On Physical Lines of Force" (1861), Maxwell notes:

> In mechanism, when two wheels are intended to revolve in the same
> direction, a wheel is placed between them so as to be in gear with both,
> and this wheel is called an "idle wheel." The hypothesis about the
> vortices which I have to suggest is that a layer of particles, acting as idle
> wheels, is interposed between each vortex.

Maxwell's most celebrated contribution to the theory of electricity and magnetism was the prediction of oscillating waves of electric and magnetic forces, called *electromagnetic waves*, which travel through space at the speed of light. These waves were theoretically discovered by Maxwell after he added a single new mathematical term, called the *displacement current*, to the equations of electricity and magnetism previously worked out by others. How did Maxwell deduce his hypothetical displacement current? When I first learned the theory of electricity and magnetism as a college physics major, I thought that the displacement current had been derived by requiring mathematical consistency and the conservation of electric charge. But, in fact, Maxwell was motivated by the demands of his mechanical model. He knew from experiments that an electric or mag-netic field can store energy. Because Maxwell had a mechanical picture of his subject, and a mechanical view of the world, such energy could only be mechanical in nature. Maxwell therefore proposed that electrical and magnetic energy was stored by stretching, or displacing an elastic medium that filled up space, just as energy is stored in a stretched rubber band. In his classic paper of 1865, "A Dynamical Theory of the Electromagnetic Field," published in the *Royal Society Transactions*, Maxwell writes:

> Electric displacement, according to our theory, is a kind of elastic yielding to the action of the force, similar to that which takes place in structures and machines owing to the want of perfect rigidity of the connexions. . . . Energy may be stored in the field . . . by the action of electromotive force in producing electric displacement. . . . [I]t resides in the space surrounding the electrified and magnetic bodies . . . as the motion and strain of one and the same medium.

When an electric force oscillated in time, the electric particles in the elastic medium oscillated in response, giving rise to the so-called displacement current. The underlying elastic medium that allowed all of this to happen was called *ether*. The ether was the material substance through which electromagnetic waves propagated, just as air is the substance through which sound waves propagate, by bumping one air molecule into the next. Again, in Maxwell's words, "We have therefore some reason to believe, from the phenomena of light and heat, that there is an aetheral medium filling space and permeating bodies, capable of being set in motion and transmitting that motion from one part to another." Maxwell's mechanical model for electricity and magnetism, including the ether, was completely fictitious, but it led him to the correct equations.

In 1931, the Belgian priest and physicist Georges Lemaître published a stunning model for the origin of the universe. It was already known at this time—both from Lemaître's own theoretical work and from contemporary telescopic observations—that the universe is evolving. It was also known that very energetic particles, called cosmic rays, were constantly bombarding the earth from outer space, although the nature and origin of these particles was still a mystery. Lemaître proposed that cosmic rays originated billions of years ago from the radioactive disintegrations of enormous atoms and had been traveling through space ever since. Each of these ancient, massive atoms, in fact, was the parent of a star. Going back still further in time, when the cosmos was smaller and denser, the universe itself began as a single, giant atom, whose gradual disintegrations into smaller and smaller pieces formed nebulae, stars, and finally cosmic rays. In "L'expansion de l'espace," published in the November 1931 issue of *Revue des Questions Scientifiques*, Lemaître writes:

> We can conceive of space beginning with the primeval atom and the beginning of space being marked by the beginning of time. The first stages . . . consisted of a rapid expansion determined by the mass of the initial atom. . . . The atom-world was broken into fragments, each fragment into still smaller pieces. . . . The evolution of the world can be compared to a display of fireworks that has just ended.

In this example, both the literal and the metaphorical pieces of the metaphor arise from the unseen world of physics. Lemaître has been called the father of the big bang model of cosmology, but his primeval atom hypothesis went far beyond any theoretical or observational evidence.

The above examples should not be taken to mean that only the most brilliant scientists—the Newtons and the Maxwells—use metaphor in their work. Metaphor and analogy are rampant in physics. A graduate student and I recently calculated how gamma rays "reflect" from a layer of cold gas. In a discussion of this problem at the blackboard, beneath the equations, we drew a picture of a wavy line moving toward a wall. The line represented a single "particle" of light, called a photon, and the wall was the surface of the medium of gas. The conversation went something like this: "A high-energy photon penetrates very deeply into the medium before it first scatters off an electron. Then the photon scatters several more times, bouncing around, losing energy, and finally works its way back up to the surface of the medium, where it escapes."

I will end with an example from the forefront of theoretical physics—the string theory. The concept of strings has emerged from highly mathematical and formal attempts to describe the fundamental forces of nature. According to current string theory, the smallest unit of matter is not a pointlike object, but a one-dimensional structure called a "string." Here are some descriptions that leading string theorists have had the courage to put into print. "Scattering of strings is described by the simple picture of strings breaking and joining at the end." "Since a string has tension, it can vibrate much like an ordinary violin string. . . . In quantum mechanics, waves and particles are dual aspects of the same phenomenon, and so each vibrational mode corresponds to a particle."

Ultimately, we are forced to understand all scientific discoveries in terms of the items from daily life—spinning balls, waves in water, pendulums, weights on springs. We have no other choice. We cannot avoid forming mental pictures when we try to grasp the meaning of our equations, and how can we picture what we have not seen? As Einstein said in *The Meaning of Relativity*, "The universe of ideas is just as little independent of the nature of our experiences as clothes are of the form of the human body."

Sometimes different pictures of the same problem provide new insights. For example, the path that the earth takes in orbiting the sun can be described either as a distant response to the sun itself, ninety-three million miles away, or as a local response to a gravitational field, filling or warping space around the sun. These two descriptions are mathematically equivalent, but they bring to mind very different pictures. As Richard Feynman comments in *The Character of Physical Law* (1965), they are equivalent scientifically but very different "psychologically," especially when we are trying to guess new laws of nature. In one picture, we focus on the two masses; in the other, on the space between them.

Physicists have a most ambivalent relationship with metaphor. We desperately want an intuitive sense of our subject, but we have also been trained not to trust too much in our intuition. We like the sturdy feel of the earth under our feet, but we have been informed by our instruments that the planet is flying through space at a hundred thousand miles per hour. We find comfort in visualizing an electron as a tiny ball, but we have also been shocked to discover that a single electron can spread out in ripples, like a water wave, occupying several places at once. We crave the certainty of our equations, but we must give names to the symbols. At the age of twenty-five, Maxwell reflected on both the service and the danger of physical analogy in a paper entitled "On Faraday's Lines of Force" (1856), published in the *Transactions of the Cambridge Philosophical Society*:

> The first process therefore in the effectual study of science, must be one of simplification and reduction of the results . . . to a form in which the mind can grasp them. . . . We must, therefore, discover some method of investigation which allows the mind at every step to lay hold of a clear physical conception, without being committed to any theory founded on the physical science from which that conception is borrowed.

When the quantum theory was being developed, in the first two decades of the twentieth century, physicists agonized over their inability to picture the wave-particle split personality of subatomic particles. In fact, physicists violently disagreed over whether such pictures were even useful. In 1913, Niels Bohr, a pioneer of quantum theory, proposed a model for the atom in which electrons orbited about a central nucleus. Max Born commented a decade later (*Die Naturwissenschaften*, vol. 27) that "a remarkable and alluring result of Bohr's atomic theory is the demonstration that the atom is a small planetary system . . . the thought that the laws of the macrocosmos in the small reflect the terrestrial world obviously exercises a great magic on mankind's mind." Referring to this same Bohr model, Werner Heisenberg warned that "quantum mechanics has above all to free itself from these intuitive pictures . . . that in principle [are] not testable and thereby could lead to internal contradictions" (*Die Naturwissenschaften*, vol. 14).

In the 1920s and 1930s, there were two competing formulations of quantum theory, eventually shown to be mathematically equivalent. Heisenberg was the architect of the highly abstract version; Erwin Schrödinger had worked out a more visual theory. In a letter to Wolfgang Pauli in 1926, Heisenberg wrote, "The more I reflect on the physical portion of Schrödinger's theory the more disgusting I find it."

Schrödinger, in his reply in the *Annalen der Physik*, wrote that he felt "repelled by the methods of transcendental algebra" in Heisenberg's theory, "which appeared very difficult" and had a "lack of visualizability." A few years later, in 1932, Professor Heisenberg ascribed the nuclear force between a proton and a neutron to the "migration" (*Platzwechsel*) of an electron between them. Where did the alphas and betas in Heisenberg's matrices or the readings from the electrometers say that an electron could migrate? Remarkably, Heisenberg's image of migrating particles as agents of force led three years later to Hideki Yukawa's successful prediction of a new elementary particle, the meson.

Ultimately, Bohr himself was frustrated in his attempts to grasp intuitively the world of the atom. In 1928, he lamented (*Nature Supplement*, April 14, 1928):

> We find ourselves here on the very path taken by Einstein of adapting
> our modes of perception borrowed from the sensations to the gradually

deepening knowledge of the laws of nature. The hindrances met with
on this path originate above all in the fact that . . . every word in the
language refers to our ordinary perceptions.

Many contemporary physicists have essentially given up trying to
describe the fundamental elements of nature by anything based on common sense. Richard Feynman has remarked that he can picture invisible angels but not light waves. Steven Weinberg, like Bishop [George]
Berkeley, seems on the brink of abandoning the material world altogether
when he says that after you have described how an elementary particle
behaves under various mathematical operations, "then you've said everything there is to say about the particle . . . the particle is nothing else but
a representation of its symmetry group" (R. Crease and C. Mann, *The
Second Creation: Makers of Revolution in Twentieth-Century Physics*, 1986).
Yet physicists still use metaphors. Cosmologists still discuss how the universe "expanded and cooled" during the first nanosecond after its birth.
Relativists still talk about the "semipermeable membrane" around a black
hole. String theorists still describe their unseen subatomic strings as
"stretching, vibrating, breaking." What other choice do we have? We must
breathe, even in thin air.

But there is a difference between metaphors used inside and outside
of science. In every metaphor, there is a principal and a subsidiary object,
the literal and the metaphorical, the original and the model. When we use
metaphors in ordinary human affairs, we usually have a good sense of the
principal object to begin with. The metaphor deepens our insight. When
we hear that "the chairman plowed through the discussion," we already
know a good deal about chairmen, committees, and tiring discussion. But
when we say that a photon scattered off an electron, what concrete experience do we have with electrons or photons? When we say that the universe
is shaped like the surface of a balloon, what do we really know about how
space curves in three dimensions?

Galileo admired Copernicus for being able to imagine that the earth
moved, against all common sense. But at least Copernicus understood
that the earth was a ball and had seen other balls move. The objects of
physics today, by contrast, are principally known as runes in equations
or blips from our instruments. Earlier physicists had an immediate and
tactile relation to their subjects. Descartes could see the disjointed image

of a pen half in water and half in air. Du Fay could rub cats' fur against copal or gum-lack or silk. Count Rumford could feel the heat in a cannon just bored. But in the last century or so, science has changed. Physics has galloped off into territories where our bodies cannot follow. We have built enormous machines to dissect the insides of atoms. We have erected telescopes that peer out to unimaginable distances. We have designed cameras that see colors invisible to human eyes. Theorists have worked out equations to describe the beginning of time. The objects of physics today are far removed from human sensory experience.

As a result, it seems to me that metaphors in modern science carry a greater burden than metaphors in literature or history or art. Metaphors in modern science must do more than color their principal objects; they must build their reality from scratch. Such substance, in the palm of a modern physicist, is often hard to let go of. Although aware that the ether was based only on mechanical analogy, Maxwell believed it existed. The year before he died, Maxwell wrote in the ninth edition of the *Encyclopaedia Britannica* (1878) that he had "no doubt that the interplanetary . . . spaces are not empty but are occupied by a material substance or body, which is certainly the largest . . . body of which we have any knowledge." If a giant of science like Maxwell was seduced by his own metaphor, what can happen to the rest of us? We ought not to forget that when physicists say a photon scattered from an electron, they are discussing that which cannot be discussed. We can see the tracks in a cloud chamber, but we cannot see an electron. Metaphors in science—although a critical part of our reasoning and discovery—should be handled with caution, and with a clear knowledge of the limits of our sensory experience of the world. We are blind people, imagining what we don't see.

Content Questions

1. In Lightman's opening anecdote, why couldn't the professor's equations alone help the students understand how the universe is expanding? (461)

2. According to Lightman, what is a metaphor in science? What does Lightman mean when he says that metaphor "is part of the process of science"? (461)

3. Even though Young's theory of light contradicts Newton's, how are both theories mechanical explanations of light? (462–463)

4. In physics, what is meant by a model? Why does Lightman call Maxwell's mechanical model of electricity and magnetism "a sustained metaphor"? (463)

5. How did Maxwell's mechanical model lead him to predict electromagnetic waves? (463–464)

6. Why does Lightman consider Lemaître's theory of the beginning of the universe to be metaphorical? What is "the unseen world of physics" from which Lightman says Lemaître's theory arose? (464–465)

7. According to Lightman, why do physicists "have a most ambivalent relationship with metaphor"? (466)

8. Why was Schrödinger "repelled by the methods of transcendental algebra" used in Heisenberg's version of quantum theory? Why does Lightman point out that Heisenberg ascribed the nuclear force between a proton and a neutron to the "migration" of an electron? (467)

9. According to Lightman, what is the difference between metaphors inside and outside of science? (468)

10. How are the metaphors used by contemporary physicists different from those used by earlier physicists such as Newton, Young, and Maxwell? (468–469)

Discussion Questions

1. When Newton and Young interpreted the behavior of light in terms of physical analogies to tennis balls and waves, what did they add to their experimental observations? (462–463) What does it mean to interpret experimental observations?

2. If Maxwell's mechanical model for electricity and magnetism was "completely fictitious," how could it lead him to the correct equations for electromagnetism? (464) If a scientific model is fictitious, is there also a sense in which it can be true?

3. Why does Lightman say that string theorists are courageous for putting into print their descriptions of how strings behave? (465)

4. According to Lightman, why can't scientists avoid forming mental pictures "when we try to grasp the meaning of our equations"? (466) Must the meaning of equations in physics always be tied to mental pictures of familiar things?

5. What does it mean to say that the two pictures of how the earth orbits the sun are scientifically equivalent but very different "psychologically"? (466) How can different pictures of the same scientific problem provide new insights?

6. What are the "service and the danger of physical analogy" in science? Why does Maxwell say that scientific investigators must remain uncommitted to theories founded on the science from which their physical conceptions are borrowed? (466)

7. Is it necessary for scientists to describe the fundamental elements of nature in terms of common sense? Does Weinberg's claim that the behavior of an elementary particle can only be described in terms of mathematical operations and symmetry groups allow for an adequate picture of the physical world? (468)

8. Why do metaphors in modern science "carry a greater burden" than metaphors in literature, history, or art? (469)

9. Why does Lightman assert that physicists who say "a photon scattered from an electron" are "discussing that which cannot be discussed"? (469)

10. If, as Lightman says, metaphors in science are a "critical part of our reasoning and discovery," how can scientists avoid being seduced by them? (469)

Suggestions for Further Reading

By the author

Lightman, Alan. *Dance for Two: Essays*. New York: Pantheon Books, 1996. Lightman explores a wide range of topics in this collection of twenty-one pieces, which includes a personal account of how he chose a career in science, a discussion of how we blind ourselves to the dangers of nuclear weapons, a whimsical fable about a world where everything is made of iron, and an examination of gravitational forces impinging on a ballerina's dance.

————. *The Discoveries: Great Breakthroughs in 20th-Century Science*. New York: Pantheon Books, 2005. This chronicle of the intellectual and emotional lives of two dozen modern scientists uses their original papers to explore the creative process of scientific discovery.

————. *Einstein's Dreams*. New York: Pantheon, 1993; New York: Vintage Contemporaries, 2004. Set in Einstein's dreaming mind during the night before he submitted for publication his paper on special relativity, these thirty brief fables portray alternative worlds, each behaving according to its own set of self-consistent principles and expressed with a striking mixture of scientific exactness and poetic metaphor.

————. *A Sense of the Mysterious: Science and the Human Spirit*. New York: Pantheon Books, 2005. Several pieces in this collection, from which the selection in *What's the Matter?* is taken, are the author's reflections on his work as both a physicist and a literary writer, exploring the ways in which science, art, and mathematics are all creations of the human spirit. Other essays pick up these themes in brief portraits of Albert Einstein, Richard Feynman, Vera Rubin, and Edward Teller.

About the topic

Pesic, Peter. *Labyrinth: A Search for the Hidden Meaning of Science.* Cambridge, MA: MIT Press, 2000, 2001. This study of the struggle of scientists to wrest secrets from nature features insights into the interplay of religion, myth, mysticism, and science, especially in the work of Einstein, Kepler, and Newton.

Von Baeyer, Hans Christian. *The Fermi Solution*: *Essays on Science.* New York: Random House, 1993; New York: Dover Publications, 2001. Von Baeyer uses fresh and illuminating images and examples to explore the ways in which scientists pursue their investigations. His subjects range from gravity waves and magnetic monopoles to Fermi's approach to problem solving and scientists' concern for the aesthetic qualities of their work.

Since the particles emitted by a black hole come from a region of which the observer has very limited knowledge . . . all he can predict is the probabilities that certain particles will be emitted. It therefore seems that Einstein was doubly wrong when he said, "God does not play dice." Considerations of particle emission from black holes would seem to suggest that God not only plays dice but also sometimes throws them where they cannot be seen.

—Stephen Hawking,
"The Quantum Mechanics of Black Holes"

STEPHEN HAWKING

Black Holes and Predictable Worlds

The power to test theories by making predictions is at the core of physics, but until recent times, cosmology—the study of the origin and structure of the universe—was considered highly speculative, with little possibility of being tested by scientific obser-vation and experiment. In the twentieth century, major technological advances in astronomy, the successful predictions of Einstein's general theory of relativity, and the formulation of the big bang theory made cosmology a major branch of modern phys-ics. These developments, along with the use of quantum theory and particle physics to investigate high-energy conditions in the early universe, contributed to the expla-nation of the evolution of the universe known as the standard model of cosmology.

Einstein's general theory of relativity, published in 1915, has been central to the investigation of large-scale structures in the universe, such as stars and galaxies. This is because its explanation of gravity allows physicists to predict what occurs in regions of space where gravitational fields are extremely strong compared to those in our solar system. In the first decades after Einstein published his theory, physi-cists discovered that some of the mathematical solutions to its equations described strange cosmological phenomena for which there was at that time no observational evidence and which Einstein himself could not accept. Among these were the gravi-tational collapse of stars into small but massive objects from which no light could escape, and a universe that is not static but expanding.

When Stephen Hawking (1942–) arrived to study at the University of Cambridge in 1962, cosmology was coming into its own as a field of scientific research. Like Einstein, Hawking is a theoretical physicist whose work depends on a combination of deep intuition about the physical world, highly developed mathematical skills, and a sound understanding of the discoveries of experimental physics. Since his early twen-ties, Hawking has been afflicted with amyotrophic lateral sclerosis (ALS), a degenera-tive neurological disease that has almost completely eliminated his ability to move and speak. To overcome these physical limitations, Hawking has developed his ability to consider complex physics problems by working out their consequences through thought experiments. Hawking has been a faculty member of the University of Cambridge since the 1970s and holds the post of Lucasian Professor of Mathematics, a position once held by Isaac Newton. In 1988, he published his first book for general readers, *A Brief History of Time: From the Big Bang to Black Holes*.

Hawking has spent his career pursuing one of the primary goals of modern physics, which is to unify the insights of the theory of relativity with those of quantum theory to form a comprehensive picture of the physical world. By applying general relativity to cosmological problems, he discovered that the beginning of the universe at the big bang and the extreme state of a star's gravitational collapse, called a black hole, are similar. Because in both cases matter is compressed into a subatomic state called a *singularity*, it is necessary to supplement general relativity with quantum theory to explain what happens at this extremely small scale. One highly important aspect of Hawking's work has been his success in applying well-established principles of physics to new areas of research, showing the self-consistency of physics as it continues to develop. Hawking demonstrated this consistency by explaining that black holes strictly obey the laws of thermodynamics and emit radiation, taking black holes out of the realm of theoretical abstractions and placing them in the world of physical things that can be measured.

In the following selection, from *The Universe in a Nutshell* (2001), Hawking describes how Newton's laws of motion and gravity led scientists to assume that the future of every event in the physical world can, in principle, be predicted. He asks us to consider how some of the implications for cosmology of general relativity and quantum theory—such as the possibility that information is irretrievably lost in black holes—call into question this fundamental assumption of classical Newtonian physics.

Black Holes and Predictable Worlds

Thehuman race has always wanted to control the future, or at least to predict what will happen. That is why astrology is so popular. Astrology claims that events on earth are related to the motions of the planets across the sky. This is a scientifically testable hypothesis, or would be if astrologers stuck their necks out and made definite predictions that could be tested. However, wisely enough, they make their forecasts so vague that they can apply to any outcome. Statements such as "Personal relations may become intense" or "You will have a financially rewarding opportunity" can never be proved wrong.

But the real reason most scientists don't believe in astrology is not scientific evidence or the lack of it but because it is not consistent with other theories that have been tested by experiment. When Copernicus and Galileo discovered that the planets orbit the sun rather than the earth, and Newton discovered the laws that govern their motion, astrology became extremely implausible. Why should the positions of other planets against the background sky as seen from earth have any correlations with the macromolecules on a minor planet that call themselves intelligent life?

This selection is taken from chapter 4, "Predicting the Future," of The Universe in a Nutshell.

Yet this is what astrology would have us believe. There is no more experimental evidence for some [scientific] theories than there is for astrology, but we believe them because they are consistent with theories that have survived testing.

The success of Newton's laws and other physical theories led to the idea of scientific determinism, which was first expressed at the beginning of the nineteenth century by the French scientist the Marquis de Laplace. Laplace suggested that if we knew the positions and velocities of all the particles in the universe at one time, the laws of physics should allow us to predict what the state of the universe would be at any other time in the past or in the future.

In other words, if scientific determinism holds, we should in principle be able to predict the future and wouldn't need astrology. Of course, in practice even something as simple as Newton's theory of gravity produces equations that we can't solve exactly for more than two particles. Furthermore, the equations often have a property known as chaos, so that a small change in position or velocity at one time can lead to completely different behavior at later times. As those who have seen *Jurassic Park* know, a tiny disturbance in one place can cause a major change in another. A butterfly flapping its wings in Tokyo can cause rain in New York's Central Park. The trouble is that the sequence of events is not repeatable. The next time the butterfly flaps its wings, a host of other factors will be different and will also influence the weather. That is why weather forecasts are so unreliable.

Thus, although in principle the laws of quantum electrodynamics should allow us to calculate everything in chemistry and biology, we have not had much success in predicting human behavior from mathematical equations. Nevertheless, despite these practical difficulties, most scientists have comforted themselves with the idea that, again in principle, the future is predictable.

At first sight, determinism would also seem to be threatened by the uncertainty principle, which says that we cannot measure accurately both the position and the velocity of a particle at the same time. The more accurately we measure the position, the less accurately we can determine the velocity, and vice versa. The Laplace version of scientific determinism held that if we knew the positions and velocities of particles at one time, we could determine their positions and velocities at any time in the past or future. But how could we even get started if the uncertainty principle prevented us from knowing accurately both the positions and the velocities at one time? However good our computer is, if we put lousy data in, we will get lousy predictions out.

However, determinism *was* restored in a modified form in a new theory called quantum mechanics, which incorporated the uncertainty principle. In quantum mechanics, one can, roughly speaking, accurately predict half of what one would expect to predict in the classical Laplace point of view. In quantum mechanics, a particle does not have a well-defined position or velocity, but its state *can* be represented by what is called a wave function (fig. 1).

A wave function is a number at each point of space that gives the probability that the particle is to be found at that position. The rate at which the wave function changes from point to point tells how probable different particle velocities are. Some wave functions are sharply peaked at a

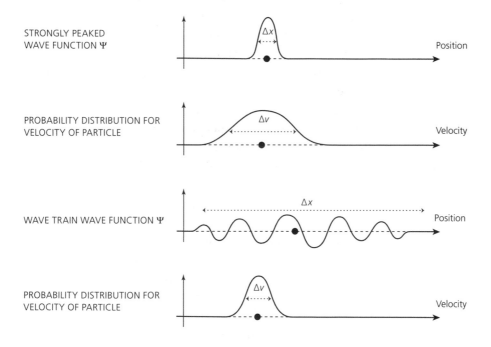

STRONGLY PEAKED
WAVE FUNCTION Ψ — Position

PROBABILITY DISTRIBUTION FOR
VELOCITY OF PARTICLE — Velocity

WAVE TRAIN WAVE FUNCTION Ψ — Position

PROBABILITY DISTRIBUTION FOR
VELOCITY OF PARTICLE — Velocity

Fig. 1. The wave function determines the probabilities that the particle will have different positions and velocities in such a way that Δx and Δv obey the uncertainty principle.

particular point in space. In these cases, there is only a small amount of uncertainty in the position of the particle. But we can also see in the diagram that in such cases, the wave function changes rapidly near the point, up on one side and down on the other. That means that the probability distribution for the velocity is spread over a wide range. In other words, the uncertainty in the velocity is large. Consider, on the other hand, a continuous train of waves. Now there is a large uncertainty in position but a small uncertainty in velocity. So the description of a particle by a wave function does not have a well-defined position or velocity. It satisfies the uncertainty principle. We now realize that the wave function is *all* that can be well defined. We cannot even suppose that the particle has a position and velocity that are known to God but are hidden from us. Such hidden-variable theories predict results that are not in agreement with observation. Even God is bound by the uncertainty principle and cannot know the position and velocity; he can only know the wave function.

The rate at which the wave function changes with time is given by what is called the Schrödinger equation. If we know the wave function at one time, we can use the Schrödinger equation to calculate it at any other time, past or future. Therefore, there is still determinism in quantum theory, but it is on a reduced scale. Instead of being able to predict both the positions and the velocities, we can predict only the wave function. This can allow us to predict either the positions or the velocities, but not both accurately. Thus in quantum theory the ability to make exact predictions is just half what it was in the classical Laplace worldview. Nevertheless, within this restricted sense it is still possible to claim that there is determinism.

However, the use of the Schrödinger equation to evolve the wave function forward in time (that is, to predict what it will be at future times) implicitly assumes that time runs on smoothly everywhere, forever. This was certainly true in Newtonian physics. Time was assumed to be absolute, meaning that each event in the history of the universe was labeled by a number called time, and that a series of time labels ran smoothly from the infinite past to the infinite future. This is what might be called the commonsense view of time, and it is the view of time that most people—and even most physicists—have at the back of their minds. However, in 1905, the concept of absolute time was overthrown by the special theory of relativity, in which time was no longer an independent quantity on its own but was just one direction in a four-dimensional continuum called space-time.

In special relativity, different observers traveling at different velocities move through space-time on different paths. Each observer has his or her own measure of time along the path he or she is following, and different observers will measure different intervals of time between events.

Thus in special relativity there is no unique absolute time that we can use to label events. However, the space-time of special relativity is flat. This means that in special relativity, the time measured by any freely moving observer increases smoothly in space-time from minus infinity in the infinite past to plus infinity in the infinite future. We can use any of these measures of time in the Schrödinger equation to evolve the wave function. In special relativity, therefore, we still have the quantum version of determinism.

The situation was different in the general theory of relativity, in which space-time was not flat but curved, and distorted by the matter and energy in it. In our solar system, the curvature of space-time is so slight, at least on a macroscopic scale, that it doesn't interfere with our usual idea of time. In this situation, we could still use this time in the Schrödinger equation to get a deterministic evolution of the wave function. However, once we allow space-time to be curved, the door is opened to the possibility that it may have a structure that doesn't admit a time that increases smoothly for every observer, as we would expect for a reasonable measure of time.

For example, suppose that space-time was like a vertical cylinder. Height up the cylinder would be a measure of time that increased for every observer and ran from minus infinity to plus infinity. However, imagine instead that space-time was like a cylinder with a handle (or "wormhole") that branched off and then joined back on. Then any measure of time would necessarily have stagnation points where the handle joined the main cylinder: points where time stood still. At these points, time would not increase for any observer. In such a space-time, we could not use the Schrödinger equation to get a deterministic evolution for the wave function. Watch out for wormholes: you never know what may come out of them.

Black holes are the reason we think time will not increase for every observer. The first discussion of black holes appeared in 1783. A former Cambridge don, John Michell, presented the following argument. If one fires a particle, such as a cannonball, vertically upward, its ascent will be slowed by gravity, and eventually the particle will stop moving upward and will fall back. However, if the initial upward velocity is greater than a critical value called the escape velocity, gravity will never be strong enough to stop the particle, and it will get away. The escape velocity is about 12 kilometers per second for the earth and about 618 kilometers per second for the sun.

Both of these escape velocities are much higher than the speed of real cannonballs, but they are small compared to the speed of light, which is 300,000 kilometers per second. Thus, light can get away from the earth or sun without much difficulty. However, Michell argued that there could be stars that are much more massive than the sun and have escape velocities greater than the speed of light. We would not be able to see these stars, because any light they sent out would be dragged back by the gravity of the star. Thus they would be what Michell called dark stars and we now call black holes.

Michell's idea of dark stars was based on Newtonian physics, in which time was absolute and went on regardless of what happened. Thus they didn't affect our ability to predict the future in the classical Newtonian picture. But the situation was very different in the general theory of relativity, in which massive bodies curve space-time.

In 1916, shortly after the theory was first formulated, Karl Schwarzschild (who died soon after of an illness contracted on the Russian front in the First World War) found a solution of the field equations of general relativity that represented a black hole. What Schwarzschild had found wasn't understood or its importance recognized for many years. Einstein himself never believed in black holes, and his attitude was shared by most of the old guard in general relativity. I remember going to Paris to give a seminar on my discovery that quantum theory means that black holes aren't completely black. My seminar fell rather flat because at that time almost no one in Paris believed in black holes. . . .

The discovery of quasars in 1963 brought forth an outburst of theoretical work on black holes and observational attempts to detect them. Here is the picture that has emerged. Consider what we believe would be the history of a star with a mass twenty times that of the sun. Such stars form from clouds of gas. As clouds of gas contract under their own gravity, the gas heats up and eventually becomes hot enough to start the nuclear fusion reaction that converts hydrogen into helium. The heat generated by this process creates a pressure that supports the star against its own gravity and stops it from contracting further. A star will stay in this state for a long time, burning hydrogen and radiating light into space.

The gravitational field of the star will affect the paths of light rays coming from it. One can draw a diagram with time plotted upward and distance from the center of the star plotted horizontally (see fig. 2). In this diagram, the surface of the star is represented by two vertical lines, one on either side of the center. One can choose that time be measured in seconds and distance in light-seconds—the distance light travels in a second. When we use these units, the speed of light is 1; that is, the speed of light is 1 light-second per second. This means that far from the star and its gravitational field, the path of a light ray on the diagram is a line at a 45-degree angle to the vertical. However, nearer the star, the curvature of space-time produced by the mass of the star will change the paths of the light rays and cause them to be at a smaller angle to the vertical.

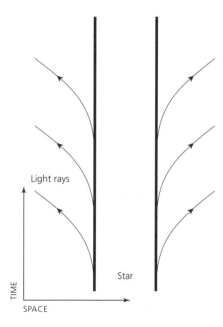

Fig. 2. Space-time around a noncollapsing star. Light rays can escape from the surface of the star (the vertical lines). Far from the star, the light rays are at 45 degrees to the vertical, but near the star the warping of space-time by the mass of the star causes light rays to be at a smaller angle to the vertical.

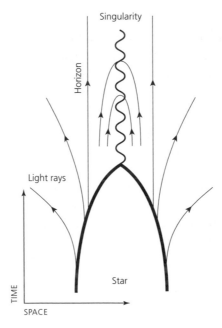

Fig. 3. If the star collapses (the lines meeting at a point), the warping becomes so large that light rays near the surface move inward. A black hole is formed, a region of space-time from which it is not possible for light to escape.

Massive stars will burn their hydrogen into helium much faster than the sun does. This means they can run out of hydrogen in as little as a few hundred million years. After that, such stars face a crisis. They can burn their helium into heavier elements such as carbon and oxygen, but these nuclear reactions do not release much energy, so the stars lose heat and the thermal pressure that supports them against gravity. Therefore, they begin to get smaller. If they are more than about twice the mass of the sun, the pressure will never be sufficient to stop the contraction. They will collapse to zero size and infinite density to form what is called a singularity (fig. 3). In the diagram of time against distance from the center, as a star shrinks, the paths of light rays from its surface will start out at smaller and smaller angles to the vertical. When the star reaches a certain critical radius, the path will be vertical on the diagram, which means that the light will hover at a constant distance from the center of the star, never getting away. This critical path of light will sweep out a surface called the event horizon, which separates the region of space-time from which light can escape from the region from which it cannot. Any light emitted by the star after it passes the event horizon will be bent back inward by the curvature of space-time. The star will have become one of Michell's dark stars, or, as we say now, a black hole.

How can you detect a black hole if no light can get out of it? The answer is that a black hole still exerts the same gravitational pull on neighboring objects as did the body that collapsed. If the sun were a black hole and had managed to become one without losing any of its mass, the planets would still orbit as they do now.

One way of searching for a black hole is therefore to look for matter that is orbiting what seems to be an unseen compact massive object. A number of such systems have been observed. Perhaps the most impressive are the giant black holes that occur in the centers of galaxies and quasars.

The properties of black holes that have been discussed thus far don't raise any great problems with determinism. Time will come to an end for an astronaut who falls into a black hole and hits the singularity. However, in general relativity, one is free to measure time at different rates in different places. One could therefore speed up the astronaut's watch as he or she approached the singularity, so that it still registered an infinite interval of time. On the time-and-distance diagram (fig. 4), the surfaces of constant values of this new time would be all crowded together at the center, below the point where the singularity appeared. But they would agree with the usual measure of time in the nearly flat space-time far away from the black hole.

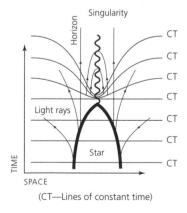

(CT—Lines of constant time)

Fig. 4.

One could use this time in the Schrödinger equation and calculate the wave function at later times if one knew it initially. Thus one still has determinism. It is worth nothing, however, that at late times, part of the wave function is inside the black hole, where it can't be observed by someone outside. Thus an observer who is sensible enough not to fall into a black hole cannot run the Schrödinger equation backward and calculate the wave function at early times. To do that, he or she would need to know the part of the wave function that is inside the black hole. This contains the information about what fell into the hole. This is potentially a very large amount of information, because a black hole of a given mass and rate of rotation can be formed from a very large number of different collections of particles; a black hole does not depend on the nature of the body that had collapsed to form it. John Wheeler called this result "a black hole has no hair." . . .

The difficulty with determinism arose when I discovered that black holes aren't completely black. Quantum theory means that fields can't be exactly zero even in what is called the vacuum. If they were zero, they would have both an exact value or position at zero and an exact rate of change or velocity that was also zero. This would be a violation of the uncertainty principle, which says that the position and velocity can't both be well defined. All fields must instead have a certain amount of what are called vacuum fluctuations. Vacuum fluctuations can be interpreted in several ways that seem different but are in fact mathematically equivalent. From a positivist viewpoint, one is free to use whatever picture is most useful for the problem in question. In this case, it is helpful to think of vacuum fluctuations as pairs of virtual particles that appear together at some point of space-time, move apart, and come back together and annihilate each other. "Virtual" means that these particles cannot be observed directly, but their indirect effects *can* be measured, and they agree with theoretical predictions to a remarkable degree of accuracy.

If a black hole is present, one member of a pair of particles may fall into the black hole, leaving the other member free to escape to infinity. To someone far from the black hole, the escaping particles appear to have been radiated by the black hole. The spectrum of a black hole is exactly what we would expect from a hot body, with a temperature proportional to the gravitational field on the horizon—the boundary—of the black hole. In other words, the temperature of a black hole depends on its size.

A black hole of a few solar masses would have a temperature of about a millionth of a degree above absolute zero, and a larger black hole would have an even lower temperature. Thus any quantum radiation from such black holes would be utterly swamped by the 2.7-degree radiation left over from the hot big bang—the cosmic background radiation. It would be possible to detect the radiation from much smaller and hotter black holes, but there don't seem to be many of them around. That is a pity. If one were discovered, I would get a Nobel Prize. However, we have indirect observational evidence for this radiation, and that evidence comes from the early universe. It is thought that very early in its history, the universe went through an inflationary period during which it expanded at an ever-increasing rate. The expansion during this period would have been so rapid that some objects would be too distant from us for their light ever to reach us; the universe would have expanded too much and too rapidly while that light was traveling toward us. Thus there would be a horizon in the universe like the horizon of a black hole, separating the region from which light can reach us and the region from which it cannot.

Very similar arguments show that there should be thermal radiation from this horizon, as there is from a black hole horizon. In thermal radiation, we have learned to expect a characteristic spectrum of density fluctuations. In this case, these density fluctuations would have expanded with the universe. When their length scale became longer than the size of the event horizon, they would have become frozen in, so that we can observe them today as small variations in the temperature of the cosmic background radiation left over from the early universe. The observations of those variations agree with the predictions of thermal fluctuations with remarkable accuracy.

Even if the observational evidence for black hole radiation is a bit indirect, everyone who has studied the problem agrees it must occur in order to be consistent with our other observationally tested theories. This has important implications for determinism. The radiation from a black hole will carry away energy, which must mean that the black hole will lose mass and get smaller. In turn, this will mean that its temperature will rise and the rate of radiation will increase. Eventually the black hole will get down to zero mass. We don't know how to calculate what happens at this point, but the only natural, reasonable outcome would seem to be that the black hole disappears completely. So what happens then to the part of the wave function inside the black hole and the information it contains about what had fallen into the black hole? The first guess might be that this part of the wave function, and the information it carries, would emerge when the black hole finally disappears. However, information cannot be carried for free, as one realizes when one gets a telephone bill.

Information requires energy to carry it, and there's very little energy left in the final stages of a black hole. The only plausible way the information inside could get out would be if it emerged continuously with the radiation, rather than waiting for this final stage. However, according to the picture of one member of a virtual-particle pair falling in and the other member escaping, one would not expect the escaping particle to be related to what fell in, or to carry away information about it. So the only answer would seem to be that the information in the part of the wave function inside the black hole gets lost.

Such loss of information would have important implications for determinism. To start with, we have noted that even if you knew the wave function after the black hole disappeared, you could not run the Schrödinger equation backward and calculate what the wave function was before the black hole formed. What that was would depend in part on the bit of the wave function that got lost in the black hole. We are used to thinking we can know the past exactly. However, if information gets lost in black holes, this is not the case. Anything could have happened.

In general, however, people such as astrologers and those who consult them are more interested in predicting the future than in retrodicting the past. At first glance, it might seem that the loss of part of the wave function down the black hole would not prevent us from predicting the wave function outside the black hole. But it turns out that this loss does interfere with such a prediction, as we can see when we consider a thought experiment proposed by Einstein, Boris Podolsky, and Nathan Rosen in the 1930s.

Imagine that a radioactive atom decays and sends out two particles in opposite directions and with opposite spins. An observer who looks only at one particle cannot predict whether it will be spinning to the right or left. But if the observer measures it to be spinning to the right, then he or she can predict with certainty that the other particle will be spinning to the left, and vice versa. Einstein thought that this proved that quantum theory was ridiculous: the other particle might be at the other side of the galaxy by now, yet one would instantaneously know which way it was spinning. However, most other scientists agree that it was Einstein who was confused, not quantum theory. The Einstein-Podolsky-Rosen thought experiment does not show that one is able to send information faster than light. That would be the ridiculous part. One cannot *choose* that one's own particle will be measured to be spinning to the right, so one cannot prescribe that the distant observer's particle should be spinning to the left.

In fact, this thought experiment is exactly what happens with black hole radiation. The virtual-particle pair will have a wave function that predicts that the two members will definitely have opposite spins. What we would like to do is predict the spin and wave function of the outgoing particle, which we could do if we could observe the particle that has fallen in. But that particle is now inside the black hole, where its spin and wave function cannot be measured. Because of this, it is not possible to predict the spin or the wave function of the particle that escapes. It can have different spins and different wave functions, with various probabilities, but it doesn't have a unique spin or wave function. Thus it would seem that our power to predict the future would be further reduced. The classical idea of Laplace, that one could predict both the positions and the velocities of particles, had to be modified when the uncertainty principle showed that one could not accurately measure both positions and velocities. However, one could still measure the wave function and use the Schrödinger equation to predict what it should be in the future. This would allow one to predict with certainty one combination of position and velocity—which is half of what one could predict according to Laplace's idea. We can predict with certainty that the particles have opposite spins, but if one particle falls into the black hole, there is no prediction we can make with certainty about the remaining particle. This means that there isn't *any* measurement outside the black hole that can be predicted with certainty: our ability to make definite predictions would be reduced to zero. So maybe astrology is no worse at predicting the future than the laws of science.

Many physicists didn't like this reduction in determinism and therefore suggested that information about what is inside can somehow get out of a black hole. For years it was just a pious hope that some way to save the information would be found. But in 1996 Andrew Strominger and Cumrun Vafa made an important advance. They chose to regard a black hole as being made up of a number of building blocks, called *p-branes*.

One way of thinking about p-branes is as sheets that move through the three dimensions of space and also through seven extra dimensions that we don't notice. In certain cases, one can show that the number of waves on the p-branes is the same as the amount of information one would expect the black hole to contain. If particles hit the p-branes, they excite extra waves on the branes. Similarly, if waves moving in different directions on the p-branes come together at some point, they can create a peak so great that a bit of the p-brane breaks away and goes off as a particle. Thus the p-branes can absorb and emit particles like black holes.

One can regard the p-branes as an effective theory; that is, while we don't need to believe that there actually are little sheets moving through a flat space-time, black holes can behave as if they were made up of such sheets. It is like water, which is made up of billions and billions of H_2O molecules with complicated interactions. But a smooth fluid is a very good effective model. The mathematical model of black holes as made of p-branes gives results similar to the virtual-particle pair picture described earlier. Thus from a positivist viewpoint, it is an equally good model, at least for certain classes of black hole. For these classes, the p-brane model predicts exactly the same rate of emission that the virtual-particle pair model predicts. However, there is one important difference: in the p-brane model, information about what falls into the black hole will be stored in the wave function for the waves on the p-branes. The p-branes are regarded as sheets in *flat* space-time, and for that reason, time will flow forward smoothly, the paths of light rays won't be bent, and the information in the waves won't be lost. Instead, the information will eventually emerge from the black hole in the radiation from the p-branes. Thus, according to the p-brane model, we can use the Schrödinger equation to calculate what the wave function will be at later times. Nothing will get lost, and time will roll smoothly on. We will have complete determinism in the quantum sense.

So which of these pictures is correct? Does part of the wave function get lost down black holes, or does all the information get out again, as the p-brane model suggests? This is one of the outstanding questions in theoretical physics today. Many people believe that recent work shows that information is not lost. The world is safe and predictable, and nothing unexpected will happen. But it's not clear. If one takes Einstein's general theory of relativity seriously, one must allow the possibility that space-time ties itself in a knot and information gets lost in the folds.

Content Questions

1. Why were the discoveries of Copernicus, Galileo, and Newton important in showing the implausibility of astrology? (477–478)

2. What is scientific determinism? How do the assumptions of determinism allow scientists to make predictions? How does chaos, a property of equations that predict the future, modify determinism? (478)

3. Why would the uncertainty principle be expected to undermine scientific determinism? How do the Schrödinger equation and the wave function allow scientists to "accurately predict half of what one would expect to predict" from the viewpoint of classical physics? (478–480)

4. What does Hawking mean by "the commonsense view of time"? With the overthrow of this view by special relativity, how is the "quantum version of determinism" preserved? (480–481)

5. How would the curvature of space-time affect the use of the Schrödinger equation in making predictions? (481)

6. In John Michell's theory, why is it necessary for dark stars to be much more massive than the sun? In this theory, what is implied about the nature of light if it can be affected by gravity in the same way as a cannonball? (481–482)

7. What is the difference between the reason that Michell says light can't escape from a dark star and the reason that Hawking says it can't escape from a black hole? (482–483)

8. What is the theoretical reason that all not stars can become black holes? (483–484)

9. What is a "singularity"? In figure 3, where are the paths of light after the star has passed the event horizon and become a singularity? (484)

10. In order to preserve scientific determinism, why is it important to be able to establish the surfaces of constant values for time, shown in figure 4? (485)

11. How does the concept of vacuum fluctuations prevent a violation of the uncertainty principle? What result of vacuum fluctuations does Hawking offer to support his discovery that "black holes aren't completely black"? (486)

12. Why does Hawking reject the possibility that information could emerge from a black hole when it has lost all of its mass through radiation? (487–488)

13. What limitation do black holes place on using the Schrödinger equation to calculate the wave function at earlier times? (488)

14. How does the Einstein-Podolsky-Rosen thought experiment demonstrate "exactly what happens with black hole radiation"? (488–489)

15. How does the p-brane model preserve scientific determinism? (489–490)

Discussion Questions

1. Unlike the predictions of astrology, how are the predictions of a scientific theory definite? (477)

2. What does it mean for a scientific theory to be consistent with other theories that have been tested by experiment? Why would scientists believe in a theory that is consistent in this way, even though there may not be any experimental evidence for it? (477–478)

3. Can determinism be scientifically verified? Why does Hawking say that scientific determinism makes the future predictable "in principle"? (478)

4. If the physical world is ruled by scientific determinism, is free will possible? (478)

5. How is it possible to claim there is determinism in quantum theory, even though the wave function can represent a particle's position or velocity only in terms of probabilities? (479–480)

6. What does Hawking mean when he says, "Even God is bound by the uncertainty principle" and can know only the wave function? (480)

7. What does Hawking mean when he says that "even most physicists" have the commonsense view of time "at the back of their minds"? (480) In light of scientific discoveries that overturn commonly held views of how the physical world operates, such as the theory of relativity, when should these views be retained or discarded?

8. How was it possible for Michell and Hawking to have a detailed description and explanation of the formation of black holes before having observational information to confirm the holes' existence? (481–485)

9. When Hawking chooses to interpret vacuum fluctuations as pairs of virtual particles, what does he mean by the picture that "is most useful for the problem

in question"? (486) Are pictures that are freely used because they help solve problems adequate for understanding how the physical world actually operates?

10. When one member of a pair of virtual particles falls into a black hole, why is our power to predict the future "reduced to zero"? (489) For determinism to be preserved, why is it necessary to be able to predict measurements?

11. What does Hawking mean by "an effective theory"? (490) If different effective theories such as p-branes and virtual particle pairs lead to similar results, how can scientists decide which to adopt?

12. Is physics possible without scientific determinism?

Suggestions for Further Reading

By the author

Hawking, Stephen. *The Illustrated "A Brief History of Time."* New York: Bantam Books, 1996. In this updated and expanded version of his best-selling book, Hawking outlines the two great and separate streams of modern physics—relativity and quantum theory—and shows how they have led to a deeper understanding of the origin and structure of the universe while at the same time offering the possibility of a unified theory of the physical world.

———. *The Universe in a Nutshell.* New York: Bantam Books, 2001. In this beautifully illustrated book, from which the selection in *What's the Matter?* is taken, Hawking provides a brief review of relativity and then launches into an exploration of topics on the frontiers of theoretical physics, concentrating on areas in which he has worked and speculating on what a theory of everything might turn out to be.

About the topic

Al-Khalili, Jim. *Black Holes, Wormholes, and Time Machines.* Bristol, UK: Institute of Physics Publishing, 1999. Based on a series of popular lectures, this book provides lively explanations of what science currently understands about the nature of time and space, black holes, and the possibility of time travel, making use of interesting analogies to express complex ideas without mathematics.

Ferris, Timothy. *The Whole Shebang: A State-of-the-Universe(s) Report.* New York: Simon & Schuster, 1997, 1998. One of the many strengths of this outstanding overview of the current state of cosmology, by one of the best science writers, is its explanation of the important relation between the science of the very large (astronomy) and the science of the very small (particle physics).

Lindley, David. *Where Does the Weirdness Go? Why Quantum Mechanics Is Strange, but Not As Strange As You Think*. New York: Basic Books, 1996, 1997. This book explores the strange phenomena of the quantum world, where the uncertainty of quantum effects is unavoidable and everyday experience does not apply, and suggests how our familiar world might arise from this subatomic realm.

Thorne, Kip S. *Black Holes and Time Warps: Einstein's Outrageous Legacy*. New York: W. W. Norton & Company, 1994, 1995. This richly detailed book by one of the world's leading cosmologists starts with an explanation of Einstein's general theory of relativity and shows how its vast implications have led the way for subsequent researchers. The wonderful prelude to the book is a futuristic story of space travel to the vicinity of a black hole.

Science can only ascertain what *is*, but not what *should be*, and outside of its domain value judgments of all kinds remain necessary.

—Albert Einstein, "Science and Religion"

ALBERT EINSTEIN

The Scientist's Responsibilities

As scientific technology has become a dominant influence on the political and economic systems of our world, it is more important than ever to raise questions about the social responsibilities of men and women of science, both as professional researchers and as private citizens. Throughout his career, Albert Einstein (1879–1955) addressed many of these questions in writings and speeches on a range of subjects outside of theoretical physics, including government, politics, Judaism, pacifism, and education.

In 1939, Einstein wrote to the president of the United States, Franklin Roosevelt, alerting him to the probability that the National Socialist regime in Germany was developing atomic weapons. At the urging of fellow scientists—many of them refugees from the worsening political situation in Europe—Einstein advised the president to form an organization to research the practical uses of uranium, the essential component of these weapons. Eminent but less widely known scientists such as Enrico Fermi and Leo Szilard recognized that Einstein's public prominence would guarantee a hearing at the highest levels of government.

Six years later, in August 1945, the result of this effort was the detonation of two atomic bombs, at Hiroshima and Nagasaki in Japan, effectively ending World War II. Forty years earlier, in 1905, Einstein had formulated the equivalence of mass and energy—the famous equation $E = mc^2$—that provided one of the fundamental principles necessary for the development of atomic technology. Along with the terrible loss of civilian lives and property, as well as the environmental destruction, the bombs provided a harrowing demonstration to the world of the way in which the theoretical work of scientists could have immense consequences. No previous event in human history so powerfully highlighted the responsibilities of scientists for an results of their research, whether pursued as an independent search for knowledge or in the service of practical objectives.

During World War I, unlike most of his scientific colleagues in Germany who participated in his country's effort to win the war, Einstein openly campaigned against its continuation. Along with his inherent antipathy to the violence of military activity, Einstein's pacifism reflected his belief that individuals cannot flourish creatively when they are caught up in what he considered senseless nationalism. This belief was a general expression of his own independent-minded pursuit of scientific knowledge and his conviction that "the representatives of the natural sciences are inclined, by the universal character of the subject dealt with and by the necessity of internationally organized cooperation, toward an international mentality predisposing them to favor pacifistic objectives." After 1919, when the experimental confirmation of an important predication of his general theory of relativity made him world-famous, Einstein was frequently called on to take positions and make statements concerning a range of social and political issues. He became involved in the unsuccessful efforts of the League of Nations to establish a stable world government, and in the Zionist movement that paved the way for the founding of the state of Israel and of Hebrew University in Jerusalem.

Einstein's pacifist views were well known when he wrote to President Roosevelt. But it is a reflection of his careful consideration of the principles underlying decisions in both scientific matters and public affairs that he chose to recommend entering the race to build atomic weapons, contrary to what many would have expected. His decision was strongly influenced by his experience during the 1930s in Germany, where Einstein had seen science, and the freedom necessary to independently pursue it, subordinated to the political ideology of National Socialism. His own work was officially rejected on the grounds that it was "Jewish science" and therefore considered not only invalid but also a corrupting influence on society. When the increasing power of the National Socialist party led to the creation of a political dictatorship, Einstein and many other intellectual leaders left Germany and settled in the United States.

The following selection is a message that Einstein sent to the Italian Society for the Advancement of Science in 1950. In it, he challenges us to think about the convictions of men and women of science concerning the value of their work, and how these convictions might influence the moral choices they make. In addition, Einstein raises questions about whether the objectivity and independent-mindedness of scientists is compatible with the interests of society, and whether scientists have a special responsibility to guide the world toward secure forms of international cooperation.

See also Einstein, pages 253–255 and 301–303.

The Scientist's Responsibilities

Let me first thank you most sincerely for your kindness in inviting me to attend the meeting of the Society for the Advancement of Science. I should gladly have accepted the invitation if my health had permitted me to do so. All I can do under the circumstances is to address you briefly from my home across the ocean. In doing so, I am under no illusion that I have something to say that would actually enlarge your insight and understanding. However, we are living in a period of such great external and internal insecurity and with such a lack of firm objectives that the mere confession of our convictions may be of significance, even if these convictions, like all value judgments, cannot be proven through logical deductions.

There arises at once the question: Should we consider the search for truth or, more modestly expressed, our efforts to understand the knowable universe through constructive logical thought as an autonomous objective of our work? Or should our search for truth be subordinated to some other objective, for example, to a "practical" one? This question cannot be decided on a logical basis. The decision, however, will have considerable influence upon our thinking and our moral judgment, provided that it is born out of deep and unshakable conviction. Let me then make a confession: for myself, the struggle to gain more insight and understanding is one of those independent objectives without which a thinking individual would find it impossible to have a conscious, positive attitude toward life.

It is the very essence of our striving for understanding that, on the one hand, it attempts to encompass the great and complex variety of man's experience, and that on the other, it looks for simplicity and economy in the basic assumptions. The belief that these two objectives can exist side by side is, in view of the primitive state of our scientific knowledge, a matter of faith. Without such faith I could not have a strong and unshakable conviction about the independent value of knowledge.

This, in a sense, religious attitude of a man engaged in scientific work has some influence upon his whole personality. For apart from the knowledge that is offered by accumulated experience and from the rules of logical thinking, there exists in principle for the man in science no authority whose decisions and statements could have in themselves a claim to "Truth." This leads to the paradoxical situation that a person who devotes all his strength to objective matters will develop, from a social point of view, into an extreme individualist who, at least in principle, has faith in nothing but his own judgment. It is quite possible to assert that intellectual individualism and scientific eras emerged simultaneously in history and have remained inseparable ever since.

Someone may suggest that the man of science as sketched in these sentences is no more than an abstraction that actually does not exist in this world, not unlike the *homo oeconomicus*[1] of classical economics. However, it seems to me that science as we know it today could not have emerged and could not have remained alive if many individuals, during many centuries, would not have come very close to the ideal.

Of course, not everybody who has learned to use tools and methods that, directly or indirectly, appear to be "scientific" is to me a man of science. I refer only to those individuals in whom scientific mentality is truly alive.

What, then, is the position of today's man of science as a member of society? He obviously is rather proud of the fact that the work of scientists has helped to change radically the economic life of men by almost completely eliminating muscular work. He is distressed by the fact that the results of his scientific work have created a threat to mankind since they have fallen into the hands of morally blind exponents of political power. He is conscious of the fact that technological methods made possible by his work have led to a concentration of economic and also of political power

1. [Economic man.]

in the hands of small minorities who have come to dominate completely the lives of the masses of people who appear more and more amorphous. But even worse: the concentration of economic and political power in few hands has not only made the man of science dependent economically; it also threatens his independence from within; the shrewd methods of intellectual and psychic influences that it brings to bear will prevent the development of really independent personalities.

Thus, the man of science, as we can observe with our own eyes, suffers a truly tragic fate. Striving in great sincerity for clarity and inner independence, he himself, through his sheer superhuman efforts, has fashioned the tools that are being used to make him a slave and to destroy him also from within. He cannot escape being muzzled by those who have the political power in their hands. As a soldier he is forced to sacrifice his own life and to destroy the lives of others even when he is convinced of the absurdity of such sacrifices. He is fully aware of the fact that universal destruction is unavoidable since the historical development has led to the concentration of all economic, political, and military power in the hands of national states. He also realizes that mankind can be saved only if a supranational system, based on law, would be created to eliminate for good the methods of brute force. However, the man of science has slipped so much that he accepts the slavery inflicted upon him by national states as his inevitable fate. He even degrades himself to such an extent that he helps obediently in the perfection of the means for the general destruction of mankind.

Is there really no escape for the man of science? Must he really tolerate and suffer all these indignities? Is the time gone forever when, aroused by his inner freedom and the independence of his thinking and his work, he had a chance of enlightening and enriching the lives of his fellow human beings? In placing his work too much on an intellectual basis, has he not forgotten about his responsibility and dignity? My answer is: while it is true that an inherently free and scrupulous person may be destroyed, such an individual can never be enslaved or used as a blind tool.

If the man of science of our own days could find the time and the courage to think over honestly and critically his situation and the tasks before him, and if he would act accordingly, the possibilities for a sensible and satisfactory solution of the present dangerous international situation would be considerably improved.

Discussion Questions

1. As a man of science, why does Einstein think that "the mere confession" of his convictions will be significant, even though he says that they are value judgments and cannot be "proven through logical deductions"? (499)

2. According to Einstein, on what basis does a scientist decide whether the search for scientific truth should depend on practical objectives? (499)

3. How could the decision that the search for scientific understanding is an independent objective influence the moral judgment of a scientist? (499)

4. Why does Einstein say that a belief in the coexistence of comprehensiveness and simplicity in scientific inquiry is, "in view of the primitive state of our scientific knowledge, a matter of faith"? (500)

5. Are extreme individualism and faith in one's own judgment reliable guides for a scientist's search for objective scientific truth? (500)

6. How would Einstein define the "scientific mentality" that he says is truly alive in the man of science? (500)

7. Are there some kinds of scientific research that a scientist should avoid because, as Einstein observes, the results have often fallen into the hands of "morally blind exponents of political power?" (500)

8. Is Einstein correct in saying that the concentration of economic and political power in small, dominant minorities can threaten the external and internal independence of a scientist? (501) Is this situation more of a threat in some kinds of political and economic systems than in others?

9. Does a scientist bear any responsibility for what Einstein calls a "tragic fate"? (501)

10. How should a scientist judge between responsibility to the independence of scientific knowledge and responsibility to his nation's political goals? (501)

11. According to Einstein, what responsibility has "the man of science" forgotten "in placing his work too much on an intellectual basis"? (501)

12. What course of action is Einstein advising that scientists take after finding the time and courage to think over their situation honestly and critically? (501)

Suggestions for Further Reading

By the author

Einstein, Albert. *Ideas and Opinions.* Reprint. New translations and revisions by Sonja Bargmann. New York: Modern Library, 1994. This standard collection of short writings, from which the selection in *What's the Matter?* is taken, represents the range of Einstein's thoughts on politics, government, education, religion, and science.

About the author

Frank, Philipp. *Einstein: His Life and Times.* Cambridge, MA: Da Capo Press, 2002. The author of this biography was a close friend and colleague of Einstein's and gives an outstanding portrayal of him both as a scientist and as a public figure deeply involved in the political and social issues of his times.

About the topic

Bronowski, Jacob. *Science and Human Values.* Rev. ed. New York: Perennial, 1990. In three loosely related essays, the author explores the consequences of separating science and technology from the values that underlie all creative human activity.

Cassidy, David. *J. Robert Oppenheimer and the American Century.* New York: Pi Press, 2005. This biography of the director of the Manhattan Project follows his career as a theoretical physicist and public figure—a career marked by fundamental conflicts between the aims of scientific research and the uses of science to further political objectives.

Powers, Thomas. *Heisenberg's War: The Secret History of the German Bomb.* New York: Alfred A. Knopf, 1993; Cambridge, MA: Da Capo Press, 2000. This investigation of whether Nazi Germany's greatest theoretical physicist chose to prevent his country from successfully developing atomic weapons provides an interesting contrast to the stories of Einstein and Oppenheimer.

Weisskopf, Victor F. *The Privilege of Being a Physicist.* New York: W. H. Freeman and Company, 1989, 1990. In this collection of lively essays, Weisskopf, an eminent physicist who was one of the key figures in the Manhattan Project, offers his views on the place of science in society and the urgent need for international cooperation in controlling nuclear weapons.

Thematic Guide

The selections in *What's the Matter?* are arranged in roughly chronological order; reading them from start to finish can provide an understanding of the ways that many of the major concepts of physics have developed over time. However, some readers may want to approach the contents more selectively, depending on their individual interests. The following guide gives suggestions for how the selections can be read and discussed in order to focus on specific topics and themes, offering numerous ways to explore the complex interplay of ideas represented in *What's the Matter?*

Part I: Topics

Many of the selections in *What's the Matter?* are concerned with the topics ordinarily included in physics courses and can supplement corresponding textbook chapters and course materials. The selections listed under each of the following headings are closely related to one another and can be read and discussed as a sequence, although each can also be read and discussed independently of the others.

Mechanics

Aristotle	Moving Things
Galileo	Falling Bodies and Projectiles
Newton	Forces
Newton	Laws of Motion
Newton	Time, Space, and Motion
Einstein	The Special Theory of Relativity
Einstein	The General Theory of Relativity
Gamow	Quantum Uncertainty

Thermodynamics/Energy

Rumford	Heat and Friction
Joule	The Mechanical Equivalent of Heat
Eddington	Entropy: The Running-Down of the Universe
Einstein	$E = mc^2$

Electromagnetism

Faraday	Induction of Electric Currents
Faraday	On the Physical Lines of Magnetic Force
Maxwell	The Science of Electromagnetism
Maxwell	Electricity and Electromotive Force
Maxwell	A Dynamical Theory of the Electromagnetic Field

Light

Newton and Young	On Light
Gamow	Quantum Uncertainty
Feynman	Quantum Behavior

The Theory of Relativity

Einstein	The Special Theory of Relativity
Einstein	The General Theory of Relativity
Einstein	$E = mc^2$
Hawking	Black Holes and Predictable Worlds

Quantum Theory

Planck	Extending the Theories of Physics
Gamow	Quantum Uncertainty
Feynman	Quantum Behavior
Heisenberg	The Copenhagen Interpretation of Quantum Theory
Polkinghorne	Quantum Perplexity and Debate
Hawking	Black Holes and Predictable Worlds

Cosmology

Eddington	Entropy: The Running-Down of the Universe
Weinberg	The Origin of the Universe
Hawking	Black Holes and Predictable Worlds

Part II: Themes

Readers of *What's the Matter?* will find many thematic connections among the selections, particularly where physicists refer to the work of their predecessors and contemporaries as they proceed with their own investigations. Each sequence of selections that follows has been arranged to facilitate the exploration of a general theme in the development of physics.

The Nature of Science and Scientific Investigation

Feynman	The Uncertainty of Science
Aristotle	The Science of Nature
Newton	Rules of Doing Philosophy
Planck	Extending the Theories of Physics
Kane	Why Physics Is the Easiest Science: Effective Theories
Weinberg	Beautiful Theories: Symmetry and Mathematics
Lightman	Metaphor in Science

Investigating the Physical World: Experiment and Observation

Feynman	The Uncertainty of Science
Newton	Rules of Doing Philosophy
Galileo	Falling Bodies and Projectiles
Rumford	Heat and Friction
Joule	The Mechanical Equivalent of Heat
Faraday	Induction of Electric Currents
Maxwell	The Science of Electromagnetism
Maxwell	Electricity and Electromotive Force
Newton and Young	On Light
Feynman	Quantum Behavior
Heisenberg	The Copenhagen Interpretation of Quantum Theory

Explaining the Physical World: Theories and Laws of Nature

Weinberg	Beautiful Theories: Symmetry and Mathematics
Aristotle	The Science of Nature
Newton	Rules of Doing Philosophy
Planck	Extending the Theories of Physics
Kane	Why Physics Is the Easiest Science: Effective Theories
Lightman	Metaphor in Science

Notes on
Key Terms and Concepts

These notes are provided to define and clarify some of the terms and concepts mentioned in *What's the Matter?* Because concepts in physics are closely interrelated, the entries are cross-referenced to help you explore different aspects of their meanings. These definitions and explanations are intended to prompt, not curtail, further thought about these central ideas. With that in mind, entries are followed by related readings in *What's the Matter?* encouraging you to return to the original texts and to consider what the authors themselves have to say. By tracing the concepts through sequences of related readings, you can explore how ideas in physics develop and change.

acceleration The rate of change of a moving object's velocity with respect to time (for example, miles per hour per second). Since velocity represents an object's speed and direction, acceleration can be the rate of change of speed, direction, or both. See also: *velocity*.
RELATED READINGS: Newton, "Forces"; Einstein, "The General Theory of Relativity"

action at a distance The idea that objects interact without any mechanical connection between them. Classical physics, although it is largely founded on mechanistic principles, attributes the operation of gravity to action at a distance. One of the central problems faced by early researchers in electromagnetism was to explain how electromagnetic effects, thought of as propagating waves, were transmitted through apparently empty space. The medium of the ether and the idea of fields were offered as hypothetical solutions to this problem. See also: *classical physics; ether; field; gravity.*
    RELATED READINGS: Faraday, "On the Physical Lines of Magnetic Force"; Maxwell, "A Dynamical Theory of the Electromagnetic Field"; Lightman, "Metaphor in Science"

big bang The generally accepted cosmological theory that the universe originated from an explosive event approximately 14 billion years ago that created space, time, and matter, and was the beginning of the universe's continuing expansion. See also: *standard model; symmetry.*
    RELATED READING: Weinberg, "The Origin of the Universe"

c A constant of nature representing the velocity of light in a vacuum, approximately 186,000 miles per second. See also: *constants of nature.*
    RELATED READING: Einstein, "The Special Theory of Relativity"

classical physics The explanation of the physical world according to Newton's laws of motion, Maxwell's laws of electromagnetism, and the laws of thermodynamics. This explanation was dominant until the early twentieth century, when the theory of relativity and quantum theory were developed. Classical physics assumes that absolute time and absolute space exist and are independent of each other. Because classical physics views the world as strictly determined by chains of cause and effect, it is sometimes described as mechanistic. Classical physics assumes that energy and momentum are continuously variable, does not take quantum effects into consideration, and provides highly accurate descriptions of the physical world at scales vastly larger than the subatomic quantum realm. Sometimes relativity physics is considered classical, because it also does not consider quantum effects and contains classical physics as a limiting case. See also: *action at a distance;*

determinism; first law of thermodynamics; second law of thermodynamics; space-time; theory of relativity; quantum theory.

RELATED READINGS: Newton, "Laws of Motion" and "Time, Space, and Motion"; Maxwell, "A Dynamical Theory of the Electromagnetic Field"; Einstein, "The Special Theory of Relativity" and "The General Theory of Relativity"; Hawking, "Black Holes and Predictable Worlds"

conservation laws Statements that in a closed system, the total quantity of momentum, energy, mass, or electrical charge remains unchanged throughout any physical process. The conservation laws for mass and energy are useful approximations, but not strictly accurate. According to Einstein's equation $E = mc^2$, some mass is converted into energy under certain conditions, so it is more accurate to say that the sum total of mass and energy is conserved. See also: *energy; first law of thermodynamics; laws of nature; mass; momentum; second law of thermodynamics; symmetry.*

RELATED READINGS: Joule, "The Mechanical Equivalent of Heat"; Eddington, "Entropy: The Running-Down of the Universe"; Einstein, "$E = mc^2$"

constants of nature Fixed numerical values that are experimentally determined and enter into numerous equations describing the physical world. Constants of nature are thought to keep the same values over time and in all locations, but new experimental data could lead us to question whether these values remain fixed in all circumstances. Three of the most important constants in physics are: c, the velocity of light and electromagnetic waves in a vacuum; G, the gravitational acceleration between any two objects and a key factor in Newton's law of universal gravitation; and h, Planck's constant, an extremely small number that occurs in many calculations of quantum mechanics and defines the least amount of energy, or quantum, that can occur in nature. See also: *c; gravity; Planck's constant; quantum; quantum theory; uncertainty principle.*

RELATED READINGS: Einstein, "The Special Theory of Relativity"; Gamow, "Quantum Uncertainty"; Kane, "Why Physics Is the Easiest Science: Effective Theories"

determinism In physics, the idea that all effects can be exactly predicted from prior causes. If the present position and velocity of an object and all the forces acting on it are known, its future path of motion, or trajectory, is predetermined and can be predicted in principle—though not always in practice—with absolute certainty. Determinism is closely identified with classical Newtonian physics and is also referred to as the mechanistic worldview. According to classical physics, complete predictability is possible because the initial conditions of an object can be measured to any degree of accuracy. In contrast, there is a fundamental indeterminism in the world as described by quantum theory. See also: *classical physics; quantum theory; uncertainty principle; wave mechanics.*

> RELATED READINGS: Newton, "Laws of Motion"; Hawking, "Black Holes and Predictable Worlds"

electromagnetic force See *forces of nature.*

electroweak force See *forces of nature.*

energy One of the fundamental concepts of physics, referring to the capacity of many kinds of phenomena in the physical world to be converted into work. When we measure changes in the condition of a physical system, including its position, mass, and temperature, we are measuring the change in energy of the system. The form that energy takes when work results from these changes can be electromagnetic, chemical, gravitational, thermal, nuclear, radiant, elastic, or kinetic. An essential characteristic of energy is that its total quantity remains the same, or is conserved, as it is converted from one form to another. Although in classical physics matter and energy were considered independent concepts, Einstein's theory of relativity demonstrated their equivalence, expressed by the equation $E = mc^2$. See also: *conservation laws; entropy; first law of thermodynamics; second law of thermodynamics; work.*

> RELATED READINGS: Rumford, "Heat and Friction"; Joule, "The Mechanical Equivalent of Heat"; Eddington, "Entropy: The Running-Down of the Universe"; Maxwell, "Electricity and Electromotive Force"; Einstein, "$E = mc^2$" and "The Scientist's Responsibilities"

entropy The measure of the amount of disorder or randomness in any closed physical system. Entropy is a consequence of the second law of thermodynamics, which states that in a closed system—one that does not receive energy from an external source—the amount of energy unavailable for maintaining order in the system increases. Inherent in entropy is the idea that an irreversible physical process will not spontaneously become more orderly unless energy is added to it. For example, that an object can go from hot to cold is not surprising; without added energy, the reverse is virtually impossible. Physical processes are irreversible because of friction and other features that dissipate energy, and in a closed system entropy always increases. If the universe as a whole is considered a closed system, it would be moving toward maximum entropy. See also: *conservation laws; energy; first law of thermodynamics; second law of thermodynamics.*

> RELATED READINGS: Joule, "The Mechanical Equivalent of Heat"; Eddington, "Entropy: The Running-Down of the Universe"

ether A transparent material once hypothesized by scientists and believed to permeate all space, providing a medium for the propagation of light and a mechanism to explain the apparent action at a distance of electromagnetic phenomena. Ether was discredited when scientists failed to detect its existence and the nonmaterial nature of fields came to be accepted. See also: *action at a distance.*

> RELATED READINGS: Maxwell, "A Dynamical Theory of the Electromagnetic Field"; Lightman, "Metaphor in Science"

field A region of space that is associated with electrically charged, magnetic, or gravitating bodies and that affects other bodies with electromagnetic or gravitational forces when they enter it. Although a field is considered to be present even when no bodies have entered it, the forces do not exist until a body enters a field and interacts with it. Mathematically, each point in a field can be assigned a numerical value for the intensity and direction of force at that point. The idea of fields has been accepted as the most useful way of explaining how forces can be exerted at a distance from an electromagnetic or gravitational source without an intervening medium such as ether. See also: *action at a distance; ether; force; gravity.*

> RELATED READINGS: Faraday, "On the Physical Lines of Magnetic Force"; Maxwell, "A Dynamical Theory of the Electromagnetic Field"

first law of thermodynamics The principle that in a closed system, the total amount of energy is completely conserved, even as it is changed from one form to another; therefore, energy is neither created nor destroyed. In particular, the first law states the equivalence between heat energy and the amount of mechanical energy into which it can be converted. See also: *conservation laws; energy; laws of nature; second law of thermodynamics.*

RELATED READINGS: Joule, "The Mechanical Equivalent of Heat"; Eddington, "Entropy: The Running-Down of the Universe"

force The action of bodies on one another, in the form of pushing or pulling, that causes them to accelerate. Forces always occur in pairs and are directly proportional to a body's mass and the acceleration produced, which is expressed by the equation force = mass × acceleration. See also: *acceleration; forces of nature; inertia; momentum; work.*

RELATED READINGS: Newton, "Forces" and "Laws of Motion"; Faraday, "On the Physical Lines of Magnetic Force"; Maxwell, "Electricity and Electromotive Force"

forces of nature The four known fundamental forces affecting the interaction of objects. Gravity is the weakest of the forces and operates between any objects that have mass. It is an attractive force with infinite range. The electromagnetic force, associated with electric charges and magnetic objects, is stronger than gravity and can both attract and repel. The strong force, most powerful of the fundamental forces but with a range confined to the diameter of the atomic nucleus, holds together the nuclei of atoms. The weak force is responsible for some forms of radioactive decay, and physicists have found that it can be unified with the electromagnetic force as the electroweak force. One of the most important areas of investigation for modern physics is the search for a theory unifying all the forces of nature. See also: *force; gravity; grand unified theory; Standard Model; theory of everything.*

RELATED READINGS: Newton, "Forces"; Faraday, "On the Physical Lines of Magnetic Force"; Maxwell, "The Science of Electromagnetism" and "Electricity and Electromotive Force"; Einstein, "The General Theory of Relativity"

G A fixed number called the gravitational constant. See also: *constants of nature; gravity.*
> RELATED READING: Einstein, "The General Theory of Relativity"

grand unified theory A theory that attempts to combine three of the forces of nature—electromagnetism, the strong force, and the weak force—into one mathematical formulation. When scientists finally discover a grand unified theory, it will be a significant advance toward a theory of everything uniting all four forces of nature. See also: *forces of nature; string theory; symmetry; theory.*
> RELATED READINGS: Weinberg, "Beautiful Theories: Symmetry and Mathematics"; Kane, "Why Physics Is the Easiest Science: Effective Theories"

gravity One of the four fundamental forces of nature, acting universally as an attractive force between objects that have mass and causing them to accelerate as they approach one another. The net gravitational force exerted on an object is referred to as its weight and is related to the object's gravitational mass. Isaac Newton first formulated the fundamental law of nature for gravity. This inverse square law states that the force of gravity is equal to the gravitational constant (G) multiplied by the product of mass$_1$ and mass$_2$, divided by the square of the distance between the two objects: $F_g = Gm_1m_2/d^2$. As the distance between two masses increases, the strength of the gravitational force between them greatly decreases. In the general theory of relativity, Albert Einstein completely reinterpreted gravity in terms of the geometry of space as it is influenced by the mass of bodies. See also: *acceleration; action at a distance; constants of nature; field; forces of nature; inverse square law; laws of nature; mass; weight.*
> RELATED READINGS: Galileo, "Falling Bodies and Projectiles"; Newton, "Forces"; Einstein, "The General Theory of Relativity"

h See *Planck's constant.*

inertia The property of an object associated with mass such that it tends to remain at rest or at the same velocity relative to a given frame of reference, unless acted on by a force. Inertia is sometimes mistakenly called a force; more accurately, it is the sluggish quality of mass. See also: *force; mass; velocity.*

RELATED READINGS: Aristotle, "Moving Things"; Galileo, "Falling Bodies and Projectiles"; Newton, "Forces"; Einstein, "The General Theory of Relativity"

laws of nature The most well-established principles in science, formulated only after many repeated, rigorous experimental observations to test hypotheses, supported by convincing quantitative data. Laws of nature are the parts of theories least likely to be discarded as new discoveries are made because their wide application to the physical world has been so thoroughly tested. However, like any scientific statements, laws of nature can change in the light of new experimental evidence and shifts in theoretical concepts. See also: *conservation laws; first law of thermodynamics; second law of thermodynamics; theory.*

RELATED READINGS: Feynman, "The Uncertainty of Science"; Newton, "Laws of Motion"; Planck, "Extending the Theories of Physics"; Kane, "Why Physics Is the Easiest Science: Effective Theories"

mass The property of a physical object, related to the amount of matter it contains, that determines how much it will be accelerated when a force is impressed on it. An object's mass is called inertial mass when it is measured by the degree to which the object can be accelerated by a force. This relationship is expressed by the equation acceleration = force/mass, and reflects our ordinary experience that in exerting the same force on different objects, those with greater mass will not accelerate as much as those with less mass.

An object's mass can also be measured by determining its gravitational mass, the force it exerts when pulled by gravity. Within a limited region where a gravitational field does not vary significantly, an object's gravitational mass is virtually the same as its weight. However, weight and mass are distinct characteristics, since under most conditions mass remains constant everywhere in the physical world, while weight depends on the distance of an object from the sources responsible for the gravitational field. An object's inertial mass and gravitational mass are always equal, an observed fact that Albert Einstein called the principle of equivalence and that became the foundation of his general theory of relativity. Like momentum, electrical charge, and energy, mass is ordinarily conserved in physical processes, although Einstein's equation $E = mc^2$ describes the conditions under which mass can be converted into energy. See also: *acceleration; conservation laws; gravity; inertia; momentum; weight.*

RELATED READINGS: Galileo, "Falling Bodies and Projectiles"; Newton, "Forces"; Einstein, "The General Theory of Relativity" and "$E = mc^2$"

mechanics The branch of physics concerned with the interaction of matter and forces. Depending on the theoretical framework being used, there are three different versions of mechanics: classical mechanics, relativistic mechanics, and quantum mechanics. See also: *classical physics; theory of relativity; quantum theory; wave mechanics.*

RELATED READINGS: Newton, "Forces," "Laws of Motion," and "Time, Space and Motion"; Einstein, "The Special Theory of Relativity" and "The General Theory of Relativity"; Gamow, "Quantum Uncertainty"

model A representation of some aspect of the physical world that cannot be directly observed or easily grasped without visual images and mathematical formulations. Models provide analogies to familiar things and help us picture physical systems, structures, or processes. Models often accompany theories, but can be revised and sometimes discarded as theories continue to develop. Even though models may not be literal representations of the ultimate underlying reality, they are useful tools for calculating the values of properties associated with phenomena and for guiding scientists in developing new ideas about the physical world. See also: *standard model; string theory; theory; wave mechanics.*

RELATED READING: Lightman, "Metaphor in Science"

momentum The quantity of motion, designated in physics by p and expressed by the equation momentum (p) = mass × velocity. An object's momentum is directly proportional to its mass and its velocity, so that a small object moving fast can have as much momentum as a large object moving slowly. According to Newton's second and third laws of motion, momentum changes only when a force is impressed on a moving object, and the total momentum of a closed system of interacting bodies is conserved. See also: *conservation laws; force; mass; velocity.*

RELATED READINGS: Galileo, *"Falling Bodies and Projectiles"*;
Newton, *"Forces"*

Planck's constant One of the fundamental constants of nature that is of
central importance in quantum theory. It was discovered by the German
physicist Max Planck in the early twentieth century. Symbolized by h,
Planck's constant is an extremely small fixed number that represents
the ratio of a subatomic object's energy to its frequency: $h = E/f$. That is,
h links the particle-like characteristic energy (E) and the wavelike
characteristic frequency (f) of a subatomic object such as an electron.
See also: *constants of nature; quantum theory; uncertainty principle;
wave-particle duality.*
RELATED READING: Gamow, "Quantum Uncertainty"

probability An expression of the likelihood that among all the possibilities for the outcome of an event, a particular possibility will actually
occur. Probabilities are usually stated in terms of percentages of the total
number of occurrences in a series of repeated events; for example, the
probability that heads will come up each time a coin is tossed is 50 percent. Probabilities are essential in physics to make predictions when
there is a high degree of uncertainty about the conditions that cause
events.

In classical physics, probabilities are used to overcome uncertainties
that result from the difficulty of making accurate observations and measurements. Even so, classical physics assumes that the world is strictly
determined by causes that can, in principle, be known with complete
certainty. For example, the second law of thermodynamics is based on
statistical probabilities for the overall behavior of immense numbers of
molecules in motion, because there is no practical way to measure the
motion of each molecule. However in quantum physics, the world can
only be described by probabilities because measurements are fundamentally uncertain and probability is an inherent part of nature. Physicists
often use a mathematical tool called a probability distribution, a graph
or an equation that represents the results of many experimental observations and shows the comparative range of values for different actual outcomes. In the version of quantum theory known as wave mechanics, the
probability distribution is derived from a mathematical expression called

a wave function. See also: *classical physics; determinism; quantum theory; uncertainty principle; wave mechanics.*

> RELATED READINGS: Eddington, "Entropy: The Running-Down of the Universe"; Feynman, "Quantum Behavior"; Heisenberg, "The Copenhagen Interpretation of Quantum Theory"; Hawking, "Black Holes and Predictable Worlds"

probability function A mathematical expression in the version of quantum theory called wave mechanics that is derived from the Schrödinger equation. The probability function can be used to calculate properties of a quantum system such as the position of particles, momentum, and energy. See also: *probability; quantum theory; wave function; wave mechanics.*

> RELATED READINGS: Gamow, "Quantum Uncertainty"; Feynman, "Quantum Behavior"; Heisenberg, "The Copenhagen Interpretation of Quantum Theory"; Polkinghorne, "Quantum Perplexity and Debate"; Hawking, "Black Holes and Predictable Worlds"

quantum The smallest unit of certain physical properties, such as energy or momentum, that can occur in nature. The quantum is the foundation of quantum physics, in which there cannot be continuous changes in the values of energy or momentum for things such as photons and electrons. Instead, these changes happen in discrete jumps (quantum leaps) from one value to the next, with no intermediate values possible. The idea of the quantum represents a radical break from classical physics, in which energy and momentum can assume any values continuously, no matter how small. The size of the quantum is defined by Planck's constant, symbolized by h. See also: *classical physics; constants of nature; Planck's constant; quantum theory.*

> RELATED READINGS: Planck, *"Extending the Theories of Physics"*; Gamow, *"Quantum Uncertainty"*

quantum theory The accepted theory of the behavior of matter and energy, particularly at the subatomic level. The basic features of quantum theory center around three principles: quantization, uncertainty, and wave-particle duality. Quantization is the idea that things such as energy and momentum occur only in multiples of specific quantities, rather than in continuously varying amounts, as is the case in classical physics.

The size of these quanta are defined by a fundamental constant of nature, Planck's constant, designated *h*.

Heisenberg's uncertainty principle places limits on simultaneously measuring particular pairs of variables, such as position and momentum, or energy and time. Consequently, quantum physics cannot predict the future state of a physical system with the absolute certainty of classical physics. Related to quantum uncertainty is the idea that quantum entities such as electrons behave as either waves or particles, depending on how they are observed. The laws of mechanics for the subatomic quantum realm are referred to as quantum mechanics or wave mechanics. See also: *classical physics; constants of nature; mechanics; Planck's constant; probability; Schrödinger equation; theory; uncertainty principle; wave function; wave mechanics; wave-particle duality.*

> RELATED READINGS: Planck, 'Extending the Theories of Physics"; Gamow, "Quantum Uncertainty"; Feynman, "Quantum Behavior"; Heisenberg, "The Copenhagen Interpretation of Quantum Theory"; Polkinghorne, "Quantum Perplexity and Debate"; Hawking, "Black Holes and Predictable Worlds"

quark The fundamental particle that makes up protons and neutrons in the atomic nucleus. See also: *standard model.*

> RELATED READING: Weinberg, "Beautiful Theories: Symmetry and Mathematics"

reductionism The idea in science that all complex phenomena can be understood only by reducing them to the smallest possible number of principles and elements, from which all phenomena can in turn be derived according to a few simple laws of nature. Physics has largely been guided by reductionism, from Aristotle's speculations on primary elements and causes, through Isaac Newton's formulation of the laws of motion that form the basis of classical physics, to the modern search for a unified theory of how the forces of nature and subatomic particles interact. See also: *forces of nature; grand unified theory; string theory; symmetry; theory of everything.*

> RELATED READINGS: Aristotle, "The Science of Nature"; Newton, "Laws of Motion" and "Rules of Doing Philosophy"; Kane, "Why Physics Is the Easiest Science: Effective Theories"

Schrödinger equation The fundamental equation of wave mechanics, formulated by the Austrian physicist Erwin Schrödinger in the 1920s. The solution to the Schrödinger equation is a mathematical expression called a wave function that contains all the information we can know about the state of a subatomic object such as an electron. See also: *quantum theory; wave function; wave mechanics.*

RELATED READINGS: Gamow, "Quantum Uncertainty"; Heisenberg, "The Copenhagen Interpretation of Quantum Behavior"; Polkinghorne, "Quantum Perplexity and Debate"; Hawking, "Black Holes and Predictable Worlds"

second law of thermodynamics A law of nature that places limitations on how much energy in any physical process can be converted to work. Although the first law of thermodynamics states that when energy is converted from one form to another, the total quantity of energy in a closed system is conserved, the second law states that over time, some of the energy is no longer in a form available for performing work. The result is that no physical process can be completely efficient because some high-temperature thermal energy is always degraded into low-temperature thermal energy and dissipated into the environment. There are several equivalent statements of the second law. The most familiar is that heat energy flows spontaneously from higher to lower temperatures.

The second law is a law of probabilities that does not preclude the extremely remote possibility that heat energy could spontaneously flow from lower to higher temperatures. Rather, it states that the probability of this happening is so low as to be virtually impossible. Because the efficient use of energy is necessary for maintaining the structural order of things, whether in inanimate or biological systems, the consequence of the second law is that things tend to lose their orderliness and deteriorate. The measure of the amount of disorder in a system is called entropy, leading to another statement of the second law: the entropy of a closed system always increases. See also: *conservation laws; energy; entropy; first law of thermodynamics; laws of nature; probability.*

RELATED READINGS: Joule, "The Mechanical Equivalent of Heat"; Eddington, "Entropy: The Running-Down of the Universe"

space-time According to the theory of relativity, the four-dimensional framework of the physical world in which events occur. It joins the three familiar dimensions of space with the dimension of time. Space-time represents the insight that, in the measurements of the same events made by observers moving relatively to one another in different frames of reference, space and time are interdependent. However, space-time should not be thought of as merely consisting of space *and* time. Instead, in the theory of relativity, space-time represents the complete union of space and time as the framework in which observations and measurements are made. It is a complete departure from the separate, independent, and absolute space and time of classical physics. See also: *classical physics; theory of relativity.*

RELATED READINGS: Newton, "Time, Space, and Motion"; Einstein, The Special Theory of Relativity"

standard model/Standard Model A term that applies to two distinct but related pictures of the physical world, one in cosmology and the other in particle physics. In cosmology, the standard model is based on a hypothetical event called the "big bang" that is thought to be the origin of the universe. Because everything that existed in the first instants following the big bang was at extremely high levels of temperature and energy, the structure of matter and its interactions as we now know them had not yet evolved. The standard model of cosmology includes what we have discovered about the very early universe and the evolution of the physical world's most elementary components—particles and forces. It represents an important synthesis of insights from two different branches of physics, since it is based on both astrophysical data and experiments conducted by particle physicists in accelerators that reproduce some of the extreme conditions immediately following the big bang.

The Standard Model of particle physics (usually capitalized) is a description of the world in terms of elementary particles—known as quarks and leptons—and the electromagnetic, weak, and strong forces. It has had outstanding success in accounting for the interactions and properties of matter and is central to several of the most important theories of physics, including quantum electrodynamics, usually referred to as QED. See also: *big bang; forces of nature; model; quark.*

RELATED READINGS: Weinberg, "The Origin of the Universe" and "Beautiful Theories: Symmetry and Mathematics"; Kane, "Why Science Is the Easiest Science: Effective Theories"

string theory A speculative model of the underlying structure of all matter and energy in the universe and a central focus of research for a growing number of physicists in the late twentieth and early twenty-first centuries. The various versions of string theory are all based on mathematical models of submicroscopic, one-dimensional elements visualized as strings of energy that vibrate in complex patterns. These patterns theoretically predict the behavior of many of the known properties of subatomic particles and their interactions. A version of string theory called superstring theory seems to hold some promise for a unified theory of the fundamental forces of nature because it incorporates the concept of supersymmetry. Due to the extremely small scale of strings, there are not yet experimental techniques for testing string theory and accumulating the quantitative data that could confirm its predictions and raise its status to a fully established theory of physics. See also: *forces of nature; grand unified theory; model; reductionism; theory; theory of everything.*

RELATED READINGS: Weinberg, "Beautiful Theories: Symmetry and Mathematics"; Kane, "Why Physics Is the Easiest Science: Effective Theories"; Lightman, "Metaphor in Science"

strong force See *forces of nature.*

symmetry A mathematical concept describing the way in which some feature of a physical system remains unchanged when the system is transformed. Symmetry is one of the most important guiding ideas in theoretical physics. It helps scientists describe fundamental patterns in the physical world and discover new patterns based on correspondences with those already known.

Symmetry is central to research in particle physics, which seeks fundamental patterns underlying the forces of nature and the array of elementary particles that are the constituents of all matter. Scientists are especially interested in exploring breaks in symmetrical patterns. These broken symmetries seem to hold the key to discovering how the world as we know it evolved from a state of greater symmetry in the conditions of extreme heat and energy following the big bang.

The concept of supersymmetry guides scientists in their ongoing attempt to find a theory of everything, such as a version of string theory that would reduce the description of all known forces and particles to one great symmetry, expressed in a relatively small number of mathematical equations. See also: *big bang; conservation laws; reductionism; standard model; string theory; theory of everything.*

RELATED READINGS: Weinberg, "Beautiful Theories: Symmetry and Mathematics"; Kane, "Why Physics Is the Easiest Science: Effective Theories"

theory In science, a coherent set of concepts, laws of nature, and models that can be used to explain and predict phenomena in the natural world. A theory provides a framework for understanding an array of related phenomena according to the same general principles, and in physics these principles must be formulated with mathematical certainty. In addition, a theory must suggest ways for scientists to test its claims repeatedly and rigorously through experimentation, and to make predictions of the results of experimental observations with a high degree of quantitative precision. Regardless of how well established a scientific theory might be, it is always subject to revision as new discoveries are made. Besides the explanations it provides, a theory is often as valuable for the fruitful questions that it raises and the directions for further investigation that it indicates. See also: *laws of nature; model.*

RELATED READINGS: Feynman, "The Uncertainty of Science"; Planck, "Extending the Theories of Physics"; Weinberg, "Beautiful Theories: Symmetry and Mathematics"; Kane, "Why Physics Is the Easiest Science: Effective Theories"; Lightman, "Metaphor in Science"

theory of everything A theory that, if discovered, would combine all four forces of nature— gravity, electromagnetism, the strong force, and the weak force—into one mathematical formulation. See also: *forces of nature; grand unified theory; string theory; theory.*

RELATED READINGS: Weinberg, "Beautiful Theories: Symmetry and Mathematics"; Kane, "Why Physics Is the Easiest Science: Effective Theories"

theory of relativity The collective name for two closely related theories developed by Albert Einstein in the early twentieth century: the special theory of relativity and the general theory of relativity. Both the special and general theories are concerned with the way in which observers measure time and space from their own frames of references, moving relative to one another. The special theory is limited to observers moving uniformly, without acceleration. The general theory of relativity extends the special theory to apply to all observers, including those that are accelerating relative to one another. Both the special and general theories of relativity do away with classical physics' framework of absolute time and space independent of each other, combining them into a new framework called space-time.

The theory of relativity is one of the foundations of modern physics and represents a fundamental departure from classical physics. However, like classical physics, the theory of relativity does not take quantum effects into consideration and describes a deterministic world dominated by discoverable laws of cause and effect. Although it leads to deeply counterintuitive ideas about the nature of space and time, the theory of relativity has been repeatedly confirmed by experiments. See also: *classical physics; determinism; quantum theory; space-time; theory.*

RELATED READINGS: Newton, "Time, Space, and Motion"; Planck, "Extending the Theories of Physics"; Einstein, "The Special Theory of Relativity," "The General Theory of Relativity," and "$E = mc^2$"; Weinberg, "Beautiful Theories: Symmetry and Mathematics"

uncertainty principle The fundamental principle of quantum theory, often called Heisenberg's uncertainty principle after Werner Heisenberg, the German scientist who first formulated it. The uncertainty principle precisely defines the amount of uncertainty that results when simultaneous measurements are made of specific pairs of variables, such as an object's position and momentum—so that the more precisely the position is known, the more uncertain the momentum, and vice versa. The amount of uncertainty in these measurements is defined by an extremely small number known as Planck's constant (h), so that effects of this uncertainty are not apparent at the scale of everyday objects, but become significant only at the subatomic scale. The uncertainty principle reflects an inherent limitation on what we can know about the physical world, rather than a technical limitation on the techniques we use to make observations. Because of the uncertainty principle, the deterministic predictability of classical physics does not apply to the realm of quantum events. Instead, probability functions are used to determine the range of possible values that variables such as position and momentum might have when an observer makes successive experimental observations of an object. See also: *classical physics; constants of nature; determinism; Planck's constant; probability; quantum theory; wave mechanics; wave-particle duality.*

> RELATED READINGS: Gamow, "Quantum Uncertainty"; Feynman, "Quantum Behavior"; Heisenberg, "The Copenhagen Interpretation of Quantum Theory"; Polkinghorne, "Quantum Perplexity and Debate"; Hawking, "Black Holes and Predictable Worlds"

velocity The rate of change of a moving object's position with respect to time (for example, number of miles northward per hour). An object's speed and velocity have the same numerical value, but velocity includes the object's direction. Velocity is usually understood to mean an object's speed and direction at an instant in time. See also: *acceleration; inertia; momentum.*

> RELATED READINGS: Galileo, "Falling Bodies and Projectiles"; Newton, "Forces"; Einstein, "The Special Theory of Relativity"

wave function In wave mechanics, a mathematical expression derived from the Schrödinger equation that specifies the state of a quantum system as it develops over time. The quantum system may consist of one or many subatomic objects, such as electrons. The wave function does not represent an actual wave, even though it is expressed in terms of the characteristics of waves such as frequency and amplitude. It is deterministic in the special sense that it contains all the information that can be known about a quantum system, such as its position, momentum, and energy.

A probability function can be derived from the wave function, giving the probability that, for example, an electron will be found in a certain position or will have a certain momentum. What the wave function does not determine is the outcome of a specific experimental measurement of a quantum system. When a measurement is made, in accordance with the necessary constraints of the uncertainty principle, the range of values represented by the wave function for such things as position, momentum, and energy is said to collapse to the actual values given by the measurement. Why a wave function collapses to any particular value is one of the enigmas of quantum physics and represents its break from the strictly deterministic explanations of classical physics. See also: *classical physics; determinism; probability; probability function; quantum theory; Schrödinger equation; uncertainty principle; wave mechanics.*

   RELATED READINGS: Gamow, "Quantum Uncertainty"; Heisenberg, "The Copenhagen Interpretation of Quantum Theory"; Polkinghorne, "Quantum Perplexity and Debate"; Hawking, "Black Holes and Predictable Worlds"

wave mechanics A widely accepted version of quantum theory based on a mathematical model of quantum events at the subatomic level—the Schrödinger equation. Experimental evidence confirms that when subatomic particles such as electrons are observed under certain conditions, they exhibit wavelike characteristics. Consequently, the Schrödinger equation can be used to describe the way in which quantum events develop over time, in terms of the familiar characteristics of ordinary waves, such as wavelength, frequency, and amplitude. This description, derived from the Schrödinger equation, is called a wave function. Although Erwin Schrödinger apparently intended his wave equation to represent the structure of physical reality, in wave mechanics it is always interpreted abstractly in terms of statistical probabilities, rather than as representing actual waves. See also: *mechanics; model; probability; quantum theory; Schrödinger equation; wave function; wave-particle duality.*

   RELATED READINGS: Gamow, "Quantum Uncertainty"; Feynman, "Quantum Behavior"; Heisenberg, "The Copenhagen Interpretation of Quantum Theory"; Polkinghorne, 'Quantum Perplexity and Debate"; Lightman, "Metaphor in Science"; Hawking, "Black Holes and Predictable Worlds"

wave-particle duality The concept at the foundation of quantum theory that things such as electrons and light behave, depending on the circumstances in which they are observed, sometimes as particles and sometimes as waves, though not as both simultaneously. Wave-particle duality and the uncertainty principle represent the fundamental break of quantum theory from the principles of classical physics and continue to raise profound philosophical questions about the meaning of quantum theory for our understanding of the physical world. See also: *classical physics; Planck's constant; quantum theory; uncertainty principle; wave mechanics.*

RELATED READINGS: Gamow, "Quantum Uncertainty"; Feynman, "Quantum Behavior"; Heisenberg, "The Copenhagen Interpretation of Quantum Theory"

weak force See *forces of nature.*

weight The net gravitational force exerted on an object, which varies depending on the object's distances with respect to the sources responsible for the gravitational field. Even though all bodies having mass exert some gravitational force on one another, an object's weight is usually considered to be the result of the nearest strong source of gravity, such as the earth or the moon. That is, since weight is a force, its measure depends on the object's location. The terms *weight* and *mass* are closely related and often mistakenly used interchangeably, but in physics they represent distinct characteristics of an object. Unlike an object's weight, the measure of its mass remains the same wherever the object is located in the universe. See also: *force; forces of nature; gravity; mass.*

RELATED READING: Einstein, "The General Theory of Relativity"

work The effort to shift energy from one physical system to another, defined by the force applied to an object and the displacement of the object while the force is being applied. For work to be performed, some or all of the force must be applied in the direction of, or opposite to, the object's displacement. See also: *energy; force.*

RELATED READINGS: Rumford, "Heat and Friction"; Joule, "The Mechanical Equivalent of Heat"

Bibliography

Asimov, Isaac. *Understanding Physics*. New York: Walker, 1966; New York: Barnes & Noble Books, 1993. This survey starts with basic elements and builds up the entire body of knowledge necessary for understanding both the history and the technical details of all major topics in physics.

Atkins, Peter. *Galileo's Finger: The Ten Great Ideas of Science*. Oxford: Oxford University Press, 2004. Among the concepts that this book covers with real insight are entropy, symmetry, and the atomic structure of matter.

Beyers, Nina, and Gary Williams, eds. *Out of the Shadows: Contributions of Twentieth-Century Women to Physics*. Cambridge: Cambridge University Press, 2006. This book profiles forty scientists who have made outstanding contributions in all areas of physics. Each chapter, written by a physicist, demonstrates that great scientific talent has nothing to do with gender.

Cole, K. C. *First You Build a Cloud: And Other Reflections on Physics As a Way of Life.* New York: Harvest Books, 1999. One of the best popular-science writers provides a fresh look at the ideas and individuals that have shaped modern physics.

Reading any of these outstanding surveys of physics along with the selections in *What's the Matter?* will provide an excellent overview of the history and content of physics.

Crease, Robert P., and Charles C. Mann. *The Second Creation: Makers of the Revolution in Twentieth-Century Physics.* Rev. ed. New Brunswick, NJ: Rutgers University Press, 1996. This is an excellent account of the scientists who created the study of particle physics and of the scientific communities in which they worked.

Cropper, William H. *Great Physicists: The Life and Times of Leading Physicists from Galileo to Hawking.* Oxford: Oxford University Press, 2001, 2004. These brief biographies of physicists from Galileo to Hawking provide not only information about their lives but also detailed discussions of their scientific work.

Dolling, Lisa M., Arthur F. Gianelli, and Glenn N. Statile, eds. *The Tests of Time: Readings in the Development of Physical Theory.* Princeton, NJ: Princeton University Press, 2003. This anthology of original papers by scientists who developed the major concepts of physics through the centuries includes helpful introductory notes for each selection.

Feynman, Richard P. *Feynman Lectures on Physics.* 3 vols. Reading, MA: Addison-Wesley, 1963–1965. Feynman's talent for making difficult scientific problems interesting is communicated on every page of these transcripts of his challenging physics course lectures.

Gell-Mann, Murray. *The Quark and the Jaguar: Adventures in the Simple and the Complex.* New York: W. H. Freeman and Company, 1994; New York: Owl Books, 1995. Ranging over the fields of physics, biological evolution, and string theory, this discussion of complex adaptive systems is by the scientist who discovered the quark.

Gleick, James. *Chaos: Making a New Science.* Reprint. New York: Penguin Books (Non-Classics), 1988. This book is an outstanding overview of the concepts and experimental methods used to investigate random patterns in nature.

Goldsmith, Barbara. *Obsessive Genius: The Inner World of Marie Curie.* New York: W. W. Norton & Company, 2004, 2005. The focus of this biography is the tireless efforts of this Nobel laureate physicist and chemist to establish her work in the scientific community of early twentieth-century Europe.

Greene, Brian. *The Fabric of the Cosmos: Space, Time, and the Texture of Reality.* New York: Alfred A. Knopf, 2004; New York: Vintage Books, 2005. This explanation of the ideas behind the latest developments in physics, particularly string theory, successfully translates difficult concepts into nontechnical and often entertaining language.

Hakim, Joy. *The Story of Science.* Vol. 1, *Aristotle Leads the Way.* Vol. 2, *Newton at the Center.* Vol. 3, *Einstein Adds a New Dimension.* Washington: Smithsonian Books, 2004, 2005, 2007. This series is a history of physics and physicists that teaches scientific content as it highlights the human story of science. Appropriate for both younger readers and adults, the books are beautifully illustrated.

Holton, Gerald, and Stephen G. Brush. *Physics, the Human Adventure: From Copernicus to Einstein and Beyond.* 3rd ed. New Brunswick, NJ: Rutgers University Press, 2001. This detailed history effectively presents the technical content of physics and explores many problems in the philosophy of science.

Kaku, Michio. *Parallel Worlds: A Journey Through Creation, Higher Dimensions, and the Future of the Cosmos.* New York: Doubleday, 2004. An excellent popular-science writer and physicist explores some of the frontiers of current cosmology.

Krauss, Lawrence M. *Fear of Physics: A Guide for the Perplexed.* New York: Basic Books, 1993, 1994. This book makes physics accessible by focusing on how physicists think about the world.

Lederman, Leon, with Dick Teresi. *The God Particle: If the Universe Is the Answer, What Is the Question?* Boston: Houghton Mifflin, 1993; reprint, New York: Dell, 1994. Lederman, a Nobel laureate and one of the great teachers of science, presents his highly personalized account of the search for fundamental particles.

Levin, Janna. *How the Universe Got Its Spots: Diary of a Finite Time in a Finite Space.* Princeton, NJ: Princeton University Press, 2002; New York: Anchor Books, 2003. This book, which blends autobiography and scientific speculation effectively, conveys the working life of a young physics researcher.

Lightman, Alan. *Great Ideas in Physics: The Conservation of Energy, the Second Law of Thermodynamics, the Theory of Relativity, and Quantum Mechanics.* 3rd ed. New York: McGraw-Hill, 2000. This book focuses on detailed explanations of just four fundamental ideas, including relativity and quantum theory, and discusses how these ideas have had an impact outside of science.

Lindley, David. *Boltzmann's Atom: The Great Debate That Launched a Revolution in Physics.* New York: Free Press, 2001. This book tells the story of one of the most important theoretical physicists of the nineteenth century and his struggle to establish the atomic basis of matter.

Newton, Roger G. *What Makes Nature Tick?* Cambridge, MA: Harvard University Press, 1993, 1994. This book focuses on the theoretical concepts that guide physicists in devising experimental methods for investigating the world.

Penrose, Roger. *The Road to Reality: A Complete Guide to the Laws of the Universe.* New York: Alfred A. Knopf Books, 2005. A leading theoretical physicist provides a challenging summary of current mathematical explanations of the universe.

Pesic, Peter. *Sky in a Bottle.* Cambridge, MA: MIT Press, 2005. Centered on the seemingly simple question of why the sky is blue, this investigation probes the ways in which science, philosophy, and art have, through the centuries, attempted an answer.

Rees, Martin J. *Just Six Numbers: The Deep Forces That Shape the Universe.* New York: Basic Books, 2000, 2001. This book by a leading astronomer describes in detail six significant numbers that define the overall properties of the universe.

Rhodes, Richard. *The Making of the Atomic Bomb.* New York: Simon & Schuster, 1988, 1995. This narrative history is both the story of theoretical physics in the early twentieth century and an account of the political situation that led scientists to construct the first atomic weapons.

Ridley, B. K. *Time, Space, and Things.* 3rd ed. Cambridge: Cambridge University Press, 1995. This is one of the best introductions to the basic concepts of physics and provides an excellent foundation for further reading in specialized topics.

Rothman, Tony. *Instant Physics: From Aristotle to Einstein, and Beyond.* New York: Fawcett Columbine/Ballantine Books, 1995. This entertaining introductory survey takes a historical approach and includes interesting problems for readers to solve.

Schrödinger, Erwin. *Nature and the Greeks; and, Science and Humanism.* Foreword by Roger Penrose. Cambridge: Cambridge University Press, 1996. In these two lecture series, a major twentieth-century physicist offers his account of the scientific picture of the world from ancient times to the development of quantum theory.

Sime, Ruth Lewin. *Lise Meitner: A Life in Physics.* Berkeley: University of California Press, 1996. This biography of one of the great researchers in atomic physics emphasizes the immense challenges Meitner faced working in a male-dominated field and surviving during the years of Nazi domination in Europe.

Taylor, John C. *Hidden Unity in Nature's Laws.* Cambridge: Cambridge University Press, 2001. This tour through the principles of physics takes as its theme the way in which scientific knowledge progresses by finding unity among different categories of phenomena.

Wilczek, Frank, and Betsy Devine. *Longing for the Harmonies: Themes and Variations from Modern Physics.* New York: W. W. Norton & Company, 1988, 1989. Using the metaphor of musical themes and variations, this book by Nobel laureate Wilczek explores the major themes of current physics.

Zinsser, Judith P. *La Dame d'Esprit: A Biography of the Marquise du Châtelet.* New York: Viking, 2006. This book tells the life story of an eighteenth-century noblewoman who played an important role in bringing the works of Newton to the French scientific community while also making original contributions of her own to physics and mathematics.

Acknowledgments

All possible care has been taken to trace ownership and secure permission for each selection in this anthology. The Great Books Foundation wishes to thank the following authors, publishers, and representatives for permission to reprint copyrighted material:

The Uncertainty of Science, from THE MEANING OF IT ALL, by Richard P. Feynman. Copyright © 1998 by Michelle Feynman and Carl Feynman. Reprinted by permission of Perseus Books PLC, a member of Perseus Books, LLC.

The Science of Nature and *Moving Things*, from PHYSICS, by Aristotle, edited and translated by Robin Waterfield. Translation copyright © 1996 by Robin Waterfield. Reprinted by permission of Oxford University Press.

Entropy: The Running-Down of the Universe, from THE NATURE OF THE PHYSICAL WORLD, by Arthur S. Eddington. Copyright © 1928 by the Macmillan Company. Reprinted by permission of Cambridge University Press.

Art Credits

FRONT COVER A feather and an apple fall at the same rate in a vacuum, demonstrating the validity of Newton's law of gravity. © Jim Sugar/Getty Images.

ii Original frontispiece from Galileo's *Dialogue Concerning the Two Chief World Systems* (1632) depicting Aristotle, Ptolemy, and Copernicus. © AIP Emilio Segre Visual Archives.

12 Medieval astronomers making observations. © Bettmann/Corbis.

28 Diagram of the geocentric universe showing Aristotle's four earthly elements surrounded by the fixed spheres of the sun, planets, and stars, 1539. © The Print Collector/Alamy.

46 Original frontispiece from Galileo's *Dialogue Concerning the Two Chief World Systems* (1632) depicting Aristotle, Ptolemy, and Copernicus. © AIP Emilio Segre Visual Archives.

68 Gravity experiment at the top of the Eiffel Tower. © Bettmann/Corbis.

98 Newton investigating the nature of sunlight with a prism. © ImageState.

116 Rumford's calorimeter, 1887. © ImageState.

136 Joule's apparatus for determining the mechanical equivalent of heat, 1872. © ImageState.

154 Time's arrow. © Photodisc.

174 Faraday in his laboratory at the Royal Institution. © AIP Emilio Segre Visual Archives.

200 Generating artificial lightning in Nikola Tesla's laboratory. © Bettmann/Corbis.

234 Marie Curie in her laboratory, ca. 1905. © Bettmann/Corbis.

252 Einstein in a classroom at Princeton University, 1940. © Lucien Aigner/Corbis.

300 Einstein's office at Princeton University, 1955. © Ralph Morse/Time Life Pictures/ Getty Images.

314 Trails left by subatomic particles in a bubble chamber detector, 1983. © Kevin Fleming/ Corbis.

336 Particle accelerator tunnel at Deutsches Elektronen Synchrotron. © Peter Ginter/ Getty Images.

360 Trails left by subatomic particles in a bubble chamber detector, 1983. © Kevin Fleming/ Corbis.

378 Particle accelerator tunnel at Deutsches Elektronen Synchrotron. © Peter Ginter/ Getty Images.

394 Array of radio telescopes. © Corbis.

412 Johannes Kepler's diagram of the planets' orbits as circumscribed Platonic polyhedrons. © Fotosearch.

440 Arabian astrologers making observations, 1513. © Stapleton Collection/Corbis.

458 Physics research laboratory at the Sorbonne, Paris, 1895. © ImageState.

474 Diagram of a black hole. © Fotostock.

496 Einstein and J. Robert Oppenheimer, director of the Manhattan Project, which built the first atomic weapons; 1947. © Alfred Eisenstaedt/Time Life Pictures/Getty Images.

BACK COVER Circle emitting electricity. © Don Farrall/Photodisc/Getty Images.